The Rorty-Habermas Debate

SUNY series in American Philosophy and Cultural Thought
Randall E. Auxier and John R. Shook, editors

The

Rorty-Habermas Debate

Toward Freedom
as Responsibility

Marcin Kilanowski

Cover image: ©Marcin Kilanowski

Published by State University of New York Press, Albany

©2021 State University of New York Press

All rights reserved

Printed in the United States of America

No part of this book may be used or reproduced in any manner whatsoever without written permission. No part of this book may be stored in a retrieval system or transmitted in any form or by any means including electronic, electrostatic, magnetic tape, mechanical, photocopying, recording, or otherwise without the prior permission in writing of the publisher.

For information, contact State University of New York Press, Albany, NY
www.sunypress.edu

Library of Congress Cataloging-in-Publication Data

Names: Kilanowski, Marcin, author.
Title: The Rorty-Habermas debate : toward freedom as responsibility / Marcin Kilanowski.
Description: Albany : State University of New York Press, [2021] | Series: Suny series in American philosophy and cultural thought | Includes bibliographical references and index.
Identifiers: LCCN 2020034952 | ISBN 9781438483559 (hardcover) | ISBN 9781438483566 (ebook) | ISBN 9781438483542 (paperback)
Subjects: LCSH: Rorty, Richard. | Habermas, Jürgen.
Classification: LCC B945.R524 K55 2021 | DDC 191—dc23
LC record available at https://lccn.loc.gov/2020034952

10 9 8 7 6 5 4 3 2 1

For Sandra, Aleksander, and Antoni

CONTENTS

From the Author	xi
Acknowledgments	xv
Introduction	1
I Opening: *First Comes Dewey*	15
II On Rorty's Sociopolitical Thought	23
III On Habermas's Theory of Communicative Action	75
IV On the Convergence of the Perspectives of Rorty and Habermas	127
V Postscript: *From Dewey to Rorty and Habermas*	191
Conclusion	201
Notes	211
Bibliography	261
Index	279

FROM THE AUTHOR

Richard Rorty and Jürgen Habermas are two of the most important philosophers of the twentieth century. There is a considerable scholarship that focuses on their philosophies, however, very little of this work pays attention to their shared commitments. Most of the existing work is focused on their points of disagreement. The general goal of this volume is thus to bridge the gap in the scholarly literature on Rorty and Habermas to show how their work converges.

This volume is intended to serve those in the social sciences and legal studies who want and need a guide to both philosophers and to the important debate and exchange that happened between them. It is meant to help graduate students and scholars of law and government that often think of the Frankfurt school as tremendously influential but also as a tradition that can at times be dense and pedantic to the point that its authors occasionally frustrate readers with seemingly impenetrable prose. It is thus important to allow students and researchers outside of the formal discipline to turn to a more accessible source. In other words, this volume's explicit aim is not to address professional philosophers. Philosophers most of the time do not need a guide on this topic. But so many others do need it. Of course philosophers can also find it challenging to read critical theory, and about the debate between Rorty and Habermas. It can also be difficult to see the potential that exists within their thought to reflect on the philosophical basis on which our societies and democracies should be grounded.

To help those both outside and within the discipline of philosophy and to make reading this volume a valuable endeavor, it is designed to be an exercise in closely reading the works of Rorty and Habermas. I will often refer to the philosophers' own words and compare them with passages of their disputants to show why I came to particular conclusions. By reading closely, I lead the reader step by step toward conclusions that change the common reading of Rorty's and Habermas's thought and of their debate.

We have many different "common readings" of situations, texts, events, and people. These are often grounded in assumptions that we no longer verify, for example, that beggars on the street are responsible for their lives, according to the saying "You've made your bed, now lie in it." We also say "Stop cheating like a gypsy" or "You are emotional like a woman." Such common readings also exist in the sciences, especially in the social sciences or the humanities, and they need to be addressed and overcome to create a chance to reach for something new. This "something new" in the case of this volume is to show that Rorty and Habermas are convergent thinkers, which runs against many superficial claims that there is only a limited affinity between them, at the level of certain general perceptions or beliefs, for example, as to the value of democratic order or to the value of freedom, and to show that this affinity happens as "conversation" conducted "with the public" and from a "scientific" or "academic" point of view. Rorty indeed said that Dewey and Habermas were his heroes, "and they always had two conversations: one with their professional colleagues on technical issues that only philosophy professors care about, and another conversation with the public." In this volume, however, both conversations will be important—those about, for example, the nature of truth or the role of rationality, as well about what basis we need for communication to occur. It will be also important to present the possible consequences of that conversation.

Academic literature is full of works with conclusions driven by research sympathies that evolve with the amount of time one spends with the subject of one's research. Even in writing this volume, I have experienced how Rorty scholars defend his view, and Habermas scholars his, both sets of scholars being very much attached to the work of the philosopher whose work they know best but at the same time read in a particular way. For these scholars the conclusion might be striking that Rorty and Habermas to a large extent speak with the same voice when they argue about the philosophical basis of their sociopolitical views, as well as when they speak about the political form they would like to put in place of the present one. In light of the exercise that this volume is and its proposed methodology, those challenged by its conclusions would need to argue in the same way, not only by presenting general claims but by also pointing to texts themselves, which at the same time should be perceived within the body of the authors' corpuses. It is certainly not enough to show one citation from one place when a particular issue was a subject of further discussion, between Rorty and Habermas, and it is important to reach for various sources to present an argument.

In the first two chapters, the reader will find a presentation of the nuances of Rorty's and Habermas's notions of truth, rationality, universality, and communication. Such a presentation is important because, as I have mentioned, I see my audience as being wider than professional philosophers, who could consider the presentation and the analysis as an overview. Indeed, the content of these two chapters will be familiar to some of my readers, however, the goal is to present the philosophies of Rorty and Habermas in as clear, careful, accessible, concise, and comprehensive a way as possible, and to proffer some criticisms in the latter part of each chapter. To present selected issues from the philosophies of Rorty and Habermas as clearly as possible, I am not getting into a discussion about interpretations of their work by other authors. One can of course see the downside of such close reading in that it does not benefit from the insights that have been hashed out in the secondary literature. However, the upside of omitting significant engagement with existing interpretative debates is brevity, conciseness, and overall clarity of presentation of the ideas of each thinker. To counterbalance the downsides, the secondary literature will be included in the footnotes to this text. I will refer there to articles and books that criticize and support the philosophical views of John Dewey, Rorty, and Habermas.

The goal is, however, not only to present what Rorty and Habermas both argued about and what they both claimed about each other but also to confront them and their views. I do so in the third chapter of this volume. In particular, I analyze whether they are right in their assessment of each other's philosophical thought. Perhaps they misread each other due to erroneous preconceptions they had before different stages of their debate or they did not listen carefully to each other's arguments. The conclusion is that American and Continental pragmatists criticized each other, illuminated each other, and to a large extent converge philosophically. This turns the page in readings of Rorty and Habermas; they were not philosophers that were fundamentally at odds with each other, but were ones that to a large extent spoke with the same voice even though they sometimes used different vocabularies. There are of course differences in their views, and I will also present them in this volume, drawing closely on the works of both philosophers.

Besides presentation of the debate that happened between Rorty and Habermas, during which they confronted each other on a number of issues, the goal of this volume is also to present their views with a question in mind: what possible meaning does their debate have for us, and what comes out of it? They share a pragmatic approach, and that is why they present their own "utopian" projects, in the positive sense of the term. What's more, their projects are aligned—as this volume will show—even though that can be difficult to realize. Both present a humane, proindividual, and communal perspective at the same time. Neither of them presents a substantial vision of how things *should be*; instead they present formal preconditions that if respected may allow us to be able to think about how things *could be*.

The crucial issue for them is to sort out on what basis to rest our societal cooperation and our politics so that the horrors of the twentieth century will not be repeated. These horrors occurred with the development of fascism and communism, which were the only "truths" for half of the twentieth century, especially in Poland and in the rest of Central and Eastern Europe. It is thus no coincidence that Rorty and Habermas, who had in mind these horrors, met for a historical debate in Warsaw after the fall of the communism when the issue at stake was, what is next? On what philosophical basis should we build our societies and relations between people? Are there any universal values that we can draw on for that project? Is there any truth that can unite us? Is rationality the cure for the madness of authoritarian regimes? Is coexistence and communication possible in societies in which people are so different, and is it feasible to dialogue across many different approaches they represent?

Out of the confrontation between Rorty and Habermas we might be able to find a new way to think about what kind of politics we need, or about freedom and responsibility, in a way that can help us to shape new democracies and to rescue those in crisis. I believe that Habermas's and Rorty's perspectives provide the opportunity for developing a new understanding of freedom, "freedom as responsibility," but this volume shows only a path toward such an understanding, the possibility of arguing in the future about a new understanding of the notion of freedom as responsibility. It is thus not the goal to present a new understanding of the notion of "freedom as responsibility" here. As the volume's subtitle suggests, I will only move "toward" it in this work.

In short, as a volume mostly for nonspecialists, from disciplines ranging from the social to the political sciences, but also for philosophers interested in the subject, it is a general introduction to Rorty and

Habermas without losing the clarity of the exposition of their ideas. The work also attempts to be an original contribution to existing debates about the level of disagreement between the two philosophers. I hope by posting questions throughout the volume and moving step by step to keep the reader interested and engaged in unpacking how Rorty's and Habermas's thought converges. Moreover, I will try to show that there is enormous potential in the pragmatic philosophical tradition to help us deal with the problems of today, especially when deciding what kind of politics we need and how we should understand and exercise our freedom.

ACKNOWLEDGMENTS

Not long ago we had to live through a severe economic crisis. At the moment we witness the crisis of a democratic system that we can observe in countries that were developing as democracies but also in those that were considered to be well established on the democratic path.[1] We are facing the crisis of building the European Union, which was supposed to rest on the idea of solidarity.[2] A number of thinkers are looking for solutions.[3] The conditions in which we live today are, however, not something new. Many scholars, such as Dewey, Rorty, and Habermas, responded to them in past. In their own specific ways they tried to explain that the problems we face do not rest only on erroneous economic or financial decisions, or on political institutions maladjusted to face existing challenges, which is often the case, but also on the philosophical underpinning of our ways of thinking: understanding concepts that we operate with, which separate us from the proper understanding of the reality around us, from realizing the net of relations in which we are entangled, the fact that we are part of them, that we start and end in others, just as others start and end in us. That prevents us from taking responsibility for the quality of these relations. I believe that it is worthwhile to turn to these philosophers and the debate between them in present conditions, as it can be a rich source of inspiration and guidance for us today.

This book is the result of the research project that started with the support of the State Committee for Scientific Research and the Kosciuszko Foundation for which I am very thankful. It was conducted at Nicolaus Copernicus University, Utrecht University, and Harvard University, where I was able to cooperate with great professors for whose support, guidance, and advice I would like to thank them in particular. I would like to thank Professor Marek Jakubowski for creating a fruitful environment for scientific research at Nicolaus Copernicus University. I would also like to thank Professor Hilary Putnam for his guidance and for making it possible for me to continue working on this volume at Harvard University, and Professors Jane Mansbridge, Roberto Mangaberia Unger, and Duncan Kennedy for more-than-enthralling discussions. I would also like to thank Professors Richard Rorty and Jürgen Habermas for consultations conducted in writing or in person during the creation of this work. I also need to thank those who reviewed or provided comments on the manuscript or parts of it during different stages of my writing. These thanks should go to Professors Randall Auxier, Bert van den Brink, Andrzej Kaniowski, Wojciech Sadurski, Andrzej Szahaj, and Lech Witkowski, as well to my friends Józefina Bartyzel, Richard Lehun, Marta Sibierska, and Paweł Puwalski. I need to also thank the anonymous reviewers selected by SUNY Press whose suggestions were very useful in the preparation of the final version of this book. Of course, I bear sole responsibility for the possible mistakes still present within it. Finally, I would like to thank my family for their support and understanding while I was working on this book. I dedicate this book to them, to my wife Sandra and my sons.

INTRODUCTION

The Specter of Auschwitz

Fascism and communism developed in the twentieth century as reactions against the inequalities of early capitalism, which facilitated race and class struggles and called for social engineering at a considerable scale. Their leaders, assigning themselves the role of the arbiters of truth, subordinated their societies to ideological moralities based, on the one hand, on class struggle, and on the other, on racial superiority.[1] Any actions that supported their historical mission were, in their opinion, justified. They created totalitarian regimes whose aim was a better future, regardless of the costs. Consequently, violence, pain, and suffering became a common experience that marked millions of people.

In the light of these experiences—still somehow vivid, from our perspective—we ask ourselves what to do in order for us and future generations to never again partake in anything like them. "[A]t times like that of Auschwitz, when history is in upheaval and traditional institutions and patterns of behavior are collapsing, we want something which stands beyond history and institutions. What can there be except human solidarity, our recognition of one another's common humanity?"[2] This question has been posed by Rorty but also by many others. All try to tackle the tragic experiences of the twentieth century in different ways. They wish, among other things, to indicate such forms of coexistence that would allow for preserving dignity within a community.[3] This is in fact what has shaped the thought of Habermas. There are also those, including Rorty, who tried to indicate forms of coexistence devoid of coercion and that do not cause suffering.

They all share a disapproval of what has happened and the desire for it to never happen again.[4] Haunted by the specter of Auschwitz, they create utopian visions of a better future, bearing in mind that someday they may spread.[5] The situation they are in is not, however, favorable. Habermas has written that today it looks like the utopian energy has expired: as if it has evaporated from historical thinking. Thus, the future does not appear optimistic. At the threshold of the twenty-first century, we encounter a somewhat terrifying picture of common life interests being threatened: the never-ending arms race, the dissemination of nuclear weapons, systematic impoverishment, unemployment, increasing social inequality in developing countries, and environmental pollution—these are the slogans that permeate public consciousness via mass media.[6] The reactions of intellectuals and of politicians equally prove their helplessness.[7] And it is by no means merely a realist perspective to accept helplessness so eagerly and let it substitute for attempts at acting for the sake of the future. Perhaps the situation is, indeed, objectively opaque. But opaqueness can still be a part of a willingness to act, of which societies are capable. The point is that Western culture should trust itself.[8] Were we, in light of Habermas's words above, indeed to talk of a surrounding opaqueness, such a situation should not make intellectuals give up. Certainly, this is not the case with thinkers, such as Rorty and Habermas, who wish for hope to take the place of knowledge in our social interactions.[9] This hope should be based on the conviction that we are able to deliberately and consciously change ourselves and our surroundings.[10] It should be followed by the renunciation of the search for the one and only truth. This renunciation is characteristic of American pragmatism, but not only of that tradition. Rorty observed that the belief that it is social consensus, and not the attitude toward nonhuman reality, that is of the utmost significance, is characteristic not only of American pragmatism but also of the works of Habermas,[11] whose thought can be also described as belonging to the pragmatist tradition.

Pragmatism

As far as Habermas is concerned, the above statement may seem surprising, though it should not be so.[12] For when we ask in what sense it can be articulated, we will have to answer that it is in the sense of the pragmatic categories and views that appear within Habermas's philosophy, which are crucial for pragmatism—despite its many guises—and in the sense he himself has used when referring to pragmatism, and when utilizing it, acknowledging his affinity with this tradition of thought.[13] In the case of Habermas's thought, the affinity lies in both the first and second case. Many of the categories appearing in Habermas's philosophy are present also in pragmatist thought; he himself is well familiar with pragmatism and has taken into consideration its output with respect to reflecting on the theory of democracy or, by and large, sociopolitical thought, though not only on those topics.[14] This output is of much importance for Habermas's theory of communicative action, which—as he himself has suggested—rests upon pragmatist presuppositions. It is the output of both American and Kantian pragmatism.[15] Habermas has interpreted American pragmatism as follows: "From the outset I viewed American pragmatism as the third productive reply to Hegel [. . .], as the radical-democratic branch of Young Hegelianism, so to speak. Ever since, I have relied on this American version of the philosophy of praxis when the problem arises of compensating for the weaknesses of Marxism with respect to democratic theory."[16] What does Habermas uncover in American pragmatism that is of so much significance? When asked about it, he has answered that it is the antielitist, democratic, and egalitarian attitude that shapes and permeates pragmatists' projects. He has added that this attitude has been more important for him than any particular essay on politics or democracy. And this is not all. Habermas's thought, just like American pragmatism, can be characterized by antipositivism, antiessentialism, fallibilism, pluralism, a critique of dualisms and industrial societies, sensitivity to ambivalences, and approaching philosophy as a tool for tackling human problems. They both can also be characterized by how they treat the categories of development and progress, and maintain hope that social change may occur. What is also common between Habermas's ideas and American pragmatism is some convergence in the approach to the discursive structure of the public sphere as something necessary for democracy to develop.[17] And Habermas has admitted to that convergence when he said that the pragmatic approach to language helped him "to develop a theory of communicative action and of rationality. It was the foundation for a critical theory of society and paved the way for a discourse-theoretic conception of morality, law, and democracy."[18]

In the light of the aforesaid convergences with American pragmatism, though not only its American variant, referring to it or "resting" on it, as Habermas himself has written, as well as in light of his articulating American pragmatism as an "American variant" of pragmatist philosophy, it seems plausible to call his own variant of sociopolitical thought "continental pragmatism."

On Sources and Crucial Issues

There has been a great deal of controversy surrounding, and many misunderstandings of, pragmatism. They are all due to, in one way or another, superficial readings of pragmatists texts and thought, based on reconstructing the considerations of other critics without verifying the value of such statements at their sources. Such problems—creating "interpretations of interpretations"—can be avoided by careful reading of the texts of the authors as such. And it is this strategy that has been adopted while writing this book. Thus, it shall include numerous references to source texts in order to minimize the possibility of understatement and overinterpretation. It is obvious, however, that all of our actions are accompanied by a preliminary interpretation of a situation, and the result of this interpretation does somehow depend on one's attitude. And this is what has happened in the case of the actions accompanying the writing of this very work.

This volume is underpinned with an intention that is reflected in both the selection of literature to be studied and the fact that only some threads found in it are to be traced and analyzed. The purpose of that is to prove the accuracy of the initial intuition that accompanied the author of these words while studying pragmatist thought, namely that the perspectives of Rorty and of Habermas are convergent. Such a statement may seem surprising for those who tend to think of Rorty as a "postmodernist," and of Habermas as a "universalist."[19] However, such a classification would not be correct, for the postmodernism of the former is not in fact such a radical departure from previous philosophical considerations, nor is the universalism of the latter blindly attached to them.[20] All this becomes clear when, while analyzing their thought, we take into consideration each word and expression. Such an approach is not an exaggeration, for the aim at stake requires particular carefulness. The aim is to prove that those who are often deemed opponents are standing in the same place and speak to a large extent in one voice.

Rorty's and Habermas's philosophical output comprises many significant works, among them those crucial for the realization of the aforesaid tasks, that is, especially, Habermas's *Theory of Communicative Action* and Rorty's *Contingency, Irony, and Solidarity*. These texts will be analyzed to a considerable extent in the following pages.

As far as the *Theory of Communicative Action* is concerned, Habermas touched upon many issues that appeared also in his previous texts. Here, however, they are reexamined in accordance with the debates in which Habermas himself has been involved.[21] Numerous polemical discussions led the philosopher to move from the categories of cognition and interest, crucial for his previous way of thinking, toward the categories of "society and communicative rationality."[22] He has realized the feebleness of the epistemological/methodological program of grounded critique. The move toward new categories culminated with the *Theory of Communicative Action*, in which Habermas presented the theory of action and of society. Its main subjects are communicative rationality, the concept of a society—embracing the theory of action and the theory of systems—and a critical theory of modernity that tries to respond to the problems of present times: the problems of postindustrial society. And these problems are just a few of all that we face, for "occasions for discontent and protest arise wherever a one-sided process of modernization, guided by criteria of economic and administrative rationality, invades domains of life which are centred on the task of cultural transmission, social integration, socialization and education."[23] Therefore, Habermas has continued to believe that social modernization should turn not only in the direction of capitalism but also in a direction that would allow for institutions hindering unrestrained expansion of economic and administrative systems to emerge from the world of everyday life.[24] He has defended the position that it is necessary for different domains of life to be based upon communicative rationality. Accordingly, he has presented a critical theory of society and wished to point out that due to communicative rationality, which is the basis for the processes of constituting an ideal communicative community, we shall come closer to the idea of conciliation and freedom. This theory is an attempt at proving that the normative concept of rationality reconstructed here—that is, communicative rationality—makes conspicuous what at the same time guides the process of modernization understood as a process of societal rationalization. This process is supposed to lead to the emergence of a more just and freer community of human beings.

It should be noted here that the work that further articulated Habermas's social theory is the volume *Between Facts and Norms*, published in 1992, which contains Habermas's deliberations on the development of the paradigm of law, the rule of law, the role of civil society, and different concepts of the political public sphere. These issues will not be presented in this book, and therefore I will pay only limited attention to the role of law in the context of the progressive "juridization" and reification of various areas of the lifeworld about which he writes in the *Theory of Communication Action*. The problems which are discussed by Habermas in *Between Facts and Norms* were not the subject of a wider debate between Rorty and Habermas, except for the issue of the type of policy we should choose after deciding on what grounds we should base our functioning in society, and on what understanding of the concepts of truth, rationality, and objectivity. They both advocate politics that Habermas has called a proceduralist deliberative politics. I will present how Habermas has understood it in the volume *Between Facts and Norms*, when it will be important to answer the question as to what kind of policy both philosophers chose. At the same time, it should be noted that Habermas tried to build on his arguments contained in the *Theory of Communicative Action* in later works, especially when it comes to the universality of valid claims or communicative rationality transcending here and now. But whether these arguments "withstand the test of strength" in direct comparison with Rorty's arguments can be observed on the pages of Habermas's *Truth and Justification* from 1998, and when analyzing the exchange of views of both philosophers contained in the work *Rorty and His Critics* from 2000. I will also refer to these two key sources when the views of Rorty and Habermas are juxtaposed later in this work.

In the case of Rorty's thought, however, the texts essential for this work, and for the realization of the task outlined in it, include *Contingency, Irony, and Solidarity* and *Objectivity, Relativism, and Truth*. When writing these books Rorty wished to initiate a transformation in our way of thinking and attitude, which is to be based on replacing the need for objectivity with the need for solidarity by incorporating detailed epistemological and semantic analyses at several points. In his opinion, what is necessary is a change in the rhetoric that our community uses, a change in its own image of itself, in its thinking, and a renunciation of elaborate edifices based on one or another understanding of truth. Moreover, in the mentioned works Rorty gave the most attention to the categories crucial for his sociopolitical perspective: contingency, irony, solidarity, and freedom. One of his objectives was, as he himself argued, to point to the possibility of presenting a liberal utopia in which "human solidarity would be seen not as a fact to be recognized by clearing away 'prejudice' or burrowing down to previously hidden depths but, rather, as a goal to be achieved."[25] This goal could be achieved not through investigation but by means of imagination, the imaginative ability to acknowledge our contemporaries as suffering fellow beings. This solidarity would be constituted not by discovering some sort of truth about our own selves but by making us sensitive to particular instances of suffering and humiliation. This process would consist in the gradual recognition of other human beings as not "other" but "one of us."

This stance held by Rorty and Habermas is rooted in the tradition of pragmatic thought, especially that of John Dewey, which Rorty explicitly pointed to, inter alia, in *Objectivity, Relativism, and Truth* as well Habermas in *Between Facts and Norms*. Rorty drew on Dewey extensively in a number of his texts, writing, for instance, that he wished to consider his thought a continuation of Dewey's stance. Though their perspectives differ in some respects, the differences are small, especially as far as the issues dwelled upon in this work are concerned.[26] For our purposes, it is important to note that what in Rorty's opinion is valuable in Dewey's perspective, and what he himself tried to extract from Dewey's philosophy and to retain in his own considerations, is an account of gradual change in humans' self-image "which has taken place in recorded history—the change from a sense of their dependence upon something antecedently present to a sense of the utopian possibilities of the future, the growth of their ability to mitigate their finitude by a talent for self-creation."[27] He also appreciated Dewey's attempts to overthrow the doctrines of representationalism; and he agreed with Dewey that they impede winning the sense of one's own independence. Rorty wanted to continue this project and to prove it is due to this greater independence that we shall be able to build a liberal society that shall realize to a greater extent, among other things, the idea of freedom.[28]

It should be added that the reception of the thought of both philosophers is also a focus of this work, but only insofar as it concerns their reading of each other and the issues in question. This research strategy has been accompanied to a great extent by the thought of Theodor W. Adorno; that is, to paraphrase, when coping with philosophies or particular thinkers, one needs to refer to their own texts.[29] The phrase "to a great extent" does not appear in the above sentence without a reason, for, as it should be mentioned, works of such authors as John McCumber, Matthew Festenstein, and Richard J. Bernstein were of much help in the initial stage of investigating the philosophical output of Rorty and Habermas.[30] It was, inter alia, while studying them that I first had the intuition of the similarities between their views. The work itself, however, in its reconstruction and critical parts rests on direct reading and analysis of Rorty's and Habermas's texts, so as to point, at the very source, to the compatibility of the central elements of their philosophical perspectives, to indicate on what basis we should rest democracies, and, additionally, to present that on the basis of their thought there is a possibility to develop an understanding of freedom as responsibility in the future. Paving the way toward such a possible understanding of freedom is yet another aim of this work.

Step by Step

In writing this book I have been accompanied by some intuitions, among these that the perspectives of Rorty and of Habermas are convergent and that we need an original reading of the dialogue between Rorty and Habermas to show the convergence of the positions of both thinkers. In other words, I will focus in this book on the dialogue between Richard Rorty and Jürgen Habermas, which has been going on intensively since the 1990s until the death of Richard Rorty in 2007. This exchange concerned fundamental philosophical issues: the nature of reality, the status of truth, the understanding of modernity, and the universality of philosophical concepts, as well as the implications of these for the issues of freedom, democracy, and the present and future of liberal societies. Adversaries have often emphasized the mutual sympathy of the two philosophers, personal and philosophical, as well as the fact that they do not differ much in practical terms, in particular regarding the social and political consequences of their positions. Their discussion took the form of a dialogue between the great philosophical traditions of European continental philosophy represented by Habermas, with particular emphasis on critical theory, and the tradition of American pragmatism represented by Rorty.

The fact that quite a bit of time has passed since the dispute was conducted between the two does not mean that the issues raised at the time have lost their relevance. Issues such as truth, reason, freedom, and the role of philosophy are timeless. Addressing these issues in this book is thus a value in itself, but there is another aim as well: to show that not only are the conclusions of the positions of Rorty and Habermas convergent but also their positions themselves, much more than both thinkers were sometimes ready to admit. I will, therefore, go against the tide of schematisms seeking to show connections between Rorty's pragmatism and Habermas's philosophy. I will, however, not limit myself to the task just mentioned; I will also try to indicate which elements of Rorty's and Habermas's positions may prove to be crucial for developing the concept of society that is modern, liberal, and based on diversity and tolerance. Therefore, I am interested in the relationship between Habermas's and Rorty's philosophy from the practical perspective too—the social and political perspective—and in the practical implications of Rorty's and Habermas's positions. To implement such a research concept I will draw basic problem areas and concepts from the philosophy of John Dewey.[31]

To show both the extent to which Rorty and Habermas are convergent with respect to philosophical perspectives and their sociopolitical views, and to show that there is a possibility of developing on their basis a new understanding of freedom as responsibility (chapter 3), first, the following pages shall be devoted to reconstructing the central threads of Rorty's and of Habermas's thought (chapters 1 and 2). These threads have been selected in such a way as to present the basis of their thinking as accurately as possible, as well as to point to the elements that are important when explaining their particular choice of appropriate political form.[32]

To speak in more detail, in the first chapter of the monograph I reconstruct Rorty's views and explain among other things the proper sense of the category of ethnocentrism used by the American pragmatist and indicate that, despite Rorty's declared belief in the compatibility of the idea of respect for private spheres with any political model, ultimately only liberal democracy turns out to be the right framework for pluralism of the private spheres. I also devote a lot of space to Rorty's key category of contingency, as well as to his specific understanding of the concept of rationality, which in his understanding is equated with tolerance, understood as patience and understanding for views that differ from his own. In this chapter I also confront the objection of relativism frequently raised against Rorty's concept and indicate that Rorty himself rejected this position. It can be said that relativism as a position can be formulated only from a universal perspective, which Rorty consistently questioned. As Rorty put it, if you have no epistemological concept, you also do not have a relativistic epistemological concept. Rorty follows a similar path, rejecting the accusation of irrationalism in his own position. I also consider other key concepts from Rorty's thought, namely the concept of solidarity being a result of specific historical, social, and institutional processes, as well as the concept of communication, understood as the replacement of coercion by persuasion. I regard his antirepresentationalism as the key to understanding Rorty's position correctly.

In the first chapter I will also present and refer to other accusations that were formulated regarding Rorty's position. The pragmatist himself referred to most of these accusations, such as the question of whether irony can lead to the erosion of a liberal society, that is, whether it can be limited to the private sphere only so that it does not threaten the values of the public sphere, such as tolerance, free communication, and solidarity. In addition to the accusations accepted by Rorty, I will also present my own criticisms. In particular, I will point to the possible inconsistency of Rorty, who seems on the one hand to insist on the division into the public and private sphere, postulating the limitation of all philosophical narratives to the latter; on the other hand, however, he treats the innovative dictionary of "liberal ironists" as the target language of the public sphere of a utopian liberal society.

In the second chapter of this volume, I will present the key categories of Habermas's philosophy, primarily on the basis of the *Theory of Communication Action* published in 1981, but also other works, among those *Truth and Justification*. Analysis of this work allows the reader to learn about Habermas's main arguments regarding the foundations on which we should base our thinking about freedom, communication, politics, and democracy. I will present the categories of the lifeworld, of communication rationality, communication action, and the role the validity claims play in it. In other words, I will start with a different approach than other researchers and I will focus primarily on the philosophical bases of Habermas's vision of democracy and politics.[33] Is there any truth as a point of reference? Can we refer to some universal values? What is the role of rationality? I will thus not focus on the question of whether Habermas's concept of democracy is possible.[34] The basis of his concept of democracy—which he called radical democracy—is his discourse theory, and that theory will be a main concern in this book when Habermas's thought will be considered.

It is important to say that Habermas has wanted his concept of radical democracy, read in terms of discourse theory, to have a practical significance, and that is why in *Between Facts and Norms* he also analyzed the role and development of the political public sphere and indicated the role of civil society, but not only as normative demand. That is why he said that the concepts of the political public sphere and civil society "are not mere normative postulates but have empirical relevance. However, additional assumptions must be introduced if we are to use these concepts to translate the discourse-theoretic reading of radical democracy into sociological terms and reformulate it in an empirically falsifiable manner."[35] He tried to do so by analyzing the role of law and the rule of law. I will not focus here on this matter, firstly because I want to present what are the necessary philosophical bases for democracy to occur in Habermas's view, and later to analyze whether they are justified in light of the debate with Rorty, who also presented in his works the necessary philosophical basis for his vision of democratic politics. Secondly, I will not focus on them because, as I have said above, they were not part of the Rorty-Habermas debate.

The first two chapters are an elaborate, but necessary, introduction to chapter 3, which is devoted not only to the confrontation of the previously reconstructed positions of Rorty and Habermas, although this will also take place, but also to demonstrate that they are not as far apart as it sometimes seemed to the thinkers themselves or to readers of their work. This chapter will be a reconstruction of the real debate between the two philosophers. Recapitulating this debate, I will draw attention to the numerous distortions that appeared in the mutual interpretations of the positions of both adversaries. In particular, I will be critical toward some elements of Rorty's interpretation of Habermas's thoughts. I will also reveal assumptions of their own positions that the philosophers sometimes have not noticed, such as the presence of a moment of idealization in Rorty's philosophy, contrary to his declarations. I will also devote my attention to considerations regarding the status of valid claims, in particular the issue of whether by raising such claims in our communicative actions, we actually refer to the universal auditorium. When referring to these matters I will point out the crucial difference between Habermas and Rorty, but I will also focus on the fundamental agreement between the two philosophers regarding the role that communication plays in building solidarity in modern, liberal societies and what formal conditions must be met for that communication to occur. Both Rorty and Habermas have agreed that communication is crucial and that certain formal foundations are necessary for it to occur. Due to these foundations, appropriate social interaction as well as creating new worlds and new languages are possible. Both philosophers list among these formal conditions the equality of the parties and freedom of speech. In their opinion, these conditions are necessary for undistorted communication to occur. In the light of their crucial role, Habermas has developed his idea of communicative rationality. Rorty, when assuming an attitude toward it, wrote that—as it appeared to him—there is a great deal of convergence between Habermas's idea of replacing subject-centered reason with communicative reason and what he called the Protagorean/Emersonian tradition.[36] This tradition refers to the thesis—as he wrote—"that human beings are on their own—that their own imagination will have to do what they hoped the gods, or a scientific knowledge of the intrinsic nature of reality, might do."[37]

Both Rorty and Habermas make use of their imagination and take things into their own hands. They present their sociopolitical utopias with the conviction that these may spread. In their own unique way, they develop perspectives thanks to which it is possible to designate the way "toward the future." Their approach combines many common elements: fundamental moral beliefs, a vision of a decentralized world, fostering pluralism of world views, seeking a compromise understood as "unforced consent," opposition to all forms of violence in social life, and the role of education in preparing individuals to participate in discourses oriented toward achieving compromise, as well as the role of hope and the vision of liberal utopia. They are also to a considerable extent compatible, as, for example, in the case of their common recognition of the primacy of the category of freedom over the category of truth. The categories of freedom and of communication—crucial elements for the thought of both philosophers—shall be discussed in more detail in the following pages.

It is important to highlight here that these crucial categories and values, which in the case of Rorty and Habermas become the basis for advocating liberal democracy, are to be found also in the thought of Dewey, one of the leading representatives of American pragmatism, who in his works devoted a great deal of time to reflecting on the relationship between philosophy and democracy. It is hardly surprising, since Dewey, as a representative of the previous generation of pragmatists, worked on presenting the benefits of liberal democracy and on developing both the philosophical and pragmatist basis for a "Great Community" or "radical democracy" built upon values such as equality and freedom, long before Rorty and Habermas. Before moving to reconstructing and critically discussing Rorty's and Habermas's thought later, it is, then, worth describing, as a means of making an introduction, the central threads of Dewey's philosophy. In the introductory description of Dewey's views, I will oppose the stereotypical approach to pragmatism. I will refer to Dewey's multiple forms of rooting the individual into social structures, and by that reject a simplified vision of pragmatism as a doctrine based on the atomist version of individualism. I will also discuss Dewey's idea of radical democracy, understood as abandoning society's orientation toward objective truth and replacing it with the idea of dialogue and education aiming at developing individual potentials. Thus presented, Dewey's thought shall constitute a background for reconstructing the life-forms that are characterized by attributing an important role to individual freedom and communication devoid of violence, as presented by Rorty and by Habermas. In other words, Dewey's perspective will constitute a peculiar anchor in this book. I will begin my considerations by presenting it, but I will also come back to it in the part that is a recapitulation of the most important findings of this work. Thanks to presenting Dewey's thought at the beginning of this volume, it shall become possible to observe later on the numerous similarities between Dewey's, Rorty's, and Habermas's perspectives. Some of these similarities shall be pointed out in the concluding section of this volume, in the context of the already analyzed thought of the two leading thinkers of American and continental pragmatism. This, however, shall be achieved only to such an extent as to see that it is possible to talk not only of convergence between Rorty's and Habermas's thought but also of convergence within pragmatist sociopolitical thought when reading Dewey's as a kind of "common root" of Habermas's and Rorty's positions.[38] Pointing to these similarities shall be the first step toward summarizing the issues most crucial for this work, which shall be highlighted toward the end of this volume.

I

OPENING

First Comes Dewey

Introduction

In some respects, much of what we encounter in the thought of modern pragmatists such as Richard Rorty or Jürgen Habermas is to be found as early as in John Dewey's philosophy and his numerous works on the crisis of liberal values.[1] It is in these works that we read of the necessity to articulate a perspective that would allow us to retain these values alongside ongoing economic and industrial development. It is in them that Dewey has indicated that values such as equality, freedom, and individual self-realization are the values that should be supported not only for the sake of individuals but also for the sake of the community in which they live. The best political form that can ensure all of this—in Dewey's opinion—is liberal democracy. In this kind of democracy, though, individuals do not realize their life plans regardless of social costs. The scope of individual freedom should be defined. When acting, we need to consider the consequences—for us, as well as for others. In other words, it is of utmost significance to act in a responsible way.

In order to briefly present Dewey's perspective, it is necessary to refer to three texts. These are *The Public and Its Problems*, *Liberalism and Social Action*, and *Individualism, Old and New*. In the first of these, Dewey defended the idea of participatory democracy; in the second, he presented a new liberalism whose values need to be negotiated in resistance to current economic and political conditions in order for it to remain valid; in the third, he discussed the development of individualism and indicated the necessity for developing its new form, corresponding to the new conditions of culture. The three aforementioned texts are to be the major source in relation to which Dewey's perspective is to be presented, though references to many other texts shall appear as well. Taking all of them into consideration, Dewey can be said to have concentrated upon classical liberalism together with its values, which lost much of its importance in light of social, technological, and economic transformations.[2] He analyzed the present-day crisis of individuality, communal relations, and the workings of the democratic structure of countries, and tried to propose a solution to this impasse.

From Crisis to New Liberalism

Dewey witnessed the crisis of both liberal values and democratic institutions. The crisis came into existence alongside the emergence of new forces of production that were not accompanied by the development of an appropriate conception of intellectuality and individuality. Liberals did not notice that the understanding of the value of freedom, individuality, and intellectuality is historically determined, which, eventually, led to social and political crises.[3] Reformulations in the realm of beliefs, needs, goals, and political and legal relations remained far behind the ongoing transformations within the external (economic) conditions of society. They were hindered by the permanence of the idea of early individualism, in accordance with which what is valuable is in concordance with activities oriented toward profit.[4] These ideas, as well as the legal institutions built upon them in the period of industrial and scientific revolution, caused only a few to be able to use the existing resources.[5]

Dewey deemed it necessary to improve the position of individuals. Such an opportunity, for him, consisted in the elimination of the old economic and political individualism, as well as in institutional changes. In his opinion, the sociopolitical and legal sphere should not be entirely dependent on the economy. Accordingly, he claimed that it is crucial to create a new vision of liberalism within which production and exchange would not determine the entirety of human interactions.[6] It would be based upon democratic social relations enabling individual development of its members and an emergence of their new consciousness.[7] Realizing such a new vision of liberalism should, in Dewey's opinion, begin with examining the interactions in which individuals are engaged,[8] with conscious perception of social reality,[9] and with determining common goals and the possibilities for achieving them.[10]

Individual and Community

Individuals, in Dewey's opinion, are a composition of habits, beliefs, and values that are social products and social facts.[11] Their existence is, from the outset, dependent on a *give-and-take* relations that connect them with others and with their surroundings, and within which the surroundings and the individuals affect each other.[12] The basic surrounding for an individual is a community. This community, according to Dewey, exists as long as there is a common, uniting action whose consequences are considered beneficial by all the persons partaking in it, and when there is an effort to preserve its effects.[13] A community and its individual members are bound by such a strong interdependence that it is impossible to draw a clear boundary between them, and, accordingly, neither of them should be treated as more important than the other.[14]

Dewey did realize that it is difficult to talk about an individual using terms different than those developed in previous conceptions. Dewey used these terms but tried to point out that the traditional sharp distinction between individuals and the community is not compatible with a more complex reality, composed of a number of relations, where it is difficult to distinguish between its parts. Dewey wrote that as long as the old constructs and habits function, the idea of harmony between individual thoughts and desires and social reality will be perceived as "conformance." If, however, we were able to reject the old way of thinking, we would have a chance to recognize the forces and networks of relations that affect us, and of which we are a part.[15]

Which Political Form?

According to Dewey, in our everyday existence composed of networks of dependencies and relations affecting our beliefs and decisions, what we are faced with is ethical and ideological pluralism.[16] Once we acknowledge it, we should resign from searching for stable and unchanging truths. In the *Quest for Certainty*, Dewey wrote that we should cease striving for certainty in our attempt to grasp the absolute basis of reality.[17] It is not the stable elements that should determine our world and our actions. We do not need unchanging truths and absolute categories to be the basis for our actions. Our actions can be undertaken not on the grounds of referring to something stable, but to something we consider necessary at a given moment. And this can be determined by analyzing our needs on the basis of everyday practice, thanks to critical reflection and intelligence.[18]

In light of the above, exercising our critical reflection and intelligence, we could ask which political form is best. Dewey answered this question in the *Public and Its Problems*, where he wrote that it is impossible to say which form of social and political system is best, at least until history reaches its end. Even the least accidental of these forms are not a manifestation of an absolute and unquestionable good but a product of certain conditions and habits existing in a given period. Dewey believed that while searching for an appropriate form it is necessary to turn toward practice. For without a practical reference, our propositions shall be but abstract and theoretical.[19] Practice is what, to a great extent, determines the number of sensible, specific solutions to the problems we are faced with, as well as what determines the choice of a political form that is most appropriate in given conditions.

Dewey made such a choice on the basis of practical observations. Since he considered it crucial to create conditions for each and every individual to participate in the process of shaping the values and institutions regulating social relations, it is democracy that he deemed the most appropriate political form. The right criterion for assessing social and political institutions is the extent to which they facilitate the development of individual talents as well as individual and community welfare. In other words, choosing democracy as the best political form is currently based, in Dewey's thought, on the idea of human development and the belief that individuals' interest should respect the welfare and integrity of the group.[20] It is democracy based on dialogue, communication, and participation that creates the conditions for individual development and for pursuing individual and common welfare. As Dewey put it, democracy should become a way of life in which individuals will act in the social and political sphere and in which they will have influence over the decisions that concern them. They would cooperate with each other even if the needs, goals, or consequences of the actions were different for each one of them, for cooperation itself would be considered a valuable element of life just as competition is considered a valuable element of sports.[21]

Radical Democracy

Democracy, as understood by Dewey, is a radical goal whose accomplishment is based on individuals' cooperation and intelligence.[22] In *Democracy Is Radical*, Dewey wrote that in his vision of democracy there is nothing more radical than insisting on using democratic methods as the means for arriving at social change.[23] And not one word says that we should approach social change through the use of violence. Dewey deemed it mistaken to believe that in such a situation, violence is unavoidable.[24] In his opinion, it cannot result in a better society and community, for violence gives rise to violence.[25] Thus, the ultimate goal, that is freedom for all, must be accomplished by means that do not contradict it.[26]

In *A Liberal Speaks Out for Liberalism*, Dewey wrote that freedom is not something that can be granted to humans by an external authority, by the proletariat, or by a fascist order. Freedom can emerge only when individuals partake in obtaining it. It is this commitment, and not some political mechanism, that is the basis for liberal democracy.[27] The emergence of freedom is a necessary condition for the full development of individuals and for their being able to act toward accomplishing common and individual welfare and happiness.[28] In Dewey's opinion, everything that contributes to the growth and self-realization of individuals must contribute to the growth of community, for the way it grows affects the way in which individuals grow themselves.[29] He believed thus, for he was aware of the fact that our actions have certain consequences not only for ourselves but also for others. Once we acknowledge the existence of these consequences, we become aware of the dependencies that reveal that we are bound with others, and in this way, the public sphere begins to emerge.[30] Thus, in Dewey's opinion, the interests of individuals and the community are equivalent and interdependent. Our private goals cannot be fully accomplished if they are not a part of common goals as well. What is good for me should be as good for others as possible.[31]

Dialogue and Education

Dewey believed that democracy emerges when unrestrained social actions are inextricably linked with vivid communication[32] or free exchange of ideas.[33] It should be conducted in the spirit of tolerance and equality,[34] and we should treat those that we disagree with as those that we can learn from. According to Dewey, such communication allows us to solve controversies and conflicts. Dewey finds a model for managing such conflicts via communication in academic community, connected with self-improvement, growth, progress, pluralism, and dialogue, which makes it truly democratic.[35] Following this as a model while forming a liberal community would allow us to pursue an effective social and political reconstruction. It would allow us to free ourselves from the burden of dogmas, stereotypes, and habits formed in the past.[36] It would give us an opportunity to directly reconcile our ideas with life practice and social and political conditions, and to do so by means of the scientific method.[37] As Dewey wrote, "Application [of a scientific method] *in* life would signify that science was absorber and distributed; that it was the instrumentality of that common understanding and through communication which is the precondition of the existence of a genuine and effective public."[38]

According to Dewey, the controversies and conflicts mentioned above should be solved by society, for it is society that knows best when they emerge.[39] For him, lack of proper education among citizens is not a reason for the society to be denied the right to decide about the direction in which state politics should be pursued, but an argument in favor of creating a proper educational system. Such an education, according to Dewey, should direct our attention to the relativity and the changeability of our perspectives and attitudes, as well as point to the networks of dependencies that constitute them,[40] to the countless relations binding us with others.[41] It enables the emergence of new needs, new intellectual habits, and new moral models and abilities to design future goals.[42] The aim of education is, according to Dewey, to develop both critical thinking, which should permeate all spheres of human life, and individuals' abilities as far as sensitivity is concerned. It should prepare for life in a community, and it should unveil the relations binding us with others, as well as make us aware of what the common good is. Consequently, there should emerge a community in which groups that are ethnically, culturally, or religiously different would not function as equal only due to the implementation of law, but due to the commonly shared respect for cultural difference and otherness of its members. This community would be pluralistic, a place where everybody benefits from unrestrained contact with others.[43]

Toward Great Community

As has been said before, education as Dewey understood it is a life process that never ends and that is connected with individuals' growth and self-realization.[44] It enables recognizing new needs and pursuing active debate.[45] It also enables the emergence of communication and cooperation,[46] without which the public cannot be constituted, and the Great Community cannot come into existence. Creating the Great Community, in Dewey's opinion, will be possible due to proper, critically oriented education, and respecting the rights of other human beings to equality, freedom, and the conditions for the free exchange of ideas.[47] The philosopher thought that achieving the fullness of human existence and creating an ideal community in the give-and-take relation is possible only through participating in the community, communication, cooperative effort, and in the sharing of beliefs and desires.

Such a project is by no means easy. However, according to Dewey, the obstacles that emerge can be overcome.[48] Thus, he has presented a twofold vision of social reconstruction, occurring within both social and individual consciousness as well as within the institutional sphere. On the one hand, by embracing the transformation of social and political consciousness through the emergence of a new individualism, communication, and reflexive and experimental intelligence, it is possible to approach ongoing problems and to present sensible prospects for their solution. On the other hand, Dewey has pointed to the necessity of proper social and political education, common actions toward governing a democratic state of which we are a part.

Utopian Project

Dewey's project, pointing to the necessity for changes in the social, political, economic, educational, and moral spheres, has faced considerable critique, often resulting from misinterpretations. Many deemed it utopian, for it was claimed to put too much emphasis on the role of intelligence and on the active participation of individuals in dialogue and cooperation, in creating individual and common welfare.[49] According to Dewey, however, such a perspective was quite realistic. He believed that it is necessary to invest all of our energies into affirming the value of our legacy.[50] He repeated that it is we who are responsible for strengthening and disseminating liberal values. In *The Need for a Recovery of Philosophy*, he wrote that it is crucial to clearly articulate our belief about the possibility of creating a democratic society based on liberal values, such as freedom, individualism, and intelligence.[51]

Alongside changes in the character of present challenges, democracy (which is only an instrument with which we tackle certain problems), liberalism, and our society should be reformulated. In light of these changes, Dewey himself pursued such a reformulation, acting against the traditional dualisms and pointing to the relativity, diversity, and processualism characteristic of our cognition as well as social and political interactions. In his reformulated vision of a liberal society, both the individuals and the community are values. In Dewey's opinion, both of them are a constant of everyday interactions, and it is through understanding their interrelations that it is possible, due to intelligence and critical reflection, to create a democratic society based upon mutual respect, equality, and dialogue.[52]

Followers

Dewey's vision of a liberal democracy was long suppressed by other visions until Rorty and Habermas, among others, returned to it in their sociopolitical thought.[53] Their role in popularizing Dewey's philosophy and pragmatist thought anew has been substantial.[54] It is thanks to them that Dewey's thought has been seriously reconsidered alongside the idea that we are "to be on our guard against using intellectual tools which were useful in a certain socio-cultural environment after the environment has changed, to be aware that we may have to invent new tools to cope with new situations."[55] What is the most important, then, is for us not to be trapped in a "shell of conventions," and for our language, thoughts, and actions to be compatible with the reality in which we live, so as to successfully tackle the problems that occur within it. It is not the only important lesson we learn from Dewey, though. Rorty claimed that what is worth preserving from Dewey's works is "his sense of the gradual change in human beings' self-image which has taken place in recorded history—the change from a sense of their dependence upon something antecedently present to a sense of the utopian possibilities of the future, the growth of their ability to mitigate their finitude by a talent for self-creation."[56] This thought is "preserved," inter alia, thanks to Rorty and Habermas, who support the idea of freeing human beings from what is to be prior to their own selves, and who point in particular to the corresponding emergence of utopian possibilities and better chances for individual self-realization.[57] They themselves exercise this freedom and create utopian projects of a liberal society and of an ideal communicative community, which should be and are touched upon later in this volume. These utopias do not depend on some absolute truths, as was the case with the totalitarian regimes of Hitler or Stalin, who "justified the imposition of total control by the State by the openly proclaimed objective of reconstructing society from top to bottom, in keeping with a dogmatic but otherwise vague notion of a new utopian order."[58] Both Rorty and Habermas argue for the necessity of establishing specific formal conditions by which each and every individual will be able to pursue their personal happiness and welfare.

II

ON RORTY'S SOCIOPOLITICAL THOUGHT

Introduction

Rorty and Dewey

In a number of texts, Richard Rorty explicitly stressed that it was John Dewey who had a sway over his thought.[1] Dewey is the philosopher Rorty admired the most and he considered himself to be a disciple.[2] He wanted to see "the charges of 'relativism' and 'irrationalism' once leveled against Dewey as merely the mindless defensive reflexes of the philosophical tradition which he attacked."[3] Being to a great extent in philosophical debt to Dewey, Rorty presented his views, which were, however, deemed as equally controversial as those formulated by Dewey. Consequently, just as Dewey did, Rorty encountered many critical responses to his work.[4] Some point to the ambiguities and contradictions appearing within his thought.[5] Several are actually worth mentioning here at the very beginning. In the case of these charges, it is also worth attending to the way in which Rorty himself takes a stance in response to them, so as to, by making further interpretive steps, resolve the doubts of his critics. At the same time, what is to be presented are the central categories and problems of Rorty's thought, which shall be discussed in more detail in the following sections.

Philosophy and the Mirror of Nature

In his now famous *Philosophy and the Mirror of Nature*, Rorty took a stand against the previous outputs of philosophy, especially of analytic philosophy. At the very beginning of the work, he claimed that the vision of mind as a great mirror, containing various accurate and inaccurate representations, a mirror that can be examined with pure nonempirical methods, has been very appealing to the philosophical tradition. He stressed that but for this vision of mind, the concept of knowledge as accuracy of representation would not be so convincing, and "the strategy common to Descartes and Kant—getting more accurate representations by inspecting, repairing, and polishing the mirror, so to speak—would not have made sense."[6] Rorty took a stand against this tradition, not wanting to be held captive by this very vision. He argued against the concept of knowledge as representation. He also objected to traditional dualisms, including that of the knowing subject and the object of knowledge. For him, knowledge does not consist in uncovering what is out there in the world. Further, he tried to dissolve the previously made distinctions, on the basis of which it was possible to talk of the objective and the subjective, of facts and values, or of true or false statements describing the world. The fact that we label some convictions as true, for Rorty, has nothing to do with the way the world is, for he believed that the fact that some people share power, and others are deprived of it, has consequences for which statements are candidates for truth, which are treated as serious candidates for discussion.[7] Thus, he rejected the traditional belief that is based on the conviction that there is some higher instance called "Truth" that can set us free.[8]

What is more, Rorty thought that we could create such a model of "I" that would be satisfactory, and that could be adjusted to fit our own needs. It is possible to presume, then, that, according to Rorty, there is no "objective truth" about what the human "I" is actually like. It is worth noticing, however, that such a stance could be justified only on the grounds of the traditional metaphysical/epistemological belief in the "really real," from which Rorty tried to break free.[9] In short, it is ambiguous as to what exactly Rorty himself contributed, for he often wrote in a way that suggested that he knew what things are really like. Still, he did become aware in his later work that he should not have spoken the way he sometimes did, "of 'pseudo-problems', but rather of problematics and vocabularies that might have proven to be of value, but in fact did not." As he wrote, "I should not have spoken of "unreal" or "confused" philosophical distinctions, but rather of distinctions whose employment has proved to lead nowhere, proved to be more trouble than they were worth."[10]

Rorty believed that the previous meditations over the essence of things or something of an intrinsic nature, which should be uncovered brought more trouble than they were worth.[11] What caused these problems were the suppositions forming the foundations for our vocabulary, whose origins have been forgotten, and which began to be treated as something to be yet uncovered. Rorty sets aside such considerations. He advocated for changing the problematics of our philosophical discussions from methodological and ontological to ethical and political.[12] As far as this project is concerned, he claimed that we have never managed to go beyond *nomos* toward *phusis*, beyond rhetoric toward logic, beyond the nominality toward the reality, beyond politics toward something less local and less contingent.[13] We have not gone beyond it, for, in Rorty's opinion, all the previous problems are historically contingent and are not, as a number of metaphysicians claim, a product of our inability to find an appropriate "theoretical glue," which, once being discovered, could be commonly accepted by our society.[14] In other words, there is nothing to go beyond. The sooner we become aware of it, the closer we will get to the emergence of a culture of irony: a culture in which beliefs will be based on the acquired experience of past generations, and no one, neither princes nor philosophers, will be able to challenge the authority of the thus obtained experience.[15] The experience or the language that we use do not reflect, in Rorty's opinion, the way the world really is. He agrees with Ludwig Wittgenstein, John Dewey, and Martin Heidegger that "investigations of the foundations of knowledge or morality or language or society may be simply apologetics, attempts to eternalize a certain contemporary language-game, social practice, or self-image."[16]

Rorty wished to break with the previous tradition holding that it is visions rather than opinions, metaphors rather than statements about facts, that form the foundations for our philosophical beliefs. What he advocated for is a metaphor of self-creation, and not of discovery. In Rorty's opinion, we should accept the fact that this metaphor is the only tool to gain control over the world. Thanks to it we will be able to reject the belief that "truth, and not just power and pain, is to be found 'out there.'"[17]

Contingency

Our liberal society has been constituted, Rorty claimed, due to the emergence and dissemination of certain metaphors. It is not the superior moral law but the sense of solidarity and loyalty that is the point of support for such a society. Solidarity and loyalty are not ahistorical facts; rather, they emerge in the course of history. They are not discovered but produced. And thus, morality is exclusively characteristic of such a liberal society or community. For Rorty, it is a historical narration and utopian speculation rather than a result of a discovery of some general rules.

Rorty is an adherent of such a liberal society. Still, although he believed that it is but a fortunate, accidental construct, he wished to reformulate its language in order to improve it. But how did he want to accomplish that task? Claiming that the society as well as its language are only accidental constructs seems to deprive us of the ability to influence its changes and to support its growth. A question arises: how are we to extend "us," and to diminish suffering? If a liberal society was only a fortunate accident, the only thing that would be left for us to do would be to wait for another coincidence that would make human solidarity expand. Meanwhile, yet another, less fortunate accident could occur and lead, for example, to popularizing anti-Semitism or racism anew.

While looking for solutions to the problems mentioned above, it is important to properly understand the intuition hidden behind Rorty's concept of contingency. When he described something as historically contingent or accidental, what he meant is that it is not rooted in any true, objective reality existing somewhere out there. Something is contingent when it arises due to a number of events in a specific historical, geographical, or political context. According to Rorty, we have much influence over the course of these events; he said "people can rationally change their beliefs and desires," and that "one can give a retrospective account of why one changed—how one invoked old beliefs or desires in justification of the new ones—rather than having to say, helplessly, 'it just happened; somehow I got converted.'"[18]

In other words, according to Rorty, we can say that we have influence over the extension of the circle of those we call "we"; this, however, does not change "the fact" that our tools are solely cultural, and that when competing with other communities or cultures and their values, we have no objective advantage over them. We do not possess any stable and unchanging point of reference, nor any universal criteria. Accordingly, Rorty, to a great extent, resigned himself from the notions of "radical critique," "delving down to the roots," as well as from the idea of "the critique of ideology." By doing so, he exposed himself to considerable criticism, for, as he himself observed, such a perspective "is criticized for not having what philosophers were employed to do: explain why our framework, or culture, or interests, or language, or whatever, is at last on the right track—in touch with physical reality or the moral law, or the real numbers, or some other sort of object patiently waiting about to be copied."[19]

Ethnocentrism

Rorty believed that we cannot take a supracultural, universal stand, for we are but products of our own culture. Therefore, he advocated ethnocentrism. Ethnocentrism, however, is yet another category that caused Rorty some trouble. He admitted that his ambiguous use of the term "ethnocentrism" provoked antagonistic responses from and distrustful attitudes in some of his critics. He wrote, This ambiguity has made me appear to be attempting a transcendental deduction of democratic politics from antirepresentationalism premises. I should have distinguished more clearly between ethnocentrism as an inescapable condition—roughly synonymous with 'human finitude'—and as a reference to a particular *ethnos*. In the latter usage, 'ethnocentrism' means loyalty to the sociopolitical culture of what the Marxists used to call 'bourgeois democracies' and what Roberto Unger calls, more neutrally,' the rich North Atlantic democracies.'"[20] Rorty considered ethnocentrism a bridge between antirepresentationalism and political liberalism.[21] Although metaphysics is said to be a voice of the past,[22] Rorty still found it useful to distinguish between what has been obtained by persuasion, and what has been obtained by force. He advocated the former, and he did not doubt the possibility of peaceful social progress. He did not doubt the values of the community in which he lived—the liberal society—claiming, moreover, that they are the only points of support on which we can rely. These values include, inter alia, equality of parties and freedom of speech. They are, at the same time, a formal basis for allowing new metaphors to emerge in the communicative sphere. Rorty believed that things are going to get better if we allow new metaphors to come into existence. It will happen once each and every one of us has the right to speak and be heard, and when no one shall claim a status superior to that of an interlocutor in a debate, as we are, as he claimed, all just human beings, all fallible, all determined by history.[23] It is the prospect of speaking and being heard, and not some universal categories or laws, that Rorty thought was the most appropriate foundation for liberal democracy.

Whichever Kind of Politics

In the light of the above, we may wonder at Rorty's writing that a plurality of different subjective perspectives is compatible with any kind of politics, even of the liberal kind.[24] In other words, according to the philosopher, there is nothing that limits us to favoring this or that kind of politics. In Rorty's opinion, it is an act of choice—good as any other—for there are no stable and unchanging criteria for making such a choice. It is important to realize, however, that in his case, this choice is not as free as he would like it to be.[25] The issue becomes clearer once we look at how Rorty argued against Heidegger and attempted to reformulate the public sphere in such a way so as to assimilate individual private spheres within it. Rorty tried to escape the threat awaiting here by finding new spaces for private endeavors and public interactions, delineating the private and the public sphere. Any excessive individual aspirations should remain within the former. The latter, as Rorty wrote, should be the space for interactions based on "moral responsibility" and supported by "moral vocabulary." In other words, Rorty believed that the private sphere should be clearly separated from the public one. By suggesting such a step, however, he contributed to narrowing the scope within which the aforesaid choice can be made, for there are but few political models where, as Rorty wished, the existence of individual private spheres, as a space for a plurality of different subjective perspectives, can be recognized and respected, and where the necessity of searching for consensus within the public sphere can be properly emphasized. The choice that we will be able to make will become more specified, and less free, than it may initially seem. In such a situation, we, alongside Rorty, will not be satisfied with "whichever kind of politics." If we wish to maintain the plurality of different, subjective perspectives, there is probably only one choice to be made, and that is liberal democracy.

This brief and only partial excursion into the previously mentioned problems is probably quite enough for our purposes at present. To a great extent, they are only signaled; yet it will be necessary to return to these issues and, among other things, answer the crucial question as to whether Rorty managed to break with the previous philosophical tradition, according to his own wishes.

Breaking with the Tradition

Rorty is an adherent of the conviction that we should free our culture from all the philosophical vocabulary amassed around the concepts of reason, truth, and knowledge. This does not mean, however, that reason, truth, and knowledge are inaccurate as such. According to Rorty, what is inaccurate are the Platonic attempts at positioning them in the center of our culture and connecting them to our understanding of what a human being is. Freeing the culture from these would allow us to cease the ongoing attempts at reaching the world as it is, and would help us resign from the project of discovering the essence of things. But is it possible? Is it possible to resign from the previous philosophical vocabulary? Jürgen Habermas, considering such attempts in *Coping with Contingencies*, wrote, "The practice of criticizing Platonist pseudo-objects moves within a conceptual frame and employs conceptual means which cannot in turn be deconstructed without depriving anti-Platonism of its own critical Sting. The radical attempt to do away with any abstraction, idealization, or concept of truth, knowledge, and reality that transcends the local hic et nunc would run into performative self-contradictions. One cannot reduce all universals to particulars, all kinds of transcendence to immanence, the unconditional to the conditional, and so on, without presupposing these same distinctions and tacitly making use of them."[26] In other words, in Habermas's opinion, if we want to manage any general, universal concepts, they need to be present in our vocabulary. Then the anti-Platonic critique comes in two stages: "First, the deconstruction of hypostatizations is intended to do justice to formerly repressed contingencies; the next and more inconspicuous move toward a new scheme of interpretation is meant to offer instruction in how to cope differently with this new kind of contingency."[27] In addition, then, Habermas points out that the anti-Platonic critique has a reconstructive dimension, and does not only aim at the simple deconstruction of idealistic abstractions. Such activities, in his opinion, are compatible with the shift from Platonism to anti-Platonism, and back. The intention of Rorty, however, was to break free from such a shift. Thus, a question, voiced inter alia by Habermas, arises as to "whether Richard Rorty can do so without merely starting the next round of the same game."[28] The answer will not be possible after reconstructing the central threads of Rorty's philosophy in this chapter. It shall be fully articulated, though, in the course of juxtaposing Rorty's and Habermas's thought in chapter 3.

The reconstruction, as it has already been mentioned in the introduction, shall be pursued with the intention of presenting the central elements of Rorty's sociopolitical thought. As we already know, he wished for the emergence of a community that would replace the idea of objectivity with the idea of unforced consensus. In such a community, having no stable points of reference, we would be left alone, but, in turn, as Rorty claimed, we would be free in remaking our own selves.[29] This freedom, which, in his opinion, cannot be reached automatically through learning the truth, as his opponents tend to think, is of primary importance for his thought.[30] It is a crucial element of his philosophical project, the lack of which he is often accused of.[31] In the following sections, it shall become apparent that Rorty did possess a project of his own—a humanist project—and that it contains valuable directions that are of practical importance.

From Contingency to Irony

Rorty claimed that none of the descriptions of the world is an accurate representation of what actually is. Since he was one of the philosophers who saw science as but one of many fields of human activity, he disagreed with those who contrasted the subjective sphere and metaphor with bare scientific facts. In his opinion, science does not uncover the truth but creates it. The truths are not discovered by philosophy, either. What we encounter within science, philosophy, or everyday life is contingency. And it is necessary for us to cope with it, to elaborate an appropriate attitude in ourselves. These issues shall be discussed on the following pages.

On Contingency

TWO APPROACHES TO TRUTH

What is crucial for Rorty's considerations is the category of truth. In *Consequences of Pragmatism*, he wrote about two approaches to truth in two traditions:

> The first tradition thinks of truth as a vertical relationship between representations and what is represented. The second tradition thinks of truth horizontally—as the culminating reinterpretation of our predecessors' reinterpretation of their predecessors' reinterpretation. . . . This tradition does not ask how representations are related to nonrepresentations, but how representations can be seen as hanging together. The difference is not one between "correspondence" and "coherence" theories of truth—though these so-called theories are partial expression of this contrast. Rather, it is the difference between regarding truth, goodness, and beauty as eternal objects which we try to locate and reveal, and regarding them as artifacts whose fundamental design we often have to alter. The first tradition takes scientific truth as the center of philosophical concern [. . .]. The second tradition takes science as one [. . .] sector of culture, a sector which, like all the other sectors, only makes sense when viewed historically.[32]

Rorty disagreed with the first approach and in the belief that truth is somewhere "out there." In his opinion, it cannot be "out there," for it cannot exist detached from the human mind. What is "out there" is the world, but not its descriptions, not statements about it as well. Only the descriptions of the world may be true or false. The world itself, not supported by any descriptive activity of human beings, is not in a position to be asserted as a proposition.[33]

According to Rorty, truth occurs only where statements do. It is only they that can be true or false. In *Consequences of Pragmatism*, Rorty also wrote that "for pragmatists, 'truth' is just the name of a property which all true statements share," and it is difficult to say much about it.[34] Elsewhere, he wrote that truth is "simply a compliment paid to the beliefs which we think so well justified that, for the moment, further justification is not needed."[35] It is not surprising then that he considered the belief, existing within Western culture, that truth corresponds to reality nothing but a worn-out metaphor. Thus, he referred to Friedrich Nietzsche, who preached that truth is "a mobile army of metaphors [. . .] a sum of human relations, which have been enhanced, transposed, and embellished poetically and rhetorically and which after long use seem firm, canonical, and obligatory to a people."[36]

As far as the world is concerned, Rorty agreed that there exists something like a blind resistance of matter. He did not, however, deem it possible to transfer this nonlinguistic stiffness referring to facts onto the truth value of sentences. It is not difficult, though, as he observed, "to run together the fact that the world contains the causes of our being justified in holding a belief with the claim that some nonlinguistic state of the world is itself an example of truth."[37] As he added, this nonlinguistic state of affairs does not show us in which language games we should engage. We should not conclude, though, that decisions with respect to the issue are made arbitrarily, or that they are an expression of something hidden inside us. Accordingly, we should not substitute the objective criteria for choosing our vocabulary with the subjective ones, with reason, will, or emotions, for "the notions of criteria and choice (including that of 'arbitrary' choice) are no longer in point when it comes to changes from one language game to another."[38] According to Rorty (so far as we have gotten in his account), changes of this kind are neither acts of will nor results of a discussion. They result from a gradual process of getting out of the habit of using certain words, and getting used to others. This process has depended on many contingent elements, on contingent beliefs and desires.

CONTINGENCY OF LANGUAGE AND SELF

Contingency is another category crucial to Rorty's philosophy. He gave a great deal of attention to it in the first two chapters of *Contingency, Irony, and Solidarity*, which contain his considerations on the contingency of language and of self. Writing about the former, he concluded that we need to abandon the hope that "a given language is 'adequate' to a task—either the task of properly expressing the nature of the human species, or the task of properly representing the structure of nonhuman reality."[39]

In the course of his considerations, Rorty referred to the philosophy of Donald H. Davidson, which aims, as Rorty claimed, at presenting language as free from the requirement to be adequate, as it was presented to be doing in the past.[40] In accordance with Rorty's understanding of communication, language should not be treated as a third element between self and reality.[41]

In light of the above, Rorty believed that our present language, as well as the science and culture of twentieth-century Europe, could be seen as something that developed as a result of many contingencies.[42] Europe has been gradually getting out of the habit of using certain words and statements, and has gotten used to using others. The process was and still is at work, alongside the emergence of statements that did not or do not have a specific place in the language game. As far as these new sentences are concerned, Rorty wrote, "If it *is* savored rather than spat out, the sentence may be repeated, caught up, bandied about. Then it will gradually require a habitual use, a familiar place in the language game. It will thereby have ceased to be a metaphor—or, if you like, it will have become what most sentences of our language are, a dead metaphor."[43] In other words, it is plausible to say that using new metaphors—their permeation of the living language of the everyday—helps them to become dead metaphors. They cease to surprise, to occur at the peripheries of language, and become something obvious, a core in itself. Still, after some time, these dead metaphors begin to serve as a basis and a background for new metaphors,[44] or, in other words, they yield them their place.[45]

Further, Rorty claimed that we are by no means equipped with the criterion for choosing between alternative metaphors, and we can no longer compare metaphors and languages with some nonlinguistic entity called "a fact," but only with each other.[46] There is no reality that would serve us as a point of reference, and we should not understand moral and intellectual progress as a story of arriving at what things are really like, but as a story of the emergence of more and more useful metaphors.[47]

Rorty stressed the contingency of self, or—in other words—the contingency of individual existence, just as eagerly as he pointed to the contingency of language, at the same time advocating for the completion of the project initiated by the Romantic poets. For him, the process of learning who we are does not consist in discovering something that exists within us objectively but in creating a new language, developing new metaphors, narrating oneself anew. In his considerations, he drew upon the thought of Sigmund Freud, "the moralist who helped de-divinize the self by tracking conscience home to its origin in the contingencies of our upbringing."[48] In Freud's and, accordingly in Rorty's, opinion, moral consciousness is but a sum of events and beliefs that are shaping us now, as well as of those that we inherit.[49] Thus, we should give up the wish for moral feeling being somehow universally fastened.

NEW LANGUAGES, NEW VOCABULARIES, NEW WAYS OF THINKING

By writing about the contingency of self and the contingency of language, which we should at last acknowledge and assimilate, Rorty directs our attention toward the importance of the emergence of new languages, new vocabularies, the shaping of new ways of thinking. These different vocabularies are treated by Rorty as tools that we can use, not knowing a priori what they can serve for. Due to these new vocabularies, we can create new descriptions of the world and of ourselves, which was hard to imagine beforehand.[50] While doing so, we should accept the idea that reality does not correspond to our descriptions of it, and the idea that the human self originates in the process of using a particular vocabulary. Once we do that, we will assimilate the idea that truth is constructed and not discovered, and that what we are equipped with is a multiplicity of descriptions and vocabularies, being our own creation; we cannot choose one of them as that referring to criteria not rooted in its very self. We cannot do that, for there are no principal, better arguments supporting this language or another. As far as the supposed superiority and neutrality of rationality are concerned, Rorty further concluded, "To accept the claim that there is no standpoint outside the particular historically conditioned and temporary vocabulary we are presently using from which to judge this vocabulary is to give up on the idea that there can be reasons for using languages as well as reasons within languages for believing statements. This amounts to giving up the idea that intellectual or political progress is rational, in any sense of 'rational' which is neutral between vocabularies."[51] Just as there is no superior point of viewing and examining our language, there are no superior arguments with which to examine the statements articulated within it. Accordingly, we cannot speak of any superior rationality that would oversee language and statements so as to distinguish between accurate and inaccurate ones, and that would, in addition, serve as a point of reference for their further growth. In short, we cannot assume that a given language or a given statement are more rational than others, for our understanding of rationality still depends on the kind of vocabulary we use.[52]

RATIONALITY

Rorty opposed "rationality" understood as acting in a methodical way, according to specific criteria. For him, these criteria are nothing but clichés that "contextually define the terms of a final vocabulary currently in use."[53] He believed that we should not seek the criteria for acting or the source of ongoing cultural changes either in ourselves or in the world, for, doing so, we would be tempted by the prospect of searching for at least some of the intrinsic nature of things, for some of the essence of the world or the self. In his opinion, this would inevitably lead to privileging one language over others.

However, Rorty did not abandon the notion of rationality altogether. The rationality that he advocated for is merely to be separated from the notion of truth. For him, rationality is "roughly synonymous with tolerance."[54] Rationality means patience and acceptance of the differences among us. It is connected with opening to the other, to dialogue, to persuasion: to persuading and being persuaded. It is an expression of coexistence and compromise arrived at in the course of dialogue. Rorty wrote in this way in many of his texts. He pointed to the fact that being rational means being able to "discuss any topic [. . .] in a way which eschews dogmatism, defensiveness, and righteous indignation,"[55] or—in other words—being "persuasive."[56] In yet another text, he stated also that being rational means accomplishing one's aims by means of argumentation and not coercion. He added that in order to investigate what being rational means for the public, it is necessary to comprehend "techniques of persuasion, patterns of justification, and forms of communication."[57] In short, being "rational," as understood by Rorty, means, more or less, being "civilized," and not necessarily "methodical."

The understanding of rationality outlined by Rorty in the above words has not been welcomed with much enthusiasm. There are many who pine for rationality in a stronger sense: connected with objective truth, correspondence to reality, with methods and certain criteria.[58] Rorty was well aware of that desire; still, he argued that we should rather settle for a "weaker" version of rationality and avoid the former, "stronger" one. We do not need to know the criteria and to act according to certain standards, via which we would measure progress. They do not constitute a value of any special kind. In his opinion, a critical vocabulary based upon such terms as "rational," "criteria," "arguments," "foundations," or "absolute" is not suitable for describing the relations between the old and the new. It becomes apparent once we realize that progress, occurring both in the lives of the individuals and of the society, appears due to the emergence and use of new words, while we still use old languages that serve us as means of communication and argumentation.[59]

RELATIVISM?

Rorty advocated the "weaker" version of rationality, in which he saw many positive aspects. However, there are also those thinkers who—just as realists do—see in it the threat of relativism and warn that relativism will corner us if we give up the affection for objectivity and the idea of rationality understood as conforming to that criteria.[60] Some accuse Rorty of contributing to creating such a threat.[61] He himself considered talking about relativism here unjustified. He viewed accusing a pragmatist of relativism as a mistake. Realists do not see that in their descriptions and assessments they follow their own thinking habits. Those realists ascribe their own wish—the wish to look at our community in which we are rooted from a universal viewpoint—to the pragmatist. As Rorty observed, realists cannot believe that the pragmatist is far from such a wish, which, for him, is the basis for philosophical thinking and every individual biography. According to realists, the essence of philosophical thinking rests on this very wish.[62] Here, however, in Rorty's opinion, realists are wrong. Rorty himself did not strive for reaching a universal point of view, nor is it his secret desire. Thus, he opposed referring to his pragmatist project as "relativism." In the essay titled "Pragmatism, Relativism, and Irrationalism," he wrote, "'Relativism' is the view that every belief on a certain topic, or perhaps about *any* topic, is as good as every other. No one holds this view. Except for the occasional cooperative freshman, one cannot find anybody who says that two incompatible opinions on an important topic are equally good."[63]

We cannot say that two opinions are equally good, for it would require us to place our own selves at a certain metalevel, or—in other words—to use a metanarration. Such a metanarration, advocating one thing, would itself prove another. Rorty is aware of the fact, and, therefore, he also opposes relativism, as it is involved with what it speaks against.

Rorty also defended himself against the assumption that he had discovered that something that was supposed to come from outside of us, it turns out, comes from inside. He opposed a view that something that used to be treated as objective turned out to be only a subjective human construct. He argued, "[W]e anti-Platonists must not accept this way of formulating the issue. For if we do, we shall be in serious trouble. If we take the distinction between making and finding at face value, our opponents will be able to ask us an awkward question, namely, have we discovered the surprising fact that what was thought to be objective is actually subjective, or have we invented it?"[64] Thus, he suggested we cease using the differentiation between discovering and finding, of making reality and discovering it, of subjective and objective, and treat them both as inventions: then there will be no reason for calling thinkers like Rorty subjectivists, or social constructionists.[65]

Rorty believed that we should give up the conviction that the world or the self have an intrinsic nature of their own. He warned, however, that his suggestion should not be treated as a stance, that the kind of philosophy he presented corresponds to the actual state of affairs. To say that "we should drop the idea of truth as out there waiting to be discovered is not to say that we have discovered that, out there, there is no truth."⁶⁶ His suggestion not to ask questions about Truth and Goodness does not rest on a theory of the essence of reality, knowledge, or human beings, which states that "there is no such thing as Truth or Goodness."⁶⁷

In light of the above, we can say that what we encounter in Rorty's pragmatist perspective is not, as the critics claim, a relativist or subjectivist theory of truth. Pragmatism, a tradition to which he himself belongs, is not "a positive theory which says that something is relative to something else."⁶⁸ Rorty once again stressed that he "does not have a theory of truth, much less relativistic one [. . .]. Not having *any* epistemology, *a fortiori* he does not have a relativistic one."⁶⁹

Rorty was well aware of the situation he was in. However, as he claimed, he could not offer any argument for his stance, which the critics called "relativism," and which he preferred to call "antifundamentalism" or "antidualism."⁷⁰ He did not justify his suggestion to abandon the old questions to which no satisfactory answers have been found by referring to predetermined criteria—common to both the old and the new language games. He believed that his perspective was one of many, and the choice between them is determined by the community in which we grow. Therefore, he claimed that if there is something a pragmatist like him can be criticized for, it is "taking his own community *too* seriously. He can only be criticized for ethnocentrism, not for relativism."⁷¹

BEYOND RELATIVISM

Rorty dismissed the accusations of being a "relativist," or even an "irrationalist," as they depend on a differentiation he himself did not accept.⁷² He was not bothered by the allegations of relativism or irrationalism.⁷³ He tried to tackle these responses by discrediting the vocabulary within which they are articulated, and he suggested simply changing the subject.⁷⁴ He claimed, then, that "the traditional Western metaphysico-epistemological way of forming up our habits simply isn't working anymore."⁷⁵ It is impossible to say anything either of truth or of rationality. The only thing we can do is rely on the justification procedures that we use within given scientific, social, or political communities.⁷⁶ Articulating a particular stance or consciously arriving at a particular belief is justifiable only in certain circumstances.⁷⁷ Our beliefs and their justifications are rooted in the social practices existing at a given time. Rorty argued, "Where these webs of belief and desire are pretty much the same for large numbers of people, it does become useful to speak of an 'appeal to reason' or to 'logic', for this simply means an appeal to a widely shared common ground by reminding people of propositions that form part of this ground. More generally, all the traditional metaphysical distinctions can be given a respectable ironist sense by sociologizing them—treating them as distinctions between contingently existing sets of practices, or strategies employed within such practices, rather than between natural kinds."[78] It is worth asking what Rorty understood to be the justification procedures that we can accept, and that our society uses or can use in certain circumstances. Rorty believed that these procedures depended not on any criteria but only on comparing one society against others. Such a justification process should be as common as possible. Comparison shall allow us to see that it is much more beneficial for everyone when a society supports itself on "toleration," "free inquiry," and "the quest for undistorted communication."[79] In other words, according to Rorty, it is necessary to compare the vocabularies that different societies use, and take into consideration what consequences they have. If, as a result of confrontation, it turns out that using our vocabulary does not bring us particular advantage, that it is not useful, we should change it.

USEFULNESS

Rorty believed that the vocabulary within which the traditional problems of Western philosophy has been formulated used to be useful, but it is no longer so.[80] Since today we have quite different goals, we should use a different vocabulary, one that will serve their realization, which will be a better tool for tackling our present problems.[81] It is important, then, for the vocabulary to be more useful, and not to better correspond to reality. We should use words as tools so as to manage the environment, and should not try and attempt to use them to reflect on the intrinsic nature of the environment. These words, or whole vocabularies, will be considered "useful or useless, good or bad, helpful or misleading, sensitive or coarse, and so on; but [. . .] not 'more objective' or 'less objective' nor more or less 'scientific.'"[82] This way we shall ultimately free ourselves from questions on the nature of the relation of humans with reality.[83]

Once we no longer treat words as representations, but as tools, the question of whether we discover or invent them becomes pointless. It is also pointless to ask if a belief corresponds to reality, or if it represents a reality of a mental or physical kind. The right question is whether our beliefs evoke willingness to act and whether they contribute to satisfying our needs as much as possible. In other words, we should ask what aims holding a given belief serves.[84] Correspondingly, according to Rorty, "to say that a belief is, as far as we know, true is to say that no alternative belief is, as far as we know, a better habit of acting."[85]

The theses analyzed above can be also applied to our descriptions. In accordance with Rorty's perspective, while describing, we do not need to ask whether we describe something as it actually is. According to Rorty, great scientists, poets, and political thinkers, when inventing descriptions of the world useful for different purposes, never create descriptions that accurately represent the world as it is in itself.[86] What these descriptions allow them to do is present certain practices and goals anew, but none of them is the privileged one, the one corresponding to reality. Thus, "no such view [...] can 'cancel' inquiry, argument, and the quest for truth—any more than it can 'cancel' the search for food or for love,"[87] for we always describe reality due to our needs and interests, and it is we that decide if they are justifiable or not. What we should be careful about, though, is being attentive to other competing descriptions, as one of them may turn out be more useful as far as our goals are concerned.

The above considerations on discovering and inventing descriptions and goals can be summarized with Rorty's words, included in the essay entitled "Relativism—Finding and Making":

> The relativity of descriptions to purposes is the pragmatists' principal argument for their antirepresentational view of knowledge—the view that inquiry aims at utility for us rather than an accurate account of how things are in themselves. Because every belief we have must be formulated in some language or other and because languages are not attempts to copy what is out there, but rather are tools for dealing with what is out there, there is no way to divide "the contribution to our knowledge made by the object" from "the contribution made by our subjectivity". Both the words we use and our willingness to affirm certain sentences using those words and not others are the product of fantastically complex casual connections between human organisms and the rest of the universe.[88]

Rorty himself is one of the pragmatists described, and, just like them, he held an antirepresentationalist view of knowledge. Here, he referred to the category of usefulness. It is important to add, at this point, that Rorty was not a cynical opportunist who chose the description that happened to sustain his egotistical interests. What he did was point to the fact that our language does not accurately reflect what is outside, that it is our own invention that we create alongside the world surrounding us. Unfortunately—for the enthusiasts of our language as a mirror of nature—we cannot separate what originates in us and what originates in the world.

THE PLACE OF "TRUTH" IN THE POLITICAL SPHERE

We can ask how Rorty's considerations of "truth" contributes to considerations concerning the public sphere. What Rorty strove for is a situation where general philosophical claims could not discredit political beliefs or aspirations.[89] In other words, there is no such thing as a philosophical claim that can capture something better than a political belief, that can capture this "something" in the world to which our beliefs should be subdued. Such claims are contingent. And so are the beliefs of those playing leading parts on the political stage. Thus, we can say that what our politics is like and "what our future rulers will be like will not be determined by any large necessary truths about human nature and its relation to truth and justice, but by a lot of small contingent facts."[90]

The way in which contingency affects a whole spectrum of sociopolitical relations and the way in which history unveils it is illustrated by George Orwell's *1984*, about which Rorty wrote,

> Orwell helps us to see that it *just happened* that rule in Europe passed into the hands of people who pitied the humiliated and dreamed of human equality, and that it may *just happen* that the world will wind up being ruled by people who lack any such sentiments or ideas. Socialization, to repeat, goes all the way down, and who gets to do the socializing is often a matter of who manages to kill whom first. The triumph of Oligarchical Collectivism, if it comes, will not come because people are basically bad, or really are not brothers, or really have no natural rights, any more than Christianity and political liberalism have triumphed (to the extent they have) because people are basically good, or really are brothers, or really do have natural rights.[91]

In short, it just so happened that Europe began to value goodwill and the idea of humanity common to us all. And it could just so happen that at some point power will be held by those following quite a different morality—antagonistic to the present one.

Rorty observed that *1984* tells a story of how bad things can go due to contingency. O'Brien, one of the main protagonists of *1984*, does not say, in Rorty's opinion, that the nature of humans, of power, or of history is an affirmation that the future is "a boot stamping on a human face," but that it just happens that it is stamping so, and that "the scenario can no longer be changed. As a matter of sheer contingent fact—as contingent as a comet or a virus—that is what the future is going to be."[92]

Orwell has convinced us, as Rorty wrote, "that there was a perfectly good chance that the same developments which had made human equality technically possible might make endless slavery possible," as "nothing in the nature of truth, or man, or history was going to block that scenario, any more than it was going to underwrite the scenario which liberals had been using between the wars. He convinced us that all the intellectual and poetic gifts which had made Greek philosophy, modern science, and Romantic poetry possible might someday find employment in the Ministry of Truth."[93] All we can do is act so as that does not happen. We can, for example, create utopian visions of the world where the values we will share shall include equality and freedom, and where the contact between people will include communication, and not violence, hoping that someday these may become quite common.[94] Such an effort is made by Rorty. He presented to us a liberal utopia and its characteristic practical attitude, in which ironism, or—in other words—an ironist attitude, is something common. He presented us with it, for there is nothing left to do in a situation in which referring to some certainties is just an illusion telling us that it will be the way toward which these certainties point.

On Irony

IRONISTS AND METAPHYSICIANS

In Rorty's thought, the aforesaid ironist attitude is juxtaposed with the commonsensical attitude. Describing them one after another, Rorty outlined the differences between them. The former is characteristic of the ironist, the latter, of the metaphysician.[95] What is the difference between them? This shall be elaborated below.

The metaphysician is the one who follows common sense and believes that there is one unchanging reality that should be discovered in the diversity of fading phenomena. He thinks that the vocabulary he has inherited and his common sense allow him to shape his relations with this unchanging reality. He assumes, as Rorty argued, "that the vocabulary which the ironist fears may be merely 'Greek' or 'Western' or 'bourgeois' is an instrument which will enable us to get at something universal."[96] Relying on this assumption, the metaphysician describes reality by means of the words that make up his final vocabulary and does not doubt it to be insufficient to describe and judge those using alternative final vocabularies.[97] For the metaphysician, the presence of a given word in his own final vocabulary is a guarantee of the word referring to something that has a true essence. The more there are such words, the more he is convinced that he is in possession of a proper language for describing reality and for discovering the way things actually are. The only thing he still needs to do is consider its consequences.

The other side of the barricade is occupied by the ironist. In her opinion, nothing has an intrinsic nature or true essence. The statement "Truth is independent of the human mind" is for her a cliché serving to inculcate the local, commonsensical, final vocabulary of the West. She is a historicist and nominalist who has rejected the view that her beliefs and desires refer to something unchanging and atemporal. Thus, she thinks that her aim should not be to find a vocabulary that represents something accurately, that the search for a final vocabulary could be a way to grasp something more than the vocabulary itself. Her final vocabulary is not final, nor does it describe something accurately. It is characterized as final, as its users cannot refer to anything outside it if the words within it are challenged.[98] She uses it to justify her own beliefs and desires. While justifying, the ironist faces contingency, all the time being aware that the words she uses to describe her own self are subject to change. She remembers, then, about the fragility and contingency of her final vocabulary and of herself.[99]

The ironist is aware of the fact that the words belonging to her language, or languages as such, are subject to change. Still, she gives up the attempt to formulate the criteria for choosing between final vocabularies. She believes that all we can do is compare these vocabularies, as there is nothing outside them that would serve as a criterion for choosing between them. Thus, Rorty wrote that "nothing can serve as a criticism of a final vocabulary save another such vocabulary; there is no answer to a redescription save a re-re-description [. . .]. Nothing can serve as a criticism of a person save another person, or of a culture save an alternative culture—for persons and cultures are, for us, incarnated vocabularies."[100] In such a situation, the ironist's preferred form of argumentation is dialectical, and the preferred unit of persuasion is a vocabulary, not a statement. Rorty called it dialectical, for he understood dialectics as a struggle between vocabularies thanks to which it is possible to redescribe reality.[101] The way to act is, then, to redescribe, and not to conclude, to change one's own image, and not to discover the way things actually are. Accordingly, we can say that by giving up an old description or a whole discourse, we make a change rather than discover a new fact.

To recapitulate, using Rorty's words, we can say that the ironist is somebody who fulfills the following conditions: "(1) [S]he has radial and continuing doubts about the final vocabulary she currently uses, because she has been impressed by other vocabularies, vocabularies taken as final by people or books she has encountered; (2) she realizes that argument phrased in her present vocabulary can neither underpin nor dissolve these doubts; (3) insofar as she philosophizes about her situation, she does not think that her vocabulary is closer to reality than others, that it is in touch with a power not herself."[102] Thus, she can "choose" her vocabulary, but when doing so, she does not refer to any neutral or universal metavocabulary, and does not wish to "fight one's way past appearances to the real." Instead, she begins to use a new vocabulary and, by that, she is gradually repudiating the old one.[103]

IRONIC THEORISTS AND LIBERAL THEORISTS

Among the ironists—both women and men—Rorty listed ironists of a special kind: ironist theorists. Those ironists do not want to understand the metaphysician's efforts to rise above the diversity of phenomena, hoping that once he takes a look from the heights, he will be enlightened with an unexpected unity: a unity that will be a proof that what he discerns is something real, something that is hidden behind phenomena and that creates them. Those ironists—ironist theorists—want to elaborate a theoretical standpoint so as to use it in the broadest extent possible. However, they do not trust the metaphor created by the metaphysicians of taking a "view from above," which allows one to "look down" on the world. Unlike those that take up this metaphor, the ironist theorists do not try to search for an ahistorical final vocabulary that is not an idiosyncratic construct. Still, they often think of themselves as the prophets of the new era. They are constantly tempted by the return to metaphysics, the attempt to uncover one grand hidden reality. Those ironist theorists still wish for "the kind of power which comes from a close relation to somebody very large" and, thus, as Rorty observed, rarely are they liberals.[104] However, their wishing for "that kind of power" does not change the fact that the purpose of both themselves and the ironist theory they invent is, after all, to understand the metaphysical longing for theorizing deeply enough to break free from it. At the same time, they stress that the ironist theory is the last thing the ironist theorist wishes or needs, and that it is a ladder that should be pushed away once we realize what made our predecessors theorize.

Is it possible, however, to push the ladder away? Let us presume that Rorty is right and that the ironist theorist will be able to push away the ladder, but will it be possible for everyone else? Perhaps it will be impossible to push it away for a long time, until language changes so that there is no place in it for metaphysical longing. Undoubtedly, during the process, both ironist theory and ironist theorists will be of use. These ironists, however, will be of a special kind: they will be liberal ironists, who among their unjustifiable desires count their personal hope for the scope of suffering to diminish, and for humiliation to cease. According to them, as Rorty stressed, there is no way to justify the fact that cruelty is horrible.

There is also no way to answer the question of when we should stand to fight injustice, and when we should succumb to our private plans of self-creation. In their opinion, the only justification for their hopes is referring to the beliefs of the liberal society in which they have happened to grow. And deep down inside, they will deem everyone who thinks that there are justifiable theoretical answers as a theologian or a metaphysician.[105]

FREEING FROM METAPHYSICAL LONGING

Analyzing the above, we can ask, why did Rorty, the ironist, want to cure the metaphysical longing for theorizing? Why did he not trust the attempts made by metaphysicians to find the unity under phenomena? The reason is that he found these attempts harmful. He claimed that they have brought more damage than benefit and more bad than good. He believed it is worth resigning from them, for, perhaps, if we accept historicism, we will become a self-aware society more devoted to human equality than our current liberal culture is, a culture that is still metaphysical in its proclivities.[106] Perhaps, thanks to that, we will be able to achieve solidarity.

Rorty was aware of the fact that all those who believe in an atemporal and unchanging order determining the purpose of human existence see ironism as antagonistic toward democracy and the idea of human solidarity.[107] It appears as such also to those certain that such an order is necessary. Rorty disagreed and assured us that it is not the case. He claimed that "hostility to a particular historically conditioned and possibly transient form of solidarity is not hostility to solidarity as such."[108] Thus, he did not oppose the solidarity characteristic of a certain community. Such solidarity, though it is perceived as a certain historical construct, is more than desirable.

However, both Rorty and Milan Kundera found it understandable that "man" longs for "a world where good and evil can be clearly distinguished, for he has an innate and irrepressible desire to judge before he understands. Religions and ideologies are founded on this desire. . . . They desire that somebody be right."[109] This desire, as Rorty argued, cannot be satisfied when we realize the relativity of our beliefs. It is, undoubtedly, a major test for human character to be able to live with the consciousness that there is no stable, unchanging point of reference or any common denominator for our desires and endeavors. As Kundera said, "[I]t is precisely in losing the certainty of truth and the unanimous agreement of others that man becomes an individual."[110] Living with consciousness of this situation is a big challenge; it requires much more of us. It requires that we take on ourselves the burden of freedom. Being willing to do so, as Rorty stated after Joseph A. Schumpeter, is an indication of being a civilized human being. He in fact quoted the words of Schumpeter on this subject: "To realize the relative validity of one's convictions and yet stand for them unflinchingly, is what distinguishes a civilized man from a barbarian."[111]

Toward an Ideal Liberal State

On Ethnocentrism

Rorty was an antirepresentationalist. He believed that there was "no way of formulating an *independent* test of accuracy of representation—of reference or correspondence to an 'antecedently determinate' reality—no test distinct from the success which is supposedly explained by this accuracy."[112] What is available to us are different descriptions, each of them positioning us in culture contingently. Thus, the categories that we use, the categories that shape our identity and account for who we are and whence we came, are of an ethnocentric character: they determine our position in time and space. This ethnocentrism is, according to Rorty, unavoidable and unquestionable. He believed that nothing and no one can escape ethnocentrism, which is the effect of cultural adaptation. We should, therefore, accept the fact that what is our starting point is the place where we live and that "we are just the historical moment that we are."[113]

In light of the above, it should be said that what shall enable us to distinguish between the attitudes we respect and the attitudes we denounce as fanatical is the local and ethnocentric tradition of a given community, or a consensus of a given culture. Thus, we will deem as rational or fanatical what "is relative to the group to which we think it is necessary to justify ourselves—to the body of shared belief that determines the reference of the word 'we.'"[114] In other words, we will be able to say that something is rational or fundamental as a result of recognizing the point of reference in our group, community, society, or culture, shaped by common tradition and consensus.[115]

According to Rorty, when we have to assume an attitude toward different beliefs or statements, we can do nothing except refer to common tradition or cultural consensus. We cannot assume an ahistorical point of view in order to, for instance, justify our choice of a democratic system that we advocate. We cannot refer to any superior truth when we try to justify our identity against the community with which we identify. We should practicably privilege our own communities and, although each of our beliefs is prone to critique, we do not have to justify everything. As Rorty put it, "We Western liberal intellectuals should accept the fact that we have to start from where we are, and that this means that there are lots of [critical] views which we simply cannot take seriously."[116]

We may ask, in what circumstances is it necessary, or, perhaps, possible, to justify our beliefs? Rorty argued that it should be done within the community to which we belong—within our *ethnos*—and it is within it that discussion is possible due to commonly shared beliefs.[117] Justification is possible within the scope in which certain beliefs are shared, and this, in turn, leads to a productive discussion. In the case of "all the rest," in the case of a "clash" of some antagonistic beliefs—as Rorty thought—there is no chance for simplifying or solving the issues in accordance with the criteria that both of the parties accept. In Rorty's opinion, a problem can be solved "if history allows us the leisure to decide such issues, only by a slow and painful choice between alternative self-images."[118] Our advantage rests in the fact that our ethnocentric liberal culture avoids the drawbacks of ethnocentrism as such, for it is open and willing to change.[119] Due to pursuing the strategy of creating the space for encounters with other cultures, it becomes possible to broaden both our culture and the horizons of thinking about our own selves.[120]

Contingent Liberal Society

Rorty claimed that recognizing our language, conscience, morality, and greatest hopes as contingent results of what used to be accidental metaphors is synonymous with accepting the identity that qualifies us for being citizens in an ideal liberal state.[121] In such a state, what counts as a liberal society is a society recognizing the fact that it is what it is not because it reflects the will of God or human nature in the most accurate way but because poets and revolutionaries of the past spoke in a particular way. For Rorty, such a liberal society is an entirely contingent creation. Just as anything else, it results from the gradual process of getting out of the habit of using certain words and getting used to new ones.

Since Rorty considered our liberal society a contingent creation, he opposed referring to any of its fixed philosophical foundations. There are no neutral, natural, superior arguments that would not be connected with contingent competing languages, that would be, to some extent, prior to them. In his opinion, we cannot point to something that is more prior and basic than something else. Thus, he claimed that liberal culture needs a better description of itself than any foundation can provide. The task that needs to be faced consists in providing culture with a vocabulary that would be its only vocabulary, that would clear it of the remnants of the obsolete vocabulary of the past. In Rorty's opinion, the institutions and the culture of liberal society would benefit more from a vocabulary of moral and political reflection based on the notions of metaphor and self-creation, and not on the notions of truth, rationality, or moral obligation. He advocated a vocabulary that includes different individual descriptions resulting from individual attempts to redescribe the world. In such a vocabulary, the choice between the descriptions of our political situation consists not in managing hard facts but in "playing off scenarios against contrasting scenarios, projects against alternative projects, descriptions against descriptions."[122]

Toward a New Liberal Discourse

Rorty opposed the idea of a transhistorical point of view, and, thus, he proposed we not try to transcend historical contingencies. He advocated for new descriptions—historical narratives on the development of liberal institutions and customs, which would aim at restraining cruelty, constituting states governed with the consent of those governed, and introducing communication that would be as free from domination as possible. It is these liberal institutions that are to be described in the subsequent pages, so as to come to what Rorty wished to tell us about restraining cruelty and introducing domination-free communication.

On Liberal Institutions

FROM DECONSTRUCTION TO ALTERNATIVE SOLUTIONS

Rorty wrote on how many want to be fed on the hope that engaging in philosophy has political implications. This hope arises in those who believe that "it is politically useful to 'problematize' or 'call into question' traditional concepts, distinctions, and institutions."[123] In Rorty's opinion, pointing toward the inconsistencies inherent in social practices, or "deconstructing" them, does not bring about any major benefit unless it is accompanied by proposals for alternative practices, with at least a sketch of a utopia of some sort—the way things could be—within which these inconsistencies would no longer exist. In other words, when exposing the internal tensions, it is necessary to offer ways of resolving them. Therefore, Rorty wrote, "We pragmatists drop the revolutionary rhetoric of emancipation and unmasking in favor of a reformist rhetoric about increased tolerance and decreased suffering. If we have an Idea [. . .] in mind, it is that of Tolerance rather than that of Emancipation."[124]

In accordance with the above, in his texts, Rorty not only "deconstructed" but also offered an alternative practice: he presented a democratic utopia.[125] In this utopia, he claimed, there would be no superior, ultimately defined truth, that would be more important than individual suffering or search for happiness. He added that for those living in this democratic utopia, "tolerance and curiosity, rather than truth-seeking, are the chief intellectual virtues."[126] Everyone would be allowed to do whatever they want, as long as it would not cause others to suffer.[127]

TOWARD TOLERANCE

According to Rorty, the traditional metaphysical and epistemological method of grounding our customs no longer stands the test of the present moment.[128] We should relinquish the ideas of "transcending the mind" toward the external perspective, from which the mind could be really seen. In this case, the alternative consists in "our minds gradually growing larger and stronger and more interesting by the addition of new options—new candidates for belief and desire, phrased in new vocabularies."[129] In other words, the alternative consists in a new vocabulary, which shall allow us to broaden our imagination and our community with what is different and with those who were beyond our scope of recognition. Alongside the emergence of such a vocabulary, what will also emerge is tolerance for difference and opposition, a new culture. According to Rorty, upbringing in such a culture, a culture that is not monolithic but tolerant for the multiplicity of subcultures and willing to listen to the neighboring cultures, is an opportunity for transcending our cultural conditioning and opening up for others. It remains an open issue whether these subcultures or neighboring cultures will do the same, whether they will be tolerant toward us, listen to our culture. Rorty responded that "if members of other cultures protest that this expectation of tolerant reciprocity is a provincially Western one, we can only shrug our shoulders and reply that we have to work by our own lights, even as they do, for there is no supercultural observation platform to which we might repair."[130] Still, we can be sure that one day such a meeting of cultures shall be possible and that there shall emerge a common ground, and their beliefs and desires shall agree with our own.

It is worth asking what Rorty's statement given above—the statement that "we have to work by our own lights"—means. It means that we should do what our liberal societies do. We should turn toward experts in different fields, "permitting them to fulfill their function as agents of love, and hoping that they will continue to expand our moral imagination."[131]

Undoubtedly, it shall involve much planning and many painful and difficult social experiments. What we should also do is act for the sake of the development of our liberal institutions and the imagination of those who govern, so that they say "we" more often, and do not refer to moral rules once they are faced with different social groups whose fate they will hold in their hands.[132] All that should, inter alia, lead to a broadening of the scope of tolerance.[133]

PROBLEMS AND PROGRESS

If we cannot refer to the superiority of our perspective and our sociopolitical model, how should we tackle the problems that we encounter? The progress of science and technology, as well as liberal reforms, have evoked social transformations, due to which some problems have been solved, while others took their place. The feudal institutions disappeared, but the colonial reign began; education became widespread, but the nuclear threat increased as well. It has become clear that both our capacities of adapting to new circumstances and our effectiveness can be used either to oppress or to free, to facilitate suffering or to diminish it, to decrease rationality that is the synonym of tolerance or to increase it. It has also turned out that rationality understood as the ability to manage our surroundings can lead to greater tolerance but does not have to.

Rorty believed that in the time of the great transformation of our culture, we were not in a position to solve its emerging problems. All we had was hope that curiosity and the desire to diminish suffering would lead to resolving at least some of them.[134] Rorty still hoped that it would become possible to solve our present problems and facilitate further progress.[135] He did not believe, however, that, being a pragmatist, one could present a given set of criteria that could be commonly accepted, or come up with a single language game that would fulfill the functions of all the previous games. Nonetheless, he wrote, "This failure to find a single grand commensurating discourse, in which to write a Universal translation manual [. . .] does nothing to cast doubt on the possibility [. . .] of peaceful social progress."[136] And thus he thought that our democratic society does not need a safety net in the form of an idea that has adequate philosophical grounds, or that is "latent" in "human reason."[137] It can do without such a safety net to such an extent that it will become possible to talk of actual progress.

Moreover, in Rorty's opinion, we can tell a story about progress and we do not need to presuppose the existence of any constant "we," any transhistorical, metaphysical subject. It is enough to refer to a local and temporary "we," meaning "something like 'us twentieth-century Western social democrats."'¹³⁸ We can speak of ourselves as a part of universal human history, however, only as long as we do it to keep up our spirits, and not to reach for metaphysical justifications of our position, so as to prove our superiority with respect to others. Further, he argued, "We Deweyans have a story to tell about the progress of our species, a story whose later episodes emphasize how things have been getting better in the West during the last few centuries, and which concludes with some suggestions about how they might become better still in the next few."¹³⁹ Improving such a situation is, in Rorty's opinion, to consist in the dissemination of a specific method of acting, thanks to which our future descriptions, universal human histories, and their categories will be better than those we rely on today. As Rorty believed, they shall become such as long as the reason for acknowledging them rest on persuasion rather than on coercion.

At this point, we can have certain doubts as to whether relinquishing unanimity will not lead us toward positions that the Nazis took.¹⁴⁰ Rorty provided all his critics that had such doubts an answer in the negative. He opposed associating ethnocentrism—which is inevitable for a pragmatist—with Nazism. In his opinion, there is a substantial difference between statements in which

> "[w]e admit that we cannot justify our beliefs or our action to all human beings as they are present, but we hope to create a community of free human beings who will freely share many of our beliefs and hopes," and saying, with the Nazis, "We have no concern for legitimizing ourselves in the eyes of others." There is a difference between the Nazi who says "We are good because we are the particular group we are" and the reformist liberal who says "We are good because, by persuasion rather than force, we shall eventually convince everybody else that we are." Whether such a "narcissistic" self-justification can avoid terrorism depends on whether the notion of "persuasion rather than force" still makes sense after we renounce the idea of human nature and the search for transcultural and ahistorical criteria of justification.¹⁴¹

Toward Limiting Cruelty and Suffering

LIBERAL UTOPIA

Rorty was an adherent of a liberal utopia, in which it is characteristic to abandon theory, to abandon attempts at enclosing within one vision all aspects of our lives, and attempts at describing it, using only one vocabulary. He believed that it is impossible to find a metavocabulary that can embrace all possible vocabularies, and, therefore, he advocated historical and nominalist culture founded on narratives. It shall be likely to emerge once the liberal utopia comes true in the name of freedom rather than in the name of the pursuit of the eternal truth. He added that such a new culture would be inhabited by people who would share the sense of contingency of their own language, their own conscience, and their society. They would be liberal ironists—people who link their commitments with a sense of contingency to those commitments.[142] The accusation of relying on relativism would lose its power, the idea of "something which stands beyond history" would become inexplicable, but the sense of solidarity would prevail.[143]

The last of the elements listed here—the sense of solidarity—should be approached with particular attention due to its role in Rorty's philosophy. The category of solidarity lies in the very center of his "new narrative" of a liberal utopia. Solidarity is what the growth of liberal institutions and customs is to lead to. It is strictly connected with diminishing suffering, with replacing coercion with persuasion.

FROM OBJECTIVITY TO SOLIDARITY

The deliberations on solidarity should commence with presenting two positions, for which it is characteristic to pursue objectivity and to pursue solidarity, respectively. Rorty remarked that a person exercising the former—the pursuit of objectivity—"distances herself from the actual persons around her" and searches for something "which can be described without reference to any particular human beings."[144] A person in the pursuit of solidarity, on the other hand, "does not ask about the relation between the practices of the chosen community and something outside that community" but is interested in the relations with people here and now.

As Rorty illustrated, the pursuit of solidarity is characteristic of pragmatists. They wish to replace the desire for objectivity with the desire for solidarity, but they are confronted with much resistance. It results partly from the fear that our traditional liberal habits and hopes will not withstand such a change. However, pragmatists—unlike realists—believe that we do not need grounding in objectivity, we do not need metaphysics or epistemology. They do not interpret truth as correspondence to reality. They see it as something that is worth referring to, that is worth believing in. They do not need epistemology to provide them with justifications in order to claim that there are natural, and not only local, procedures for justifying beliefs. And thus they do not need any explanation of the relationship between beliefs and objects. For them, the gap between truth and justification is not something that one should build a bridge over.[145]

Their primary concern does not revolve around the way in which we shall define words such as "truth," "rationality," "knowledge," or "philosophy" but around what our society's own image is to look like.[146] According to pragmatists, these issues should be presented in the categories of morality and politics rather than epistemology or metaphysics. Rorty said, "If we could ever be moved solely by the desire for solidarity, setting aside the desire for objectivity altogether, then we should think of human Progress as making it possible for human beings to do more interesting things and be more interesting people, not as heading towards a place which has somehow been prepared for humanity in advance. Our self-image would employ images of making rather than finding."[147] For Rorty, solidarity is not a fact at which one can arrive by abandoning one's "prejudice." In his opinion, it is not to be discovered, but created. It is possible thanks to making ourselves sensitive to particular instances of the suffering and humiliation of people whom we deem strangers. In consequence, it will be more difficult for us to dismiss people who are different from us with a statement "They do not feel it as *we* would" or "There must always be suffering, so why not let *them* suffer?"[148] It will happen also on account of our imagination, the ability to see strangers as our brothers who suffer.[149]

Rorty believed that making us more sensitive and widening the scope of our imagination is not a task for theory but for such literary genres as ethnographic description, reports, comics, and fictionalized documentary. In addition, Rorty emphasized "in particular, the novel." In his opinion, it is the writers that play an exceptional role here, for they can help us remain alert to "the springs of cruelty in ourselves."[150] And thus it can be added that their works should become one of the crucial elements of "sentimental" education. Such an education should not be based on ingraining moral truths or assigning moral obligations, which have nothing to do with love, friendship, trust, or social solidarity,[151] but should make us sensitive to the suffering of others and should build emotional links, and not another rational argument.[152]

PAIN, SUFFERING, AND HUMAN SOLIDARITY

The ability to acknowledge fellow human beings who suffer is connected with the ability to see the pain that exists in the world. This pain controls us in the same way the world controls us—even though we have de-deified it and begun to create it, and not to discover it. This control is visible, as it can lead us to self-destruction. But that sort of control and power over us is not the sort we can appropriate by adopting and then transforming its language, thereby becoming identical with the threatening power and subsuming it under our own more powerful selves. This latter strategy is appropriate only for coping with other persons—for example, with parents, gods, and poetic precursors. For our relation to the world, to brute power and to naked pain, is not the sort of relation we have to persons. Faced with the nonhuman, the nonlinguistic, we no longer have an ability to overcome contingency and pain by appropriation and transformation, but only the ability to *recognize* contingency and pain.[153]

The world, then, is full of contingency and pain. This pain—the suffering—is a translinguistic phenomenon; it remains autonomous of the attempts at describing it. It can be described in a number of ways. It is also possible, in these descriptions, to dismiss the right to feel it, but this does not change the fact that it will still exist, it will still be experienced, to a lesser or to a greater extent. It is the ability to experience it—to suffer—that, according to Rorty, is common to all people. Apart from that, there is nothing truly human that would not be an effect of education or socialization, except for the ability "to speak a *particular* language, one which enables us to discuss particular beliefs and desires with particular sorts of people."[154] In other words, apart from the ability to suffer, there is nothing to refer to as something existing in us and something characteristic of us. We are what the circumstances and we ourselves made of us. Any criteria—or standards for rationality based on criteria—are created by us, and not discovered in us.[155] Accordingly, as Rorty claimed, referring to Freud, compassion and mercy are not values that determine our common core. They are feelings that arise in very specific contexts and toward particular people.[156] Rorty treaded on this path even further, writing also that "one can be humane without being universalist, without believing either that it is 'rational' to be concerned with the sufferings of others or that there is a 'common humanity' which binds you to those others."[157] It is possible, then, to want to relieve others' suffering, not having a universal answer to the question why we want to do that.

Rorty was against the traditional understanding of "human solidarity" as something existing inside each and every one of us and as something strictly connected with humanity, whose presence we should supposedly uncover in others. What does it mean for us? "This means that when the secret police come, when the torturers violate the innocent, there is nothing to be said to them of the form 'There is something within you which you are betraying. Though you embody the practices of a totalitarian society which will endure forever, there is something beyond those practices which condemns you.'"[158] In short, there is no neutral method for defending the liberal claim that cruelty is the worst thing we do.[159] For Rorty, whether one is a decent human being depends only on historical circumstances, on the short-term consent on which practices are deemed just and which are not deemed so, and on which attitudes we deem as normal and which are not considered so.¹⁶⁰ Of course, as has already been said, Rorty did not approve of opportunism. He did not claim that the only thing left for us to do is to adapt to the existing circumstances and take care of our own interests. He advocated something quite contrary: actively and creatively changing our vision of the world and of ourselves. What he did claim was merely that "being decent" shall not always mean the same thing, since we cannot rely on any independent, ahistorical, external criterion of decency.

SOLIDARITY IS CONTINGENT

Rorty rightly asserted that "at times like that of Auschwitz, when history is in upheaval and traditional institutions and patterns of behavior are collapsing, we want something which stands beyond history and institutions." He asked, "What can there be except human solidarity, our recognition of one another's common humanity?"¹⁶¹ For Rorty, there is nothing apart from solidarity. However, solidarity does not stand outside of history and institutions. It is created, and it does not rest on any natural grounds, for—as it has already been said—Rorty claimed that it is not possible to talk of any common humanity or universal human nature. He could be listed in the ranks of historicists, who believe there is nothing "deeper" than historical conditioning of a society, nothing that would determine the essence of being human.¹⁶² Everything depends to the same extent on the context, and not on the existence of something like "human nature" or "the deepest level of the self." Once we acknowledge that, we are forever freed from theology and metaphysics, "from the temptation to look for an escape from time and chance."¹⁶³

It is worth noticing that Rorty, while deliberating on solidarity, referred to the work of Wilfrid Sellars and his analysis of morality as "we-intention," in which the basic concept consists in the idea of "one of us." Rorty—on the basis of these reflections—claimed that our sense of solidarity is and will be stronger if "those with whom solidarity is expressed are thought of as 'one of us', where 'us' means something smaller and more local than the human race."¹⁶⁴ This smaller and more local group—the "we"—exists with relation to "others," whom we have excluded, often deeming as worse than us. Our relationship with them rests on which similarities and which differences we find most crucial. This, in turn, depends on the final, contingent vocabulary that we use.

In both Sellars's and Rorty's perspectives, solidarity should be treated as a product that comes into being in the course of history, and not as an ahistorical fact that has been discovered.¹⁶⁵ As Rorty added, the idea of human solidarity is just a fortunate, accidental product of modernity, and "human solidarity" in light of contingency is only a rhetorical turn.¹⁶⁶

Rorty remarked, however, that this concept does not lose anything of its significance because of being a product. At the same time, he wrote that what we need is the ability to acknowledge the differences as irrelevant, when contrasted with the similarities, especially with respect to the experience of suffering, humiliation, or cruelty. Thus, we will strive for greater human solidarity and for further moral progress.[167] This shall come true once we will be able, even only via our imagination, to identify with others, belonging to different religions and living in different corners of the world, who have been recognized by our ancestors as so alien that they were not able to identify with them.[168] Still, in defending such a thesis, as Rorty again noted, we are not able to refer to something more "real" or less elusive than historical contingencies.

Communication

TOWARD AGREEMENT

Having presented Rorty's views on the new narrative of the development of liberal institutions and aims, comprising diminishing suffering, expanding human solidarity, and using persuasion rather than coercion, it is necessary now to provide an element without which they shall not come into existence. They shall be possible due to the introduction of domination-free communication and the compliance with certain procedures. This domination-free communication is for Rorty an element of the utmost importance. Thus, in his view, liberal society calls for, first and foremost, freedom and openness in discussion. His ideals can be realized through persuasion and reform, an encounter between the existing linguistic practices and the proposals of new ones, and not through violence or revolution.[169] In addition, he claimed that liberal society is a society "which is content to call 'true' whatever the upshot of such encounters turn out to be."[170]

Accordingly, for Rorty, the only political goal that is possible to accept is the ultimate victory of persuasion over coercion. However, its realization will be feasible only when we act in a particular way. Rorty argued that the pragmatists advise us that we should choose between two hypotheses, and to not continue to worry about whether any of them are true. We should put aside theoretical deliberations, and start asking practical questions about "whether we ought to keep our present values, theories, and practices or try to replace them with others."[171] In order to find an answer, it is necessary to approach our own communities with ample criticism, compare them with other real or possible groups, and try to present the advantages of some of them over the others. And, when doing that, we should trust our own beliefs, and use them as a prism through which we should test the beliefs and opinions present in other cultures that we encounter.[172]

All that shall be possible if our actions will include a certain linguistic competence, the ability to search for compromise and to cooperate with other participants of the language game, and to not proceed in accordance with previously learned rules.[173] And the result shall consist of freely achieved agreement on common goals, such as equality of life opportunities or diminishing suffering, and agreement on the means that should be used in order to make these plans come true. In the perspective sketched out by Rorty, it is also important to include among the goals creating scenarios that—once implemented—would serve "diminishing human suffering and increasing human equality" as well as "increasing the ability of all human children to start life with an equal chance of happiness."[174] It is important to arrive at an agreement that will be the glue of liberal society, an agreement that our goal is "to let everybody have a chance at self-creation to the best of his or her abilities, and that that goal requires, besides peace and wealth, the standard 'bourgeois freedoms.'"[175]

"EQUALITY OF OPPORTUNITY" AND THE "STANDARD BOURGEOIS FREEDOMS"

"Equality of opportunity" is nothing else but creating conditions and chances for the full self-realization of individuals. Rorty thought that in his ideal society, the certainty of creating opportunities for growth is necessary, and "would not be based on a view about universally shared human ends, human rights, the nature of rationality, the Good for Man, nor anything else. It would be a conviction based on nothing more profound than the historical facts which suggest that without protection of something like the institutions of bourgeois liberal society, people will be less able to work out their private salvations, create their private self-images."[176] In Rorty's opinion, these institutions should ensure typical bourgeois freedoms.

In order to accomplish the goal—that is, "to work out [. . .] private salvations" or "create [. . .] private self-images"—or, using Dewey's words, to achieve a full self-realization of individuals, certain conditions must be met. Among them, Rorty listed peace, wealth, and "bourgeois freedoms": in other words, liberal freedoms. He advocated them not because they are underpinned with any sort of agreement on the more basic issues but because they are desirable.[177] What is desirable, then, is, for instance, free and open discussion, one of the elements of political freedom. It is not to be a discussion devoid of ideologies but, as Rorty wrote, "simply the sort which goes on when the press, the judiciary, the elections, and the universities are free, social mobility is frequent and rapid, literacy is universal, higher education is common, and peace and wealth have made possible the leisure necessary to listen to lots of different people and think about what they say."[178]

It is crucial to stress that for Rorty, freedom, as discussed above, does not occupy a privileged position. Freedom is one of many values. As it has already been said, history points out that freedom is something we should support. And it is by the practice and comparison of the results of our actions that we can prove that the institutions based on liberal freedoms allow for individual growth to the fullest extent.[179]

Objections

Two Basic Objections

There are two basic objections that can be put forward with respect to the suggestion that the glue of a society, supporting the ideal liberal society, is but an agreement, that its purpose consists in equalizing opportunities for self-creation in accordance with its possibilities, and that the realization of this purpose requires liberal freedoms: "The first is that as a practical matter, this glue is just not thick enough—that the (predominantly) metaphysical rhetoric of public life in the democracies is essential to the continuation of free institutions. The second is that it is psychologically impossible to be a liberal ironist—to be someone for whom 'cruelty is the worst thing we do', and to have no metaphysical beliefs about what all human beings have in common."[180] Such objections are not uncommon among the readers of Rorty's texts.[181] They concern the lack of metaphysical convictions in his philosophy, both when he spoke of his vision of the world, as well as when he spoke of the attitude of the liberal ironist. It is important here that Rorty himself was well aware of them, and tried to reply. It was the way in which he responded to them that determines whether we can consider them overcome or—using a less defensive/offensive language—whether the doubts of his critics are cleared up.

Attempt at Answering the First Objection: Does the Concept of Irony Contribute to the Weakening of Liberal Society?

As far as the first objection is concerned, Rorty pointed to the fact that it is connected with the prediction of what would happen if the place that in our public rhetoric is occupied by metaphysics were overtaken by ironism. The critics think that the widespread victory of the ironical conception and, by that, "the general adoption of antimetaphysical, antiessentialist views about the nature of morality and rationality and human beings, would weaken and dissolve liberal societies."[182] In the opinion of those in doubt, a freely accomplished agreement that is not based upon any metaphysical convictions is not feasible.[183] They think that without this "metaphysical foundation" for our free institutions that are to realize liberal goals, it is impossible to talk of their—or others'—existence being justified. They think the "glue" would not be thick enough to hold up our everyday practices. And, therefore, all those sharing these doubts cannot accept the attitude of an ironist.

Rorty took a stand with respect to these doubts and concluded that perhaps it is right to think that assuming an ironist attitude should result in weakening and disintegrating liberal societies; still, he believed there is at least one reason to consider such a statement false: the history of the decline of religious faith. In his opinion, this decline has not weakened liberal societies, it has, in fact, strengthened them. The willingness to "endure suffering for the sake of future reward was transferable from individual rewards to social ones, from one's hope for paradise to one's hopes for one's grandchildren."[184] Accordingly, he thought that the decline of metaphysics should not lead to weakening and disintegrating liberal societies; on the contrary, especially after assuming the attitude of an ironist, it should make them more self-critical and committed to the idea of human equality.[185]

The way in which Rorty answered the first objection, instead of clearing up these doubts, causes more of them. It is doubtful whether the willingness to endure suffering for the sake of future individual reward has been indeed transferred onto the willingness to endure suffering for the sake of a social reward to be received today. The majority of the members of our societies still expect such an individual reward; the difference is that they expect the reward here and now, and with as little suffering and as little sacrifice as possible. Correspondingly, claiming that the perspective within which the individual reward was expected has changed into one privileging the pursuit of social reward does not sound convincing. It is doubtful whether each and every day we all wake up with the hope that we will create a better world for our grandchildren. Thus, it is impossible to agree with Rorty that it is false to prognosticate the weakening of liberal society in a situation in which the ironist conception would conquer the hearts of the public, for both the description of the decline of some attitudes and of the emergence of new ones that Rorty presented is questionable; also, the analogy he employed is not convincing enough to defend his stance.[186] We do not know, then, whether the decline of metaphysics would not lead to weakening liberal societies. And, most certainly, we do not know whether such a decline, even if it did occur, would actually result in our willingness to work toward the best possible future of our children.

In his further deliberations on the subject, Rorty said that he did not think any change in scientific or philosophical conviction could disintegrate the social hope that inhabits modern liberal societies, the hope that "life will eventually be freer, less cruel, more leisured, richer in goods and experiences, not just for our descendants but for everybody's descendants."[187] In his opinion, this hope, or this liberal society, does not rest on any philosophical foundations.[188] According to Rorty, it is not the "foundations" that bind the society together but the common vocabularies and hopes, which are purely contingent constructs. In the case of a liberal society, this "hope" or—as Rorty has written—social glue consists in creating opportunities for the full growth of individuals and in ensuring liberal freedoms, supported by the institutions of a liberal state.[189]

We may ask whether our social hope that "life will eventually be freer, less cruel, more leisured, richer in goods and experiences, not just for our descendants but for everybody's descendants"[190] indeed does not rest on any philosophical foundations and that it is, as Rorty wrote, "ludicrous" when some of us believe that liberal societies are bound together with philosophical convictions. As an answer, it needs to be said, it is difficult to agree with Rorty that liberal culture needs an "improved self-description rather than a set of foundations."[191] Undoubtedly, an improved self-description, one that would seem adequate in light of new challenges, is very desirable. But an adequate "set of foundations" is desirable as well. Rorty did not share such an opinion. He perceived all kinds of willingness to look for the foundations in liberal culture as a result of the scientism of the Enlightenment, which, in turn, is a remnant of the religious need to back human projects up with some sort of force beyond human reach. He believed such a search must be connected with claims of objectivism. But is it indeed a must? Not necessarily, for it is possible to talk of the foundations characteristic of a given community, or a given culture. These foundations are also the basis of a liberal society. They rest on certain philosophical convictions, and social hope is deeply connected with them. It is these convictions that support the vision of what our lives could look like. Thanks to these philosophical convictions, a liberal society is coherent in spite of the awareness of the contingency of these foundations—their locality. One needs to agree with Rorty that such a society is not as strong as its philosophical foundations, but its strength is determined by how much its philosophical convictions and values have spread. It is this dissemination of certain values and beliefs in a given community that makes a particular form of cultural life strong.

The issue of the existence of certain philosophical foundations for a liberal society is crucial also in the case of discussing the topic of justifying our choice of a society based on liberal values. Rorty believed that if we are to talk of such a choice, it should be made on the basis of a result that we arrive at, comparing it with other forms of social organization, and not referring to the philosophical foundations of such a society. Still, Rorty is not entirely right. It is necessary to notice that when observing the different ways of organizing societies, we will be doing so from a particular perspective, we will be comparing particular elements. We will choose to compare the elements that play a particular role for us. For liberals, making such a comparison will play out differently than for someone who compares their own model with ours. What we will pay attention to will indicate what we deem as most basic for our liberal vision of the world and of society. Referring to foundations is, then, inevitable, even though it will not require referring to something universal but rather to the value of our community or—in other words—to its philosophical foundations.[192] It is these foundations that our hope rests on. Can ironism threaten it?

Answering the question as to whether the adoption of ironism by the public would cause the weakening and decline of liberal society depends, to a great extent, as Rorty claimed, on whether we are able to imagine a culture in which nominalism and historicism would be a part of public rhetoric. Rorty tried to present us such a culture. In his "ideal liberal society," the rhetoric of the public, by means of which we would socialize the young, would no longer be metaphysical but would be borrowed from nominalists and historicists. In such a society, nominalism and historicism would not be the property of intellectuals but would become a part of the final vocabularies of all people. According to Rorty, such a society would on the one hand be composed of intellectual-ironists, and on the other, of nonintellectual, rational nominalists and historicists. The latter would be rational nonmetaphysicians, well aware of the fact that they are composed of many contingencies, and would not experience any discomfort because of that. A member of such a society would not search for any justification of, for example, his or her sense of human solidarity, as he or she "was not raised to play the language game in which one asks and gets justifications for that sort of belief."[193] In case of doubts with respect to public rhetoric, in such a culture, he or she would turn to actual alternatives and programs rather than look for definitions and rules. Still, most importantly from the perspective of understanding Rorty's thought is to see that assuming ironism would not require such an individual, just as it does not require

Rorty himself, to opt for creating a public rhetoric that would itself be ironist. Rorty believed that it is possible and desirable to create such a liberal culture in which the rhetoric of the public is nominalistic and historicist. He does not claim, however, that it is possible or necessary to create a culture in which the public rhetoric should be ironist. As he stressed, he could not "imagine a culture which socialized its youth in such a way as to make them continually dubious about their own process of socialization."[194] Thus, it seems that he opposed creating a culture whose public rhetoric would be ironist. Irony should remain something private. And, what is more, "irony is, if not intrinsically resentful, at least reactive."[195]

Responding to the above, it could be said that we can imagine a culture in which nominalism and historicism would be a part of public rhetoric. But is it possible to imagine a culture in which irony would not affect the public sphere? Rorty believed that the fact that "philosophers are waxing ironic over real essence, the objectivity of truth, and the existence of an ahistorical human nature" is unlikely to "arouse much interest, much less do any damage," especially to somebody whose sense of life depends on the liberal hope.[196] Rorty does not see any problem at this point. But a close reader should discern one. The problem is whether the ironist philosophers and their views can threaten social hope, whether the individual, private beliefs of the philosophers have a negative effect upon the members of a liberal society; in other words, whether they affect the public sphere. It seems that Rorty answered in the negative, and such an answer is directly connected with the division into the private and the public that he introduced. His line of reasoning shall become clearer once we discuss his attempts at answering the second of the objections mentioned above, that is, the question whether ironism can be reconciled with solidarity.

Attempt at Answering the Second Objection: Is Ironism to Be Reconciled with Solidarity?

As far as the second of the objections is concerned, Rorty argued that it is plausible to say that it is connected with the conviction that "there is something about being an ironist which unsuits one for being a liberal, and that a simple split between private and public concerns is not enough to overcome the tension."[197] Those who say so believe, as Rorty claimed, that the division into the private and the public spheres, which he himself advocated, would not withstand, since no one is able to divide his or her own self into a private creator of the self and the public liberal. They have doubts whether it is possible for ironism to be reconciled with solidarity. Rorty believed that it can be. In his opinion the ironist should be occupied with the creation of new narratives in her private sphere, for irony should be connected with what is private only. Thus, Rorty viewed the development of ironist thought as to a great extent indifferent to public life and political issues. He said, "Ironist theorists like Hegel, Nietzsche, Derrida, and Foucault seem to me invaluable in our attempt to form a private self-image, but pretty much useless when it comes to politics."[198] Even though they are useless, there is nothing that would prevent them from being liberals. In Rorty's opinion, they could be liberal ironists. He believed that being an ironist did not prevent one from being a liberal, for the continual, and often contingent, attempts at self-description can, but do not have to, pose a threat to one's liberalism. This is possible, since, in terms of our final vocabularies, we are able to distinguish between our private and our public vocabularies. As Rorty wrote, "[T]he ironist's final vocabulary can be and should be split into a large private and a small public sector, sectors which have no particular relation to one another."[199] The former should, in Rorty's opinion, serve to construct redescriptions of private goals, the latter to create descriptions for public purposes. On the one hand, then, there is the private vocabulary, which results from individual self-creation and which is not connected with public actions, and on the other, the public vocabulary. For a liberal, the latter is a vocabulary that requires awareness of the different means by which people are humiliated. Accordingly, as Rorty argued, the liberal ironist, while acting within the public sphere, needs to try to get acquainted, also by means of her imagination, with alternative final vocabularies, "not just for her own edification, but in order to understand the actual and possible humiliation of the people who use these alternative final vocabularies."[200] For the public vocabulary, even though—just as the private one—it is subject to change, it is contingent and does not contain any stable element, it should, in Rorty's opinion, turn to what lies beyond language: to suffering. Such a vocabulary can be used to describe how in the course of our actions we inflict suffering on others. According to Rorty, the users of such a vocabulary are aware of the fact that they should avoid such actions. By assuming such a vocabulary and using it, they agree on suffering being the worst thing we can do.[201]

Of course, in Rorty's opinion, everyone can have a different vocabulary for public purposes. It does not pose any problem as long as these vocabularies coincide to such an extent that all of them contain words connected with the need for acknowledging the presence of others and respecting them. However, as Rorty also pointed out, these coinciding words, including "kindness," "decency," and "dignity," do not create a vocabulary that all humans can arrive at in the course of reflection on their own nature. As Rorty remarked, such a reflection "will not produce anything except a heightened awareness of the possibility of suffering. It will not produce *a reason to care* about suffering. What matters for the liberal ironist is not finding such a reason but making sure that she *notices* suffering when it occurs."202 For her, this suffering does not contain in itself any message that can be discerned. The ability to identify with those suffering by means of imagination, or the desire to avoid the actual and the possible humiliation of others, are not more real, nor more "essentially humane."203

Summing up, it can be said that there is a substantial difference between the ironist and the metaphysician, though both of them can be liberals. Rorty favored the liberal ironist, who while using her vocabulary does not refer to anything about universal human nature.204 He believed that the final vocabulary of the liberal ironist does not need to be dominated by the metaphysical rhetoric of liberalism, for it is not what she shares with the rest of humanity. For the liberal ironist, acknowledging the common susceptibility to humiliation is the only social bond needed. It is both this "bond" as well as sharing the values of the liberal community that create the emergence of human solidarity. For the sake of a brief answer to the above questions, connected with the two objections, Rorty claimed that it is possible to reconcile ironism with human solidarity, and the ironist can be a liberal as well. In light of the division within our final vocabulary, according to Rorty, there is no reason to fear that private philosophical convictions threaten social hope, at least, as he clarified later on, from the side of those like Dewey who are moderate pragmatists, being at the same time a moderate version of ironists and not the radical kind.205 However, the possibility of making such a division in the first place might seem quite questionable. The issue shall be discussed in the next section.

On Division into the Private and the Public

Blaming the Truth

Bearing in mind what we previously discussed, it can be said that Rorty feared the category of truth, as he thought that looking through its prism results in our being less friendly toward those who do not share this truth with us, less tolerant to their otherness, and more prejudiced. Still, sometimes Rorty did not seem such a pessimist about the influence of referring to the category of truth. He said, "What would it be like to be less fuzzy and parochial than this? I suggest that it would be to become less genial, tolerant, open-minded, and fallibilist than we are now."[206] By writing that we would be less friendly, he did not make—at least not at this point—a concrete critical statement on the category of truth as inevitably leading to intolerance. He did think, however, that it may happen, and thus he wrote, "Suppose that we had the sort of 'weapons' against the fascists of which Dewey was said to deprive us— firm, unrevisable, moral principles which were not merely 'ours' but 'universal' and 'objective'. How could we avoid having these weapons turn in our hands and bash all the genial tolerance out of our own heads?"[207] Rorty answered in the negative. He feared that relying on the category of truth today may become a nail in our coffin tomorrow if the category is used by some sort of a new totalitarian regime. He also thought that the vocabulary of the previous era was an example of that and, accordingly, was less liberal and less tolerant. He regretted that such a vocabulary served as a foundation for the rhetoric of the Enlightenment, which provided further grounds for the natural sciences, which, in his opinion, was a proof of cultural stagnation.

Rorty understood that searching for universal and objective truths was—and still is—an attempt at tackling our own finitude. He did not disapprove of this attempt, but he thought that such projects should be undertaken only within the private sphere. And the private sphere should be separate from the public one. Accordingly, we should not try to reconcile the two, as metaphysicians from Plato to Marx used to do.

The Private and the Public

The distinction between the private and the public that Rorty wished to maintain is a manifestation of the belief that there is an us-only space and a space in which we enter into interactions with others. It can be claimed that both spaces, in Rorty's opinion, have their rules. He recognized the individual need for a sense of autonomy, and, at the same time, for self-description through challenging one's own self and searching for a new "I." He was also aware of the fact that societies are not quasipeople, that they are comprised of them and, if they are to function in harmony, it is necessary to create space that will be free from the actual pursuit of self-creation.[208] Therefore, the private sphere, being the space for self-creation, should be, in Rorty's opinion, separate from the public sphere, which is the space for social interactions and compromises that shape a society's sense of responsibility and solidarity.

In our private space, we can be individualists and we can create our own constructs concerning ourselves and the world; still, it would be inappropriate to believe that these are the only right constructs, and to organize public space in accordance with them. Therefore, Rorty argued that the likes of a Nietzsche or a Heidegger should privatize their projects, their pursuit of the sublime. They should consider them as irrelevant to politics, and, by that, possibly be in a position to be reconciled with a sense of human solidarity, supported by the development of democratic institutions. This "amounts to the request that they resolve an impending dilemma by subordinating sublimity to the desire to avoid cruelty and pain."[209] Otherwise, we will be faced with the threat that, once again, somebody will start seeking a "new human" on a global scale, which happened in Hitler's Germany and in Mao Zedong's China. And this is something Rorty wanted to avoid.

It is worth noticing that Rorty was aware of the fact that his distinction between private and public is but one of many. There have been many perspectives on the division between the private and the public. We can follow Plato and look for something stable and eternal in ourselves, something that we share with others. In consequence, we can arrive at the conclusion that only specific social or political solutions are right, for it is only they that reflect the order that exists inside ourselves. We can also follow Foucault and presume, as Rorty proposed, that if there is nothing universally human about us, and our subjective point of view is an effect of some accidental forces affecting us, we should give up all social institutions, for there is no basis for their existence (their different types do nothing but limit the freedom of individuals and are a manifestation of "power relations"). However, in Rorty's opinion, such a perspective leads to anarchism. On the one hand, then, we encounter an attempt to incorporate the private into the public, and, on the other, an attempt to incorporate the public into the private. Rorty did not approve of either due to his commitment to liberal values, such as freedom and individualism, as well as to the institutions of democratic states that support them.[210]

Can We Make Such a Division?

At this point, it is worth asking whether or not we are willing to agree with Rorty and assume that the division between the private and the public is indeed possible. Is the fact that while acting we should think of others, we should take into consideration their final vocabularies, not an encouragement for us to consider the arrangements from the public sphere while shaping our own private vocabulary? And does it not mean that, at the same time, we are not able to make a clear distinction between what is private and what is public? Indeed, it is hard to imagine ourselves being able to use a final vocabulary including both the private and the public sphere but acting only in accordance with one of them. It is hard to imagine ourselves hating enemies on the one hand, and acting so as not to humiliate them and not to make them suffer on the other. Finally, it is hard to imagine a nationalist using a private vocabulary full of expressions of hostility toward foreigners, their beliefs, their culture, and their religion while praising liberal freedoms for everyone in their public vocabulary. In short, it is difficult to picture a situation in which, on the one hand, we describe ourselves and others in our private vocabularies—and these descriptions would have nothing to do with someone's present or prospective suffering—and, on the other hand, we consider causing suffering the worst thing we can do. Fortunately, the doubts that arise in the discussion of the division between the private sphere and the public sphere are cleared up to some extend within Rorty's works. While reading them, we encounter fragments that point to the relations between private and public vocabularies. They point to the private part of the final vocabulary affecting the public one—and the other way around—to the public context influencing the shaping of the private vocabulary.

As far as the influence of the private part of the final vocabulary on its public counterpart is concerned, it is worth noticing that Rorty said that "every specific theoretic view comes to be seen as one more vocabulary, one more description, one more way of speaking."[211] It needs to be added, however, that apart from it being one more way of speaking, it is also undoubtedly one more way of acting. Rorty himself viewed language as a means of communication, a tool for social interaction, and a way humans enter into relations with one another.[212] It seems feasible, then, to say that it is impossible to create an individual, private vocabulary somewhere on the side—a vocabulary that would not affect others, that would not affect the public sphere. Rorty himself should have agreed, as he noted that "getting rid of the idea of 'the view from Nowhere'—the idea of a sort of knowing that has nothing to do with agency, values, or interests—might have considerable cultural importance." And, further, he stated, "It would probably not change our day-to-day ways of speaking, but it might well, in the long run, make some practical differences. For changes of opinion among philosophical professors sometimes do, after a time, make a difference to the hopes and fears of nonphilosophers."[213] What is more, Rorty pointed to the process by which old vocabularies and old metaphors are gradually being replaced by new ones. These are created by the ironists (such as Rorty) questioning the vocabularies and metaphors that exist. They pursue their private attempts at self-creation and influence the shape and nature of the public sphere when their "redescriptions" begin to be disseminated. Such influence by individuals and their descriptions on the public sphere, which Rorty referenced, results in the decline of religious faith, which—in Rorty's opinion—has already occurred, inter alia, due to the influence of scientific discoveries and the work of philosophers.[214] It can be said, then, that thanks to creative individuals, in the course of history, some vocabularies are pushed out by others. And even though it is often difficult to determine the extent to which the private shapes the public, it is certain that the process does occur.[215] And was is acknowledged also by Rorty, when he pointed to the changes within "the public vocabulary" that we use.[216]

While investigating Rorty's thought, it is also worth noticing that the public context shapes the private vocabulary. This issue becomes clearer when Rorty himself—after Wittgenstein—pointed to the idea that there are no private languages, that "you cannot give meaning to a word or a poem by confronting it with a nonlinguistic meaning, something other than a bunch of already used words or a bunch of already written poems."[217] Rorty, when paraphrasing Wittgenstein, also wrote that every poem requires a great dose of cultural "stage-setting." In other words, each and every one of our utterances lives in a certain context and is strictly connected with it. Thus, Rorty thought that metaphors are novel uses of old words, which is possible only when there is the background of the old words used in the old, well-known way.[218] Accordingly, it seems plausible to state that the private portion of our final vocabulary is created within the public context, the context that is constructed by the public vocabulary.

Proving that private language affects the public one and comes into existence in the public context is to be considered an argument for the presence of relations between the private sphere and the public sphere. It is worth noting that Rorty also goes that direction in an interview with the titled "Toward a Post-Metaphysical Culture."[219] He admitted that private beliefs or private languages describing anew how creators see themselves penetrate public language and influences how we behave toward others. Rorty said, "I don't think private beliefs can be fenced off [from the public sphere]; they leak through, so to speak, and influence the way one behaves toward other people."[220] Such reasoning can also be presented within Rorty's text when he himself wrote about the relationship between theory and practice. For Rorty, pragmatism does not include any serious division into theory and practice, "all so-called 'theory' which is not wordplay is always already practice."[221] In consequence, Rorty repeated Dewey's idea that theory should be supported if it is likely to facilitate practice.[222] Still, caution is desired, as theory can do much wrong. It is visible, as Rorty noted, "when you weigh the good and the bad the social novelists have done against the good and the bad the social theorists have done," for then "you find yourself wishing that there had been more novels and fewer theories."[223] For Rorty, writers are those who describe how things are, and bring the problems of other people closer to us, while theoreticians are those who try to describe in a new way, to create new visions and theories that they would like to share to be recognized by others, and to penetrate and unite with a public discourse. These theorists for Rorty are often philosophers but also poets or activists who want to "invent a new language because they want to invent a new self."[224] They often want to synthesize this language describing the new self with the public discourse. He added, however, that he did not think that they are "synthesizable."[225] And by saying that he again created confusion in light of what he has said previously about the concepts of the "new self," developed when Hitler or Mao Zedong were in power, when their private languages almost completely took over the public discourse.

Rorty's Inconsistence?

In light of what has been said on the division into the private and the public spheres, which Rorty advocated, as well as of the fact that it is possible to find in Rorty's thought a confirmation that we can talk of the influence of the private vocabulary on the public one and of its shaping in the public context, it is quite plausible to conclude that Rorty was inconsistent. This inconsistency for some can be visible when, on the one hand, Rorty wrote, "[F]or us ironists, theory has become a means to private perfection rather than to human solidarity,"[226] and on the other hand when he presented us with his proposal for a vocabulary based on particular words that are to draw our attention to the suffering around us, and that are to contribute to the implementation of an ideal liberal society. He also claimed that ironists such as himself treat theories as idiosyncrasies, while elsewhere he himself offers a theory that has certain connections with the public sphere.[227] He presented to us a new vocabulary, a new language, by means of which he told the story of the division into the private and the public and of an ideal liberal society, hoping that in the future, it could push out the old order. Rorty's ambition was to make it a vocabulary of a liberal society—of the ideal liberal society "in which ironism, in the relevant sense, is universal."[228] It might seem, however, for some, that according to his own philosophy, this should be considered a private affair, aimed at one's own self-creation. And, thus, Rorty should not argue about his final vocabulary, to make others abandon the old vocabulary that they use and to replace it with a new one. Rorty, however, seems to do otherwise. He presented his point of view, discussed the objections to it, and focused on its advantages. Rorty's position—based on his claim that private idiosyncrasies should remain private—is in this respect challenged with his own proceedings. Of course, Rorty could say that it is dialogue and freedom that are the basic elements of his philosophy, and thus it is not inappropriate that he had his works published or that he tried to debate with those who criticized his ideas. He would certainly say that it is important to debate, and not to resort to violence. As long as we debate, no wrong will happen. It needs to be said, though, that if such a debate—a debate on private final vocabularies—is pursued in the public, it is inevitable for those private vocabularies to permeate the public one. Even though, according to Rorty, philosophers ought to privatize their projects, while pursuing a public debate they do publicize them. They may assure us that their intentions are quite the opposite, but, still, their actions have some specific consequences. Thus, saying that the theories they preach have no significance for the public sphere, that they are their private business only, or that it is "very unclear what impact, if any, this will ever have on public discourse" does not sound convincing.[229] All that is uttered out loud in the course of dialogue ceases to be a private affair of the utterer, and becomes a part of the public sphere: it begins to function as an element of the "sphere" of communication, which is as vast as there are disputants and listeners within it.[230] Whether that will have a small or large impact is a matter for observation, but have an impact it certainly does. And Rorty in fact admitted to a certain extent that what appears in the public sphere over the centuries "actually turns out to have a certain impact."[231]

In light of the above it is worth adding that restricting our private idiosyncrasies to the private sphere, so that they do not intertwine with the public sphere, which actually, as it turned out, was not fully Rorty's point of view, could be realized only when the particular members of our communities were deprived of their right to voice their opinions, the right to speak of their world-visions freely, and the right to their own final vocabularies. And it is needless to argue that this would cause much harm to society. The conclusion to the above is, then, as follows: it is impossible to separate the private sphere from the public one if, at the same time, dialogue and freedom of speech are to be maintained. Interactions between the spheres exist, which Rorty himself admitted, and are necessary for social harmony and individual growth. In other words, this is not the way to defend both the private and the public sphere against threats.

Unjustified Fears

The private sphere influences the public one, and vice versa, and they cannot be separated definitively. By separating the private from the public sphere, Rorty wished to diminish the threat that may result from a too expansive dissemination of one's private visions of the world. As was already mentioned, what he had in mind, in fact, when he was advocating such separation was the radical sense of irony, evident in ironist intellectuals or theoreticians that should be privatized. Irony as a fallibilist civic virtue does not have to be privatized. In his contribution to the Library of Living Philosophers focusing on his philosophy, Rorty explained that the confusion as to what he meant appeared because his "description of the liberal ironist was badly flawed," and that he "conflated two quite different sorts of people: the unruffled pragmatist and the anguished existentialist adolescent."[232] He had in mind two conflicting senses of irony, a radical version, and a more moderate version. In light of that, we can say that what he wanted to point out was rather the need to diminish the threat coming from the ironist in the strong sense and not from the liberal ironists—ironist in the weak sense.

Rorty was anxious also about rationality and justification, which he viewed as strictly connected with the category of truth. However, these fears are not justified. Rationality or justification are not to be avoided. They are tools that can be used for different purposes. In order to support such a claim, it is worth referring to what Rorty wrote about Orwell: "He convinced us that there was a perfectly good chance that the same developments which had made human equality technically possible might make endless slavery possible."[233] The same developments—intellectual and poetic gifts—"which had made Greek philosophy, modern science, and Romantic poetry possible might someday find employment in the Ministry of Truth."[234] When he was writing these words, Rorty should have become aware of the fact that intellectual gifts, such as argumentation, rationality, or justification, may also serve different purposes: both philosophy and science, as well as torturers. The way intellectual gifts are to be utilized depends on humans themselves, and not on the nature of the gifts, which, supposedly, makes us use them in a particular way.

What has been said above about rationality and justification is relevant also with respect to the category of truth. Even if somebody is an adherent of an objective truth, it is not directly connected with the necessity of acting in any particular way. It is not the category of truth—or any other category—that is responsible for its particular usage. None of the visions of the world connected with certain convictions and categories determines a particular action, regardless of whether it preaches the existence of an objective reality or its construction by individuals.[235] We can insist either on the objective existence of the world or its entirely social or cultural nature. It does not matter whether we are convinced about the fact that we know the objective truth or that everything is a product of culture. Our actions do not depend on our belief in the objective and universal nature of our reality or its cultural constitution, but on the way we use these beliefs. Therefore, opposing any reference to the category of objective truth and having the conviction that our beliefs are entirely cultural in nature should not be a solution for all those whose aim is to realize liberal ideas to a fuller extent and not to make others suffer. In order to protect liberal values we should not oppose particular visions of the world but act in the name of changing the individual interests that threaten them, influencing the way of utilizing individual beliefs.[236] The game revolves around the way in which a given belief is to be used and what cultural and political positions its adherents are to take.[237]

Is It Already "As Good"?

When commenting on Rorty's philosophical arguments, it is worth noting that he opposed the ideas of the Enlightenment, assuming that today they are only a ladder that should be thrown away. He said, "Therefore I urge that whatever good the ideas of 'objectivity' and 'transcendence' have done for our culture can be attained equally well by the idea of a community which strives after both intersubjective agreement and novelty—a democratic, progressive, pluralist community of the sort of which Dewey dreamt."[238] Rorty added that once we realize that, there is a fair chance for the emergence of a culture that "could be [. . .] every bit as self-critical and every bit as devoted to human equality as our own familiar, and still metaphysical, liberal culture—if not more so."[239]

Referring to the above, it can be said that it was only Rorty's supposition that such a culture would come into existence once we followed the path he proposed. He was convincing us that such a culture would be based on intersubjective understanding and innovation. It is interesting, however, that this culture would be as much—or even more—"self-critical" and devoted to human equality as our familiar, metaphysical, liberal culture. On the basis of these words, it can be said that Rorty remarked that our culture is not "as bad" as it could seem. Accordingly, we can ask ourselves whether it is justifiable for us to try to "change" our culture and our vocabulary if we think that "now everything is good." Should such attempts be based on the slogan "Let us change the direction of our journey, and then, perhaps, our culture will be 'more' self-critical and devoted to human equality than it is now"? It seems difficult to encourage "throwing the ladder away," abandoning the old vocabulary and utilizing a new one, if the results are to be "as good" as what we have now. Reading these fragments, we are quite confused; we had thought that Rorty had "important" motifs for throwing the ladder away.

All Categories Are Good—As Long as They Bring Us Advantage

When talking about "throwing the ladder away," Rorty discussed abstract categories, which have paved the way for political and cultural transformations. He discussed them using the past tense, as he did not believe we still needed them. Such a statement is acceptable once we assume that these categories no longer bring us any advantage. However, it seems that they may still come in handy. If a bit of rhetoric is useful, it seems right to retain it, especially if it can be used to pursue particular purposes as far as changing ways of thinking and attitudes. For liberal pragmatists, any area of rhetoric leading to a liberal goal should be good.[240] However, Rorty did not put forward such a claim, though he could have, for he himself argued that beliefs are the tools of successful practice.[241] He could have followed this path if he had been aware of the fact that the category of truth can still bring us advantages if it is used appropriately and that it need not be dangerous. He did not follow this path, though by agreeing that there is a possibility of being faithful to the category of truth, and at the same time considering freedom a value to be protected, he contributed to the idea that the category of truth no longer seems so dangerous. He said that he recommended "the picture of the self as a centerless and contingent web to those with similar tastes and similar identities," and that he did not recommend it to those with

> a similar vocation but dissimilar moral identities—identities built, for example, around the love of God, Nietzschean self-overcoming, the accurate representation of reality as it is in itself, the quest for "one right answer" to moral questions, or the natural superiority of a given character type. Such persons need a more complex and interesting, less simple-minded model of the self—one that meshes in complex ways with complex models of such things as "nature" or "history". Nevertheless, such persons may, for pragmatic rather than moral reasons, be loyal citizens of a liberal democratic society. They may despise most of their fellow citizens, but be prepared to grant that the prevalence of such despicable character types is a lesser evil than the loss of political freedom.[242]

On the basis of the above, it can be said that those believing in the existence of objective truth can be good citizens of a liberal state as long as they accept the role of freedom. The category of truth need not be dangerous, or become the means of realizing the interests of a particular class or race, if we also rely on the value of freedom and agree that our interactions should be based on typical liberal freedoms.[243] Referring to an absolute truth would not require depriving others of the freedom of speech. What is more, it is possible to imagine that those who knew it would lead others toward it, being well aware that if the other party reached it on their own, the truth would be fully discovered and accepted. It is only the certainty of knowing the truth without a simultaneous respect for the freedom of another person that may result in using the category of truth in a harmful way. Preaching the one and only truth may become a basis for an oppressive ideology if adherents believe that since they already know the truth, all the other opinions are not worth being heard, and what need be done is make the "only" truth commonly accepted, regardless of what it takes.

Conclusion

The problems connected with the use of the category of truth to which Rorty pointed can be avoided. When Rorty's fear of the category of truth and of rational justification will disappear, it will not be necessary to introduce a proposed division into the private and the public sphere, which, as it has already been said, is hard to maintain. It needs to be admitted that people depend on each other to a great extent, and their actions are never private enough not to influence others. The only solution is to seek harmony between the private sphere and the public sphere. And sometimes Rorty was aware of this, for in spite of the distinction between the private and the public that he introduced, he said that it was advisable to "seek a balance between our idiosyncratic, private fantasies and our public dealings with other people. He who finds this balance could be called 'wise.'"[244]

In spite of all the ambiguities and inconsistencies, Rorty still has something important to tell us. He believed that the idea of truth as responsibility toward reality may be gradually replaced with the idea of what we begin to believe in free and open encounters, in the course of domination-free discussions. As a consequence of these discussions, we will label any of their results as "true" or "good." The only overall criterion for truth that is needed in their course is the idea of "undistorted communication." However, Rorty wrote that he did not think "there is much to be said about what counts as 'undistorted' except 'the sort you get when you have democratic political institutions and the conditions for making these institutions function.'"[245]

Rorty believed that the turn in history has made it easier for us to replace the category of truth with the category of freedom. In his opinion, it is freedom that is now crucial for thinking and for social progress.[246] He believed that if we take care of freedom, the truth will take care of itself.[247] This thought becomes more comprehensible if we listen to what Rorty had to say in analyzing Orwell's *1984*, and especially in light of the following passage from it: "The obvious, the silly, and the true had got to be defended. Truisms are true, hold on to that! The solid world exists, its laws do not change. Stones are hard, water is wet, objects unsupported fall towards the earth's centre."[248] While commenting on the quote, Rorty claimed that it is, inter alia, on its account that Orwell is read as a realist philosopher, a defender of common sense against the educated ironists. It is assumed that what is crucial for Orwell is the classic opposition between unreal appearances and bare reality. Rorty, however, sought to offer a different interpretation: he stressed that Orwell's output in making the public sensitive to the instances of cruelty and humiliation "is not usefully thought of as a matter of stripping away appearance and revealing reality. It is better thought of as a redescription of what may happen or has been happening—to be compared, not with reality, but with alternative descriptions of the same events."[249] While presenting this alternative interpretation, Rorty argued that "it does not matter whether 'two plus two is four' is true, much less whether this truth is 'subjective' or 'corresponds to external reality'. All that matters is that if you do believe it, you can say it without getting hurt. In other words, what matters is your ability to talk to other people about what seem to you true, not what is in fact true."[250] What matters the most is "the freedom to be honest with one another and not be punished for it."[251] For the sake of a short recapitulation, it can be said that in his philosophy Rorty proposed a shift from epistemology to politics, from explaining the relation between "reason" and reality to explaining the ways in which political freedom has changed our understanding of the goals of human cognition. And, as he himself claimed, Dewey was willing to take a step toward freedom, which he followed, but from which Habermas has hung back.[252] But is Rorty right?

III

ON HABERMAS'S THEORY OF COMMUNICATIVE ACTION

Introduction

From Radical Criticism to Reform

Richard Rorty said that today nonanalytic philosophy, with some exceptions, is dominated not by social hope but by despair about the condition of the world. As he noted, "Because the typical member of this tradition is obsessed with the idea of 'radical criticism', when he or she turn to politics it is rarely in a reformist, pragmatic spirit, but rather in a mood either of deep pessimism or of revolutionary fury. Except for a few writers such as Habermas."[1] We should agree with Rorty that, indeed, Jürgen Habermas is not somebody interested only in criticism. He is most certainly a reformist. His own critical analysis of the contemporary world has not made him lose hope—which, unfortunately, is the case with critical theory—in reform being possible. As far as critical theory is concerned, he has stated,

> The research program of the 1930s stood and fell with its historical-philosophical trust in the rational potential of bourgeois culture—a potential that would be released in social movements under the pressure of developed forces of production. Ironically, however, the critiques of ideology carried out by Horkheimer, Marcuse, and Adorno confirmed them in the belief that culture was losing its autonomy in postliberal societies and was being incorporated into the machinery of the economic-administrative system. The development of productive forces, and even critical thought itself, was moving more and more into a perspective of bleak assimilation to their opposites.[2]

The drawbacks of critical theory include, at least as Habermas has presented it, the concept of truth it has assumed. In his opinion, it was and is impossible for it to be reconciled with the fallibilism characteristic of scientific work. It was a concept based on an idea of instrumental reason oriented toward success only. Moreover, critical theory does not appreciate the achievements of bourgeois democracy.[3] Unlike the representatives of critical theory, Habermas has continued to believe that "the formal features of bourgeois systems of law and constitutions, of bourgeois political institutions in general, demonstrate a conceptual structure of moral-practical thought and interpretation which must be considered superior in relation to the built-in moral categories of traditional and legal political institutions."[4] Such a structure is superior since it is based on ideas that, in Habermas's opinion, are worth preserving. What is more, this structure is the ground that allows us to tackle moral-practical issues.[5]

Pointing to the drawbacks of critical theory, Habermas has stressed that they still can be handled. In his opinion, it is crucial to get rid of its normative deficiencies by turning to the idea of "communicative agreement" inherent in language theory. Thus, the philosopher presents his position as revolving around the intuition that any linguistic communication includes the pursuit of agreement. Acknowledging this phenomenon is an important step in the direction of the idea of communicative rationality. The next step is to use this concept in social and institutional conditions.[6] However, as Habermas has remarked, one needs to be cautious at this point not to fall into the traps of fundamentalism or linguistic transcendentalism.

Habermas put forward his beliefs in *The Theory of Communicative Action*, which is to serve as an introduction to explaining the normative basis for a critical theory of society. As far as the theory of communicative action itself is concerned, Habermas said, "The theory of communicative action is meant to provide an alternative to the philosophy of history on which earlier critical theory still relied, but which is no longer tenable. It is intended as a framework within which interdisciplinary research on the selective pattern of capitalist modernization can be taken up once again."[7] An alternative to the philosophy of history, in Habermas's opinion, this theory is also to have a reformist nature. How does it manifest itself? Habermas argued in *The Theory of Communicative Action* that describing its significance can aid us in accomplishing the goal of reviving the communicative opportunities that have been lost. This shall be possible through acknowledging the role of communicative action and communicative rationality, based on the concept of validity claims. This rationality, in Habermas's opinion, is deeply rooted in the social life-form. Thanks to rationality and communicative action, it becomes possible to rationalize different world-visions, to rationalize systems of actions, and to rationalize society. In his magnum opus, Habermas also presented other crucial elements of the theory of action, such as action oriented toward mutual understanding or to the symbolically structured lifeworld. He reconstructed these, discussing the important ingredients of the sociological theories of society. While doing so, he departed from earlier attempts that consisted in foregrounding the critical theory of society by means of a methodological perspective or of an epistemological perspective.

The Structure of the Theory of Communicative Action

To a great extent, Habermas referred to the crucial elements of the theory of communicative action from the point of view of the history of social theory. In heading in the direction of analyzing the sociological origins of the theory of social rationalization, Habermas wished also to expose the commonness of the concept of communicative rationality.[8] As far as the path he followed is concerned, he said, "This is the path I shall follow—not with the intention of carrying out historical investigations; rather, I shall take up conceptual strategies, assumptions, and lines of argument from Weber to Parsons with the systematic aim of laying out the problems that can be solved by means of a theory of rationalization developed in terms of the basic concept of communicative action."[9] At the same time, Habermas opposed the philosophy of mind based on the subject-object model. He argued that its conceptual frames do not allow for referring to the issue of rationalization in a way that can be satisfactory. Following the history of Weber's thesis on social rationalization, Habermas exposed the limits of the approach based on the theory of mind and presented arguments for a change of paradigm. He proposed a change in the understanding of the role of action and a shift from goal-oriented action to communicative action. In Max Weber's thought, among the three types of rationality that emerged after the decline of traditional visions of the world, it is only goal-oriented rationality that has found an embodiment in the institutions of contemporary society. Habermas criticized such a stance, since he believed that it would be a mistake to investigate the rationality of the systems of action only in terms of goal-oriented rationality. This criticism was for him a starting point for further analysis of the concept of communicative action, beginning with the social theory of George H. Mead and Émile Durkheim, about whom he wrote, "On the basis of Mead and Durkheim, I attempt to develop an evolutionary perspective for the increasing reflexive fluidity of world-views, for a continuing process of individuation, and for the emergence of a universalistic moral and legal system through the simultaneous detachment and liberation of communicative action from institutionally frozen contexts."[10] It is Mead and Durkheim who, in Habermas's opinion, have created the categories that have enabled the freeing of the theory of rationalization from the aporias of the philosophy of mind—who contributed to the emergence of a new paradigm, which is not an abstract invention. Mead has accomplished that with his theory of communication and with treating action as symbolic interaction; Durkheim—with the theory of social solidarity, presenting the normative grounds for intersubjective agreement.

When writing about Mead, Habermas pointed also to his analysis of the origins of self and of society, and proved their significance for his own theory. Socialization is here depicted as a process of individualization, the shaping of identity as connected with assimilating the normative structures of intersubjective nature, and the private as something that is subject to intersubjective interpretation and criticism. In the case of Durkheim, Habermas pointed, among other things, to his theory of religion, which, in turn, allows one to discern in the common consciousness the translinguistic roots of communicative action, having a symbolic nature. Thus, it is possible to take them into consideration while analyzing communicative action guided by norms. According to Habermas, analyses of Mead's and Durkheim's concepts allow for the reconstruction of the structure of the original medium used for coordinating social actions, that is, linguistic interaction guided by norms.

This is a précis of what Habermas has written on some social theories. It is, however, sufficient in this context, for it is not his analyses of social theories that are of the greatest importance to us; what matters the most is the fruit that they bring: the purposes that some of these ideas can serve. These deliberations are pursued in the introduction to *The Theory of Communicative Action*, as are some further reflections on issues of a systematic nature. At the beginning, Habermas presents us with the formal-pragmatist approach characteristic of the theory of communicative action. Then he elaborates on the concept of the lifeworld and makes a clear distinction between the miscellaneous or "rationalized" lifeworlds— which are reproduced via communicative action—and the formally organized systems of action, based on steering media, so as to further investigate the tendencies of the connection of lifeworlds and systems to disappear. Finally, having combined research on the history of theory with systematic analysis, Habermas pointed to the tasks that the present-day critical theory of society encounters. It is these elements of *The Theory of*

Communicative Action that are to be the object of our further deliberations. They are particularly important for understanding Habermas's concepts and their reformist potential.

Central Problems in the Theory of Action

The Theory of Communicative Action revolves, obviously, around the idea of communicative action, which, as the author wrote, "provides access to three intertwined topic complexes: first, a concept of communicative rationality that is sufficiently skeptical in its development but is nevertheless resistant to cognitive-instrumental abridgments of reason; second, a two-level concept of society that connects the 'lifeworld' and 'system' paradigms in more than a rhetorical fashion; and finally, a theory of modernity that explains the type of social pathologies that are today becoming increasingly visible, by way of the assumption that communicatively structured domains of life are being subordinated to the imperatives of autonomous, formally organized systems of action."[11] In this chapter, these three topic complexes are to be reconstructed in the above order. This shall allow us to delve into the basic elements of Habermas's theory of communicative action deeply enough so as to point to the particular portions of it that are important for accomplishing the task set forth at the beginning of this book.

Communicative Rationality and Communicative Action

What is crucial for Habermas's thought and our further deliberations is the concept of communicative rationality, by means of which, as he himself has claimed, it is possible to explicate the idea of reconciliation and the idea of freedom. He claimed that the theory of action, whose starting point already contains a project for an ideal communicative community, is more than well-suited for that purpose. As far as its role is concerned, he said, "This Utopia serves to reconstruct an undamaged intersubjectivity that allows both for unconstrained mutual understanding among individuals and for the identities of individuals who come to an unconstrained understanding with themselves."[12] According to Habermas, creating conditions for the emergence of an ideal communicative community shall take us closer to realizing the idea of reconciliation and of freedom, to building a community based on mutual communication, in which there will be no coercion. He based his "Utopia"—a road sign of a sort—on the concepts of communicative rationality and communicative action. He argued that once such an action occurs it shall become possible for the rationality inherent in it to break free, and, by that, it shall be possible to erase the archaic core of rationality. Accordingly, there will be more space for rationalizing world-visions, for universalizing law and morality, and for a quicker process of individualization. Thus, the utopia, which has only pointed to certain possibilities, shall begin to be actually implemented.

Such a project sounds more than interesting. In order to understand it properly, it is necessary to pay close attention, first, to the concepts of rationality, especially communicative rationality, and then to the concept of communicative action.

COMMUNICATIVE RATIONALITY

In the first chapter of *The Theory of Communicative Action*, which is concerned with giving a preliminary definition of rationality, Habermas begins the exposition of his perspective on rationality by sketching out his understanding of the idea. He argued that it is symbolic expressions—linguistic and nonlinguistic, communicative and noncommunicative actions—that embody knowledge that can be rational. In the case of the original action and its means of expression, one who aims at communicating something articulates a thought. In the case of the latter, one deliberately interferes with the world. Both types of expression and the connected actions—communicative and teleological—that embody fallible knowledge can be subject to criticism. Such criticism shall refer to the claim that the acting subject connects with his or her expression, as long as it has been aimed as a statement or as a purposeful action. As Habermas said, "For *A* does not make an assertion unless he makes a truth claim for the asserted proposition *p* and therewith indicates his conviction that his statement can, if necessary, be defended. And *B* does not perform a goal-oriented action, that is, he does not want to accomplish an end by it unless he regards the action planned as promising and therewith indicates his conviction that, in the given circumstances, his choice of means can if necessary be explained."[13] Thus, in the first case, action is accompanied by a truth claim that is crucial for statements concerning the state of affairs in the world; in the second, action is accompanied by a claim for a positive result or effectiveness as far as rules for action allowing for one's integration with the world are concerned. Habermas then goes on to say, "With his assertion, *A* makes reference to something that *in fact occurs* in the objective world; with his purposive activity, *B* makes reference to something that *should occur* in the objective world. In doing so both raise *claims* with their symbolic expressions, claims that can be criticized and argued for, that is, *grounded*. The rationality of their expressions is assessed in light of the internal relations between the semantic content of these expressions, their conditions of validity, and the reasons (which could be provided, if necessary) for the truth of statement or for the effectiveness of actions."[14] The rationality of the expression in question can be either criticized or justified. Next Habermas argued, "An expression satisfies the precondition for rationality if and insofar as it embodies fallible knowledge and therewith has a relation to the objective world (that is, a relation to the facts) and is open to objective judgment. A judgment can be objective if is undertaken on the basis of a *transsubjective* validity claim that has the same meaning for observers and nonparticipants as it has for the acting subject himself. Truth and efficiency are claims of this kind."[15] As Habermas claimed, tackling rationality through criticizing it has certain drawbacks. Such an approach is too abstract, for it does not articulate the important distinctions, and it is too narrow, since the expression "rational" is used not only in the context of expressions that can be true or false, effective or ineffective.

Referring to the first of the drawbacks, Habermas argued that the cognitive concept of rationality can be presented in two distinct ways. It is possible to talk of cognitive-instrumental rationality, which is connected with the successful self-maintenance "made possible by informed disposition over, and intelligent adaptation to conditions of contingent environment."[16] It is also possible to talk of communicative rationality. As Habermas puts it, the concept "carries with it connotations based ultimately on the central experience of the unconstrained, unifying, consensus-bringing force of argumentative speech, in which different participants overcome their merely subjective views and, owing to the mutuality of rationally motivated conviction, assure themselves of both the unity of the objective world and the intersubjectivity of their lifeworld."[17] In turn, while referring to the latter drawback, he said that though, indeed, justified statements and effective actions are proofs of rationality, there are also other types of expression that can rest on valid arguments, even though they are not followed by truth claims or claim for success in accomplishing a goal. Someone can be called rational also "if he is following an established norm" or "if he makes known a desire or an intention, expresses a feeling or a mood, shares a secret, confesses a deed, etc."[18] These actions, regulated by norms, or the articulations of inner states, have "the character of meaningful expressions, understandable in their context, which are connected with criticizable validity claims."[19] It is also the case that in these rational behaviors the possibility of the intersubjective recognition of criticizable validity claims, in terms of their normative righteousness or subjective honesty, is quite crucial. Habermas stressed that "with these expressions the speaker can refer not to something in the objective world but only to something in a common social world or in his own subjective world."[20] His or her expressions can be justified or criticized, by thus fulfilling the condition for rationality.

In light of the above, it is obvious that Habermas paid particular attention to communicative rationality. He argued that by acknowledging its presence and its role in the process of shaping a consensus, we overcome the abstractness of approaches based only on the cognitive-instrumental function of our actions and cognitive processes. In other words, in his *Theory of Communicative Action*, Habermas observed that rationality is a concept that is not restricted to the expressions connected with validity and efficacy claims. To this point, he wrote,

> actions regulated by norms, expressive self-presentations, and also evaluative expressions, supplement constative speech acts in constituting a communicative practice which, against the background of a lifeworld, is oriented to achieving, sustaining, and reviewing consensus—and indeed a consensus that rests on the intersubjective recognition of criticizable validity claims. The rationality inherent in this practice is seen in the fact that a communicatively achieved agreement must be based *in the end* on reasons. And the rationality of those who participate in this communicative practice is determined by whether, if necessary, they could, *under suitable circumstances*, provide reasons for their expressions. Thus the rationality proper to the communicative practice of everyday life points to the practice of argumentation as a court of appeal that makes it possible to continue communicative action with other means when disagreements can no longer be repaired with everyday routines and yet are not to be settled by the direct or strategic use of force.[21]

Acknowledging other kinds of expressions means obtaining a more accurate picture of linguistic actions creating communicative practice aimed at consensus. This consensus shall be accomplished every time by means of criticizing validity claims that accompany our expressions. Agreement reached in the course of such a criticism shall be based on relevant arguments.

ARGUMENTATION

The deliberations on communicative rationality are based on the crucial—for Habermas's philosophy—concepts of argumentation, rational action, and validity claims. And these need to be discussed in more detail, for this shall determine the proper understanding of the concept of communicative rationality per se.

Starting with the concept of argumentation first, it is worth observing that its place in Habermas's philosophy is strictly connected with his theory of argumentation. The aim of this theory is to reconstruct formal-pragmatist premises and the conditions for rational behavior. For Habermas, within the frames of this theory, argumentation is a type of utterance in the course of which the interlocutors present opposing validity claims and try to refer to them by means of arguments, either agreeing or criticizing. These arguments comprise certain reasons and are strictly connected with certain validity claims. Habermas distinguishes between three aspects of utterances that use arguments. They can be conceived of as a *process*, in the course of which the interlocutors need to assume that the act of communication between them shall be free from coercion, and if there is to be a coercion of some sort, it shall be the coercion to use better arguments and no other. In this case, the only motivation will be to cooperate in the search for truth. Argumentation can also be conceived of as a *procedure*, a form of interaction, during which the interlocutors thematize validity claims and, assuming a hypothetical attitude, "test with reasons, and only with reasons, whether the claim defended by the proponents rightfully stand or not."[22] Utterances using arguments can also be conceived of as *creating* apt arguments, thanks to which "validity claims can be redeemed or rejected."[23]

Accordingly, Habermas claimed that the basic intuition connected with argumentation can, in the processual aspect, be characterized "by the intention of convincing a *universal audience* and gaining general assent for an utterance; from the procedural perspective, by the intention of ending a dispute about hypothetical validity claims with a *rationally motivated agreement*; and from the product perspective by the intention of grounding or *redeeming* a validity claim with arguments."[24] However, as Habermas stressed, any argumentation requires the form of organization that lies at the basis of the cooperative search for truth. It is "learning processes—through which we acquire theoretical knowledge and moral insight, extend and renew our evaluative language, and overcome self-deceptions and difficulties in comprehension" that rely on these arguments.[25] And the aim is to shape intersubjective beliefs with better arguments.[26]

RATIONAL ACTION AND VALIDITY CLAIMS

In Habermas's opinion, the theory of argumentation serves to explain both the rationality of expression and the rationality of subjects able to communicate and act. In the theory, the ability to properly argue is an expression of the ability to act rationally, which is characteristic of a person who can, among other things, provide reasons for his or her expressions. Therefore, Habermas calls "rational" those who in the cognitive-instrumental domain articulate justified beliefs and act effectively. Their rationality is connected then with the ability to learn on the basis of their mistakes, as well as their ability to challenge hypotheses and overcome failures, which result from intervening in the world. In this case, the medium shall consist in theoretical discourse, within which validity claims are a point of discussion.

In Habermas's opinion, we call "rational" also those who in the moral-practical domain can justify their actions by referring to existing normative contexts. They act commonsensically and they do not indulge in their affections, neither do they motivate their actions with bare interest but instead try to assess a conflict from a moral point of view without a bias, and resolve it by means of a consensus. In this case, the medium consists in *practical discourse*, with the help of which it is possible to hypothetically test whether the norm guiding the action can be validated or not. Thus, this discourse serves an exchange of arguments, their topics being the claims for normative righteousness.

We encounter a rational attitude not only in the cognitive-instrumental or moral-practical domains but also when we are faced with evaluative expressions, expressions articulating inner states, and explicative discourse. Thus, we call "rational" also those who interpret their set of needs according to culturally rooted standards of evaluation and who are able to be critical with respect to those standards. Moreover, in Habermas's opinion, we can call rational also someone who is willing to break free from illusions that rest not on mistakes with respect to facts but on misunderstandings of his or her own experiences, as well as someone who is willing to pursue consensus and, in case of disturbances in communication, is willing to challenge linguistic rules.

In light of what has been said above, Habermas wrote that "rationality is understood to be a disposition of speaking and acting subjects that is expressed in modes of behavior for which there are good reasons or grounds. This means that rational expressions admit of objective evaluation. This is true of all symbolic expressions that are, at least implicitly, connected with validity claims (or with claims that stand in internal relation to a criticizable validity claim). Any explicit examination of controversial validity claims requires an exacting form of communication satisfying the conditions of argumentation."[27]

To be in accordance with the above, all rational expressions need to be *implicitly* or *explicitly* connected with criticizable validity claims. As it has already been said, these claims are connected with particular discourses— forms of argumentation. Habermas distinguishes between theoretical discourse and the related claim for truth and effectiveness (articulated via cognitive-instrumental expressions); practical discourse and the related claim for righteousness (articulated via moral-practical expressions); aesthetic criticism and the related claim for adequacy (articulated via evaluative expressions); therapeutic criticism and the related claim for honesty (articulated via the expressions of experiences); and explicative discourse and the related claim for comprehensibility or correctness. All of the above forms of argumentation differ from each other with respect to the relevant validity claims. These validity claims, at first presented hypothetically, are criticizable, and by that they can be intersubjectively accepted or not.[28]

VALIDITY OF EXPRESSION AND JUSTIFICATION

According to Habermas, validity claims are one of the categories that make it possible to grasp the essence of the discourse theory of truth. He listed three categories: *"conditions of validity* (which are fulfilled when an utterance holds good), *validity-claims* (which speakers raise with their utterances, for their validity), and redemption of a validity-claim (in the framework of a discourse which is sufficiently close to the conditions of an ideal speech situation for the consensus aimed at by the participants to be brought about solely through the force of the better argument, and in this sense to be 'rationally motivated')."[29] And these categories as well as the discourse theory of truth comprise an intuition that—as Habermas wrote—is quite simple:

> Validity-claims are explicitly thematized only in non-trivial cases, but it is precisely in these cases that there are no rules of verification available which would make it possible to decide directly whether certain conditions of validity are fulfilled or not [. . .]. Rather a play of argumentation is required, in which motivating reasons take the place of the unavailable knock-down arguments. If one accepts this description, it becomes clear that the following difficulty arises in the attempt to explain what it means to say that an utterance is valid. An utterance is valid when its conditions of validity are fulfilled. According to our description the fulfillment or non-fulfillment of conditions of validity, in problematic cases, can only be ascertained by means of argumentative redemption of the corresponding validity-claims. The discourse theory of truth, then, explains what it means to redeem a validity-claim by an analysis of the general pragmatic presuppositions of the attainment of a rationally-motivated consensus.[30]

And therefore Habermas argued that the occurrence of validity claims is related to the redemption—or fulfilling—of the conditions for the rightness of a given expression. A validity claim can be articulated *explicitly* or *implicitly*. The interlocutor can accept it, discard it, or ignore it.[31] It is the discursive "compensation" for validity claims that determines whether a given expression, a given utterance, is to be considered justified. In other words, a sentence will be justified if the discussion as well as its results are based on previously respected validity claims, which are an important element of communication. As Habermas remarked, "[G]rounding descriptive statements means establishing the existence of states of affairs; grounding normative statement, establishing the acceptability of actions or norms of actions; grounding evaluative statements,"[32] establishing the choice of particular actions or norms of values that are, in turn, a reference point for the evaluations articulated; "grounding expressive statements, establishing the transparency of self-presentations; and grounding explicative statements, establishing that the symbolic expressions have been produced correctly."[33] The process of grounding—or justifying—will require resolving the conflict over validity claims via "discursive" conditions—when "the meaning of the problematic validity claim conceptually forces participants to suppose that a rationally motivated agreement could in principle be achieved, whereby the phrase 'in principle' expresses the idealizing proviso: if only the argumentation could be conducted openly enough and continued long enough."[34] As Habermas claimed, in the course of argumentation (in theoretical, practical, or explicative discourse), the interlocutors also need to assume that they have ensured the conditions for an ideal situation of linguistic communication, conditions that are as close to the ideal of undistorted communication as possible.

Accordingly, it can be said that once we are provided with the conditions for facilitating dialogue, once all the parties use their argumentation for the sake of, for instance, establishing the rightness of their stances, once they assume the possibility of arriving at agreement in the course of eliminating secondary arguments and choosing better ones, we will partake in the process of justifying. Eventually, a stance containing validity claims shall be justified if this is to be universally accepted.

UNIVERSAL ACCEPTANCE

Due to argumentation for or against criticizable validity claims, it is possible to arrive at rationally motivated agreement, universal acceptance, and, we need to add, public universal acceptance. It will be possible due to the willingness to be criticized, to exchange arguments, to adjust one's own beliefs, to learn on the basis of one's own mistakes, to cooperate while searching for the truth, and to convince the other participants of the discourse by means of apt reasoning. For Habermas, it is precisely the accuracy of reasoning that is the manifestation of the strength of an argument; this strength is expressed, inter alia, whether it convinces the participants of the discourse or not, whether it motivates accepting given validity claims.[35]

This shaping of intersubjective beliefs by means of better argumentation, convincing the public, and accomplishing rationally motivated agreement deserving universal acceptance of all those interested can occur, in Habermas's opinion, pursuant to communicative action. And it is precisely communicative action that shall be discussed next. However, before that, it is important to point to yet another issue: the warning put forward by Habermas.

While writing about the idea of validity, Habermas warned against the danger of substituting it with the idea of acceptability. He himself used the concept of acceptability; however, he understands it as agreeing with others given reasons and arguments. Universal acceptance is, then, based on reasons, and not on, for example, coercion. Were we to talk of coercion determining such a universal acceptance, it would be only the coercion created by virtue of better argumentation. In other words, one should not equate the idea of validity with the idea of acceptability, just as legality should not be equated with social obligation. Such legality, in Habermas's opinion, transcends the limits of space and time, and the reasons connected with it should be as rational and as independent of the circumstances as possible. Accordingly, he wrote about a certain kind of "unconditionality" and "impartiality":[36] "The theory of communicative action aims at the moment of unconditionality that, with criticizable validity claims, is built into the conditions of processes of consensus formation. *As claims* they transcend all limitations of space and time, all the provincial limitations of the given context."[37] However, Habermas argued that this moment, saved and stored in the discursive concepts of fallible truth and morality, "is not an absolute, or it is at most an absolute that has become fluid as a critical procedure. Only with this residue of metaphysics can we do battle against the transfiguration of the world through metaphysical truths."[38] These words sound controversial, and so does the entire issue of the universality of validity claims. This should be discussed in more detail; however, this will take place once we deliberate on other crucial concepts in the theory of communicative action. The next one to be discussed is communicative action itself.

COMMUNICATIVE ACTION

Communicative action, according to Habermas, belongs to a much broader group of linguistic actions. He distinguished between actions oriented toward success and actions oriented toward understanding. The former includes instrumental actions and strategic actions; the latter, communicative action. These two basic forms of actions exist within social interactions connected with reasons; subjects, while speaking and acting, draw on their knowledge and at least implicitly utter the claim for validity or for success. They differ in the mechanisms of coordinating action. In the first, these involve fulfilling sets of interests; in the latter, they involve the pursuit of achieving understanding.[39] As far as instrumental action and strategic action are concerned, Habermas said, "We call an action oriented to success *instrumental* when we consider it under the aspect of following technical rules of action and assess the efficiency of an intervention into a complex circumstances and events. We call an action oriented to success strategic when we consider it under the aspect of following rules of rational choice and assess the efficacy of influencing the decisions of a rational opponent. Instrumental actions can be connected with and subordinated to social interactions of a different type—for example, as the 'task elements' of social roles; strategic actions are social actions by themselves."[40] Actions oriented toward understanding, including communicative actions, are quite different from the above. Habermas talks of communicative action when the interlocutors agree on their actions in the course of a process of reaching a consensus, not minding the possibilities of achieving a success. Thus, what he calls communicative actions are those forms of social interaction in which "plans of action of different actors are co-ordinated through an exchange of communicative acts, that is, through a use of language [. . .] oriented towards reaching understanding."[41] In the course of such an action, the interlocutors position success in the foreground. They aim at "their individual goals under the condition that they can harmonize their plans of action on the basis of common situation definitions,"[42] that they can come up with a common scope of acting. Negotiating these definitions is an important element of the processes of communication that occur in communicative action.

Habermas observed that in dividing linguistic action into action oriented toward success and action oriented toward understanding, we encounter a difficulty connected with the fact that, on the one hand, communicative acts by which the speaker and the listener arrive at an agreement are treated as a mechanism of coordinating action, and, on the other hand, that not every instance of interaction mediated by language constitutes an example of action oriented toward understanding. In order to avoid this difficulty, Habermas claimed that the use of language as oriented toward understanding is the original mode of arriving at agreement, and implying something or contributing to a particular understanding of something is an intermediate mode—a parasite on the original one. As Habermas noted, it is precisely this division that John Austin introduced, distinguishing between illocutions and perlocutions.[43]

Austin, as Habermas highlighted, distinguished between locutionary, illocutionary, and perlocutionary acts. Locutions serve to express states of affairs. By means of locutionary acts, the speaker performs certain activities—he or she states, promises, or commands. Such an act always occurs alongside communicative intention, so that the listener can understand and accept an utterance. It is in itself sufficient, for "the communicative intent of the speaker and the illocutionary aim he is pursuing follow from the manifest meaning of what is said."[44] In turn, perlocutionary acts serve the speaker to bring about a particular effect in the listener. They occur when "a speaker acts in an orientation to success and thereby instrumentalizes speech acts for purposes that are only contingently related to the meaning of what is said."[45] Building on these distinctions, Habermas claimed that "the three acts that Austin distinguishes can be characterized in the following catch-phrases: to say *something*, to act *in* saying something, to bring about something *through* acting in saying something."[46]

Taking into consideration the above—and using the terminology introduced by Austin—Habermas argued that communicative action, which is his central focus, differs from strategic interactions in the fact that all the participants pursue it in order to realize illocutionary purposes—in order to reach understanding. This understanding, emerging in the course of the process of arriving at agreement, must be accepted by the participants as valid. Habermas said to this end that "[p]rocesses of reaching understanding aim at an agreement that meets the conditions of rationally motivated assent to the content of an utterance. A communicatively achieved agreement has a rational basis; it cannot be imposed be either party, whether instrumentally through intervention in the situation directly or strategically through influencing the decisions of opponents."[47] This agreement can be reached in the course of interaction consisting in criticizing validity claims. Agreement is here an intersubjective acceptance of these claims put forward by the speaker within an utterance. Agreeing with one of them, the speaker accepts also the other two claims presented implicitly.

This understanding, reached communicatively and rationally, emerges within shared normative agreement, sharing of propositional knowledge, and mutual trust in their respective subjective honesty. It is measured according to three criteria, as the interlocutors "cannot avoid embedding their speech acts in precisely three world-relations and claiming validity for them under three aspects."⁴⁸ A reference to something in the objective world, something in the social world, and something in the subjective world are used by the speaker and by the listener as somewhat of an interpretative framework, within which they develop common definitions of their situation connected with acting.

To sum up, it can be said that communicative action, strictly connected with Habermas's idea of communicative rationality, is based on a cooperative process of interpretation, with respect to what counts, which are only those linguistic acts with which the speaker connects criticizable validity claims. Habermas said that "only those speech acts with which a speaker connects a criticizable validity claim can move a hearer to accept an offer independently of external forces. In this way they can be effective as a mechanism for coordinating action."⁴⁹

Lifeworld and System

Generally speaking, we can distinguish between three dimensions inherent in the concept of communicative rationality: "[F]irst, the relation of the knowing subject to a world of events or facts; second, the relation to a social world of an acting, practical subject entwined in interaction with others; and finally, the relation of a suffering and passionate subject [. . .] to its own inner nature, to its own subjectivity and the subjectivity of others."⁵⁰ In Habermas's opinion, we are able to observe these three dimensions when we analyze the process of communication from the perspective of its participants. In this process, yet another role is played by the lifeworld, on which the process of reaching an understanding is based. In other words, the deliberations on communicative rationality and communicative action need to be supplemented with the concept of the lifeworld. This lifeworld is a constituent of mutual understanding as such. It is the place where the speaker and the listener meet, and where they can put forward claims and criticize them. Systematic referencing of these actions creates formal conceptions of the world. In Habermas's opinion, it is due to them that the participants of communication, coming from a common lifeworld, communicate with each other with respect to something in the objective, in the social, and in the subjective world. Both the concept of the lifeworld as well as the formal conceptions of the world need to be discussed in more detail.

LIFEWORLD — IMPLICIT KNOWLEDGE AND CONTEXT

The lifeworld consists of nonproblematic convictions that are its hidden grounds, convictions that are self-evident, as well as the faculties mastered in a naïve way. According to Habermas, it is present only in a prereflective form. The concept of action as oriented toward understanding allows us to comprehend these hidden grounds that Habermas called "knowledge not articulated explicitly" and that appear in the cooperative processes of interpreting.[51] Habermas hopes that in the right circumstances, the participants of strategic or communicative actions, wishing to reach success or to reach understanding, will be able to identify when they are trying to understand each other, and when the attempts at understanding are to fail on the basis of this pretheoretical, intuitive, and implicit knowledge.

Communicative action, as already discussed above, depends on implicit knowledge. However, it is also dependent on situational contexts, which are the components of the lifeworld of interacting participants. Habermas wrote,

> If the investigations of the last decade in socio-, ethno-, and psycholinguistics converge in any one respect, it is on the often and variously demonstrated point that the collective background and context of speakers and hearers determines interpretations of their explicit utterances to an extraordinarily high degree. Searle has taken up this doctrine of empirical pragmatics and criticized the long dominant view that sentences get *literal meaning* only by virtue of the rules for using the expressions contained in them. So far, I have also construed the meaning of speech acts as literal meaning in this sense. Naturally this meaning could not be thought independently of contextual conditions altogether; for each type of speech act there are *general* contextual conditions that must be met if the speaker is to be able to achieve illocutionary success. But these general contextual conditions could supposedly be derived in turn from the literal meaning of the linguistic expressions employed in the standard speech acts. And a matter of fact, if formal pragmatics is not to lose its object, knowledge of the conditions under which speech acts may be accepted as valid cannot depend *completely* on contingent background knowledge.[52]

Habermas continued this deliberation, referring, inter alia, to John R. Searle, according to whom, in Habermas's account, it is impossible to present the conditions for rightness independent of context, and "if we begin to vary relatively deep-seated and trivial background assumptions, we notice that the (only) seemingly context-invariant conditions of validity change meaning and are thus by no means absolute."[53] Accordingly, it can be said that the literal meaning of an expression is of a relative nature, and that this meaning depends on the background, which is made of changeable and implicit knowledge.[54] Habermas responded by stating, "The fundamental background knowledge of the acceptability conditions of linguistically standardized expressions if hearers are to be able to understand their literal meanings, has remarkable features: It is an *implicit* knowledge that cannot be represented in a finite number of propositions; it is a *holistically structured* knowledge, the basic elements of which intrinsically define one another; and it is a knowledge that *does not stand out at our disposition*, inasmuch as we cannot make it conscious and place it in doubt as we please."55 It needs to be added that in the course of the processes of reaching understanding, the interlocutors use reliable definitions of situations, and by doing so they use a certain consensus, provided by the lifeworld connected with a given cultural tradition, or they negotiate over new definitions. New definitions are developed in the case of new situations emerging from the lifeworld. When it happens, those undertaking communicative actions do not exercise a position from outside the world. They cannot exercise it also with respect to language as a medium for the processes of reaching understanding, marked by culture. The same concerns, the cultural patterns for interpretation, evaluation, and expression, are transmitted via this language. According to the culturalistic concept of the lifeworld, these patterns are "resources" for interpretative actions of interaction participants, who negotiate between themselves over the definitions of situations, and who try to arrive at a consensus on something existing in the world.

LIFEWORLD AND FORMAL WORLD-CONCEPTS

"Language and culture are constitutive for the life-world itself. They are neither one of the formal frames, that is, the world to which participants assign elements of situations, nor do they appear as something in the objective, social, or subjective worlds. In performing or understanding a speech act, participants are very much moving within their language, so that they cannot bring a present utterance *before themselves* as 'something intersubjective.'"56 In other words, the category of lifeworld has a status different from one of the formal world-concepts, by means of which the participants of communication collectively define their situations.

However, we may ask where these formal concepts originated. For Habermas, they are an effect of the process of learning. In his deliberations, he used the idea developed by Jean Piaget, who delineated the levels of cognitive development that do not differ from each other due to new contents but that refer to higher and higher levels of the ability to learn. Habermas said on this subject, "Thus, for Piaget there is cognitive development in a wider sense, which is not understood solely as the construction of an external universe but also as the construction of a reference system for the *simultaneous* demarcation of the objective and social worlds from the subjective world. Cognitive development signifies in general *the decentration of an egocentric understanding of the world.*"⁵⁷ Habermas wanted to describe the emergence of new structural properties of world-images as transformations in the systems of categories in a similar manner. These transformations, connected with the process of passing onto new levels of learning—going from the mythical through the metaphysical and religious into the modern way of thinking—lead to the emergence of a system of reference for the formal concept of the three worlds. In the course of this process, as Habermas noted, we can "form a reflexive concept of 'world' and open up access to the world through the medium of common interpretive efforts, in the sense of a cooperative negotiation of situation definitions."⁵⁸ Undertaking these interpretative efforts, the members of communicative community distinguish between the objective world, their intersubjectively shared social world, and their subjective worlds. The division into the three worlds results from common assumptions in a system of coordinates "in which situation contexts can be ordered in such a way that agreement will be reached about what the participants may treat as fact, or a valid norm, or a subjective experience."⁵⁹ In other words, these concepts "together with criticizable validity claims [. . .] form the frame or categorical scaffolding that serves to order problematic situations—that is, situations that need to be agreed upon—in a lifeworld that is already substantively interpreted."⁶⁰

However, according to Habermas, the lifeworld cannot be described in such a way: it cannot be viewed from the outside, for we and linguistic actions are but its part. He also claimed that "communicative actors are always moving *within* the horizon of their lifeworld" and "cannot refer to 'something in the lifeworld' in the same way as they can to facts, norms, or experiences."⁶¹

To conclude the deliberation on the relation between the lifeworld and the formal world-concepts, Habermas wrote, "In a sentence: participants cannot assume *in actu* the same distance in relation to language and culture as in relation to the totality of facts, norms, or experiences concerning which mutual understanding is possible."⁶² It can be added that it is precisely due to the forms of intersubjectivity that the participants of communication can reach understanding. And it also needs to be said, once again, that it is not possible as far as the lifeworld is concerned.

NARROWNESS OF CULTURALISTIC CONCEPT OF LIFEWORLD

As presented above, Habermas's concept of a lifeworld has been outlined from a culturalistic perspective, according to which the patterns for interpretation, evaluation, and expression serve as resources for the interpretative actions of interacting participants. However, the lifeworld comprises not only cultural certitudes but also individual skills, intuitive knowledge, and socially consolidated practices. In other words, the lifeworld comprises also society and identity. Accordingly, Habermas remarked that "the actor is at once both the *initiator* of his accountable actions and the *product* of the traditions in which he stands, of the solidary groups to which he belongs, of socialization and learning processes to which he is exposed. Whereas *a fronte* the segment of the lifeworld relevant to a situation presses upon the actor as a problem he has to resolve on his own, *a tergo* he is sustained by the background of a life-world that does not consist only of cultural certainties."[63] What Habermas has deemed narrow are perspectives that rely on a culturalistically narrowed world-concept, one based on the theory of socially constructed reality. Communicative action is not only a process of reaching understanding, not only a process of interpretation, within which "cultural knowledge [. . .] is thus exposed to a test" but also encompasses "processes of social integration and of socialization."[64] In this process, the interlocutors communicate with each other with respect to something in the world, reproducing their cultural knowledge, and, by that, creating, proving, and renewing their membership in their social groups and their own identity. Accordingly, Habermas said, "The lifeworld is 'tested' in quite a different manner [. . .]: these tests are not measured directly against criticizable validity claims or standards of rationality, but against standards for the solidarity of members and for the identity of socialized individuals."[65] In other words, communicative actions influence also the bonds of solidarity and the competence of socialized individuals. According to Habermas, then, we need to revise the narrow culturalistic understanding of the lifeworld and view the everyday practices of communication as rooted in the context of the lifeworld, comprised of cultural traditions, legitimate orders, and socialized individuals.

THE ROLE OF SYSTEMS

Communicative actions do influence the bonds of solidarity, but this influence is not the only relation they have to socialized individuals and not the only way in which social integration is ensured. Habermas sees the perspective that acknowledges only their influence on the bonds of solidarity, and does not acknowledge that they also include systematic mechanisms, as wrong. Thus, he does not accept a perspective within which societies are transformed into lifeworlds. In his opinion, it "screens out everything that inconspicuously affects a socio-cultural lifeworld from the outside."[66] If we view society as a lifeworld, we accept a threefold fiction, for we assume the autonomy of individuals acting, the independence of culture, and the transparency of communication. In such a perspective, social actors are of sound mind and act in accordance with criticizable validity claims, culture is independent of external pressures, and violence does not occur. On this point, Habermas said,

> These three fictions become apparent when we drop the identification of society with the lifeworld. They are convincing only so long as we assume that the integration of society can take place *only* on the premises of communicative action—leaving space, of course, for the alternatives of acting strategically when consensus breaks down. This is the way things look to the members of a sociocultural lifeworld themselves. In fact, however, their goal-directed actions are coordinated not only through processes of reaching understanding, but also through functional interconnections that are not intended by them and are usually not even perceived within the horizon of everyday practice. In capitalist societies the market is the most important example of a norm-free regulation of cooperative contexts. The market is one of those systemic mechanisms that stabilize nonintended interconnections of action by way of functionally intermeshing action *consequences*, whereas the mechanism of mutual understanding harmonizes the action *orientations* of participants.[67]

Therefore, Habermas deems it right to see society as a certain system that needs to fulfill the conditions necessary for preserving the sociocultural lifeworlds, for perceiving them as entities that develop in the course of evolution and grow to be systems and lifeworlds. As he put it, "Every theory of society that is restricted to communication theory is subject to limitations that must be observed. The concept of the lifeworld that emerges from the conceptual perspective of communicative action has only limited analytical and empirical range."[68] The above understanding of the concept of society is, in Habermas's opinion, proven by the theory of social evolution. He understands this social evolution as a process that results in differentiating the system and the lifeworld. This process is characterized, on the one hand, by the increase in the rationality of the lifeworld, and, on the other, by the increase in the complexity of social systems. Our next step shall be presenting both of them.

RATIONALIZATION OF THE LIFEWORLD

Habermas understands the lifeworld as equivalent to the processes of reaching an understanding, which the actors of communicative action develop. The lifeworld of those actors always originates from more or less nonproblematic beliefs that form the background. Problematic situations, which require arriving at an agreement, as well as their resolutions, become a part of the assumptions of a nonproblematic lifeworld. This is possible due to the formal structure composed of three world-concepts and the accompanying validity claims. They store the interpretations of the past generations, a basis for situation definitions, which the participants use. These definitions become a solid ground for arriving at an agreement. However, the situation changes with the decentration of worldviews. When writing about decentration, Habermas referred to the concept used by Piaget in order to point to the evolutionary perspective, which we can use if we want to talk of the historically universal process of the rationalization of worldviews. The concept of decentration serves Habermas to elucidate the intrinsic relations between the structures of worldviews, the lifeworld as a context for the processes of reaching understanding, and the possibilities of rational control over one's life. As he wrote, "The more the world-view that furnished the cultural stock of knowledge is decentered, the less the need for understanding is covered *in advance* by an interpreted lifeworld immune from critique, and the more this need has to be met by the interpretative accomplishments of the participants themselves, that is, by way of risky (because rationally motivated) agreement, the more frequently we can expect rational action orientations."[69] In Habermas's opinion, rationally oriented actions are to lead to the rationalizing of worldviews and eventually to the rationalizing of the lifeworld itself. In a rationalized and decentered lifeworld, understanding is no longer to be ensured by interpretations that are immune to criticism and supported by tradition but by rationally pursued agreement.[70] The lifeworld is then to be perceived as rationalized once it rests on understanding reached in the course of communication.

Due to the differentiation and shaping of its structural components, the lifeworld presented by Habermas is subject to the processes of ongoing rationalization. The greater the extent to which these processes emerge, the more likely it is for our interactions to occur in an environment where there are the conditions for the rational pursuit of understanding, that is creating a consensus, which, as Habermas said, "rests *in the end* on the authority of the better argument."[71] This process points to the historical transformations that tend toward rationalizing the lifeworld; these "can be systematized under three perspectives: (a) structural differentiation of the lifeworld, (b) separation of form and content, and (c) growing reflexivity of symbolic reproduction."[72] According to Habermas, the differentiation of the lifeworld leads to continual, critical references to the tradition and to the pursuit of cooperative processes of interpretation. He has stressed that these tendencies are a proof of releasing "the rationality potential inherent in communicative action."[73] He has also added that "corresponding to the differentiation of culture, society, and personality, there is a differentiation of form and content,"[74] which manifests itself in modern societies by the gradually firmer recognition of the rules of legal order and of morality, which correspond to the particular life-forms to a lesser and lesser extent. However, "the cognitive structures acquired in the socialization process are increasingly detached from the content of cultural knowledge with which they were at first integrated in 'concrete thinking.'"[75] And as far as the mechanism of making the symbolic reproduction more reflexive is concerned, Habermas pointed to the process of education and its formalization that "means not only a professional treatment of the symbolic reproduction of the lifeworld, but its *reflective refraction* as well."[76]

At this point, it needs to be stressed that Habermas remarked that the rationalization of the lifeworld is of an ambiguous nature. And, therefore, he said that "what some celebrate as institutionalized individualism [. . .], others abhor as a subjectivism that undermines traditionally anchored institutions, overloads the individual's capacity for decision making."[77]

DEVELOPMENT OF LAW AND MORALITY— AN ASPECT OF THE RATIONALIZATION OF THE LIFEWORLD

According to Habermas, the process of rationalizing the lifeworld is connected with its structural differentiation, which is accompanied by an increasing systemic complexity. The increase occurs alongside introducing a new systemic mechanism, which next needs to be institutionalized or—in other words—needs to be "anchored" in the lifeworld, being a subsystem that defines the existence of the social system as a whole. Such an institutionalization requires a rearrangement of the existing institutionalized moral and political solutions and a change in the way of resolving conflicts to make it more consensual.

Therefore, the structural differentiation of the lifeworld consists also in the development of law and morality, which are to serve the process of resolving conflicts, so that the process of mutual understanding is not disturbed and so that the social integration of the lifeworld does not collapse. Due to their development, we are to reach a postconventional level, at which, according to Habermas, morality and legality are divorced.[78] At this level, "morality is deinstitutionalized to such an extent that it is now anchored only in the personality system as an *internal* control on behavior."[79] Moreover, the social component of the lifeworld—the system of institutions—grows independent of personality and culture, and the legal order is increasingly dependent on "formal procedures for positioning and justifying norms."[80] The emergence of legal institutions of this kind—institutions that embody moral consciousness—is necessary for the emergence of a higher level of integration in the course of social evolution and for the constitution of conditions crucial for creating an institutional framework for class societies organized in accordance with political or economic rules.[81]

The development of law and of morality can be perceived as aspects of the rationalizing of the lifeworld. The process of rationalization and of law reaching a higher level of development ought to occur alongside generalization of motivations and values. Habermas, referring to Talcott Parsons, understands this process as "the tendency for value orientations that are institutionally required of actors to become more and more general and formal in the course of social evolution."[82] This process of generalizing both motivations and values is a condition crucial for releasing the rationality potential inherent in communicative action. This potential will be realized in the course of the ongoing process of their generalization and of the shrinking of the areas of the nonproblematic. This generalization will, in due time, reach the level at which "*abstract obedience to law* becomes the only normative condition that actors have to meet in formally organized domains of action."[83]

This generalization of values, as Habermas stressed, leads to releasing two opposite tendencies in the domain of interaction. Alongside the ongoing process of generalizing motivations and values, communicative action is being freed from concrete, traditionally transmitted, normative patterns of behavior.[84] In consequence, the burden of social integration is put on the linguistic process of shaping a consensus.[85]

CONTINGENCY AND IDEOLOGIES

Habermas remarked that what is characteristic of the abovementioned process of reaching understanding in its modern form is, on the one hand, the fact that "communicative actions are increasingly detached from normative contexts and become increasingly dense, with an expanded scope for contingencies," and, on the other, that "forms of argumentation are institutionally differentiated, namely, theoretical discourse in the scientific enterprise, moral-practical discourse in the political public sphere and in the legal system, and aesthetic criticism in the artistic and literary enterprise."[86]

Forms of argumentation—as one of the abovementioned elements characteristic of the modern pursuit of understanding—have already been discussed. However, at this point yet another element appears for the first time: extending the domain of what is contingent. As Habermas stressed, the process of detaching communicative process from the norms of a particular place and time results precisely in extending the domain of what is contingent, a domain that constitutes the space for communicative action. As Habermas argued, "[T]he scope of contingency for interaction loosed from normative contexts that the inner logic of communicative action 'becomes practically true' in the deinstitutionalized forms of intercourse of the familial private sphere as well as in a public sphere stamped by the mass media."[87] Alongside the extension of the domain of contingency, the importance of communication increases, and the ongoing process of rationalization is more and more visible. The rationality potential so far released in the sphere of the profane ceases to be neutralized and restricted within certain limits, for the difference between the levels of the sacred and the profane—which has always been there—disappears. In other words, the secularization of the bourgeois culture and extension of the domain of rationality results in diminishing the role of the sacred. What is also diminished is the threat of ideologization of certain contents and of imposing structural limitations on communication. In consequence, the religious-metaphysical culture, which has been based on barbarian injustice and that has strengthened its position by means of an ideological interpretation of the world, loses these characteristics.

In Habermas's view, the increasingly rationalized world loses its structural capacities for creating ideologies. However, these are still present, and are accompanied by the ambition to cover the whole spectrum of problems that surround us. In his written work on this issue, Habermas pointed out that ideologies emerge in light of observable distortions and deficiencies, originating from the lifeworld alongside social modernization. They rely on the wish for moral or ethical renewal of the political, public sphere and for reviving politics, which has been reduced to purely administrative activities. They also manifest themselves in the ideals of autonomy and participation, which are, to a great extent, present in the radical-democratic and socialist movements. Even though their contents differ from those of the ideologies having their roots in the nineteenth century, they share with them the form of all-embracing visions of order aimed at presenting a global interpretation. This form, as Habermas wrote, "has to break down in the communication structures of a developed modernity. When the auratic traces of the sacred have been lost and the products of a synthetic, world-picturing power of imagination have vanished, the form of understanding, now fully differentiated in its validity basis, becomes so transparent that the communicative practice of everyday life no longer affords any niches for the structural violence of ideologies."[88]

According to Habermas, rationalization leads to uncovering the interrelations between systems and the lifeworld, which results in the disappearance of grounds for creating ideologies. In consequence, the societies of late capitalism develop a functional equivalent for previously created ideologies. Instead of satisfying the needs for interpretation by means of ideologies, "we have the negative requirement of preventing holistic interpretations from coming into existence."[89] And, therefore, we need to come to terms with the fact that what we are faced with is colloquial knowledge that is dispersed, or, at least, "never attains that level of articulation at which alone knowledge can be accepted as valid according to the standards of cultural modernity."[90]

On the basis of the above, we are provided with a sketch of a vision in which knowledge is dispersed and, with that, it is impossible for a superior narrative to emerge, a narrative that could be claimed more important than others. The basis for interaction no longer relies on a vision of total order but on an elaborate communicative structure.

TWO TYPES OF ACTION AND THE TWO MECHANISMS OF THEIR COORDINATION

What is characteristic of the process of reaching understanding in its modern form is freeing communicative action from normative contexts and from particular value orientations. In Habermas's opinion, this leads to the emergence of action oriented toward success and action oriented toward understanding, as well as to the emergence of "corresponding mechanisms of action coordination."[91] As he noted, "On the basis of increasingly generalized action orientations, there arises an ever denser network of interactions that do without directly normative steering and have to be coordinated in another way."[92] Satisfying the growing need for coordination can be achieved via linguistic pursuit of understanding or via the mechanisms that decrease the effort required for communication as well as the risk of misunderstanding. These mechanisms either condense or replace the linguistic pursuit of understanding. On the one hand, then, we dispose of linguistically communicative media, and on the other, of steering media.

The linguistic media of communication include reputation or value commitment. They allow us to bring the linguistic pursuit of understanding to a higher level, but they do not replace it. As Habermas argued, these media "relieve interaction from yes/no positions of critcizable validity claims only *in the first instance*. They are dependent on technologies of communication, because these technologies make possible the formation of public spheres, that is, they see to it that even concentrated networks of communication are connected up to the cultural tradition and, *in the last instance*, remain dependent on the actions of responsible actors."[93]

At the points where we encounter reputation or moral authority, action coordination proceeds by means of resources familiar to the linguistic means of accomplishing a consensus. As Habermas stressed, "[M]edia of this kind cannot uncouple interaction from the lifeworld context of shared cultural knowledge, valid norms, and accountable motivations, because they have to make use of the resources of consensus formation in language."[94]

The media that unburden the linguistic pursuit of consensus include money and power. They allow actors to influence the decisions of other participants of interaction while omitting the linguistic processes of accomplishing a consensus. Coordinating action via steering media—and not via language—leads to uncoupling interaction from the context, that is, the lifeworld. This context is debased and ceases to be necessary for coordinating action.

In such circumstances, action coordination—detached from the previously introduced, intrinsic communicative consensus and from the lifeworld—no longer requires sensible and responsible participants. The communicative media deprived of their linguistic nature by money and power create more and more complex networks of interaction, which no longer need to be transparent, and for which no one needs to be responsible.

Dangers and the Possibility to Overcome Them

Freeing communicative actions from normative contexts leads to both extending the scope of what is contingent as well as rationalizing the lifeworld. Due to this ongoing rationalization, the threat of ideology collapses. However, it needs to be added that at the same time, other threats arise. The lifeworld is being permeated by systemic imperatives that cause communicative action to adjust to the formally organized scopes of acting. Therefore, Habermas claimed that the communicative infrastructure he has presented "is threatened by two interlocking, mutually reinforcing tendencies: *systemically induced reification* and *cultural impoverishment*."[95]

REIFICATION AND CULTURAL IMPOVERISHMENT

In Habermas's opinion, the processes of reaching understanding and of rationalization result in "a deepened culture of reflection and feeling."[96] The circumstances of socialization and structuring of the lifeworld change. This change, however, is twofold. On the one hand, after freeing communicative action from the shackles of tradition and from obligatory consensus, a need for coordinating actions arises. On the other hand, there emerge organizations of a new type, based on communicative media, which influence separating the processes of acting from the processes of communicating, and coordinate them by means of generalized instrumental values, such as money and power. The steering media—that is, money and power—"replace language as the mechanism for coordinating action. They set social action loose from integration through value consensus and switch it over to purposive rationality steered by media."[97] We are, therefore, faced with the following paradox: the rationalization of the lifeworld and the rationalization of everyday communication—for which language is the original and irreplaceable medium of reaching understanding—enables "a kind of systemic integration that enters into competition with the integrating principles of reaching understanding."[98] Habermas added that due to the growing "complexity of subsystems of purposive-rational action, in which actions are coordinated through steering media such as money and power,"[99] the rationalized lifeworld begins to depend on more and more complex, formally organized domains of action, which influence it and disintegrate it. It can be said that once the rationalized lifeworld allows for the emergence and growth of subsystems, their autonomous imperatives—due to their growing complexity—turn against it. This can be exemplified with the mechanism of linguistic pursuit of understanding being replaced with communicative media deprived of their linguistic character.

In consequence, the lifeworld and the systems become uncoupled, which, in turn, leads to reification: social integration and systemic integration become uncoupled as well. This process begins with the differentiation of two types of action coordination, which are exercised either by means of pursuing a consensus between the participants or by means of functional action relations, and proceed up to the moment when the systemic mechanisms begin to permeate the processes of undertaking action and enter the very forms of social integration. This happens, for due to the process of reification, the lifeworld begins to depend on systemic imperatives, which leads to its colonization.[100] The moral-practical aspects, so far existing in the sphere of private life and in the political public sphere, are colonized by systemic imperatives, such as monetarization and bureaucratization, which are followed by annihilation of traditional life-forms and which seem to "overstep the boundaries of normality when they instrumentalize an influx from the lifeworld that possesses its own inner logic."[101] These imperatives devastate both the private and the public sphere. They work by means of systemic constraints that instrumentalize the communicatively structured lifeworld. This is followed by a collapse of the relational networks within the lifeworld and their growing to resemble the formally organized spheres of the capitalist economic and bureaucratic systems of the state apparatus.[102]

The processes of reification, occurring within the lifeworld, are not comprised only of the repressive influence of economy and state apparatus.[103] They consist also of a number of other conflicts that emerge in areas such as cultural reproduction, social integration, and socialization. The deficiencies lying at their base "reflect a reification of communicatively structured domains of action that will not respond to the media of money and power."[104] These domains require a mechanism for reaching understanding as a means of action coordination. Otherwise—when the reproduction of the lifeworld relies on the rules of systemic integration—a number of pathologies occur.

At this point, it needs to be added that the deformation discussed above should not be limited to either the rationalization of the lifeworld or the increasing density of a system itself. The secularization of worldviews or the structural differentiation of a society do not themselves lead to inevitable pathological side effects. Therefore, it needs to be stressed that "the rationalization of contexts of communicative action and the emergence of subsystems of purposive rational economic and administrative action are processes that have to be sharply distinguished analytically."[105] Accordingly, Habermas said, "It is not the uncoupling of media-steered subsystems and of their organizational forms from the lifeworld that leads to the one-sided rationalization or reification of everyday communicative practice, but only the penetration of forms of economic and administrative rationality into areas of action that resist being converted over to the media of money and power because they are specialized in cultural transmission, social integration, and child rearing, and remain dependent on mutual understanding as a mechanism for coordinating action."[106] As a result of reification, which destroys the lifeworld, the practices of everyday life are deformed. This, in turn, leads to cultural impoverishment, which is the second of the dangers Habermas listed. This process occurs due to one-sided rationalization of everyday communication, which results from the autonomization of media-steered subsystems. These subsystems, being rationalized outside the horizon of the lifeworld—and alongside their imperatives—intrude into the indigenous domains of the lifeworld, creating at the same time a reality devoid of norms. Consequently, cultural impoverishment and lifeworld impoverishment are to be observed. The lifeworld is cut off from the vivid and continuous cultural tradition.

The deformation has its cause in the one-sided rationalization of the processes of everyday communication; however, it needs to be added that its cause also lies in the development and differentiation of science, morality, and art, which begin to be subject to the processes of autonomization. Once theoretical discourses, practical-moral discourses, and aesthetic criticism are differentiated, they are overtaken by experts. The elitist separation of expert cultures from the general sets of relations of communicative action results in the cultural impoverishment of the communicative practice of the everyday. What the culture acquires thanks to specialist knowledge and reflection, then, permeates everyday practices with great difficulty.[107]

PROVING THE THESIS ON REIFICATION—JURIDIFICATION

The internal colonization thesis proclaims that in the course of capitalist progress the subsystems of economy and state grow more and more complex and permeate the areas of lifeworld reproduction ever more deeply. This thesis may seem unconvincing. In order to prove it, Habermas has explored the phenomenon of the juridification of communicatively structured domains of action, and has pointed out that the more power the rules of market economy and the commandments of mass consumption gain over leisure or culture, the more important juridification of informally regulated spheres of the lifeworld is. Bureaucracy and judicial control concern greater scopes of activity.[108] In other words, social integration is transformed into systemic integration, which takes the form of the processes of juridification and, in consequence, leads to reification. Accordingly, Habermas wrote that "in the face of the changing and steadily increasing volume of positive law, modern legal subjects content themselves in actual practices with legitimation through procedure, for in many cases substantive justification is not only not possible, but it is also, from the viewpoint of the lifeworld, meaningless. This is true of cases where the *law serves as a means for organizing media-controlled subsystems* that have, in any case, become autonomous in relation to the normative contexts of action oriented by mutual understanding."[109] On the basis of the above, it can be said that this type of law does by itself take the role of a steering medium, alongside the media of money and power.[110] It is "relieved of the problem of justification; it is connected with the body of law whose substance requires legitimation only through formally correct procedure."[111]

LEGAL INSTITUTIONS

However, at this point, it is worth adding that apart from law as a steering medium, Habermas talks also of law in the context of the existence of legal institutions. By making such a distinction, he points to legal institutions, which are one of the social components of the lifeworld and whose function is merely regulative.[112] Due to functional requirements, they are oriented toward reaching understanding, a basis for coordinating action. They encompass norms "that cannot be sufficiently legitimized through a positivistic reference to procedure."[113] It is also due to the fact that they belong to the lifeworld itself, and that they are—together with the informal rules for acting—a backup for communicative action. Therefore, as Habermas noted, "as soon as the validity of *these* norms is questioned in everyday practice, the reference to their legality no longer suffices," and they require "substantive justification."[114] Accordingly, these norms and contexts of action should be protected against the influence of systemic imperatives. On this, Habermas said, "The point is to protect areas of life that are functionally dependent on social integration through values, norms, and consensus formation, to preserve them from falling prey to the systemic imperatives of economic and administrative subsystems growing with dynamics of their own, and to defend them from becoming converted over, through the steering medium of the law, to a principle of sociation that is, for them, dysfunctional."[115] Habermas argued further on this issue, especially in his book *Between Facts and Norms*, but as was said in the introduction, they were not part of the Rorty-Habermas debate, thus here they are only mentioned and not analyzed further.

OVERCOMING DANGERS

In short, in the course of our deliberation, we have reached a point where we can see that it is possible to overcome the dangers that Habermas has listed for us. On the one hand, the point is to protect certain domains of the lifeworld against reification, against dependence on systemic imperatives, and on the other hand, to prevent cultural impoverishment. Therefore, in the two domains in which it is possible, law as a medium needs to be replaced with an understanding-oriented procedure for regulating conflicts, and the lost means of expression and communication need to be revitalized.[116] For it does not need to be the case that the processes of modernization are accompanied by the feeling that "with the one-sided canalization and destruction of possibilities for expression and communication in private and in public spheres, changes are fading that we can bring together again, in a posttraditional everyday practice, those moments that, in traditional forms of life, once composed a unity—a diffuse one surely, and one whose religious and metaphysical interpretations were certainly illusory."[117] The theory of reification, formulated by means of the concepts of system and lifeworld, also needs to be supplemented with, as Habermas puts it, the cultural dimension of modernity. This should allow us to explain cultural impoverishment and "the conditions for recoupling a rationalized culture with an everyday communication dependent on vital traditions."[118] Habermas has articulated such an impoverishment, pointing to the systems intervening in those lifeworld domains that should be regulated only by means of communication. According to him, the conditions for recoupling include those that support and maintain the possibility of vital communication and vital tradition to be used. In other words, we should not forget about the norms, values, and processes of reaching understanding that determine the cultural dimension of modernity, and we should not allow systemic imperatives to colonize them, which results in a decay of traditional life-forms and the possibility of communicating. We need to bear in mind that the processes of reaching understanding, around which the lifeworld revolves, need a reference to its cultural grounds and that "in the communicative practice of everyday life, cognitive interpretations, moral expectations, expressions, and valuation have to interpenetrate and form a rational interconnectedness via the transfer of validity that is possible in the performative attitude."[119] And all that is to be pursued so as to create the conditions for a culture of "reflection and feeling."[120]

There is still one more way to tackle such a danger. What needs to be done is a coupling of expert culture with the lifeworld, for the distance between it and the public sphere has become a serious problem.[121] With the differentiation of science, ethics, and art, they have become autonomous, they have grown specialized and detached from the tradition that is still the basis for our interactions.[122] As Habermas has put it, "What the cultural sphere gains through specialized treatment and reflection does not *automatically* come into the possession of everyday practice without more ado. For with cultural rationalization, the lifeworld, once its traditional substance has been devalued, threatens rather to become *impoverished*."[123] And, therefore, in the name of preventing the impoverishment of everyday life, we need to make sure that the reflexive output of experts becomes a part of communicative processes.[124]

COMPETITION OF SOCIAL INTEGRATION PRINCIPLES

Habermas stresses that what we are faced with is not a competition of types of action oriented toward reaching understanding with actions oriented toward success but a competition of the principles of social integration. On the one hand, there is the mechanism of linguistic communication oriented toward validity claims, and, on the other, steering media, devoid of any traces of language, by means of which systems of success-oriented actions are differentiated. Habermas advocates the mechanism of linguistic communication oriented toward validity claims. It is around this mechanism that he constructs his social theory, based on the concept of social rationalization. A crucial element here is the concept of reason, which Habermas reconstructs in the spirit of communicative rationality. This reconstructive procedure is accompanied by a question of "whether a reason that has objectively split up into its moments can still preserve its unity."[125] The unity of reason, in the opinion of Habermas, is possible.[126] A more elaborate answer that the philosopher has provided, referring to formal pragmatics—to validity claims and argumentation theory—shall be presented further on in this work. Before that, however, we need to discuss a number of issues that have already appeared here but, as it has been signaled, still need to be elaborated. Accordingly, the following pages shall draw our attention to the issue of ambition and the universality of action theory as well as its universal validity claims. This shall allow us to see Habermas's idea at its fullest, and help us make out its stronger and weaker points.

Constructing a Theory

Toward Universal Validity of Our Understanding of Rationality

Habermas has aimed at presenting his theory of communicative action—a germ of a social theory—that could play an important part in preserving what is most precious: the lifeworld. In the case of constructing a theory, he has been and is well aware of the risk of it being connected only with a particular perspective, which will be culturally and historically determined. He also has been and still is aware of the fact that actions oriented toward reaching understanding—which, for him, are the basis for the functioning of a rational society—do not always occur in communicative practices. He has continued to believe, however, that these problems can be avoided once the basic concepts are construed in such a way "that the concept of rationality they implicitly posit is encompassing and general, that is, satisfies universalistic claims."[127] If this requirement is to be realized, we would need to prove, as Habermas noted, that the internal rational structure of the processes of reaching understanding is "universally valid":[128] "This is a very strong requirement for someone who is operating without metaphysical support and is also no longer confident that a rigorous transcendental-pragmatic program, claiming to provide ultimate grounds, can be carried out."[129] However, this has not discouraged Habermas, and he still has attempted to present such a requirement.

Proof

Calling for the acknowledgement of the universal validity of our understanding of rationality is inevitably linked with the burden of providing proof for it. For Habermas, however, the burden does not seem too heavy, for he thinks that proving the universality of the concept of communicative rationality is feasible, and it is possible without referring to grand philosophical traditions. In Habermas's opinion, if we rely on ahistorical reconstructive analysis, the theory of communicative action can be proved with respect to the rational substance of communicative structures, which are deeply rooted in anthropological terms. Reconstructive actions embrace—alongside intuitional, or, in other words, pretheoretical knowledge of subjects competent at judging, acting, and speaking—also systems of collective knowledge transmitted via tradition. These activities are aimed at acquiring knowledge about the conditions that need to be fulfilled in order to grasp the basis of rationality, on which experiences, judgments, actions, and linguistic pursuit of understanding rely, so that those who share this kind of worldview are able to rationally control their lives. Such reconstructive actions make us, then, as Habermas has stressed, shift from conceptual to empirical analysis and search for rationality structures symbolically embodied in worldviews. The burden of proving his theory of social communication rests on the concept of communicative action.[130] Trying to prove its significance, Habermas has pointed to Mead and written that in his reconstruction, communicative action is of crucial importance and that "there are empirical reasons—and not merely methodological prejudgments—for the view that the structures of linguistically mediated, normatively guided interaction determine the starting point of sociocultural development."[131]

Accordingly, it can be said that the starting point for Habermas consists in the concept of lifeworld, composed of nonproblematic convictions—implicitly articulated knowledge. Habermas would like to point to the universal—going beyond cultures and eras—importance of this concept. Its universal validity relies on rationality structures symbolically embodied in worldviews. According to Habermas, these structures are of universal nature—they transcend cultural particularities.

Rationality structures that delineate the modern understanding of the world should not be, as Habermas stresses, accepted as universally accurate without a test, just as they should be perceived from a historical point of view. The test is carried out when present knowledge becomes problematic. It can be said that at the beginning the lifeworld is preconceived, that is, it consists of a certain preunderstanding and intuitional cognizance. These elements form certain knowledge on which we rely when we enter into numerous interactions with each other. It is also on what everyday communicative practice silently relies. And this silence is to be broken only with the appearance of a concrete problem: then things known become "something in need of being ascertained."[132] In other words, the need of ascertaining—of testing—arises when a portion of knowledge, a nonthematized background, becomes doubtful, when we need to come to an agreement with respect to what has become problematic. This portion of knowledge is, then, "set loose after having been enclosed in complex traditions, in solidaric relations, in competences."[133] In the test, the knowledge that is our nonthematized background is granted the status of explicitly articulated knowledge. What we can count on however, with respect to testing and acquiring explicit knowledge, is a coherent worldview, and nothing else. This worldview consists of "cultural knowledge," by means of which the linguistic community interprets the world and makes reference to reality in its language.

No Ultimate Justifications—No Fundamentalist Claims

In light of the above, the theory of communicative action cannot be said to fall into the trap of fundamentalism. Such objections, voiced inter alia by Rorty, are, as Habermas has argued, made in view of a universalistic claim. Reconstructing the concept of reason in the spirit of communicative rationality needs to be supported with this claim, even though it departs from "the foundationalism of traditional, transcendental philosophy, which requires a justification."[134] Being aware of the fact that the concept of communicative reason is accompanied by the menace of transcendentalism, Habermas has said that the supposed similarities between his formal-pragmatic approach and the classical transcendental philosophy are illusory. Therefore, he has answered in the negative to the questions he himself has posed: "Is not such a theory of rationality open to the same objections that pragmatism and hermeneutics have brought against every kind of foundationalism? Do not investigations that employ the concept of communicative reason without blushing bespeak universalistic justificatory claims that will have to fall to those—only too well grounded—metaphilosophical doubts about theories of absolute origins and ultimate grounds?"[135] The theory of communicative action does not seem to include fundamentalist claims, for its aim consists in successful coherence. The theory does not seem to exhibit claims for transcendental justification, since—as Habermas has claimed—we need "no foundation and no justification in the sense of a transcendent grounding."[136] In Habermas's opinion, the theory of action, which identifies communicative reason "by way of structural characteristics and conceptualises it as procedural rationality—instead of mystifying it as fate—is protected against the danger of dogmatically overstating its claims precisely through being formalised."[137]

Are Validity Claims Universal?

In spite of Habermas's belief that the theory of communicative action does not put forward any fundamentalist claims, its crucial—and, at the same time, controversial—element consists in validity claims, which, in his opinion, are of universal character. It is this view of which he wished to convince the readers of *The Theory of Communicative Action*. In order to do that, he proceeded with his deliberations, during which he juxtaposed the mythical and the modern understanding of the world, which is based, as he claimed, on the universal structures of rationality.

As he described the modern understanding of the world, Habermas pointed to the importance of linguistic communication and cultural transmission, which this communication releases. As he put it, "[U]nder the presupposition of formal world-concepts and universal validity claims, the contents of a linguistic worldview have to be detached from the assumed world-order itself. Only then can we form the concept of cultural tradition, of a temporalized culture, whereby we become aware that interpretations vary in relation to natural and social reality, that beliefs and values vary in relation to the objective and social worlds."[138] Accordingly, today, in the processes of communication, we start with formal suppositions of something held in common. As Habermas has stressed, these are necessary for us to be able to refer to something in the objective world, identical for all the observers, or for us to be able to refer to something in the social world, which we intersubjectively share. These suppositions on something common are updated with claims for propositional and normative rightness as well as by referring them to particular expressions. In such a situation, saying that a statement is true means that the state of affairs described exists in the objective world. And recognizing a given action as right, taking into consideration the existing normative context, means that it deserves being accepted and that it constitutes a legitimate ingredient of the social world. Habermas has stressed that the validity claims he lists can be criticized and, further, that they rest on the formal conceptions of the world. They presuppose "a world that is identical for *all possible* observers, or a world intersubjectively shared by *members*, and they do so in an abstract form freed of all specific content."[139] What is also required with respect to validity claims is assuming a rational attitude by the other party during the communicative processes in which they occur.

Accordingly, the modern understanding of the world includes the development of formal world-concepts that are presupposed at the beginning of communication as something common. These presuppositions are updated alongside validity claims. As Habermas wrote, "Actors who raise validity claims have to avoid materially prejudicing the relation between language and reality, between the medium of communication and that about which something is being communicated. Under the presupposition of formal world-concepts and universal validity claims, the contents of a linguistic worldview have to be detached from the assumed world order itself. Only then can we form the concept of a cultural tradition, of a temporalized culture, whereby we become aware that interpretations vary in relation to natural and social reality, that beliefs and values vary in relation to the objective and social worlds."[140] In other words, according to Habermas, it is not the contents that are universal but the formal structures: what is deemed universal is a preconceived world order, which needs to be accepted in order for rational communication to occur. In the course of evolution, there emerges a formal concept of an objective, external world, a social world, and an internal world, which are but abstract constructs. It is, however, still an unresolved issue whether our understanding of the world is granted a claim for universality. Thus Habermas himself made it his objective to answer the question whether—and in which aspects—the standards of rationality can aspire to universal validity. He tried to answer it by presenting arguments both for and against the universalistic position. What shall be elaborated on here is only the first series of arguments by means of which Habermas wished to arrive at the "pros" of taking the universalistic position. What shall not be analyzed, on the other hand, is the whole of the "dispute" as well as the quandary as to whether Habermas does indeed fight off the objections of the opponents to the universalistic view.[141] What is most important is whether his line of reasoning and the arguments it involves convince us that "rationality standards can aspire to universal validity," and that there are no alternative standards of rationality. If they existed, it would undoubtedly be difficult to state that any one of them can be endowed with universal validity.

It needs to be said that at the starting point of his deliberations, Habermas rightly observed that the reasons and the criteria that we use while describing and acting depend on the context of a particular place and time. What is characteristic of these reasons and criteria is that they are "ours," and when we utilize them in order to describe others, those others will appear the way these criteria and reasons allow. Habermas has been well aware of that; he argued that only hermeneutic ruthlessness toward one's own presuppositions can prevent us from criticism without self-criticism and from making the mistake of imposing one's own—supposedly universal—cultural standards onto others. He is also aware of the fact that a given context is determined by language, via which we describe our surroundings and relations we enter into. This language, the linguistically articulated worldview and life-forms, that is, the everyday practice of socialized individuals, are for Habermas, "concepts that refer on the one hand to something particular [. . .]. On the other hand, they refer to totalities; for members of the same culture the limits of their language are the limits of the world. They can broaden the horizon of their form of life in an ad hoc manner, but they cannot step out of it; to this extent, every interpretation is also a process of assimilation. Inasmuch as worldviews refer to totalities, we cannot get behind them as articulations of an understanding of the world, even if they can be revised."[142] Although Habermas acknowledged the above, at the same time, he continues to believe that criteria such as truth, rightness, and honesty do not depend on context. In his opinion, the fact that the context determines the criteria on the basis of which members of different cultures in different times and in different ways assess the validity of expressions does not mean that "the ideas of truth, of normative rightness, of sincerity, and of authenticity that underlie (only intuitively, to be sure) the choice of criteria are context-dependent in the same degree."[143] Worldviews, as he wrote at another point,

> owing to their reference to totality [. . .] are indeed removed from the dimension in which a judgment of them according to criteria of truth makes sense; even the choice of criteria according to which the truth of statements is to be judged may depend on the basic conceptual context of a world-view. But this does not mean that the idea of truth might itself be understood in a particularistic way. Whatever language system we choose, we always start intuitively from the presupposition that truth is a universal validity claim. If a statement is true, it merits universal assent, no matter in which language it is formulated.[144]

The paragraph above encompass a number of issues that need elaboration. Beginning with the last statement, it needs to be said that it can be understood as follows: if given languages embrace validity claims for truth, a statement that is considered true in one of them will undoubtedly deserve being accepted also in other languages. It can also be understood like this: if a statement is true in one language, it deserves being accepted also in other languages. Taking such a stance, simultaneously, we would have to show the reference point for all languages with respect to which it is possible to assess the rightness of statements. The first interpretation surely corresponds with Habermas's intuitions, as he claims that the rightness of statements or beliefs can be stated only within a particular language: it can be stated only in the language in which the existence of an objective world has been presumed and in which the idea of truth—a basis for choosing criteria—has been intuitionally assumed. Accordingly, even if we always intuitionally presume that truth is a universal validity claim, about which we have not been convinced yet, we cannot claim that a statement accepted as true shall deserve being universally accepted in the latter understanding.[145] It needs to be said, then, that accepting a statement as true is to be possible only within our linguistic system, which we are unable to transcend.

In his further deliberations on mythical thinking, Habermas quoted a passage on the division into closed and open cultures, borrowed from Robin Horton. Cultures that are termed "closed" can be characterized by a lack of conscious choice, and the sacredness of beliefs, as well as fear of questioning them. Open cultures, on the other hand, include those in which we are conscious of the possibility of choice, in which we are able to challenge the absolute and the sacred, and in which we are not that afraid to do so. Habermas recalled and referred to those concepts, for, as he wrote, "this dimension of 'closed' *versus* 'open' seems to provide a *context-independent standard for the rationality of worldviews.*"[146] Accepting such a division, he claimed that what distinguishes closed cultures from open ones is the fact that the latter lack references. Habermas added that what we need is precisely a more complex system of references allowing us to grasp "the simultaneous differentiation of *three* formal world-concepts."[147] He referred to the observations of Horton and Ernest Gellner, of whom he noted, "[T]he two authors provide concurring descriptions of the increasing categorical separation among the objective, social, and subjective worlds, of the specialization of cognitive-instrumental, moral practical, and expressive types of questions, and above all of the differentiation of the aspects of validity under which these problems can be dealt with." Then they stress "the increasing differentiation between linguistic worldview and reality."[148] In this perspective, worldviews are crucial with respect to the entire spectrum of processes of reaching understanding and of socializing, in the course of which their participants refer to the common social world, to the experiences connected with their subjective world, as well as to the objective world.[149] These views constitute both the processes of reaching understanding as well as of socializing individuals. They are crucial for forming and ensuring identity. They provide individuals with basic categories and presuppositions, which cannot be revised, for then the identity of individuals and of social groups is to be disturbed. Habermas added that "this *identity-securing knowledge* becomes more and more formal along the path from closed to open worldviews; it attaches to structures that are increasingly disengaged from contents that are open to revision."[150]

In Habermas's opinion, the above considerations allow for a subtler defense of the universalistic position. However, it is possible to ask whether the division into closed and open cultures, among which three formal world-concepts arise and claims are differentiated, can indeed be a measure of rationality that is independent of context. Habermas accepts the division; however, it is hard to overlook the fact that he described closedness and openness from the point of view of the Western world. He proved the closed character of mythical thinking, using precisely the categories of the Western mind.

What is more, Habermas pointed to the formulation of the modern—open—understanding, in which the three formal world-concepts are more and more common and are a nonrevisable basis for constructing the identities of individuals and of social groups. Still, instead of concluding that these images are metaphors that died of literality, Habermas heads toward saying (referring to the descriptions and "observations" of Gellner and Horton, which images are to support the utilization of the concepts of "closed-open" in anthropological terms): "Scientific rationality belongs to a complex of cognitive-instrumental rationality that can certainly claim validity beyond the context of particular cultures."[151] This claim may come as a surprise, since it is not very well justified in the earlier part of Habermas's deliberations. His argument that he has accounted for this claim in relation with his thesis that each linguistically articulated worldview and each cultural life-form encompass a concept of rationality that cannot be compared with anything else is also not very convincing.[152] If we were to state that he succeeds, it would be only by the virtue of the Western point of view.[153]

The same can be said of Habermas's attempt at pointing to the universal validity of the concept of rationality, which he pursued in *The Theory of Communicative Action* by showing that one theory—the theory of rationalization formulated within the categories of communicative action—solves or can solve problems that have emerged on the grounds of other social theories. He argued that "thus for any social theory, linking up with the history of theory is also a kind of test; the more freely it can take up, explain, criticize, and carry on the intentions of earlier theory traditions, the more impervious it is to the danger that particular interests are being brought to bear unnoticed in its own theoretical perspective."[154] Should we agree? Referring to the quotation, it needs to be said that it is doubtful that the deliberate criticism and continuation of the intentions of earlier theoretical traditions have chased away the threat of articulating particular interests in a given theory, for they will be pursued via the language of our culture. It is also hard to agree with the claim that deliberate explanations are to be the criterion for determining the universal validity of our concept of rationality. Thus, it can be said that the theory presented by Habermas is but one of the paradigms present in the social sciences, which are, as he himself has written, "internally connected with the social contexts in which they emerge and become influential. In them is reflected the world- and self-understanding of various collectives; mediately they serve the interpretation of social-interest situations, horizons of aspiration and expectation."[155]

Referring to Habermas's deliberations presented here, it can be said that the defense of the universalistic position and the attempt at pointing to rationality as transcending the contexts of particular cultures is pursued by Habermas by means of the categories that he is to defend against the accusation of belonging to a particular culture. Thus, it is difficult to agree with the statement that appears at the end of his considerations, concerning "the justified claim to universality on behalf of the rationality that gained expression in the modern understanding of the world."[156] Perhaps Habermas is right that "we are implicitly connecting a claim to *universality* with our *Occidental understanding of the world*,"[157] but it needs to be added that it is difficult to state that such a claim should be accepted as universal outside of "our Occidental understanding of the world." In short, Habermas's reasoning here is not convincing enough to make us agree that validity claims are of a universal character. All we can state, then, is that validity claims are elements characteristic of our culture and our language. Reading the very last lines of *The Theory of Communicative Action*, one is left with the impression that Habermas is also aware of that "the test case for a theory of rationality with which the modern understanding of the world is to ascertain its own universality would certainly include throwing light on the opaque figures of mythical thought, clarifying the bizarre expressions of alien cultures, and indeed in such a way that we not only comprehend the learning processes that separate 'us' from 'them', but also become aware of what we have unlearned in the course of this learning."[158] Habermas, however, does not offer us a proposition of such a test.[159]

Toward Social Theory

The analysis of general structures of reaching understanding that Habermas presents in *The Theory of Communicative Action*, as he noted, is not a means of continuing the theory of cognition with different tools. His theory of communicative action is not a metatheory but a germ of a social theory "concerned to validate its own critical standards."[160] After shifting our paradigm via the theory of communication, Habermas wished to present "the formal properties of the intersubjectivity of possible understanding" that are subject to historical change and "can take the place of the conditions of the objectivity of possible experience."[161] As he wrote, these forms—the forms of mutual understanding—each and every time represent "a compromise between the general structures of communicative action and reproductive constraints unavailable as themes within a given lifeworld."[162]

Social Theory—Societal Rationalization

The concepts of communicative action and of lifeworld are the basic categories of the general social theory constructed by Habermas. He said,

> It is only with the turn back to the context-forming horizon of the lifeworld, from within which participants in communication come to an understanding with one another about something, that our field of vision changes in such a way that we can see the points of connection for social theory within the theory of communicative action: This concept of society has to be linked to a concept of the lifeworld that is complementary to the concept of communicative action. Then communicative action becomes interesting primarily as a principle of sociation [*Vergesellschaftung*]: Communicative action provides the medium for the reproduction of lifeworlds. At the same time, processes of societal rationalization are given a different place. They transpire more in implicitly known structures of the lifeworld than in explicitly known action orientations.[163]

According to the above, communicative action is connected with societal rationalization. Therefore, Habermas argued that the concept of societal rationalization can be formulated, starting with "the perspective of action oriented to reaching understanding and referring to the lifeworld as the common background knowledge presupposed in real action."[164] The point of reference for societal rationalization is to consist in the potential of rationality, located in the validity foundations of speech, which can be activated depending on the level of the rationalization of knowledge embedded in worldviews. In other words, according to Habermas, societal rationalization is to depend on the level of rationalization of knowledge and the potential of rationality located in the validity foundations of speech, on rationalization of the significant spheres of social life, that is knowledge and speech.

The rationalization of these spheres occurs due to action oriented toward understanding, which serves the institutionalized production of knowledge—specialized according to cognitive, normative, and aesthetic validity claims—and it permeating to the level of everyday communication, which results in it substituting for traditional knowledge, which has so far functioned as a means of controlling interactions. The practices of everyday life are rationalized. However, if rationally oriented actions are to be possible in a particularly interpreted lifeworld, and if they are to lead to the progression of a rational way of living, cultural transmission needs to fulfill certain formal criteria. Habermas enumerated such criteria and formal conditions thanks to which it is possible to rationalize mutual references between the participants of interactions and to rationalize their ways of living.[165] These references are deemed rational as long as the consensus accomplished results from the process of reaching understanding leading to coordination of social activities. During the process, rationally motivated agreement is accomplished. It is measured with criticizable validity claims.

Therefore, Habermas has presented the process of reaching understanding as oriented toward arriving at a consensus based on intersubjective recognition of validity claims, which are subject to critical revisions and which allow for updating the actors' references to the world. It is by means of analyzing these elements as well as fulfilling certain presuppositions that Habermas presents "structural properties of processes of reaching understanding," which are the starting point for the processes of societal rationalization.[166] As he put it, it is in these formal properties where "the rationality of worldviews and forms of life would have to be found."[167]

The Ideal of the Fully Rational Life-Form—Utopianism

It needs to be presumed that, according to Habermas, it is possible to talk of the process of societal rationalization: the rationalization of the practices of everyday life. However, it is a process based only on formal rules, not accompanied with the pursuit of success, that is, constituting an ideal community. The perspective offered by Habermas "does not extend to the concrete shape of an exemplary life-form or a paradigmatic life history. Actual forms of life and actual life histories are embedded in unique traditions."[168] In other words, the perspective—with its crucial concepts of communicative rationality and validity claims connected with a decentered understanding of the world—has its consequences for all those who search for an ideal of a fully rational life-form. In his theory, Habermas proves that the attempts to depict a good life in material, substantial terms are wrong; however, he deems them the mistakes of the modern era, a utopianism. In his opinion, since life-forms are composed of worldviews, which are more or less decentered, are particular "language games," "historical configurations of customary practices, group membership, cultural patterns of interpretation, forms of socialization, competences, attitudes, and so forth,"[169] it would be pointless to evaluate them as a whole. He wrote, "We tacitly judge life form and life histories according to standards of normality that do not permit an approximation to ideal limit values. Perhaps we should talk instead of a balance among non-self sufficient moments, an equilibrated interplay of the cognitive with the moral and the aesthetic-practical."[170] In accordance with the above, we should not introduce the idea of a good life from the procedural concept of rationality, with which we are left in the decentered understanding of the world of the modern era, so as to point to an equivalent of what we have lost.[171] Accordingly, "because the idealizing presupposition of communicative action must not be hypostatized into the ideal of a future condition in which a definitive understanding has been reached, this concept must be approached in a sufficiently skeptical manner."[172] And therefore, Habermas has clearly opposed the insinuation that he has designed "a rationalistic social utopia": "Nothing makes me more nervous than the imputation—repeated in a number of different versions and in the most peculiar contexts—that because the theory of communicative action focuses attention on the social facility of recognised validity-claims, it proposes, or at least suggests, a rationalistic utopian society. I do not regard the fully transparent society as an ideal, nor do I wish to suggest any other ideal."[173] At another point, he added that he means neither an ideal of a society that has become fully transparent, nor a society that has become homogenized and unified.[174] He thinks that it would be wrong to believe, on the basis of a formal idea of a society, created in certain historical conditions, "that we have thereby also formulated the ideal of a form of life which has become perfectly rational—there can be no *such* ideal."[175]

Thus, it needs to be said that in consequence, we cannot expect social theory to construct "a system of needs," that is, a certain totality of a life-form. It is also impossible to make predictions on the value of competing life-forms. Therefore, domination-free communication can be considered a condition necessary for a dignified life, but it cannot be considered as an ample condition for historical articulation of a successful life-form. And thus, describing the development of a given society by means of particular dimensions—among which Habermas refers to "the reflexivity and complexity of social systems on the one hand, and to the social forces of production and forms of social integration on the other"—one society can, by means of comparison, "be superior to another with reference to the level of differentiation of its economic or administrative system, or with reference to technologies and legal institutions"; however, "it does not follow that we are entitled to value this society more highly *as a whole*, as a concrete totality, as a form of life."[176]

To sum up, it is worth referring to two quotes: the words of Albrecht Wellmer that Habermas himself quoted, and a fragment of Habermas's text. Wellmer wrote that "we can specify only certain *formal conditions* of a rational life—such as *a universalistic moral consciousness, a universalistic law, a collective identity that has become reflexive,* and so forth. But insofar as we are dealing with the possibility of a rational life in the substantial sense, with the possibility of a rational identity, there is no ideal limit value describable in terms of formal structures. There exists rather only the success or failure of the efforts to achieve a form of life in which the unconstrained identity of individuals, along with unconstrained reciprocity among individuals, becomes an experienceable reality."[177] In turn, since it is impossible to point to the best life-form, Habermas wrote that we do not have any prospects for such life-forms, even in abstracto. We know only that "if they could be realized at all, they would have to be produced through our own combined effort and be marked by solidarity, though they need not necessarily be free of conflict. Of course, 'producing' does not mean manufacturing according to the model of realizing intended ends. Rather, it signifies a type of emergence that cannot be intended, an emergence out of a cooperative endeavor [. . .]. This endeavor is fallible, and it does fail over and over again."[178]

Cooperative Effort

Habermas thinks that despite the fallible—and still unsuccessful—nature of cooperative effort, we can nevertheless make a normative distinction, that is, present the universal conditions for everyday communicative practice as well as the conditions for acting with respect to the processes of discursive will-formation.[179] Accordingly, he has offered a perspective that he himself has labeled as utopian, based on the formal conditions of undistorted intersubjectivity. He has not suggested any particular way of life. A utopian perspective is embedded in communicative rationality—the "utopianism" of the theory of communicative action—and is restricted merely to presenting the formal conditions for human communication.[180] Habermas has continued to believe that among these structures of undistorted intersubjectivity "can be found a necessary condition for individuals reaching an understanding among themselves without coercion, as well as for the identity of an individual coming to an understanding with himself or herself without force."[181]

Taking that into consideration, it is hard to accuse Habermas's theory of utopianism in the traditional sense: the sense of delineating a concrete but hardly real vision of a brave new world.[182] In his opinion, it is impossible to construct such an ideal vision, for we do not have access to all of the knowledge necessary for realizing such a project. In consequence, just as the theory of communicative action cannot deviate into "the fundamentalist wilderness," neither can the sciences preoccupied with the cultural tradition, social intervention, and socialization. And pragmatism and hermeneutics have grown aware of that. As Habermas has said of the social researcher, "The totality of the background knowledge constitutive for the construction of the lifeworld is no more at his disposition than at that of any social scientist—unless an objective challenge arises, in the face of which the lifeworld as a whole becomes problematic. Thus a theory that wants to ascertain the general structures of the lifeworld cannot adopt a transcendental approach; it can only hope to be equal to the *ratio essendi* of its object when there are grounds for assuming that the objective context of life in which the theoretician finds himself is opening up to him its *ratio cognoscendi*."[183] In the case of a social theory that relies on the theory of communicative action, what is left to do is assume a critical attitude toward preunderstanding that originates from its own social surroundings.

Communication—Premises and Arguments (Ethics of Discourse)

Cooperative effort, about which Habermas has written, is to rest on communication. In order to advocate for it and the understanding that results from it, we need to presuppose certain fringe conditions so that communication and understanding can emerge. In other words, if in the course of the process of communication we expect to reach an agreement, the constitution of which shall not be affected by anything except for rational argumentation and mutual kindness as well as open-mindedness of the dialogue parties, we need to presume that it is possible for an ideal communicative situation to occur. All of that corresponds to the program of the ethics of discourse that—as Habermas discussed—is briefly presented in the following fragment of Thomas McCarthy's text:

> Communication that is oriented toward reaching understanding inevitably involves the reciprocal raising and recognition of validity-claims. Claims to truth and rightness, if radically challenged, can be redeemed only through argumentative discourse leading to rationally motivated consensus. Universal-pragmatic analysis of the conditions of discourse and national consensus show these to rest on the supposition of an "ideal speech situation" characterized by an effective equality of chances to assume dialogue roles. This unavoidable (but usually counterfactual) imputation is an "illusion" constitutive of the very meaning of rational argumentation. . . . Thus the universal-pragmatic conditions of possibility of rationally justifying norms of action or evaluation have themselves a normative character.[184]

In other words, discourse aims at arriving at a consensus: arriving at understanding. In order for that to happen, we need to pursue communication in accordance with the rules of the ethics of speech, by means of speech acts, which are connected with given validity claims. What also needs to be fulfilled is the condition of an ideal speech situation. It comes down to the necessity of dialogue between equal parties, cooperatively aiming at resolving a problem, and to the existence of a cooperative attitude. In short, within the ethics of discourse, "those who understand themselves as taking part in argumentation *mutually suppose*, on the basis of the pre-theoretical knowledge of their communicative competence, that the actual speech situation fulfills certain, in fact quite demanding, preconditions."[185] These are the communicative assumptions that, according to Habermas, each of us needs to exercise intuitively if we are to participate in the argumentative procedure. He added that "we are made to assume—in a somewhat transcendental sense—that these are met to a satisfactory extent, when hindered by given empirical limitations."[186]

Habermas has claimed that linguistic communication, for the sake of which proper conditions were ensured, encompasses the potential of building bonds and understanding by articulating valid reasons connected with validity claims. Given expressions have valid reasons if they are apt or they bring about success (cognitive dimension), credible or comprehensible (practical-moral dimension), wise or convincing (evaluative dimension), truthful and self-critical (the dimensions of articulating inner states), and full of understanding (hermeneutic dimension).[187] These reasons are to be referred to if we want to assess the rationality of particular people's actions. Then we need to answer the question of whether they act rationally in general, whether their expressions have valid reasons. And "when there appears a systematic effect in these respects, across various domains of interaction [. . .], we also speak of the rationality of a *conduct of life*."[188] And in sociocultural conditions, allowing for such a conduct of life, "there is reflected perhaps the rationality of a lifeworld shared not only by individuals but by collectives as well."[189]

Communication, History, and the Unity of Reason

Habermas has continued to defend the position that rational communication contributes to the development of an emancipated society. He remarked, however, that it would be a mistake to assume that an emancipated society should rely only on domination-free communication. In his opinion, that would be too much of a simplification.[190] For emancipation consists not only in communication free from domination but also in the ongoing historical process connected with releasing the potential of reason and rationalizing the lifeworld:

> The release of a potential for reason embedded in communicative action is a world-historical process; in the modern period it leads to a rationalization of life-worlds, to the differentiation of their symbolic structures, which is expressed above all in the increasing reflexivity of cultural traditions, in processes of individuation, in the generalization of values, in the increasing prevalence of more abstract and more universal norms, and so on. These are trends which do not imply something good in themselves, but which nevertheless indicate that the prejudices background consensus of the life-world is crumbling, that the number of cases is increasing in which interaction must be coordinated through a consensus reached by the participants themselves.[191]

So as to clarify his point, Habermas discussed particular historical processes, which serve as examples of releasing the potential of reason and which facilitate the rationalization of the lifeworld. He wrote,

> I would not speak of "communicative rationalization" if, in the last two hundred years of European and American history, in the last forty years of the national liberation movements, and despite all the catastrophes, a piece of "existing reason", as Hegel would have put it, were not nevertheless also recognizable—in the bourgeois emancipation movements, no less than in the workers' movement, today in feminism, in cultural revolts, in ecological and pacifist forms of resistance, and so forth. One must also bear in mind the rather more subcutaneous transformations

in patterns of socialization, in value-orientations—for example, in the diffusion of expressive needs and moral sensitivities, or in the revolutionizing of sexual roles, in an altered subjective significance of waged work, and so on.[192]

Going even further, it is worth noticing that the whole historical progress alluded to above, connected with extending the scope of what is coordinated by means of understanding reached by the participants of communication themselves, leads to constituting the unity of reason. It can be said that this unity emerges in the course of our communicative practice, in the process of reaching understanding. Of course, Habermas is critical of the attempts at searching for the unity of reason in the field of what is theoretical, for they lead back to metaphysics and to enchanting the world anew. He wrote that "such attempts would have to lead back to metaphysics, and thus behind the levels of learning reached in the modern age into a re-enchanted world."[193] And Habermas's own intentions are not, as he put it, "to conjure up the substantial unity of reason" and "to make [him]self an advocate of such a regression."[194] As far as the unity is concerned, he stated, however, that "in the communicative practice of everyday life, in which cognitive explanations, moral expectations, expressions and evaluations interpenetrate, this unity is in a certain way *always already* established."[195] Accordingly, it seems that it would be plausible to say that the unity in question is produced in the course of reaching understanding. Thus, we can agree with Habermas, who argued that reason can still be a guard of unity. The unity of reason in the diversity of voices—in a modern society of diversified life-forms—is to emerge in the course of communication.[196]

Toward Modern Society

For the sake of a brief recapitulation of the aforementioned themes concerning communication, it can be said that what Habermas wrote about communicative rationality does not contribute to designing an ideal world, nor is it a representation of something supposedly good per se. What he said about it results from both the unavoidable presuppositions that we need to put forward if our actions are to lead us to understanding, as well as observations of certain historical processes. By investigating them closely, it is possible to notice the ongoing dissemination of the idea of reaching understanding and the ongoing rationalization of the lifeworld, which is not a law but a historical fact. This process leads to the shaping of modern society, so different from traditional ones. In such a society, communicative action is freed from strictly normatively determined contexts, the patterns of socialization are disseminated, and the processes of individualization and identity construction are strengthened.[197]

Recapitulation

In the communicative theory of society, the basic issue consists in the distinction between two types of action. Habermas distinguished between purposive-rational actions and communicative actions. The former actions contribute to the development of productive forces and improve our material status. They are oriented to success. The latter actions allow for domination-free communication and consensual regulation of social conflicts. They are connected with pursuing understanding. These two types of action are followed by two different types of rationality: instrumental on the one hand, and communicative on the other. These two types of action and of rationality delineate different patterns of organizing social relations, that is, systems and the lifeworld. Systems include economy or bureaucracy; the lifeworld—society and culture, the institutions that are connected with them, and the human personality as grasped in the social dimension.

In his deliberations, Habermas draws our attention to a particular problem: the fact that success-oriented, rational actions and instrumental rationality are the foundations not only of systems but also of the lifeworld; in other words, the lifeworld is being colonized by systems. Accordingly, law as an institution is being replaced with law as a medium, and the political sphere as well as political and legal institutions begin to depend to a greater and greater extent on the rules of instrumental rationality. This rationality, as Habermas discussed, should not be the only criterion for evaluating our institutions and actions. However, this is precisely what happens, and purposive-rational actions connected with instrumental rationality begin to determine human behavior. Accordingly, the way of perceiving social progress is distorted: it is measured only within the scope of controlling the forces of nature and the scope of productive forces. In order to prevent it, we should take into consideration, as Habermas has suggested, the existence of communicative rationality connected with domination-free communication and consensual regulation of social conflicts, so that moral and political progress, measured with individualization and emancipation, can be possible.[198] It is also important to create the right conditions for communication during which free and equal individuals can reach understanding. For Habermas, just as for John

Dewey and for Rorty, the issue of the utmost importance rests not on discovering some sort of one and ultimate truth but on the occurrence of free and undistorted communication.[199] Thus, it can be said after Rorty that Habermas sees that "freedom has changed our sense of what human inquiry is good for."[200] Rorty was, however, mistaken when he claimed that it is a shift toward acknowledging the growing importance of freedom, "from which Habermas hangs back."[201] It shall become more obvious in the next chapter, once we juxtapose previously presented themes in the thought of Rorty and of Habermas.

IV

ON THE CONVERGENCE OF THE PERSPECTIVES OF RORTY AND HABERMAS

The Convergence

The two preceding chapters presented the central threads of Richard Rorty's and Jürgen Habermas's thought. And these do not seem as different from each other as some critics have claimed. It is interesting to speculate on whether the two philosophers would share this view themselves. Have they understood the perspectives they present in relation to each other? If not, in what respects? Perhaps the differences they see between their perspectives depend only on misinterpretations of each other? The answers to these questions shall appear in this chapter. What seems most interesting, though, is whether in light of the major or minor differences between them, one can say that in terms of sociopolitical thought their perspectives converge. In context of their acknowledgment of the worth of democratic institutions, Rorty himself wrote, "We do not disagree about the worth of traditional democratic institutions, or about the sorts of improvements these institutions need, or about what counts as "freedom from domination." Our differences concern *only* the self-image which a democratic society should have, the rhetoric which it should use to express its hopes."[1] The answer to "this most interesting question" shall gradually emerge in the course of our considerations in this chapter, while we ponder whether in the case of Rorty and Habermas we are actually confronted only with different kinds of rhetoric. It is this thread that is worth beginning with. And in order to state whether, indeed, there is a difference between them of this kind—a difference which, according to Rorty, was "merely philosophical" in nature and is manifested in different ways of articulating one's hopes—it will be necessary to pay attention to those elements that are essential for their sociopolitical thought and that form its foundations. Our findings at this point shall allow us to paint a more accurate picture of their perspectives, and allow us to refer to the mentioned agreement on the worth of democratic institutions, the improvements they need, and the understanding of what freedom from domination is.

Different Rhetoric

Undoubtedly, both Rorty and Habermas have their own philosophical projects that sometimes reflect some of the other's intentions. As Habermas said, "Richard Rorty precipitated a pragmatic turn in epistemology, in which, despite all our differences, I was able to discern some of my own intentions."[2] It seems, however, that this is not the case when Habermas argues that philosophy is significant in sociopolitical terms, just as John Dewey did when he constructed his philosophy around the needs of democratic society. The true importance of philosophical concepts, for him, resides in their political implications. Rorty, however, wanted to see his philosophical thought as, to a great extent, neutral with regard to public life and political issues. This is why he—as an "ironist intellectual"—is accused of suppressing genuine conversation and constraining creativity.[3] Some of these accusations, as he claimed, "come from know-nothings—people who have not read the books against which they warn others, and are just instinctively defending their own traditional roles." However, he continued, "the same accusations are made by writers who know what they are talking about, and whose views are entitled to respect,"[4] the most important among them being, as Rorty suggested, Habermas.[5]

Habermas has criticized Rorty since—as Rorty claimed—he finds the ironist line of development disastrous for social hope. Moreover, Habermas sees the critique of the Enlightenment and the idea of rationality as damaging the bonds between the members of a liberal society. For Habermas—as Rorty himself observed—though agreeing with Nietzschean criticism of the "subject-centered reason" of traditional rationalism, sees him as leading us to a dead end. It is, in Habermas's opinion, an example of "the bankruptcy, for purposes of human "emancipation" of "philosophy of subjectivity," that is—as Rorty characterized it—"the attempt to spin moral obligation out of our own vitals, to find deep within us, beyond historical contingencies and the accidents of socialization, the origins of our responsibility to others."[6] However, according to Habermas, this emancipation is important, and this is why he thinks that "this refusal of the attempt to emancipate" has made "philosophical reflection at best irrelevant, and at worst antagonistic, to liberal hope."[7] He tries to replace the "philosophy of subjectivity" with a "philosophy of intersubjectivity" by substituting the old, subject-centered concept of "reason," common to both Immanuel Kant and Friedrich Nietzsche, with "communicative reason."[8] It is by means of this concept of communicative reason that he wishes to rebuild a certain form of rationality—communicative rationality—connected with dialogue and everyday pursuit of consensus. In other words—referring to communication free from domination—he wishes to update rationalism.

Rorty remained skeptical about such a project. He thought that according to Habermas the task of philosophy in this respect is to "supply some social glue which will replace religious belief, and to see Enlightenment talk of 'universality' and 'rationality' as the best candidate for this glue."[9] This is something Rorty could not consent to. He did not want to update universalism or rationalism: he wished to remove them and replace them with something else. He was driven by the desire to poeticize culture and the Romantic hope for the possibility of new languages that would contribute to the creation of new worlds. Thus, according to Rorty, there is a tension between this hope and the belief in the necessity for everyday pursuit of democratic consensus, characteristic of Habermas: "Professor Habermas looks principally at the need for consensus in this world now, whereas I am obsessed by the possibility of the disclosure of new worlds. My deep wish for everything to be wonderfully, utterly changed keeps me from saying that truth is idealized rational acceptability. After all, you can only idealize what you have already got. But maybe there is something you cannot even dream of yet."[10] One can say, then, that not only do Rorty and Habermas use different kinds of rhetoric but they also have different hopes and attitudes toward such essential issues as the importance of rationality and the understanding of truth as idealized rational acceptability. Rorty disagreed with, among other things, the way in which Habermas sees their very role and significance. However, this, as well as other objections that may emerge while studying the theory of communicative action, are well recognized by Habermas himself.

Rorty's Fear of Idealization

Habermas has written that "there is a more serious question: whether the concepts of communicative action and of the transcending force of universalistic validity claims do not reestablish an idealism."[11] He knows it is not easy to "counter the suspicion that with the concept of action oriented to validity claims the idealism of a pure, nonsituated reason slips in again, and the dichotomies between the realms of the transcendental and the empirical are given new life in another form."[12]

Rorty feared this kind of "idealism of a pure, nonsituated reason," as well as the idea of "truth as idealized rational acceptability." He feared idealization, rationalization, and the idea of truth, as well as universality.[13] Rorty replaced the pursuit of objectivity present in classical philosophy with the pursuit of solidarity in the linguistic community of which he happened to be a member. He had a very specific objective he wished to accomplish, being aware of his contextual roots in the "here and now." As Habermas said, "[H]e must not dream of an ideal community of all those who communicate, freed from their provinciality [...]. He must rigorously avoid every idealization, and it would be for the best if he did without the concept of rationality altogether. For 'rationality' is a limit concept with normative content, one which passes beyond the borders of every local community and moves in the direction of a universal one."[14] But is Rorty right in doing so?

Idealized Rational Acceptability

After seeking to answer this question through a careful reading of Rorty's and Habermas's texts, one can say that in the case of the numerous controversies between them we are confronted with a kind of "commotion." It is due to the fact that Rorty misconceived some of the categories used by Habermas, which manifested itself in Rorty claiming that Habermas's universalism and rationalism is that of the Enlightenment. That would point to the fact that his understanding of these concepts was quite "traditional," whereas the concepts themselves were not "traditional" at all. Not noticing the difference—or not trying to notice it—Rorty opposed the ideas of truth and rationality present in Habermas's thought, understanding them in the classical way. Accordingly, Habermas was labeled by Rorty as an adherent of Platonism and Greek thought. As Rorty put it,

> I take Platonism and Greek thought generally to say, The set of candidates for truth is already here, and all the reasons which might be given for and against their truth are also already here; all that remains is to argue the matter out. I think of romantic [...] hope as saying, Some day all of these truth candidates, and all of these notions of what counts as a good reason for believing them, may be obsolete; for a much better world is to come—one in which we shall have wonderful new truth candidates. If one holds the Greek view, then it is reasonable to define truth in terms of idealized rational acceptability in the manner of Habermas, Peirce, and Putnam. But that definition will be useless once

one starts thinking of languages and truth-candidates as constantly in the process of change.[15]

In the above quote, Rorty distinguished Platonism and Greek thought on the one side from Romantic hope on the other. Platonism and Greek thought are characterized by the belief that the collection of candidates for the truth is already given, and that there are arguments for and against them. Romantic hope, however, is characterized by the hope of a better world. Strikingly, Rorty placed Habermas and Hilary Putnam among the adherents of the "collection of candidates for the truth that is already there" stance, since they write about the category of truth and define it as "idealized rational acceptability." Rorty did that believing that thinking about truth is impossible without at least some objectivity. For him, "Habermas thinks [...] that when you assert S you claim truth, you claim to represent the real, and that reality transcends context."[16] Such attempts by Habermas, as well as reference to the notion of an ideal epistemic situation, was for Rorty, as he also repeated in *Philosophy and Social Hope*, no more useful than talking about correspondence with reality or any other notion that was previously used when speaking about truth.[17] But such an interpretation of Habermas's reasoning is not accurate. He has tried to say something different. Advocating the necessity for idealizing the creation of such concepts as truth or validity does not need to lead to false objectivistic conclusions. That is why he said that when we use the concept of reality "we presuppose something transcendent."

When classifying Habermas and Putnam as those claiming that there is both the collection of candidates for truth and all the arguments for or against them, it is important to notice that they define the concept of truth as "idealized rational acceptability." For him and Putnam, this truth, however, is not something constant, as Rorty wrongly claimed.[18] Habermas has explained that the objections presented by Rorty in the past prompted him "to revise the discursive conception of rational acceptability by relating it to a pragmatically conceived, nonepistemic concept of truth, but without thereby assimilating 'truth' to 'ideal assertibility.'"[19] For Habermas the Truth is a feature of propositions in a particular language. Truth is susceptible to a ceaseless process of changes that cannot be predicted. According to Habermas, recognizing something as true is possible only within a specific language. In other words, what is true is what has been recognized as true within a given community as a result of a rational dialogue. Habermas attempts here to combine the language-transcendent understanding of reference with the language-immanent understanding of truth as ideal assertibility.

As he said, "On this view a statement is true if and only if, under the rigorous pragmatic presuppositions of rational discourse, it is able to withstand all efforts to invalidate it."[20] It is not very problematic then to determine the concept of truth in light of ongoing changes as "idealized rational acceptability." For what is hidden in the concept of truth as idealized rational acceptability is the thought that "an idealization of this sort, which conceives of truth as acceptability grounded in reasons under certain demanding conditions, would constitute a perspective that would in turn point beyond the practices of justification that are contingently established among us, one that would distance us from these practices."[21] It is a step in this direction that Habermas finds necessary. On this issue, he refers to the work of Hilary Putnam, who justifies the idealizing, construction of concepts with the following:

> [I]f the distinction between a conception that is held to be true here and now and a conception that is true, that is, one that is acceptable under idealized conditions, collapses, then we cannot explain why we are able to learn reflexively, that is, are able also to *improve* our own standards of rationality. The dimension in which self-distancing and self-critique are possible, and in which our well-worn practices of justification can thereby be transcended and reformed, is closed off as soon as that which is rationally valid collapses into that which is socially current. [...] can we explain the possibility of the critique and self-critique of established practices of justification at all if we do not take the idea of the expansion of our interpretive horizon seriously *as an idea*, and if we do not connect this idea with the intersubjectivity of an agreement that allows precisely for the distinction between what is current "for us" and what is current "for them"?[22]

According to Habermas, the answer is negative, for he claims that idealizing is necessary. In his opinion, everyday practice oriented toward understanding is "permeated with unavoidable idealizations."[23] As he has stressed, referring to idealization here has nothing to do with the ideas remaining in opposition to reality. It refers only to "the normative contents that are encountered in practice, which we cannot do without, since language, together with the idealizations it demands of speakers, is simply constitutive for socio-cultural forms of life."[24] One may add—treading beyond the words of Habermas—that if there were no idealization, it would never be possible to break free from the ideological embraces of fascism or communism during their domination; it would never be possible to create another language that, in our opinion, would describe reality in a different or better way.²⁵ In order to create such a new language, we need a certain idealized vision of what kind of world could emerge as a result of popularizing such a language. Introducing a division into what is current "for us" and "for them" also involves some sort of idealization. Rorty introduced this division and, at the same time, he provided a basis for stating that idealizing strategies are also present in his philosophy.

Presence of Idealization in the Philosophies of Habermas and Rorty

Though Rorty "must not dream of an ideal community of all those who communicate, freed from their provinciality" and "should not let himself be lured out of his participant perspective even when the price he has to pay for this is admitted ethnocentrism,"²⁶ we have the impression that, de facto, this is what Rorty did. For this reason, Habermas has cast doubt upon whether Rorty was successful in ending the existing "philosophical language game," as he wished to. Habermas has had the impression that Rorty only began another round of the very same game. He is inclined to such a view because of a rule present in Rorty's philosophy: to diminish human suffering and increase human equality. He finds this rule too unrealistic a demand in light of pragmatic standards according to which Rorty would wish to act: "How could we convince people to implement these maxims in general practices if we could only appeal to the promotion of each one's happiness, instead of finding out, from a moral point of view, the right thing to do? The moral point of view requires us to perform another idealization, namely to imagine you and me as members of the inclusive community of human beings and to strive for the role of a fallible, yet impartial, judge on what would be equally good for everybody."²⁷ In reference to the above, it is important to notice that Rorty did not write about "diminishing human suffering and increasing human equality" as rules that would be "universally followed." However, it is possible to say, quoting Habermas, that Rorty presented some sort of "moral point of view," though Rorty himself, even if he agreed on such a label, would have added that it is the point of view of his own community. However, we need to agree with Habermas that Rorty himself idealized when he wrote about "others" who at present are outside of our community with hope that perhaps one day they will become a part of it.²⁸ Thinking about potential "others" as about members of our community requires an idealization: imagining a community broader than ours, a community that will grow as a result of dialogue and not through the use of violence or making somebody suffer.

Rorty indeed claimed that it is better to deliberate and refer to what is justifiable for a particular "auditorium," and that it is desirable to reject the idea of a universal and ideal auditorium, but, at the same time, he also claimed that "some auditoria are morally and politically better than others." The belief that they are "better" is not, however, followed by a belief that the argumentation used within them is better or worse.[29] He is undoubtedly right. We speak from the perspective of a particular auditorium and we use arguments that are most persuasive for a particular auditorium. Although we present them from the perspective of the auditorium we belong to, while using them, we may refer to some image of what this auditorium could be like. We construct a certain idealized model of an auditorium that will be, for instance, bigger than the present one, and will speak with one voice about the issues crucial to its functioning. And it is only with respect to such an idealized model that we may recognize some auditoria as morally or politically better than others. And Rorty accepts the possibility of such an evaluation. We have to state, then, that from his perspective, this is possible due to the idealized vision of community that he presented: a vision of community that is expanding with time thanks to the tolerant and rational behavior connected with settling the differences in the course of communication and renounce using violence and causing suffering.[30] From Rorty's point of view advising people to be rational means here to try to convince them that we share enough beliefs and desires that can be the basis "to permit agreement on how to coexist without violence."[31] Being rational means for Rorty acquiring a larger loyalty, because any agreement "creates a form of community, and will, with luck, be the initial stage in expanding the circles of those whom each party to the agreement had previously taken to be "people like ourselves."[32]

They Do Not Differ That Much

Ultimately, despite his fear and initial misunderstanding of certain threads of Habermas's thought, Rorty discerned that when it came to idealizing the concept of rational acceptability, his opinions did not differ that much from those of Habermas: "Habermas is right that the difference between the attempt common to him, Putnam, and Peirce—the attempt to idealize the notion of rational acceptability—and my attempt to build utopian social hope is not all that great. My attempt amounts to thinking of the contrast between the merely justified and the true not as the contrast between the actual and the ideal, but simply as the contrast between justification to us as we are here and now and justification to a superior version of ourselves, the version we hope our descendants will exemplify."³³ After overcoming these obstacles, often connected with imprecise interpretations of each other's opinions, both Habermas and Rorty discerned that in the abovementioned issue the difference between them was not that great. Rorty then had nothing to fear with regard to Habermas's work on idealization, for it is not connected with the "old-style" idealism: with the idealism of a "pure, nonsituated reason" that Rorty feared. Habermas, when writing about this kind of idealism, does not try to point to absolute truths outside the community he is in. The difference between him and Rorty rests in the fact that, as Rorty himself said, on the one hand, there is the "justification for ourselves," and on the other, the justification "for the better version of ourselves." Of course, Rorty claimed that he proceeded only with the former; but we have to say that, though not admitting it, he also proceeded with the latter: he idealized and presented a better version of ourselves. He did not admit it, for—as Habermas wrote—a contextualist such as Rorty "must exercise caution in order not to take that which he may assert as a participant within a specific historical linguistic community and a corresponding cultural form of life and translate it into a statement made from the third-person perspective of an observer."³⁴

Therefore, it can be said that the issue with one of the differences between them has been somehow resolved, and that—as Rorty himself stated—the difference is not that big.³⁵ We can say that it resides in naming what Rorty and Habermas *do* rather than *in what they do*. Is this also the case when it comes to the hopes that motivate them? Shall we agree with the aforementioned words of Rorty on this issue?

New Worlds

As has already been said, Rorty claimed that, unlike Habermas, he was not interested in the necessity for consensus in our present world but rather was occupied with the thought of the possibility of discovering new worlds. This was, according to Rorty, and as Habermas rightly observed, due to the fact that "our vocabularies serve the creative function of letting us see situations and problems in a different—and one hopes a more convenient—useful, and efficient way. It is up to us language-using animals to produce new and better vocabularies in a similar way as we have always produced new and better tools."³⁶

Rorty suggested that we free our culture from all philosophical vocabulary constructed around the categories of reason, rationality, truth, and knowledge, and thereby wrest these categories from their central place.³⁷ He suggested we do away with the dualisms that are the legacy of Plato. The objectivity of cognition amounts to the intersubjectivism of compliance, and the validity of a given belief to its acceptability. At the same time, he suggested we replace the vocabulary we have inherited with a new one. He wanted a new narration that would inhere in poeticizing the culture.

Rorty's project, thus outlined, is close also to that of Habermas, who—as it has already been said—advocates perceiving the category of truth as changeable, and, at the same time, departing from its classical conception. He agrees, as he himself wrote, with Rorty's "penetrating criticism of realist conceptions of 'truth as correspondence'" and accepts "the Deweyan proposal to explain 'truth as warranted assertability.'"³⁸ He therefore agrees on wresting the category of truth from its central place in our culture. As he put it, "For my own part, in any case, I have said goodbye to the emphatic philosophical claim to truth."³⁹ Like Rorty, he does not want to present "one grand truth," neither is he a maker of a "Weltanschauung"; he would like, instead, to "produce a few small truths."⁴⁰ He regards such a work as "constructive," and he compares it to puzzle work in which other theories are its pieces. These pieces are useful in the game, depending on their strength and plausibility. It can be said then that Habermas, as an adherent of creating new theories, or at least, as he himself said, "contributing to them," is also, like Rorty, an adherent of creating new languages.⁴¹

Creating New Worlds

But creating new languages is connected, according to Habermas, with an obstacle: the problem of their justification. As he observes, since, according to Rorty, new language is to be more suitable for the present conditions of living, and validation of a new language is to depend on expediency, it cannot be provided with the validation it would obtain if it results from the deconstruction of the old and illusory language. This new language is not, in Habermas's opinion, that new at all. He said, "If we look at it more closely, the new language appears, however, neither new nor particularly functional. The conceptual frame which Rorty introduces for 'coping' and 'problem solving' is well known from nineteenth-century naturalism, when people like Spencer extended the Darwinian conception of mutation, selection, and adaptation from the field of biology to the social and cultural sciences (without much success, by the way). The language game of the survival of the fittest may at best count as one among several more or less established vocabularies, so that we need reasons why we should prefer this one."[42] Then a question arises: why should we choose this and not another language game—a given narration? What, in Rorty's case, would be the justification for choosing a particular vocabulary? Should it rest on the general success of science? As we recall, according to Rorty, each vocabulary should be regarded as one of many, and the conflicting theories and languages, if they are affirmed—rooted—within their contexts, should not be treated as competing but as different: "They cannot compete for anything but the satisfaction of context-depending needs. 'Good' theories fit the needs at certain times and places; if they keep fitting they will adapt to different times and places."[43] In short, according to Rorty, theories and languages do not need any validation apart from the potential for reproduction and functional efficacy. But if that indeed was the case, Rorty would not be able to present any arguments justifying his calling for rejecting Platonism. Referring to its lack of functionality—as Habermas noted—will not aid Rorty, for its present functional usefulness is ample validation for the further existence of this tradition. But Rorty does not notice this functional usefulness. To answer the question, Why should we change the present language and replace its common sense with something else?, he somehow justified the attempt at departing from placing particular categories in the center of our culture. For it should be done, among other things, because of philosophical problems connected with the dualisms present in this culture and because of the hope that perhaps Charles Darwin pointed to a new moral world waiting to be discovered. What would this world be like? Rorty replied, "We will never find out unless we try. I think that the romantic hope of substituting new common sense for old common sense is a reason for skepticism about the latter. Such hope amounts to saying the world is still young. The cultural evolution of our species is just beginning. We do not have any idea yet of the possibilities, but we need to take full advantage of people like Luther, Copernicus, Galileo, Darwin, and Freud, because they give us our chances. They are our chances to transform the candidates for truth and thereby make previous patterns of justification obsolete."[44]

According to Rorty, such new worlds need significant time to achieve their full glory. They evolve as a result of transformations occurring in the language itself, and they emerge within it as do prominent spots on the sun's surface, as "protuberances." Ostensibly, despite a certain convergence, there is some tension between Rorty and Habermas, for the former is motivated by Romantic hope, and the latter by the need for consensus. Habermas wrote about this point of difference in *Philosophical Discourse of Modernity*, after a brief introduction:

According to Rorty, science and morality, economics and politics, are delivered up to a process of language-creating protuberances *in just the same way* as art and philosophy. Like Kuhnian history of science, the flux of interpretations beats rhythmically between revolutions and normalizations of language. He observes this back-and-forth between two situations in all fields of cultural life: "One is the sort of situation encountered when people pretty much agree on what is wanted, and are talking about how best to get it. In such a situation there is no need to say anything terribly unfamiliar, for argument is typically about the truth of assertions rather than about the utility of vocabularies. The contrasting situation is one in which everything is up for grabs at once—in which the motives and terms of discussion are a central subject of argument. [...] In such periods people begin to toss around old words in new senses, to throw in the occasional neologism, and thus to hammer out a new idiom which initially attracts attention to itself and only later gets put to work." One notices how the Nietzschean pathos of a *Lebensphilosophie* that has made the linguistic turn beclouds the sober insights of pragmatism; in the picture painted by Rorty, the renovative process of linguistic world-disclosure no longer has a *counterpoise* in the testing processes of intramundane practice. The "Yes" and "No" of communicatively acting agents is so prejudiced and rhetorically overdetermined by their linguistic contexts that the anomalies that start to arise during the phases of exhaustion are taken to represent only symptoms of waning validity, or aging processes analogous to processes of nature—and are not seen as the result of *deficient* solutions to problems and *invalid* answers.[45]

Habermas disagrees with Rorty, who claimed that there is no *counterpoise*. In Habermas's perspective, it is the participants of communication that resolve problems, noticing the deficiency of solutions and the invalidity of answers. They are not left to the "natural" processes of the arising vitality of new narrations and the diminishing of the previous "vital powers."

Rorty also believed that in this respect he differed from Habermas. He saw Habermas as someone who was willing to presume that the languages of science and technology, of law and morality, of economics and politics find revival in metaphorical trails, but he deemed it too big a step to admit that they are subject to the process of protuberances that make up language. When referring to this issue, he wrote that Habermas "wants world-disclosure always to be checked for 'validity' against intramundane practice. He wants there to be *argumentative* practices, conducted within 'expert cultures,' which cannot be overturned by exciting, romantic disclosures of new worlds. He is more afraid of the sort of 'romantic' overthrow of established institutions exemplified by Hitler and Mao than of the suffocating effect of what Dewey called 'the crust of convention' (e.g., the possibly suffocating effect of traditional divisions between 'spheres of culture')."[46] The above words of Rorty's are convincing only to a certain extent. Is it possible, though, to disagree with them completely? In accordance with them, Habermas would wish for the existence of argumentative practices that cannot be "overturned." Such an interpretation does not seem right, though. The argumentative practices can be "overturned," and Habermas wrote at length about such a danger. This sort of situation may take place when a system and actions aiming at success enter those areas of the lifeworld that should be regulated with communicative action: the pursuit of understanding via the use of arguments. Additionally, those "argumentative practices" are necessary, according to Habermas, for a free and rational communication between parties and for a consensus achieved in its course. Certain formal conditions need to be met during the processes of reaching understanding in order for that to happen. He does not say, however, that these processes are insusceptible to ongoing changes.

In other words, when presenting Habermas's thought, Rorty misinterpreted some issues. We need to note, though, that Rorty rightly observed that Habermas wants to check the "validity" of world-disclosures against intramundane practice; however, it also has to be stated that this process is reciprocal. For Habermas claims that what we are faced with is interaction ongoing between the processes of discovering the world and the intramundane processes of learning. This process is symmetrical and results in the interpenetration of knowledge about language and knowledge about the world. And thus, "while one enables the acquisition of the other, world-knowledge may, in turn, correct linguistic knowledge (as Putnam convincingly argues). Relevant parts of a world-disclosing language that first enables speakers and actors to look at, cope with, and interpret in a specific way anything that might occur to them can well be revised in the light of what they have learned from their innerworldly encounters."[47] Therefore, Habermas proposed that Rorty should depart from "the misleading idea about the inclusive nature of world-disclosing languages."[48] Rorty, however, did not seem to stick to this "misleading idea" as much as it could be presumed on the basis of the aforementioned quotes. As an effect of deliberation, at a certain point, he actually stated that the relation between the processes of learning and processes of discovering the world is as complex as Habermas suggests.[49] Thus, he agreed that there is a sort of feedback between the two areas. He also wrote, "I just want to say that sometimes you can easily integrate world disclosure with learning processes, but sometimes it is harder. Sometimes you get an epiphany—something that is not so much a response to an antecedent challenge as a sudden upsurge of the indescribably strange and wonderful."[50] Habermas would agree that there is the described possibility of the occurring of the phenomena of protuberances that construct language. Those protuberances would not be, from such a perspective, only an effect of intramundane encounters. They would stem from the closely connected and continuously affecting symbiotic processes of discovering the world and the intramundane processes of learning. Therefore, they should be regarded as dependent, to a lesser or greater extent, on the processes of reflection upon the solutions that turned out deficient, or the answers that ceased to be valid.

It can be said then that Rorty recognized the importance of "intramundane encounters" and their results, which affect further interactions, and would have agreed that we partake in the processes of "discovering" the world. Thus, it can be presumed that he would have been ready to agree with Habermas on this issue.[51] Did he, however, agree completely?

Validity Claims

The feedback between linguistic circumstance and the results of the processes of learning—the feedback that makes learning possible—is indebted, according to Habermas, to "the context-transcending range and context-bursting force of criticizable claims to validity on the intersubjective—but fallible—recognition on which our daily communicative practices depend."[52] In other words, the relation between the processes of discovering the world and the intramundane processes of learning depends on the idealizing presumption of the existence of validity claims. They are one of the formal conditions that have to be met in order for undistorted communication and the process of learning to be possible. The analysis of these claims points to, as Habermas wrote, "the idea of an intact intersubjectivity, which makes possible both a mutual and constraint-free understanding among individuals in their dealings with one another and the identity of individuals who come to a compulsion-free understanding with themselves. This intact intersubjectivity is a glimmer of symmetrical relations marked by free, reciprocal recognition."[53] Habermas continues to believe that it is this intact intersubjectivity that makes the idealizing presumption of the existence of validity claims, "transcending the context," or—in other words—"transcending the horizon of the present context," possible. This "transcending" is possible, according to Habermas, because

> even in the most difficult processes of reaching understanding, all parties appeal to the common reference point of a possible consensus, even if this reference point is projected in each case from within their own contexts. For, although they may be interpreted in various ways and applied according to different criteria, concepts like truth, rationality, or justification play the *same* grammatical role in *every* linguistic community. [...] all languages offer the possibility of distinguishing between what is true and what we hold to be true. The *supposition* of a common objective world is built into the pragmatics of every single linguistic usage.[54]

Accordingly, we can say that Habermas wishes to present the concept of reason as connected with both transcendent and context-dependent validity claims. And "the validity claimed for propositions and norms transcends spaces and times."[55] He stated, however, that validity claims are raised here and now—in specific contexts—and that the universal presuppositions of communicative action must not be treated as the key to achieving ultimate understanding.[56] Thus, he argued that the idea of communicative reason is haunted by the spectrum of a transcendental illusion, and the idealizing presuppositions need to be treated with some skepticism. He also added that the "pragmatic presuppositions of communicative action suggest the objectivistic fallacy according to which we could take up the extramundane standpoint of a subject removed from the world, help ourselves to an ideal language that is context-free and appears in the singular, and thereby make infallible, exhaustive, and thus definitive statements."[57]

Habermas knows that what he has to say on the above issue is by no means an alternative to cautious, admittedly ethnocentric contextualism. The contextualist concept of language, of which Rorty is an adherent, "is impervious to the very real force of the counterfactual, which makes itself felt in the idealizing presuppositions of communicative action."[58]

Rorty against the Idea of Communicative Rationality

Rorty was against the idea of validity claims and communicative reason. Rorty claimed that we should do away with the belief that "'reason' names a healing, reconciling, unifying power—the source of human solidarity." He believed that there is no such "source" and that "the idea of human solidarity is simply the fortunate happenstance creation of modern times," and this is why "we no longer need a notion of 'communicative reason' to substitute for that of 'subject-centered reason'. We do not need to replace religion with a philosophical account of a healing and unifying power which will do the work once done by God."[59] According to Rorty, and unlike in Habermas's thought, the concept of rationality cannot be useful in expressing the essence of secular cultures. He deemed it useless in light of the existence of accident and contingency. Recognizing this concept as a "healing and uniting power" may, moreover—in his opinion—lead to promoting, regardless of the price, one right option and to the emergence of different fundamentalist attitudes. But is he right? It is worth asking the question whether it is indeed the category of rationality that is responsible for the emergence of such attitudes. Habermas provided the answer:

> In specific situations it is quite true that terrorist activities may be connected with the overextension of one of these cultural moments, that is, with the inclination to aestheticize politics, to replace politics with moral rigorism, or to subjugate politics to dogmatic doctrines. But these almost intangible connections should not mislead us into denouncing the intentions of an intransigent Enlightenment as the monstrous offspring of a "terroristic reason". Those who link the project of modernity with the conscious attitudes and spectacular public deeds of individual terrorists are just as short-sighted as those who claim that the incomparably more persistent and pervasive bureaucratic terrorism practised in obscurity, in the cellars of the military and the secret police, in prison camps and psychiatric institutions, represents the very essence of the modern state (and its positivistically eroded form of legal domination) simply because such terrorism utilizes the coercive means of the state apparatus.[60]

In short, the fact that a "terrorist" refers to the rationality of his or her actions and beliefs does not mean that what rationality results in is terrorism. Thus, we cannot blame the category of truth for the pathological contexts in which it happens to appear.

To consider the concept of communicative rationality as involved in the attempt at articulating the one and only right and true, and thus opposing the plurality and diversity of voices, is not proper either. Habermas has written about the unity of reason—the unity of reason in the diversity of its voices—but it is not the unity of a theoretical perspective of some kind that is meant here; what is meant by Habermas is the unity that is accomplished in the course of actions oriented toward consensus, the unity that is produced via communicative actions and the accompanying, previously presumed, validity claims. When writing about unity, Habermas also added that he is against talking about diversity and difference only. He described such attempts as follows: "Repulsion towards the One and veneration of difference and the Other obscures the dialectical connection between them. For the transitory unity that is generated in the porous and refracted intersubjectivity of a linguistically mediated consensus not only supports but furthers and accelerates the pluralization of forms of life and the individualization of lifestyles. More discourse means more contradiction and difference. The more abstract the agreements become, the more diverse the disagreements with which we can *nonviolently* live."[61] It is not then undisputable unity that is in question but forming provisional unities that are to change over time. Their production is not an effect of the communication process and the agreement that follows. If we were aware of the temporariness of the unity, there would be no reason for fear or doubt, such as that of Rorty's, that it may be absolutized and, accordingly, enforced. The idea of unity does not need to entail the fear of coercive integration of diversity.[62] Therefore, Habermas has claimed that moral universalism should not be regarded as negating individualism but as facilitating it. And ascribing identical meanings should not be regarded as a violation of metaphorical ambiguity but as a prerequisite for it. Thus, the unity of reason should not be regarded as a limitation on the diversity of voices, for it does not impede the "increasing willingness to live in pluralism" for which Rorty cares so much.[63] And it seems that Rorty understood Habermas, because in *Rorty and His Critics* he said, "I agree with Habermas that it is as pointless to prize diversity as to prize unity."[64] In light of the above, Rorty should agree with Habermas's understanding of unity, for he himself wrote about its form existing in the diversity of voices, about agreement emerging in spite of the diversity of private goals: "I want to see freely arrived at agreement as agreement on how to accomplish common purposes (e.g., prediction and control of the behavior of atoms or people, equalizing life-chances, decreasing cruelty), but I want to see these common purposes against the background of an increasing sense of the radical diversity of private purposes, of the radically poetic character of individual lives, and of the merely poetic foundations of the 'we-consciousness' which lies behind our social institutions."[65] Undoubtedly, this easily achieved agreement should first be connected with acknowledging that creating "new worlds" is sensible and that it should unite us despite our diversity and plurality.

Necessary Communicative Rationality

Habermas does not think that the concept of communicative rationality has anything to do with one correct representation of reality.[66] When he wrote about communicative rationality he did not mean marking out a highway to truth but defining the conditions for undistorted communication. Rorty understood rationality in a similar way; ultimately, he stated that his understanding of rationality is related to such concepts as curiosity, persuasion, and tolerance. In other words, instead of understanding the concept of rationality through the prism of the concept of truth, he presented it in the context of the concept of communication and, accordingly, wrote,

> To put all this another way, I should like us to detach the notion of rationality from that of truth. I want to define rationality as the habit of attaining our ends by persuasion rather than force. As I see it, the opposition between rationality and irrationality is simply the opposition between words and blows. To analyze what it is for human beings to be rational is (and here I take up a familiar theme from Habermas's own work) to understand techniques of persuasion, patterns of justification, and forms of communication. There is, it seems to me, considerable convergence between Habermas's substitution of communicative reason for subject-centered reason and what I am calling the Protagorean/ Emersonian tradition.[67]

Though initially he did not wish to recognize the necessity for talking about communicative rationality, he eventually admitted that it did play a significant role in his own work.[68] He perceived it as the practice of achieving our aims through argumentation, which is a counterweight to the alternative means of achieving aims—that is, by "force" or violence. Rorty's understanding of rationality was then close to what Habermas has presented as communicative rationality.[69] With respect to this "closeness," Rorty claimed that there is a far-reaching convergence of communicative rationality and the tradition of Protagoras and Emerson, the latter tradition of which he was an adherent. It is expressed, inter alia, in articulating what conditions should be satisfied in order for free and tolerant communication to occur.[70] Such an articulation of rationality in Rorty's philosophy is what Habermas himself has pointed to:

> Rorty even specifies the conditions for the required context of free and tolerant discussions. While granting equal access to all relevant persons, information, and reasons, this form of communication should rule

out any kind of exclusionary and repressive mechanisms, propaganda, brainwashing, and so on. In stressing the open, inclusive, nonrepressive features of a communication within a more and more idealized auditorium, Rorty approaches willy nilly my description of "rational discourse" and Putnam's formula of truth as "rational acceptability under idealized conditions". Within this kind of "superassertability", Rorty unintentionally slides, however, back into the domain of what he calls a "Platonist culture."[71]

The above assessment by Habermas is to a great extent right. We can find some specification of formal conditions for undistorted communication also in Rorty's thought. In other words, we are faced with a certain idealized image of rational discourse: presenting ideal conditions for unconstrained dialogue. Thus, undoubtedly, Rorty unconsciously moved toward what he has wished to part with forever. It does not seem plausible, though, to accordingly state that Rorty was heading for the sphere of "Platonic culture"—unless the term is being used here in order to point out that he moved toward yet another "involvement" in the necessity of introducing some idealization—constructing an abstract model that is to serve as a signpost specifying how to behave on the path ahead of us.

Therefore, we can after all say that in this respect Rorty and Habermas seem to agree. For both, communicative rationality is a certain "uniting force." As a "healing element," it is not some concrete knowledge or truth. It is but formal rules that should be consulted to enable communication. Habermas acknowledges their importance, and so did Rorty.[72] We need to add, though, that what Rorty did not do is point to the universal element existing within them: he did not point, as Habermas does, to the universality of validity claims for the normatively charged concept of communication, which "operates with validity claims that can be redeemed discursively and with formal-pragmatic presuppositions about the world, and links understanding speech acts to the conditions of their rational acceptability."[73] Rorty wrote, "The principal differences between Habermas and myself concern the notion of Universal validity. I think that we can get along without that notion and still have a sufficiently rich notion of rationality. We can keep all that was good in Platonism even after we drop the notion of universal validity. Habermas thinks that we still need to keep it."[74] And he repeated that claim when responding to Habermas in *Rorty and His Critics* by saying, "I argued that the switch to 'communicative rationality' should lead us to drop the idea that when I make an assertion I am implicitly claiming to be able to justify it to all audiences, actual and possible."[75]

Difference

According to the above, both Rorty and Habermas care for freely accomplished agreement and maintenance of "the diversity of voices." Habermas does also recognize the role of change and contingency; thus, in his opinion, agreement that we arrive at is temporary, and the points of dispute have to be discussed all over again in the process of communication.[76] In the course of his debates with Rorty, he said that he developed "the idea that discourses remain embedded in the context of lifeworld practices because it is their function to reestablish a partially disrupted background understanding."[77] Therefore, communicative reason, about which Habermas has written, treats almost everything, even the conditions for the emergence of our own linguistic medium, as contingent. Almost everything, but not everything. And this is where the difference between Rorty and Habermas lies.

Habermas does not believe that "the whole is the false, that everything is contingent, that there is no consolation whatsoever. [...] It [communicative reason] neither announces the absence of consolation in a world forsaken by God, nor does it take it upon itself to provide any consolation. It does without exclusivity as well. As long as no better words for what religion can say are found in the medium of rational discourse, it will even coexist abstemiously with the former, neither supporting it nor combatting it."[78] We can say, then, that Habermas, in spite of his awareness of the existence of contingency, is against thinking about its totality and thinking about it as something ubiquitous and all-embracing.[79] He differs in this respect from Rorty, for he has continued to believe that "for everything that claims validity *within* linguistically structured forms of life, the structures of possible mutual understanding in language constitute something that cannot be gotten around."[80] Of course, "the reality facing our propositions is not 'naked', but is itself already permeated by language. The experience against which we check our assumptions is linguistically structured and embedded in contexts of action."[81] Therefore, he wrote about transcendence as related to recognizing in other languages the same significant element of consensus, that is, validity claims. And it is an element necessary for communication in general. In other words, according to Habermas, validity claims are the formal condition for communication in all languages, and thus he could write about their "universality."

Rorty did not accept the fact that we are to recognize the universality of validity claims: that they transcend contexts on which we are dependent and that they universally serve as a formal condition for communication and achieving a consensus.[82] Accordingly, he also did not agree with

Habermas's belief that in every language there is "the possibility of distinguishing between what is true and what we hold to be true" and that "the *supposition* of a common objective world is built into the pragmatics of every single linguistic usage."[83] Rorty believed that such a claim is disputable in light of what he called the contingency of language, and this is also why it is absent in his poeticized culture of a liberal utopia.[84] In his opinion, as far as the changing vocabularies are concerned, it is difficult to maintain the prerequisites crucial for communicative rationality, such as the concept of unconditionality and universal validity. On this point, he wrote, "I think that the notions of unconditionality and universal validity run into trouble when you go from one set of truth candidates to another—that is, when you go from the propositions taken seriously before an intellectual revolution to those taken seriously after the revolution. I think it is hard to preserve the notions of unconditionality and universal validity across such changes in vocabulary."[85] Rorty was critical of the attempts at maintaining them. He believed that universalism inclined Habermas toward replacing ahistorical rooting with convergence that is to be the guarantee for "rationality" of communication. Though Habermas is willing to abandon the problem of harmony between the human subject and the object of cognition, he insists, according to Rorty, that the process of communication should be regarded as convergent, as one in the course of which "the transcendent moment of universal validity bursts every provinciality asunder."[86]

Rorty was suspicious about the idea of "universal validity": about the idea of universal validity claims upon which the "convergence" is to rest. He believed that Habermas is motivated by the desire to maintain the traditional narrative of "asymptotic approach to *foci imaginarii*."[87] He claimed that it is possible to do without universal validity claims, for this idea provokes many a problem.[88] As far as this observable difference between him and Habermas is concerned, Rorty said, "But compared to the similarities between my Emersonian secularist romanticism and his notion of rationality as the search for undistorted communication rather than as an attempt to get from appearance to reality, this difference may not be so very important."[89] Undoubtedly, Habermas would also agree with that, considering the aim that they both wish to achieve. He has not feared, as many critics of Rorty do, that departing from the classical concept of truth is synonymous with the threat of the very foundations of our culture falling apart.[90] Unlike Rorty, he has wished, however, to point to validity claims to support the idea of undistorted communication, but this appears to the author of *Philosophy and the Mirror of Nature* too far a step.

Issue of Understanding Human Nature

Heading toward the end of our considerations concerning possible differences between the perspectives of Rorty and of Habermas, it is worth adding something that has not yet been discussed: that there is no significant tension between them with respect to the issue of understanding human nature, even though one may have such an impression after reading some portions of Rorty's texts. And so, as Rorty wrote in *Contingency, Irony, and Solidarity*, liberal freedoms "require no consensus on any topic more basic than their own desirability."[91] Subsequently, he stated that Habermas has a different opinion in this respect, that Habermas did not trust the "literary" concept of philosophy, and thus that he has maintained that liberal political freedoms require some roots in what is universally human. And in *Moral Identity and Private Autonomy*, he stated that "Habermas would like to ground moral obligation, and thus social institutions, on something universally human."[92] Rorty wrote so because he regarded Habermas as a philosopher who thinks "in terms of something deep within human beings, which is deformed by acculturation," though Habermas has agreed that "the self, the human subject, is simply whatever acculturation makes of it."[93] One can have doubts as to whether Rorty was right. Habermas does not seem to seek what is universally human, what resides deeply within human beings. He has written about unconditionality and universality, but not in the context of supporting the idea of ahistorical human nature.[94] Unconditionality and universality concern certain elements that are the formal conditions for communication and that are necessary for enabling it. Through these concepts Habermas has wished to voice his intuition that it is possible to talk about some universal elements of language as a communicative tool. And when it comes to understanding human nature, Habermas could possibly agree with Rorty that "we have to give up the idea that there are unconditional, transcultural moral obligations, obligations rooted in an unchanging, ahistorical, human nature."[95]

To Recapitulate: Much in Common

It is worth emphasizing that Rorty's opinions on the different hopes motivating him and Habermas, as quoted above, cannot be considered right. Habermas, like Rorty, wants to construct new languages, and Rorty, like Habermas, was concerned about the opportunities for undistorted communication and attitudes winning over in free and open encounters: for arriving, at least somewhat, at a consensus.[96] Therefore, it can be said that both perspectives have much in common.

What is more, both Rorty's and Habermas's thought involve an important element: idealization. Here, however, there is a bit of a difference between them: namely, it is only Habermas that has recognized the existence of this element. When pointing to the need for idealization, he has talked about the formal necessity for using such idealizations, both in the case of presuming an ideal speech situation, as well as in the case of possessing some idealized image of the community we constitute and the community we could constitute. When talking about an "ideal speech situation," he has pointed to the necessity for the existence of certain conditions essential for undistorted communication to emerge. It may be achieved when we accept the significance of a series of elements. What is more, Habermas has also observed that when entering a dialogue with validity claims, we presuppose a certain communicative community and we perceive others as its potential members. These elements of idealization are also to be found in Rorty's project of an "extended community," established in the name of greater solidarity and equality, as well as in the project of forming the conditions for undistorted, rational communication. Rorty himself, however, did not agree with this stance on the implicit elements of idealization that are to be found in his philosophy. This is why Habermas in his "Coping with Contingencies: The Return of Historicism" argued that he is still trying to convince his opponents, the contextualists, "that they are not sufficiently critical of the remaining elements of idealization in the tacit presuppositions of their own striking arguments."[97]

At this point, it has to suffice to note that in spite of his initial suspicions, Rorty eventually became aware of the fact that in the theory of communicative action, Habermas did not regard rationality and truth in the old sense: as correspondence of words and things. Rorty admitted that certain conditions are necessary for communication—as a counterweight for violence—to take place. The "new worlds" about which Rorty was concerned are constructed precisely by means of communication and reformulating our beliefs and attitudes in conducive circumstances. This communication results in agreement that should be as far-reaching as possible. And it is this idealized, far-reaching agreement—rational acceptability—that we should think about when engaging in communicative action.

For both Rorty and Habermas, arriving at an agreement as a result of communicative action oriented to understanding leads to the extending of our community. However, when he was writing about communication, Rorty did not use concepts such as "communicative rationality" or "communicative reason," which are characteristic of the work of Habermas. He found replacing "subject-centered reason" with "communicative reason" as a misleading formulation of the same thought that he himself held, that is: "A liberal society is one which is content to call 'true' (or 'right' or 'just') whatever the outcome of undistorted communication happens to be, whatever view wins in a free and open encounter."[98] But since Habermas explicitly said what he understands by the categories of reason and rationality, Rorty seems to be wrong when stating that the concept of "communicative reason" is a misleading formulation of the same thought that he himself held. However, taking notice of the latter part of Rorty's statement, it is sufficient that he wrote that what is implicit in this concept is a thought with which Habermas agrees. Thus, it can be said that the difference between the two philosophers is not that significant. It rests, to a great extent, on the fact that Rorty and Habermas have used different vocabulary to describe the same intuitions. Then we need to agree with Rorty when he claimed—in the portion of the text quoted at the beginning of this chapter—that the difference between them resides to a great extent in different ways of expressing their hopes, and thus it is a difference in the rhetoric used. But was he also right when he claimed that there is no conflict between them when it comes to democratic institutions and the understanding of what freedom from domination is? We shall take a closer look at this issue.

What Kind of Politics?

By investigating the supposed "tension" between Rorty's Romantic hope and Habermas's need for consensus, we have found out that it is not that significant. It may seem so, for both Rorty and Habermas sometimes misconceived each other's opinions, often somehow overinterpreting them, and then arrived at the wrong conclusions. This impression of a "tension" appears also due to the fact that some concerns are not articulated by Rorty and Habermas explicitly enough, even though they are an important component of their views. This articulation, however, does not seem possible (the issue with justifying the universality of Habermas's validity claims); otherwise, it would imply recognizing the planned radical project as not so radical at all (the issues of idealization in Rorty's philosophy). Having pointed to these issues and having discussed them, as well as having acknowledged a number of other elements, it can be said that the differences in the attitudes of the two philosophers are not that significant. Those that do exist result from the fact that Habermas's and Rorty's considerations are guided by either the thought of a serious change in the current philosophical *vocabulary* or the desire to point to the *minor*, but still noticeable, universal elements.[99] Unfortunately, neither can be accomplished in a satisfactory way.[100] In spite of those minor differences, the philosophers are de facto in the very same position, delineate the same formal conditions necessary for unconstrained communication, and wish for the realization of the same objective: the extending of the community of solidarity and arriving at a greater consensus. These minor differences do not affect in a negative way the possibility of claiming that the two philosophers are in agreement to a great extent, as far as the foundations of their sociopolitical perspectives are concerned.[101]

What is more, it is worth noticing that Rorty himself held that the discrepancies between Habermas's attempt at reconstructing a certain form of rationality and his own proposal of poeticizing culture are not reflected in any sort of difference in politics. He maintained that Habermas's statement that possible dangers can be avoided if the decisions concerning changes in public institutions are made in the course of "communication free from domination" is a reformulation of a traditional thesis of liberalism that "the only way to avoid perpetuating cruelty within social institutions is by maximizing the quality of education, freedom of the press, educational opportunity, opportunities to exert political influence, and the like."[102] And he was right when he formulated Habermas's position in this way. When answering the question of how political power that may lead to the moral unity of a society is to be obtained and how violence resulting from the bourgeois revolution is to be transformed, Habermas has referred to the categories of freedom from domination and freedom of argumentation as tools of reaching understanding. Freedom from domination is what is presumed by those engaging in argumentation.[103] By insisting on free communication and argumentation as paths for resolving conflicts without coercion, Habermas has expressed at the same time his "resistance to reformist interventions that turn into their opposite, because the means by which they are implemented run counter to the declared aims of social integration."[104]

The above, however, is not sufficient to make the claim that there is indeed no "political difference" between Rorty and Habermas. This issue needs to be investigated more carefully. Accordingly, now that we have considered the central threads of the sociopolitical thought of Rorty and of Habermas, it is worth trying to resolve the issue of what political form we would, in their opinion, choose after wresting the categories of truth and of human nature from the central position in our culture. Do they both recognize the value of traditional democratic institutions, as Rorty claimed, and do they identify the points to be repaired? What ought our politics to be like? When answering that question it is worth reaching out for Rorty's *The Priority of Democracy to Philosophy* and Habermas's "Three Normative Models of Democracy" as well his *Between Facts and Norms* to the extent to which Habermas argues in it in favor of an appropriate form of democracy that we should put in place. Thus I will not refer here to his analysis of the theories and developments of the public political sphere or the rule of law present in that work, despite the fact that Habermas focuses on them a great deal, because they were not the subject of the debate between Rorty and Habermas.

Democracy

For Rorty, democracy is of the utmost importance; thus, he wrote about its primacy over philosophy. Looking for constant and unchangeable truths should no longer be at the center of our culture. Regarding himself an adherent of parliamentary democracy and of the welfare state, Rorty wished to praise them, but "only on the basis of invidious comparisons with suggested concrete alternatives, not on the basis of claims that these institutions are truer to human nature, or more national, or in better accord with the Universal moral law, than feudalism or totalitarianism."[105] Undoubtedly, Habermas, who has also opposed discussing democracy in terms of universal moral rights, would agree. In "Three Normative Models of Democracy," he presented his procedural definition of democracy and its deliberative politics that is to better correspond to complex social and political relations. He discussed this kind of politics after offering outlines of two other kinds of politics—liberal and republican—from which he then distanced himself.

Habermas pointed out that from the liberal perspective, the task of a politician is "bundling together and pushing private interests against a government apparatus specializing in the administrative employment of political power for collective goals."[106] From the republican perspective, however, politics is to reflect the fundamental aspects of ethical life. It is to be the environment in which community members recognize their mutual dependency and act "with full deliberation as citizens, [and] further shape and develop existing relations of reciprocal recognition into an association of free and equal consociate under law."[107] From this perspective, as Habermas observed, what is of much significance is communication that validates the formation of the opinions and will of the citizens, as well as political discourse that enables disputes on values, needs, deficiencies, and changes within them. However, the problem that is identified by the philosopher is the tendency of present-day republicans to impose ethical limitations on this political discourse and perceiving the process of communication through communitarian ideology, regarding the democratic process as dependent on the virtues of citizens devoted to public well-being. He said,

According to the communitarian view, there is a necessary connection between the deliberative concept of democracy and the reference to a concrete, substantively integrated ethical community. Otherwise one could not explain, in this view, how the citizens' orientation to the common good would be at all possible. The individual, so the argument goes, can become aware of her co-membership in a collective form of life, and therewith become aware of a prior social bond, only a practice exercised with others in common. The individual can get a clear sense of commonalities and differences, and hence a sense of who she is and who she would like to be, only in the public exchange with others who owe their identities to the same traditions and similar formation processes.[108]

Habermas cannot agree with such a communitarian vision, for he argued that while working toward compromises between conflicting interests and values, what are recognized are the interests and values that are not fundamental to the identity of the whole community.

Rorty also could not agree that there exists some sort of essential relation between the concept of democracy and a specific integrated ethical community. At the same time that he was arguing with communitarians on the aforementioned issue, he was also against Michael J. Sandel's stance that we have to be in possession of an explanation of "the nature of the moral subject," something that is "in some sense necessary, non-contingent and prior to any particular experience."[109] Rorty did not believe that human beings have a natural, ahistorical center that can be localized and enlightened in the course of any philosophical investigation. In his opinion, "we can dismiss the distinction between an attribute of the self and a constituent of the self, between the self's accidents and its essence, as 'merely' metaphysical."[110] Rorty, as a liberal-democratic philosopher, did recognize the possibility of developing the theory of the human "I" corresponding to the institutions that he supported, but this does not mean that at the same time he justified these institutions through reference to any stronger premises. He privileged politics, and to it he adjusted philosophy: "If one wants a model of the human self, then this picture of a centerless web will fill the need. But for purposes of liberal social theory, one can do without such a model."[111] According to Rorty, we cannot talk of a certain "I," its nature as moral subject, and its inherent ahistorical moral truth whose discovery would be necessary for social survival. It was, in his opinion, useless to look for philosophical justification of our identity in a liberal society. According to Rorty, such an identity, like the whole of liberal democracy, does not need philosophical justification.[112]

Liberal Democracy without Philosophical Justification

When it comes to the necessity for philosophical justification, Rorty referred to John Rawls who—as he argued—following Dewey, showed us how liberal democracy can do without it. He believed that "philosophy in the classical sense as the search for truth about a prior and independent moral order cannot provide the shared basis for a political conception of justice."[113]

In Rorty's opinion, truth representing an order previous to ours is not and should not be connected with democratic politics. This is why Rawls, as Rorty wrote, "puts democratic politics first, and philosophy second," and maintains the Socratic commitment to free exchange of opinions, but resigns from the Platonic possibility of universal understanding.[114] According to Rorty, such an attitude is thoroughly historicist and antiuniversalist.[115] And it is an attitude he himself advocated. Thus he was against attempting to uncover the "philosophical foundations of democracy," the need for which is described by Sandel in *Liberalism and the Limits of Justice*. In the case of the conflict between democracy and philosophy, it is democracy, in his opinion, that has the primacy. Rorty perceived it as an experiment due to which generations are granted the opportunity to learn something significant. And it shall not be a philosophical or religious truth, supposedly uncovered via democratic revolutions, but a lesson that "social institutions can be viewed as experiments in cooperation rather than as attempts to embody a universal and ahistorical order."[116] This cooperation can occur, according to Rorty, thanks to certain conditions favorable for communication. This communication is to lead to reaching understanding and extending our community. In short, it is communication, and not justification founded on truth that can be uncovered and disseminated, that should be our support.

Rorty explicitly declared that he rejected justification, however de facto he himself did so in his written work, when he argued in favor of cooperation based on conditions favorable for communication. As Habermas has argued, one needs to do that to plan to expand the circle of members of a community and in order to think about greater solidarity with others. Habermas said that if "something is 'true' if and only if it is recognized as justified 'by us' because it is good 'for us', there is no rational motive for expanding the circle of members. No reason exists."[117] This is why Habermas has desired to defend the formal conditions that are necessary for communication. He has argued that "the universal discourse of an unbounded community of interpretation" is "unavoidably assumed" by anybody and "all participants must de facto accept them [the presuppositions of communication] whenever they assert or deny the truth of a statement."[118] In other words, as Rorty said, Habermas thinks "that the demand to maximize the size of the community is already, so to speak, built into communicative action."[119] Rorty responded that we can only rely on our culture and that we have no "natural" ground to stand on when we defend the communicative approach and our democratic politics against the opponents of dialogue. He argued that democratic politics cannot destroy the intellectual bases of dogmatism, totalitarianism, or authoritarianism, because he did not think that, for example, dogmatism has an "intellectual basis." We should abandon the hope that philosophy can stand above politics, that philosophy can find "politically neutral premises, premises which can be justified to anybody, from which to infer an obligation to pursue democratic politics."[120] He did not think that philosophy can be politically neutral and at the same time relevant. In consequence, democratic principles are just one kind among others. He believed that this is the right course that will allow us to be more inclusivist and that "there is nothing to be gotten right or wrong here. At this level of abstraction, concepts such as truth, rationality, and maturity are up for grabs. The only thing that matters is which way of reshaping them will, in the long run, make them more useful for democratic politics."[121] When responding to Habermas, Rorty also said that "we do not treat each with respect because we are rational. Rather, 'rationality' is, in our culture, one of our names for our habit of listening to the other side—treating most of our interlocutors with proper respect. There is no faculty called 'reason' which tells us to listen to the other side (tells the slave-owner to listen to the slave, or the Nazi to listen to the Jew). Rather, there are social virtues called 'conversability,' 'decency,' 'respect for others,' 'toleration,' and the like."[122]

Proceduralist Deliberative Politics

For Rorty, listening to the other side is crucial, and so is reaching a consensus that we should be more inclusivist. But this is also what Habermas cares about. For Habermas it is important to reach agreement, which can be achieved in the course of numerous communicative expressions of rational forming of political will, on the basis of forms of argumentation that allow talking about the presence of proceduralist deliberative politics. In this proceduralist politics, based on discourse theory, the formation of the will of democratic citizens rests not on previously established ethical beliefs but on the rules of communication enabling better argumentation, and on the procedures providing the processes of reaching understanding with clarity. Habermas wrote, "According to this proceduralist view, practical reason withdraws from universal human rights, or from the concrete ethical substance of a specific community, into the rules of discourse and forms of argumentation. In the final analysis, the normative content arises from the very structure of communicative actions."[123] In formulating his proceduralist view, Habermas has used some elements of the liberal view (the pursuit of compromises between conflicting interests, fairness provided for with the right to vote) and of the republican view (the formation of will present in the form of ethicopolitical discourse, the processes of negotiation based on understanding among all citizens), and combined them in the concept of the ideal procedure of negotiating and making decisions.[124] This ideal procedure, which "establishes a network of pragmatic considerations, compromises, and discourses of self-understanding and of justice, grounds the presumption that reasonable or fair results are obtained insofar as the flow of relevant information and its proper handling have not been obstructed."[125] Being the base for deliberative politics, the ideal procedure can lead to success, but that success depends not "on a collective acting citizenry but on the institutionalization of the corresponding procedures and conditions of communication, as well as on the interplay of institutionalized deliberative processes with informally developed public opinions."[126] Thus in Habermas's perspective, the democratic deliberative process has normative features, but there are more of them than in the case of the liberal model, though still fewer than in the case of the republican one. It includes elements of both views and combines them in a novel way; it integrates them in the concept of an ideal procedure for deliberation and decision making. Thus, we are faced with a concept of democracy that does not have to "represent the whole in a system of constitutional norms mechanically regulating the interplay of powers and interests in accordance with the market model," nor "operate with the notion of a social whole centered in the state and imagined as a goal-oriented subject writ large."[127] It is oriented toward a process of political opinion- and will-formation, conceiving the constitutional principles as giving an answer regarding institutionalized form of the process. In light of that, Habermas added, "Discourse theory altogether jettisons certain premises of the *philosophy of consciousness*. These premises either invite us to ascribe the praxis of civic self-determination to one encompassing macro-subject or they have us apply the rule of law to many isolated private subjects. The former approach views the citizenry as a collective actor that reflects the whole and acts for it; in the latter, individual actors function as dependent variables in system processes that move along blindly."[128] Habermas has rejected limitation of the self-realization of an individual and the idea of some collective entity deciding on what is the best for him or her. He is aware of the fact that what is favorable for effective control over social relations does not necessarily need to be favorable for human freedom.[129] He is aware that what is conducive to the effective management of social relations does not necessarily favor human freedom. Thus, he has advocated individual freedom and self-realization, and the need for specifying the code of social conduct, and accordingly, a specific vision of a society, different from the existing one, due to its connection with the procedural concept of democracy: "With the discourse ethic as a guiding thread, we can indeed develop the formal idea of a society in which all potentially important decision-making processes are linked to institutionalised forms of discursive will-formation."[130] Habermas highlighted that the proposed concept of democracy rests on the formal idea of a society that is not an ideal of life-form. Such an ideal, as it has already been said, does not exist. According to Habermas, the idea of a dignified life cannot be derived from the formal concept of reason that we are provided with, together with the decentered understanding of the world in the modern era. We can only outline specific formal conditions for a reasonable life. They enable—through the process of linguistic communication—identification and interpretation of problems occurring within our decentered society. In the course of this process, a "popular sovereignty"—as Habermas put it—and "communicative power" come into existence. This power results from "the interactions between legally institutionalized will-formation and culturally mobilized publics. The latter for their part find a basis in the associations of a civil society quite distinct from both state and economy alike."[131] The emerging sovereignty rests upon democratic procedures. And, as Habermas noted, it is proper institutionalization of these procedures and conditions for communication that determines the pursuit of deliberative politics in accordance with the theory of discourse.[132]

It is largely due to this institutionalization of proper procedures and discourse conditions, about which Habermas has written, that "Romantic intellectuals" like Rorty find in the democratic institutions in which he or she participates the possibility of developing relations with a more considerable number of human beings.[133] As Rorty said, we should only "point out the practical advantages of liberal institutions in allowing individuals and cultures to get along together without intruding on each other's privacy, without meddling with each other's conceptions of good."[134] These democratic political institutions constitute a community that—in Rorty's opinion—is the only goal we need. This community is not a means of realizing a goal: it is the goal itself.[135] The goal is to preserve and improve one's own self, to preserve and improve the civilization. Rorty believed that "it would identify rationality with that effort, rather than with the desire for objectivity."[136] It would not require, then, foundations more solid than mutual loyalty during the realization of this historic goal. According to Rorty, there would be no more questions about human nature, or the goal or meaning of human life. We would rather ask questions about "what we can do so as to get along with each other, how we can arrange things so as to be comfortable with one another, how institutions can be changed so that everyone's right to be understood has a better chance of being gratified."[137] In such an ideal community, in such an ideal society—as Rorty argued—first of all, discussion would be favored, and the discussion on public matters would concern the issues of "how to balance the needs for peace, health, and freedom when conditions require that one of these goals be sacrificed to one of the others, and how to equalize opportunities for self-creation and then leave people alone to use, or neglect, their opportunities."[138] In other words, the discussion would concern the way in which to utilize our freedom and the way in which we should institutionalize proper procedures in order to develop the sense of community within which we would be able to tackle problems by means of communication. Communication in such a community should be undistorted, and it shall be such if there are "democratic political institutions and the conditions for making these institutions function."[139] We need to remember, then, that this "futuristic Romanticism"—of which Rorty's discussion about conflict-free coexistence with each other is full—is, as Rorty himself highlighted, not of much use "until you have established the standard institutions of constitutional democracy" that allow communication thanks to which it would be possible to arrive at a consensus in a democratic way.[140]

For Rorty as for Habermas communication is a key. It is crucial for the "the interplay between democratically institutionalized will-formation and informal opinion-formation," and thus for deliberative politics.[141] Thanks to such institutionalizations of democratic procedure, there appears to be a chance for reasonable outcomes. Habermas has added that "deliberative politics acquires its legitimating force from the discursive structure of an opinion and will-formation that can fulfil its socially integrative function only because citizens expect its results to have a reasonable *quality*."[142] Such discursive structure relies on "*higher-level intersubjectivity* of processes of reaching understanding that take place through democratic procedures or in the communicative network of public spheres."[143]

It should be added that the concept of communication is the basis for Habermas's vision of deliberative democracy, in which the parties communicate, and come to an agreement, based on communication rationality. He called such a vision radical democracy. The occurrence of such radical democracy is crucial for the possibility of a law-abiding state. Habermas has suspected that "in the age of a completely secularised politics, the rule of law cannot be had or maintained without radical democracy." In this democracy, legitimacy of law is guaranteed by the deliberative procedure introduced, the result of which is unknown, because contemporary pluralistic and multicultural societies are unable to develop one substantive ethical basis for themselves. Deliberation refers to a process in which rational, moral, and equal citizens, through multiple acts of communication, exchange arguments with the intention of achieving mutual understanding of their different points of view. It is worth noting here that in his considerations, Habermas has gone further than Rorty and has presented an analyses of different concepts of the political public sphere, or what role the law could play in it. Such analyses are, however, outside of the focus of this book, thus they are not going to be presented here.[144]

On the basis of the aforementioned, it can be said that both philosophers have unanimously acknowledged the worth of democratic institutions and freedom from domination. Moreover, the "kind of politics" that both Habermas and Rorty support has been "proceduralist deliberative politics" based on the institutionalization of proper procedures and creating conditions for free communication, even though they differ on the need to present justifications for making such a choice. We should of course have in mind that Habermas has claimed that if we want to avoid domination, conflict, or violent clashes, "then we *must* engage in a practice of reaching understanding, whose procedures and communicative presuppositions are not at our disposition."[145] Habermas in that regard has said more than Rorty and has argued that argumentative practices are a point of convergence for disputants no matter how diverse they are. He has argued that at least intuitively they can meet to reach an understanding because "in all languages and in every language community, such concepts as truth, rationality, justification, and consensus, even if interpreted differently and applied accordingly to different criteria, play *the same grammatical role*."[146]

Besides mentioned difference, Rorty and Habermas argued that in particular conditions, it is possible to arrive at agreement without coercion. But it must be added that in order for that to happen, it is necessary to satisfy one more condition: responsible usage. And such responsible usage of the sphere of freedom from domination can be an expression of a new understanding of the category of freedom: freedom as responsibility. One small step toward explicating how the perspectives of Rorty and of Habermas could contribute to the development of such a new understanding of freedom will be made in the next part of this volume.

Toward Freedom as Responsibility

The reflections centering around the concept of freedom found in Habermas's and Rorty's work concern both how broadly it should be understood and who should decide on its particular usage. Thus, these considerations correspond to what Isaiah Berlin wrote in "Two Concepts of Liberty." It is worth briefly recalling Berlin's own view to begin our investigation.

Two Concepts of Liberty

In "Two Concepts of Liberty," Berlin wrote about two definitions of freedom and its two meanings:

> The first of these political senses of freedom or liberty (I shall use both words to mean the same), which (following much precedent) I shall call the "negative" sense, is involved in the answer to the question "What is the area within which the subject—a person or a group of persons—is or should be left to do or be what is able to do or be, without interference by other persons?" The second, which I shall call the "positive" sense, is involved in the answer to the question "What, or who, is the source of control or interference that can determine someone to do, or be, this rather than that?"[147]

In the case of the negative understanding of freedom, being free means that no one interferes in our own business. Freedom thus understood is synonymous with "freedom *from*": from interference in our actions. The larger the sphere of noninterference, the fuller is our freedom. Berlin noted that people should be allowed to live their lives the way they wish. Should that not happen—as Berlin wrote, referring to Mill—"civilisation cannot advance; the truth will not, for lack of a free market in ideas, come to light; there will be no scope for spontaneity, originality, genius, for mental energy, for moral courage."[148] However, the freedom that he wrote about should not be unlimited. We need to surrender some of our freedom in order to retain the rest. We cannot be completely free, for we will begin to inhibit the freedom of others in the name of our own freedom, or the other way around. The problem is then to determine how vast the sphere of freedom should be.

The abovementioned problem can be analyzed from yet another perspective. Berlin argued that devotees of freedom presume "that there ought to exist a certain minimum area of personal freedom which must on no account be violated; for if it is overstepped, the individual will find himself in an area too narrow for even that minimum development of his natural faculties which alone makes it possible to pursue, and even to conceive, the various ends which men hold good or right or sacred."[149] What is this minimum? We will find a definite answer not in Berlin's writings but in referencing the tradition of liberal thought within which the freedom of conscience, speech, opinion, and property is protected.

Additionally, in "Two Concepts of Liberty," Berlin also discussed how concepts of freedom derive directly from beliefs concerning the self, the person, or the human being. He added that the definitions of "human being" and of "freedom" can be manipulated, depending on one's needs.[150] And this manipulation as well as the threat it poses occur together with the arrival of those that believe they "know better." Then the questions "Who is to decide what I am to be and what I am allowed and not allowed to do?" and "Who controls me?" become of great importance. Trying to answer them, and not concentrating on "What am I allowed to be and what am I allowed to do?," is a manifestation of the "positive" sense of freedom.

Due to the above division, Berlin pointed to an important issue: "The freedom which consists in being one's own master, and the freedom which consists in both being prevented from choosing as I do by other men, may, on the face of it, seem concepts at no great logical distance from each other—no more than negative and positive ways of saying much the same thing."[151] But there is a difference between them: it results from the fact that "negative" and "positive" concepts of freedom developed in different historical directions. It may be explained by the metaphor of self-governance beginning to live a life of its own.[152] As a result, considerations concerning being one's own master have changed into considerations in terms of the categories of "higher" and "lower" human nature, as well as into constituting the conviction that one has to live up to the former, "true" nature. And thus, there has appeared the concept of true "self," transcendent and sovereign supervisor, as opposed to the empirical tangle of desires and passions that are to be leashed and repressed. Today, as Berlin observed, this concept can be understood as "something wider than the individual (as the term is normally understood), as a social 'whole' of which the individual is an element or aspect: a tribe, a race, a Church, a State [...]. This entity is then identified as being the 'true' self which, by imposing its collective, or 'organic', single will upon its reluctant 'members', achieves its own, and therefore their, 'higher' freedom."¹⁵³ The pursuit of this "higher nature" and "higher freedom" is believed to justify coercion or violence used in the name of interest that is not recognized by all.¹⁵⁴

The thus understood "positive" concept of freedom—"freedom to"—to act in the only right way—appears to the adherents of the "negative" concept as a "specious disguise for brutal tyranny."¹⁵⁵ It is perceived as such by Berlin, but also by Rorty and by Habermas, who oppose subjugating our culture to absolute truths and deem the fully rational form of life a utopia.¹⁵⁶ Undoubtedly, they would agree with Berlin that

> [o]ne belief, more than any other, is responsible for the slaughter of individuals on the altars of the great historical ideals—justice or progress or the happiness of future generations, or the sacred mission or emancipation of a nation or race or class, or even liberty itself, which demands the sacrifice of individuals for the freedom of society. This is the belief that somewhere, in the past or in the future, in divine revelation or in the mind of an individual thinker, in the pronouncements of history or science, or in the simple heart of an uncorrupted good man, there is a final solution.¹⁵⁷

Rorty—Against the "Positive" Version of Freedom

Rorty, just like Berlin, recognized the threat connected with the pursuit and imposition of one right way of thinking and acting. He was against anyone being granted the right to determine the best code of conduct for us all, referring to some kind of truth about human beings. Since he understood human subjectivity as "a contingent product of contingently existing forces" lacking a center, he could not accept the existence of universal human nature.¹⁵⁸ He believed that we are not able to distinguish some sort of central, ahistorical, noncontingent core within ourselves and use it for justifying certain political settlements and social institutions. We cannot treat it as a reference point for solutions in the public sphere.

Accordingly, Rorty did not agree with enforcing onto us what it is. Rorty considered all voices concerning human nature or our common core private ways of describing the world, means of individual self-creation that should take place in the private sphere, and not in the public. For it may lead us to a vision of "creating a new kind of human being," just like the one we were faced with in the case of Hitler or Mao Zedong.¹⁵⁹ In Rorty's opinion, the intellectuals' desire for their own selves to serve as a model for other human beings is what leads to their attitude toward politics becoming antiliberal. When they begin to think that "human beings have a moral duty to achieve the same inner autonomy as he himself has achieved, then he begins to think about political and social changes which will help them do so. Then he may begin to think that he has a moral duty to bring about these changes, whether his fellow citizens want them or not."[160] Such an attitude poses a significant threat to the freedom of an individual. Therefore, Rorty concluded, "The compromise advocated in this book amounts to saying: *Privatize* the [...] attempt at authenticity and purity, in order to prevent yourself from slipping into a political attitude which will lead you to think that there is some social goal more important than avoiding cruelty."[161] Rorty wished to avoid such "slippage." Accordingly, he found the longing for total revolution and the demand for our institutions to embody our autonomy as a symptom of nostalgia that among the citizens of liberal democracy should be restricted to their private lives. Rorty also tried to rid us of the arguments of all those believing they know what "higher freedom" is when he argued that looking for the public and political equivalent for autonomy that we find, for instance, in Nietzsche's or Foucault's thought, cannot be embodied by social institutions. For autonomy is not something, as he emphasized, "which all human beings have within them and which society can release by ceasing to repress them."[162] Moreover, in his opinion, autonomy is not something that everyone aspires to; the overwhelming majority follows the "beaten tracks," thinks and acts in ways they have been socialized. It is intellectuals that pursue "constructing themselves anew," describing themselves in new ways, making attempts at their self-creation. These attempts, however, are made only by some, and they are successful only in some cases.[163]

Common Moral Convictions

Rorty opposed using "universalistic notions like 'the nature of the self' or 'our essential humanity' as fulcrums for criticism of social institutions or common moral convictions."[164] He wrote that "we have to give up the idea that there are unconditional, transcultural moral obligations, obligations rooted in an unchanging, ahistorical, human nature" characteristic of our community, in which moral rules depend upon the moral identity of its members.[165] With the above in mind, Rorty tried to refute the claims of some of his critics that social practices and institutions shall not survive without a traditional basis comprising transcultural and transhistorical concepts of "rationality" and "morality." He opposed them, for he did not agree that "unless the younger generation has the same attachment to firm moral principles as we have [...] the struggle for human freedom and human decency will be over" or that "unless there is something absolute, something which shares God's implacable refusal to yield to human weakness, we have no reason to go on resisting evil."[166] As a pragmatist, he believed that the unshaken moral rules to which his opponents refer are simply "abbreviations of old practices" that have become popularized, certain models of behavior that have been approved of, and collections of "the habits of the ancestors whom we most admire."[167] And he did not worry that he was not able to present any historical basis for his moral judgments, which, in his opinion, stem from emotions and conventions.[168]

Beyond Truth—Advocating Pluralism

Rorty believed that his critics must be inconsolable because of the increasing number of voices advocating departing from such categories as human nature and ceasing to pursue "ultimate solutions."[169] The knowledge that it is impossible, not only in practice but as a rule, to arrive at clear and certain answers can, as Berlin observed, drive into madness those that search for one all-embracing system guaranteed to last for all eternity. He knew that the desire for something more is a deep and incurable metaphysical need. The desire for a guarantee that, as Berlin wrote, "our values are eternal and secure in some objective heaven is perhaps only a craving for the certainties of childhood or the absolute values of our primitive past."[170] It is important that at the same time he noted that this longing may be disastrous. He argued that the desire "to allow it to determine one's practice is a symptom of an equally deep, and more dangerous, moral and political immaturity."[171] For what he deemed mature is being aware of the fact that "principles are not less sacred because their duration cannot be guaranteed" and that they can be unshakably supported even though we are aware of their relativity.[172] And this is, in his opinion, the characteristic of a civilized human being.[173]

Berlin advocated pluralism, about which he said, "[W]ith the measure of 'negative' liberty that it entails, [it] seems to me a truer and more humane ideal than the goals of those who seek in the great disciplined, authoritarian structures the ideal of 'positive' self-mastery by classes, or people, or the whole of mankind."[174] Rorty and Habermas have shared similar opinions; they have been well aware of the fact that in the context of plurality, it is difficult to talk about some constant and unchangeable center.[175]

Decentered Vision of the World

What we are faced with is, then, as Habermas has claimed, a "decentered" vision of the world. This lack of a center, however, does not need to pose a threat for constructing individual or group identities. Habermas sees decentralization as the opportunity for further rationalization of societies, and not as a threat to it. In his view, it may serve to highlight the inner dependencies between the structures of visions of the world (culture, society, personality), the living world as a context for the processes of reaching understanding and the possibilities of rational control over one's life. Furthermore, in *Theory of Communicative Action*, Habermas wrote, "The more the worldview that furnishes the cultural stock of knowledge is decentered, the less the need for understanding is covered *in advance* by an interpreted lifeworld immune from critique, and the more this need has to be met by the interpretive accomplishments of the participants themselves, that is, by way of risky (because rationally motivated) agreement, the more frequently we can expect rational action orientations."[176] Thus, the rational orientation of action is possible thanks to the processes of communication, even in spite of the plurality of beliefs and interests: "The action-coordinating role of processes of reaching understanding, which proceed by means of the criticism of validity-claims, does not conflict therefore with the pluralism of life-forms and interest. The fact that modern societies are differentiated in terms of life-forms and interest-positions, and are becoming increasingly differentiated, is a fact which does not put action oriented to reaching understanding out of service."[177] Thus, it can be said that due to the advancing differentiation of life-forms and sets of interests, the process of communication continues and must continue, and it is accompanied by the awareness of the impossibility of arriving at stable and unchangeable solutions. Our only point of support is the shaky grounds of rationally motivated understanding.[178] In other words, we need to accept the necessity for constant verification of our beliefs and of the rightness of our actions in the world of contingency characterized by ceaseless changes. Living in such a decentered world requires our constant willingness to engage in dialogue on points of dispute. It is possible by way of unceasing questioning and the ability of rational argumentation to allow us to arrive at agreement.

The only thing we can do in such a world is not to cease to make the effort to arrive at agreement, thanks to which we will be able to tackle the arising problems. The thinker who exemplifies a person constantly struggling with such problems, living in the shadow of contingency—a civilized human being, as Berlin would put it—is Habermas. He himself has written that these problems belong to his own history and may be troublesome, but in the end, when we find a solution, we can feel genuinely happy.[179] As he has highlighted, there is a theme in his thought, a kind of fundamental intuition:

> The motivating thought concerns the reconciliation of a modernity which has fallen apart, the idea that without surrendering the differentiation that modernity has made possible in the cultural, the social and economic spheres, one can find forms of living together in which autonomy and dependence can truly enter into a non-antagonistic relation, that one can walk tall in a collectivity that does not have the dubious quality of backward-looking substantial forms of community.
>
> The intuition springs from the sphere of relations with others; it aims at experiences of undisturbed intersubjectivity. These are more fragile than anything that history has up till now brought forth in the way of structures of communication—an ever more dense and finely woven web of intersubjective relations that nevertheless make possible a relation between freedom and dependency that can only be imagined with interactive models. Wherever these ideas appear [...] they are always ideas of felicitous interaction, of reciprocity and distance, of separation and of successful, unspoiled nearness, of vulnerability and complementary caution. All of these images of protection, openness and compassion, of submission and resistance, rise out of a horizon of experience, of [...] "friendly living together". This kind of friendliness does not exclude conflict, rather it implies those human forms through which one can survive conflicts.[180]

It has been Habermas's intuition, then, that by relying on communicative processes it is possible to develop such social relations that shall preserve their original differentiation and shall provide as much space for individual freedom as possible. Despite the differentiation, in his opinion, it is possible, in the course of reaching understanding, to achieve some unity and develop some "dependency," for a relation between freedom and dependency is probable. And it is a result of the ongoing reproduction of cultural knowledge, of belonging to a community and one's own identity.

Reaching Understanding and Reproduction

In the course of reaching understanding, the participants of interaction depend on their cultural knowledge. Together with this process, this knowledge is being reproduced. As a result, the continuity of tradition and coherence of knowledge are ensured. This continuity and coherence can be measured by the rationality of the knowledge recognized as valid. The process of reaching understanding also involves the process of reproducing one's membership in a community; it enables social integration of the lifeworld, and this in turn allows for coordinating communicative actions and ensures the sustainability of group identities. Habermas wrote that "the coordination of actions and the *stabilization of group identities* are measured by the *solidarity* among members."[181] As a result of ongoing interactions, the participants' own identities are also being reproduced. In their course, they are subject to socialization that guarantees that "newly arising situations are connected up with existing situations in the world in the dimension of historical time: it secures for succeeding generations the acquisition of *generalized competences for action* and sees to it that *individual life histories are in harmony with collective forms of life*. Interactive capacities and styles of life are measured by the *responsibility of persons*."[182]

The aforementioned processes of reproduction occurring during everyday communicative practices can be measured by the rationality of the knowledge used, the solidarity of its members, and the accountability and responsibility of particular persons. In their course, the symbolic structures of the lifeworld are reproduced.[183] This takes place due to the maintenance of valid knowledge, of group solidarity, and of educating responsible community members. As far as this is concerned, Habermas said, "Under the functional aspect of *mutual understanding*, communicative action serves to transmit and renew cultural knowledge; under the aspect of *coordinating action*, it serves social integration and the establishment of solidarity; finally, under the aspect of socialization, communicative action serves the formation of personal identities."[184] Communicative action and reaching understanding by its means are, then, immensely important. It is thanks to them that a relation between freedom and dependency is possible. From this perspective, it is possible to talk about freedom only in the context of social relations. The awareness of these relations constitutes our cultural knowledge, the sense of solidarity toward the members of our community, and individual identity resting on the responsibility for functioning within it. A lack of this awareness and of communication is disastrous in all the abovementioned areas and, according to Habermas, eventually has tragic consequences. Resigning from the pursuit of reaching understanding may, in his opinion, lead individuals to conflict, objection, sickness, suicide, crime, or revolution and rioting—as Habermas listed.[185] It can also be added that it usually so happens that individuals choose strategic actions, at the same time affecting, to a great extent, the possibility of reproducing the lifeworld, which, in consequence, is then reproduced in a more or less restricted way, or is reproduced only within a given group, for the relations with others determine strategic actions. Accordingly, it results in what Habermas writes about in his work.

Toward a Compromise

In a decentered world, what we can rely on is communication. It is thanks to communication that we are able to engage in interactions with others, that cultural knowledge is reproduced, community solidarity is created, and the identities of responsible individuals are constructed. Rorty would agree with this assessment. Just like Habermas, he opposed "backward-looking substantial communities." He also acknowledged the importance and role of communication, of creating and extending social solidarity, and of emerging individuals responsible for social interaction. He would also like our communities to depend upon successful interactions contributing to a consensus and to be motivated by openness and compassion. And all this should not be pursued in the name of arriving at one universal truth but at recognition and respect for diversity: "I want to see freely arrived at agreement as agreement on how to accomplish common purposes (e.g., prediction and control of the behavior of atoms or people, equalizing life-chances, decreasing cruelty), but I want to see these common purposes against background of an increasing sense of the radical diversity of private purposes, of the radically poetic character of individual lives, and of the merely poetic foundations of the 'we-consciousness' which lies behind our social institutions."[186] According to Rorty, "[T]his is the question of whether notions like 'unforced agreement' and 'free and open encounter'—descriptions of social situations—can take the place in our moral lives of notions like 'the world', 'the will of God', 'the moral law', 'what our beliefs are trying to represent accurately', and 'what makes our beliefs true.'"[187]

Rorty answered in the affirmative. At the same time, he wanted to suggest how liberals could "convince our society that loyalty to itself is morality enough, and that such loyalty no longer needs an ahistorical backup."[188] Thus, he provided us with a version of morality related to the previously presented arguments of Berlin, according to which moral obligation, moral duties, moral rules, and moral choice are characteristic of a certain community. While doing that, he referenced the thought of Wilfrid Sellars, Michael Oakeshott, and Sigmund Freud. And thus, while writing about the concept of moral duty (or moral obligation), Rorty referred to it as Sellar's "we-intentions"; Sellars identifies "'obligation' with 'intersubjective validity' but lets the range of subjects among whom such validity obtains be smaller than the human race."[189] Sellars regarded moral obligation as real or potential intersubjective consensus within a given group of interlocutors. This consensus was for him only a fortunate product of certain historical circumstances.[190]

Both moral obligation and moral rules are characteristic of a given community. Moral principles, though, as Rorty wrote, referencing Oakeshott, "only have a point insofar as they incorporate tacit reference to a whole range of institutions, practices, and vocabularies of moral and political deliberation."[191] These are not their justifications, but rather reminders or—in other words—"abbreviations for such practices."[192] Oakeshott's views are in this respect related to Rorty's, especially since he claimed that "we can keep the notion of 'morality' just insofar as we can cease to think of morality as the voice of the divine part of ourselves and instead think of it as the voice of ourselves as members of a community, speakers of a common language."[193] Then, as Oakeshott wrote, it is not "a system of general principles nor a code of rules, but a vernacular language."[194] He also added that his language is not "a device for formulating judgments about conduct or for solving so-called moral problems, but a practice in terms of which to think, to choose, to act, and to utter."[195]

In short, morality was regarded by both Sellars and Oakeshott as a contingent product of humans and of societies.[196] This was also Rorty's opinion; he considered the unshaken defense of our moral convictions an issue of identifying ourselves with contingency, and he found the feeling of moral obligation deprived of universality idiosyncratic and historically conditioned, a product of time and accident. Accordingly, he considered moral choice an issue of "compromise between competing goods rather than as a choice between the absolutely right and the absolutely wrong."[197] Thanks to these local and ethnocentric compromises we are able to distinguish between those individual attitudes that we respect and those we damn as fanatical. And we find fanatical the attitudes that can be relativized with respect to common convictions, or a group in relation to which we will feel obliged to justify our identities.

The aforesaid compromise requires, as Rorty wrote, a common language by means of which we will pursue dialogue and due to which we will be able to describe the moral identity that liberal society requires from its citizens.[198] The vocabulary that serves to pursue the ever-changing compromises that construct political discourse should be, in Rorty's opinion, "banal" and characterized by the "intelligibility of the marketplace or the courtroom."[199]

Concrete Values

Advocating universally understood and familiar, "banal" language is undoubtedly synonymous with advocating certain values that are its foundations. These shall not be more real or better than other values.

Rorty thought that thinking about Truth does not facilitate saying something true, thinking about Good does not facilitate acting in a good manner, and thus also thinking about Rationality does not facilitate being rational. These theoretical considerations do not aid our solving of current problems.[200] Thus, he regarded making a statement in our language or consciously arriving at a conviction as an act connected only with a certain context in which it appears, and he claimed that "all that matters for liberal politics is the widely shared conviction that [...] we shall call 'true' or 'good' whatever is the outcome of free discussion."[201] It is worth adding, though, that for a liberal every such result will be "true" or "good" when it does not violate basic values existing within the communicative space of a community. Those values are hidden behind postulates so that the concepts of "free and open encounter" and "freely reached understanding" could take a place in our moral lives. These values include freedom of speech, freedom of action, and equality of parties. They form the foundations for formal conditions crucial for undistorted communication. Acting in accordance with them is necessary for communication to actually occur and to be rational, for argumentation to appear in its course, and for agreement to be achieved.

We also find in Habermas's thought that the equality of interlocutors and the freedom of speech are basic values. In his opinion, an inherently egalitarian relation of reciprocity is inbuilt into communicative action. It is from this relation that meaning of validity claims stems, and this, in turn, leads to the emergence of the ideas of freedom and equality.[202] Habermas considers these validity claims as universal. It is problematic, however, to justify their universality, as was discussed in chapter 2. Questioning that universality, Rorty said, "The increased communication between previously exclusivist communities produced by [...] contingent human developments may gradually *create* universality, but I cannot see any sense in which it recognizes a previously existent universality."[203] Accordingly, it is also problematic to detach validity claims from cultural values. Yet, Habermas has pointed to such a distinction; he has claimed that the standards that guide action have a claim for universality, while cultural values do not. "The circle of intersubjective recognition that forms around cultural values does not yet in any way imply a claim that they would meet with general assent within a culture, not to mention universal assent."[204] Cultural values appear together with validity claims, but they do not transcend, as validity claims do, to the truthfulness and rightness of local limitations: "Cultural values do not count as universal; they are, as the name indicates, located within the horizon of the lifeworld of a specific group or culture. And values can be made plausible only in the context of a particular form of life."[205] It appears that we have to agree with Habermas when he argued that cultural values are characteristic of a given culture and that they can be made plausible in the context of a particular life-form. However, taking into account the above considerations, it seems that it is also the case for validity claims: they should be perceived within the lifeworld corresponding to a given culture. Habermas should then say that claims for truthfulness or rightness demand the right to transcend local limitations, and not that they do transcend them. Taking a step further, it should also be said that the values of equality and freedom that are strictly connected with the very idea of communicative action are characteristic of our community and language. They should not be regarded as something occurring with each and every communicative action, for what we rely on during such an action are the values and language of our culture in a given place, in a given time.

Responsibility to Our Community

Rorty thought that it is impossible to go beyond the relative values of different communities in order to refer to unbiased criteria that could aid us in assessing these values. He maintained that there is no point of view detached from the one of our historical community.[206] Thus, "humanity" was for him a concept belonging to biology rather than to morality, and "there is no human dignity that is not derivative from the dignity of some specific community."[207] Accordingly, he also claimed that liberals "should try to clear themselves of charges of irresponsibility by convincing our society that it need be responsible only to its own traditions, and not to the moral law as well."[208] At yet another point, he said that there is "nothing to be responsible to except persons and actual or possible ahistorical communities."[209] Rorty found such an approach to be an alternative way of explaining the nature of intellectual and moral responsibility.

As Rorty noted, our sense of responsibility within the communities we belong to is, to a great extent, an effect of the process of education. It consists in inciting and supporting the idiosyncratic interests and developing the individual abilities of each and every human being. This is why he said, "People like Habermas and myself cherish both the idea of human fraternity and the goal of universal availability of education. When asked what sort of education we have in mind, we often say that it is an education in critical thinking, in the ability to talk over the pros and cons of any view."[210] The aim of the education is also to "shape people into individuals endowed with a sense of moral responsibility";[211] and as he added, there is nothing wrong with the "networks of power" that take part in the process of achieving this aim.[212]

Habermas has also acknowledged the role of such "shaping" by means of socialization. He has continued to believe that individuals are subject to socialization in the course of interactions during which their group identities are constructed and their actions are coordinated.[213] The former are measured by the solidarity of group members, while the harmonization of individual biographies with collective forms of life is measured by the responsibility of particular persons.[214] This process of constructing and coordinating that occurs in supportive, common action and incessant cooperative effort, as Habermas wrote, "places the responsibility on our shoulders without making us less dependent on 'the luck of the moment.' Connected with this is the modern meaning of humanism, long expressed in the ideas of self-conscious life, of authentic self-realization, and of autonomy—a humanism that is not bent on self-assertion."[215] What we need are responsible individuals aiming at self-realization. However, what we should keep in mind is that Habermas has argued in favor of validity claims and that Rorty "cannot get outside of philosophy without using philosophy to claim validity for his thoughts. Rorty would not be the scrupulous and sensitive, suggestive, and stimulating philosopher that he is were he to insist solely on the rhetorical role of the re-education."[216]

For Us to Be Better

We should be responsible toward our community. Thus, Rorty suggests we reject the intuition according to which there is something external that we are responsible to "in favor of the thought that we might be better than we presently are—in the sense of being better scientific theorists, or citizens, or friends. The backup for this intuition would be the actual or imagined existence of other human beings who were already better (utopian fantasies, or actual experience, of superior individuals or societies). On his account, to be responsible is a matter of what Peirce called 'contrite fallibilism' Rather than of respect for something beyond."[217] In response to the above, we might ask, how could we become better when having as a reference point imagined human beings or real ones that have already become better? Undoubtedly, by doing things better or by having better beliefs. But can we state that some beliefs are better than others? Rorty said that "the ideal of 'the better argument' makes sense only if one can identify a natural, transcendental relation of relevance, which connects propositions with one another so as to form something like Descartes' 'natural order of reason.' Without such a natural order, one can only evaluate arguments by their efficacy in producing agreement among particular persons or groups."[218] At the same time, Rorty claimed that a pragmatist believes his or her opinions are better than those of, for instance, a realist, but he or she does not claim so due to their being in accordance with some nature of things of which he or she has a better perception.[219] In other words, according to Rorty, we are not able to determine whether our position or our beliefs are better than others by maintaining that they are closer to reality. They will be "better" if what we learn today is only an intermediate station on the way to better beliefs: beliefs that will serve our goals.[220] These beliefs will be better if they are more useful. But what would they be useful for? As Rorty argued, pragmatists, when faced with such a question, have nothing to say apart from "useful for creating a better future." When asked, in what respects is it to be better?, they can only say something as ambiguous as that this future is to include more of what we deem good and less of what we deem bad. But what do they understand as "good"? All that Rorty can answer is, after Whiteman, "diversity and freedom" or, after Dewey, "progress."[221] In short, our beliefs will be better and will lead to a better future if they are related to recognizing such categories as diversity, freedom, and development.

Undoubtedly, according to Habermas, it can also be said that we shall become better. He has also maintained that there are better ways of speaking and acting, thanks to the formation of our beliefs by better argumentation in the course of cooperative action. He wrote that "*all* arguments, be they related to questions of law and morality or to scientific hypotheses or to works of art, require the *same* basic form of organization, which subordinates the eristic means to the end of developing intersubjective conviction by the force of the better argument."[222]

According to Habermas, it is cooperative action that should lead to achieving a rationally motivated understanding or—in other words—constituting a consensus that shall be based on "authority of the better argument."[223] Such a consensus achieved in the course of argumentation is, in his opinion, possible, for he has affirmed that in everyday life no one would exchange moral arguments if they intuitively did not "start from the strong presupposition that a grounded consensus could in principle be achieved among those involved."[224]

Just like Habermas, Rorty also advocated for the possibility of arriving at consensus. He believed that it is possible to use "better arguments" as long as they are related to the categories of freedom, equality, and growth of individuals, which are supported by our community. Finally, he also asserted that it is possible to justify new beliefs and desires.[225] What we need for such justification is, according to Habermas, creating appropriate conditions for undistorted communication. This communication would allow its participants to, as Habermas argued, realize particular possibilities of a better and less threatened life, according to their own needs and judgment, and out of their own initiative.[226] According to Habermas, the aim would be not only to arrive at what everyone would deem a better life but also to arrive at a life that would be "less threatened." Would Rorty also agree? Would he support and justify those of the "new beliefs" that can be, in his opinion, justified, and that concern a "less threatened life"?[227]

Not to Hurt

On the basis of Rorty's argument that any result of a free discussion can be referred to as "true" or "good," it can be presumed that it is not important what the results of such a discussion are, and that for a liberal the essential issue is simply to ensure freedom of speech. Thus, in such an approach, it is important that some sort of agreement can appear as a consequence of dialogue and argumentation used in light of commonly shared values of freedom of speech and equality of parties. But would Rorty agree that a result of a free discussion can be called as "good" and "true" if the discussion would be concluded with the conviction that it is right to hurt others, and that it is necessary to go from words to action"? As a liberal, he would not agree, since for him it is not only free discussion but also everything that is settled in its course that is a value in itself. For a liberal like Rorty, the worst thing we can do is hurt. He believed that we should make our societies more sensitive to human suffering. It is with human sensitivity and imagination that he hopes to improve human relations. It is they that make moral progress possible.[228] He was thus in consensus with Habermas, who also continues to believe that compassion, care, devotion, and openness result in forms of humanity thanks to which it is possible to survive conflicts.[229] And all this may, in his opinion, occur in our decentered culture, "a deepened culture of reflection and feeling" in which we make the cooperative effort "to moderate, abolish, or present the suffering of vulnerable creatures."[230] In short, we will not refer to all the results of discussion as "good" or "true"; we will regard as such the result that remains in accordance with the rule guiding the actions of liberals such as Habermas or Rorty.

They would answer in the negative to the question of whether while arriving at agreement we should be guided only by better descriptions, better arguments, and expressions connected with certain validity claims partaking in the process of communication. In both Rorty's and Habermas's opinion, it is not only new languages, or new ways of speaking and better arguments, that are to lead us to agreement; it is also openness, compassion, sensitivity, and a refusal to hurt others.[231] In other words, we should be guided by better arguments, and some may even be perceived as intrinsically better in light of the suffering of vulnerable people, but we should be also guided by sensitivity that will allow us to be closer to such people and not only to build theories of the use of reason.

Resigning from Violence

"Resigning" from violence and hurting others will be possible once we realize that others suffer the same way we do. This sort of awareness shall make it possible to identify with other human beings. It is through this identification with those "their ancestors had not been able to identify with—people of different religions, people on the other side of the world, people who initially seem disturbingly different from 'us'" that moral progress and extending our community to include those who used to be outside it is possible.[232] In such an extended community, "immoral action" means indeed "the sort of thing *we* don't do."[233] In liberal community, what counts as such an action is precisely causing others to suffer.

The very fact of recognizing suffering and the awareness of its existence do not suffice, though. What is also important is being conscious of the consequences of our actions that may cause such suffering. According to Rorty, it is different descriptions of suffering, such as we find expressed in books, that should help us to become less cruel.[234] They are essential for liberal hope and for the problem of reconciling this kind of hope with private irony. They can be divided, as Rorty divided them, into those entailing social practices and institutions, and those aiding us in recognizing the consequences of our private idiosyncrasies. Books of the former kind make us see how social practices that we deem natural make us cruel; books of the latter kind, however, show us "how our attempts at autonomy, our private obsessions with the achievement of a certain sort of perfection, may make us oblivious to the pain and humiliation we are causing."[235]

Toward Responsible Freedom

Having discussed a number of important issues, it is worth observing that freedom, which is an essential element constituting liberal society, is, from Rorty's and Habermas's perspectives, "delimited." We may say that freedom is a compromise, and are just like our societies, which—as Rorty wrote—"are not quasi-persons, they are (at their liberal, social democratic best) compromises between persons."[236] It is a compromise concerning formal rules necessary for the existence of our societies as well as the values that underlie them. We may become better when we are all equal, when freedom of speech and freedom of action, among other things, are regarded as values. These freedoms are necessary for undistorted communication to occur, for full self-realization of individuals to be possible, and for better beliefs and better actions to take place.

From a pragmatic perspective, the category of freedom is then connected with attention paid to the key values of our community. Advocating them is strictly connected with responsibility for acting in accordance with them. Although the category of freedom is "delimited" by other values vital for a liberal community that we are responsible for, it should not be described as "freedom from responsibility." Such a description could suggest that there is some basic, primary freedom. However, such a freedom does not exist. It is not an entity to be arrived at or possessed. Neither is it a natural, essential, or inherent feature of human beings. Accordingly, there is no freedom that should be restricted in order for it not to threaten the freedom of others, or that should be to some extent "sacrificed" in the name of social or communal good. Freedom is a cultural value, and specifying the scope of its validity depends upon social context. Our choice of this value and the fact that we understand it are related to the kind of society we function in and we were brought up in. From a pragmatic perspective, this upbringing consists in highlighting the practical benefits of procuring freedom of speech and action, both for an individual, as well as for a community. Here, the process of education comprises pointing to the benefits for both parties and to the reciprocal nonreducible dependencies that occur between them. Due to education, we discover that the scope of possible benefits shall depend on responsible action in the sphere of individual and communal relations. Individual development and social progress are also dependent upon responsibly following the formal rules that underlie our interactions. This development and this progress are, in other words, subject to responsibility for our actions and for the consequences these actions can have with respect to others, as well as for whether they limit the freedom of others and whether they make others feel humiliated or hurt.[237] In the case of our actions, it is necessary then to recognize others that may be affected by them in a given way. In short, what we are faced with within the pragmatic perspective is education oriented toward responsible freedom. Such a perspective provides the opportunity for developing a new understanding of freedom: "freedom as responsibility."

The next step to be taken is connected with a return to Dewey's thought; he pointed out that it is impossible to clearly distinguish between the individual and the community. He claimed, as it has already been said, that as long as the old constructs and old habits prevail, the idea of harmony between individual thoughts and desires and social reality will be perceived through the category of adjustment. However, if we relinquish the old ways of thinking, we will have the opportunity to recognize the forces that influence us and the networks of relations that we are involved in.[238] Then we will no longer think with categories of "my freedom" versus "their freedom." We will understand freedom as a category referring to both the individual and the community, which should be advocated for and respected in the name of communal and individual good. Such freedom we could call freedom as responsibility. It will require following formal rules based on the values of freedom of speech and equality, providing us all with the equal opportunity for growth and undistorted communication. It will be possible to tread in this direction within present pragmatist thought as long as it is also accompanied, inter alia, by a departure from the old sharp division into the private and the public spheres, which in the end, as was said earlier, Rorty was not an adherent of, as he saw that both spheres influence each other. Both spheres influence and interact with each other, and Habermas is also aware of that situation. That is why he wrote that "a sphere for a privately autonomous pursuit of individual interests and life plans cannot be delimited *once and for all* from the public sphere oriented to 'the common wealth,' any more than the 'intimate sphere' can be delimited like a core inside the wider private sphere."[239] Of course this does not mean that we should not protect private and civic autonomy, what the system of rights simultaneously calls for from us. Habermas has argued that these two forms of autonomy coexist and presuppose each other, but the issue as to how the private and public spheres and powers and responsibilities within them must be divided depends on the circumstances and social context.

To Take Responsibility

As Berlin observed, "[T]he necessity of choosing between absolute claims is then an inescapable characteristic of the human condition. This gives its value to freedom."[240] Such a choice is not easy, for it is made with the awareness of the relativity of our beliefs. However, despite their relativity, we can still firmly hold them. And this is, as Berlin argued, quoting the words of Joseph A. Schumpeter, "what [has] distinguished a civilized man from a barbarian."[241] It is somewhat analogous to Rorty's view, when he said that "the liberal societies of our century have produced more and more people who are able to recognize the contingency of the vocabulary in which they state their highest hopes—the contingency of their own consciences—and yet they have remained faithful to those consciences."[242] He referred to that as "freedom as the recognition of contingency."[243]

This kind of freedom is related to the presence of a diversity of voices, which, however, does not mean that it is related to the presence of chaos. Within this diversity, there still exists, as Habermas has claimed, the possibility of preserving the unity of reason. For, despite the diversity, it is possible to reach understanding by means of dialogue. Still, the contents that we express should not be treated as constant and unchangeable, as reflecting some sort of truth. Assuming such an attitude is not easy, since it requires both parties to treat their beliefs as open to doubt and discussion.[244]

For both Rorty and Habermas, the aforesaid dialogue is possible due to specific values. These values delimit the relations between what is important for individuals and their obligations toward the community. The fact that there is nothing constant in ourselves that would connect us with others does not mean, as Rorty believed, that we have no obligations. Rorty suggested we recognize all the diverse attitudes in the private sphere (often contradictory with respect to each other) as related to the same moral obligations in the public sphere. Therefore, he claimed that his position was underpinned with a certain moral intention according to which, due to our disenchantment with the world, we, the residents of a liberal state, become "more pragmatic, more tolerant, more liberal."[245] Habermas has expressed himself in a similar manner; he sees in decentration the possibility of our becoming more tolerant, more supportive, more rational, and more open to dialogue and more responsible for it.[246]

Turning to particular values means delimiting "negative" freedom and determining its extent. Therefore, Rorty and Habermas would agree with Berlin that "[t]he extent of a man's, or a people's, liberty to choose to live as he or they desire must be weighed against the claims of many other values, of which equality, or justice, or happiness, or security, or public order are perhaps the most obvious examples."[247] They take into consideration these "other values" and, at the same time, they make the effort of delimiting the "negative" conception of freedom. Those opposing its positive understanding by those who would like to impose on us "freedom of a higher order," through the use of one or another abstract categories, such as class, race, or nation, advocate pluralism. They believe that only in a pluralistic and decentered world is it possible for a human being to be free. Accordingly, they proceed with the thought of Dewey, according to whom "communal and public disenchantment is the price we pay for individual and private spiritual liberation."[248] This liberation allows us to recognize our responsibility for our own community and its identity, for the values that underlie it, such as freedom of speech or equality, and that are necessary for undistorted communication to occur. This liberation is accompanied by the opportunity for developing an understanding of the concept of freedom as responsibility. This freedom seems necessary for the completion of the aim of liberal societies. This aim is not "to invent or create anything, but simply to make it as easy as possible for people to achieve their wildly different private ends without hurting each other."[249] Conditions favorable for this shall be created when our culture is based on dialogue instead of coercion, and when we resign from violence.

Therefore, it can be said that the idea that Rorty and also Habermas have is to make us better in relation to one another, more responsible toward one another, more conscious of our actions and their consequences, as well as help us become more aware of the fact that while pursuing them, we may make mistakes, and our responsibility should consist also in our ability to admit it. We will be better—our deeds will be better—if we support undistorted relations between people and educate members of our community to be responsible, aiming at a greater consensus by means of new, more accurate descriptions and more successful argumentation.[250] These will be more effective by bringing us and others more of a benefit, for it is only in this way that it is possible to benefit in the future and to procure further individual and social growth.

Toward Liberal Utopia

In light of the last three sections in this chapter, it has become clear that there is not much difference between Rorty and Habermas as far as the foundations of their sociopolitical thoughts, recognizing the value of democratic institution, or understanding the category of freedom from domination are concerned. Then it can be asked, where is this supposed to lead us? The answer is, to liberal utopias based on social hope and liberal society in which philosophers and philosophy have a very particular role to play.

Social Hope

Rorty thought that the metaphysical and epistemological method of establishing our habits, traditional in the West, is no longer effective, or—in other words—it no longer fulfills its function. Accordingly, he suggested that we should assume that our sense of community is based only upon common hope in cooperation with one another.[251] In order to sustain this hope, the members of a modern society "need to be able to tell themselves a story about how things might get better."[252] He also added that these societies are dependent on "the existence of reasonably concrete, optimistic, and plausible political scenarios."[253]

Recently, social hope, as Rorty himself observed, has become much more difficult. Because of the tragic events of World War II, it is more difficult to provide a convincing account of this sort, and "as the century has darkened we find it less and less possible to imagine getting out of our present trap."[254] And even our wealthy democracies do not provide many reasons for optimism. Our culture of liberal democracies "has become very conscious of its capacity for murderous intolerance and thereby perhaps more wary of intolerance, more sensitive to the desirability of diversity, than any other of which we have record,"[255] and they still create the opportunities for self-criticism and reforms.

Fortunately, in Rorty's opinion, contemporary liberal society contains some institutions for self-repair. This is why Rorty regarded "Mill's suggestion that governments devote themselves to optimizing the balance between leaving people's private lives alone and preventing suffering" as, to a great extent, the final statement in the conceptual revolution within Western social and political thought.[256] Rorty believed that Dewey's generation was perhaps the last to fully trust in the future; he himself, though, did not lose all hope, and he presented his liberal utopia as an alternative, as a new vocabulary that would serve to tackle the current difficulties.[257] Good pragmatists, the inhabitants of this utopia "would not think of themselves as realizing the true nature of humanity [...], but simply as being happier and freer, leading richer lives, than the inhabitants of previous human communities."[258] They would become a part of their community as "equal inhabitants of a paradise of individuals in which everybody has the right to be understood but nobody has the right to rule,"[259] for we are all human beings, all fallible and all determined by history, and none of us can exercise a right to a higher status than that of an interlocutor in a conversation.[260]

Habermas has also not given up on this hope; he has presented a utopian project of a perfect communicative community underpinned with the values of freedom of speech and equality of parties participating in dialogue. Despite the numerous works that assert that utopian enthusiasm has been exhausted, in his *Theory of Communicative Action*, Habermas undertook to present a utopia and reconstructed the concept of reason in the context of communicative rationality, thereby pointing out that it is possible to rationalize worldviews. However, he has not been surprised by the fact that those talking of the "exhaustion" gain more and more adherents.[261] In his opinion, there are some firm reasons for the popularity of that view. Previous social utopias, strictly connected with historical thinking, being an element of political disputes since the nineteenth century, aroused realistic expectations. They depicted scientific and technological progress as an opportunity for rational control over nature and society. However, these expectations were undermined by numerous historical incidents of a destructive nature that would not have been possible on such a scale but for science and technology.[262] The forces from which modernity derived its consciousness and its utopian visions of a better future did not bring, in consequence, autonomy, but dependency; instead of emancipation, repression emerged; irrationality replaced rationality; and the new forces of production contributed to destruction instead of construction.[263] Habermas wrote about these high hopes and their loss in what follows:

> Eighteenth-century philosophers still hoped to develop unflinchingly the objectivating sciences, universalistic foundations of morality and law, and art, each according to its own inner logic, and *at the same time* to free the cognitive potentials built up in this way from their esoteric forms and to use them in practice, that is, in rationally shaping the conditions of daily life. Enlighteners cast in the mold of Condorcet had the extravagant expectation that the arts and sciences would promote not only the control of natural forces, but also interpretations of the world and of ourselves, moral progress, the justice of social institutions, even the happiness of humankind. The twentieth century has left little of this optimism intact.[264]

Further on, he said, "There is a difference of opinion as to whether we should hold fast to the intentions of the Enlightenment [...] or should give up the project of modernity as lost."[265] Habermas has not resigned from this project and has deemed the opinions of the early postmodern era premature. For him, we still argue in the same way about potential directions for further development, and the utopian energies of the past are still present: there is still some will to create programs that could improve the current situation. Of course, he has continued to think that we have witnessed a departure from the illusions of designing definite and all-embracing scenarios of social and political life-forms. For instance, in his opinion, the utopia that emerged around the potential of a labor-based society has been exhausted. However, he does not think that we should abandon modernity and its project altogether. We should rather "learn from the aberrations which have accompanied the project of modernity and from the mistakes of those extravagant proposals of sublation."[266]

Thus, we see that both Habermas and Rorty have insisted on maintaining some of the "intentions" of the Enlightenment. They do it insofar as the categories of communicative rationality—understood as tolerant and undistorted communication—and of progress are crucial for their thought. Both have claimed that it is still possible and beneficial to create new utopias. At the same time, they have recognized that it is impossible to discover a better, ideal form of life. In this respect, the difference between them is not so significant, and it could actually be said that it rests on the fact that one of them explicitly declared that he did not abandon the project of modernity and continues to pursue it, albeit not in the way his predecessors did, while the other one pursued it but called it something different.

Liberal Society

Habermas, just like Rorty, has advocated for the idea of a liberal society and has put forward concrete proposals concerning the nature of our institutions and values that ought to motivate our actions. Rorty rightly recognized these similarities, pointing to their convergent understanding of rationality. Rorty, like Habermas, related this rationality to "the political and moral virtues of rich, tolerant societies and the superior sort of audiences which become possible in such societies."[267] What is also characteristic of the two philosophers is their views on anxiety and distrust of liberal democracy. Rorty wrote that Habermasians and pragmatists cannot comprehend how it is possible for one to say that "May 1968 refutes the doctrine of parliamentary liberalism." In their opinion, this doctrine may be overthrown only by a better idea of how to organize a society. They believe that "no event—not even Auschwitz—can show that we should cease to work for a given utopia. Only another, more persuasive, utopia can do that."[268]

Accordingly, Rorty, as a pragmatist, disagreed with those that treat some events as evidence for the "bankruptcy" of the long-term efforts at social reform.[269] He did not interpret political, economic, or technological incidents as symptoms of shifts in the course of history, thereby questioning the idea of a "universal history of humanity." He said that "a willingness to see these as probably just more of the same old familiar vicissitudes is required to take the Dewey-Habermas line, to persist in using notions like 'persuasion rather than force' and 'consensus' to state one's political goals."²⁷⁰ Rorty took this line and thus became a part of the intellectual tradition of possible progress that—as he believed—would lead to "a planetwide democracy, a society in which torture, or the closing down of a university or a newspaper, on the other side of the world is as much a cause for outrage as when it happens at home."²⁷¹ Therefore, he insisted on a vision of a utopian future in which "cultural traditions will have ceased to have an influence on political decisions. In politics there will be only one tradition: that of constant vigilance against the predictable attempts by the rich and strong to take advantage of the poor and weak."²⁷² In such a future, society shall be as multicultural as it is today, and it shall affirm its identity not in the course of systematic processes of excluding others, but it shall draw it from "its willingness to enlarge its imagination and merge with other groups, other human possibilities, so as to form the barely imaginable, cosmopolitan society of the future."²⁷³ It is worth noticing that by taking this line and writing about "joining with other groups" and about the possibility of "one tradition," Rorty converged with the motivation that underlies Habermas's thinking, that is, the reconciliation of a torn-apart era of modernity and the idea "that without surrendering the differentiation that modernity has made possible in the cultural, the social and economic spheres, one can find forms of living together in which autonomy and dependency can truly enter into a non-antagonistic relation [...] that one can walk tall in a collectivity."²⁷⁴ This dignity (or walking tall) would rest upon such values of our community as freedom and equality; and it is thanks to acting in accordance with them that progress would be possible.

Communication and Complications

Both Rorty and Habermas have claimed that in order to talk about progress related to social reforms, releasing the potential of reason and rationalization of the lifeworld, or the ongoing improvement of the situation of the West, it is necessary for a certain condition to be satisfied, that is, unconstrained dialogue—undistorted communication—to emerge between the members of a given community and between the communities. Such a communication shall create unity between them as long as they resign from the use of violence against one another. The history of humanity, as Rorty wrote, "will be a universal history just in proportion to the amount of free consensus among human beings which is attained."²⁷⁵

It is obvious that Rorty advocated the idea of undistorted communication. We need to add, though, that he had doubts as to whether it is possible to communicate and to arrive at a consensus in any situation.[276] He believed that we do not have to respond to each and every argument by referring to the categories within which it has been presented: "Accommodation and tolerance must stop short of a willingness to work within any vocabulary that one's interlocutor wishes to use, to take seriously any topic that he puts forward for discussion. To take this view is of a piece with dropping the idea that a single moral vocabulary and a single set of moral beliefs are appropriate for every human community everywhere."[277] According to Rorty, avoiding discussion on, for example, what people should be like is not an expression of overt disregard for the spirit of accommodation and tolerance, so significant in democracy. He simply wanted to point out that "human beings are center less networks of beliefs and desires."[278] Since there is no center, the only thing that we can do is recognize the fact that we have different vocabularies and different views dependent upon our historical situation. These vocabularies do not have to correspond to one another "to make possible agreement about political topics, or even profitable discussion of such topics."[279] And Rorty added that he seems to be "as provincial and contextualist as the Nazi teachers who made their students read *Der Sturmer*, the only difference is that I serve a better cause. I come from a better province."[280] He believed that he is morally superior by belonging to this "better province," but those who do not "are no less coherent in their use of language."[281]

What is more, there are people who, in his opinion, are not sensible enough to cooperate, and there is no way of convincing them to do so. In such a situation, "we can only say 'Sorry, we cannot work with you.'"[282] Rorty also thought we should say to these people:

> There are credentials for admission to our democratic society, credentials which we liberals have been making more stringent by doing our best to excommunicate racists, male chauvinists, homophobes, and the like. You have to be *educated* in order to be a citizen of our society, a participant in our conversation, someone with whom we can envisage merging our horizons. So we are going to go right on trying to discredit you in the eyes of your children, trying to strip your fundamentalist religious community of dignity, trying to make your views seem silly rather than discussable. We are not so inclusivist as to tolerate intolerance such as yours.[283]

In light of that retort, it is clear that he believed that we should give up on the attempt to enlarge everyone's moral identity, "and settle for working out a modus vivendi—one which may involve the threat, or even the use, of force.[284]

As Rorty observed, Habermas has continued to believe that it is possible to do more in the above case. In *Theory of Communicative Action*, Habermas indicated that it is thanks to communicative rationality related to universal validity claims that a successful cooperation and communication in general are possible.[285] In seeking for understanding, parties involved have to refer to validity claims, because by their means they are able to position their claims in the three concepts of the world they presumed at the beginning of their discussion: objective, social, and subjective.[286] Habermas has claimed that these are essential elements of the theory of communicative action in order to highlight that language has the potential of reason that may be manifested in communicative action aiming at arriving at agreement or—in other words—that we may talk of rational contents of the structures of reaching understanding. In Habermas's opinion, these structures, which he refers to as "anthropologically deep-seated," are observable when we pursue the analysis describing "structures of action and structures of mutual understanding that are found in the intuitive knowledge of competent members of modern societies."[287] We are faced with this "intuitive knowledge possessed by subjects capable of speech and action, a knowledge which the growing child has to learn in order to be able to use it in communicative action as an adult" when we try to answer the question of "how a use of language oriented to reaching understanding is possible."[288] It is thanks to the process of education that it is possible to develop such a level of awareness that allows for successful cooperation and communication. Here, Habermas began with the trivial assumption "that subjects capable of speech and action cannot help but learn."[289] These processes contribute to better cooperation and understanding, better communication and integration.

However, Habermas has realized that a society is subject to evolution and that "higher levels of integration cannot be established in social evolution until legal institutions develop in which moral consciousness on the conventional, and then postconventional levels is embodied."[290] Thus, he has not maintained that all of a sudden everyone shall be equally rational, reflective, and critical, and that they shall act according to rules enabling undistorted communication. He has been well aware of the fact that the process of communication is connected with certain problems, that "the growing pressure for rationality that a problematic lifeworld exerts upon the mechanism of mutual understanding increases the need for achieved consensus, and this increases the expenditure of interpretive energies and the risk of dissensus."[291] We are faced with such a situation when, for example, a validity claim is not recognized as problematic, and an utterance is not questioned. Habermas has pointed to the possibility of such a situation: "In a therapeutic dialogue directed to self-reflection, some important presuppositions for discourse in the strict sense are not fulfilled: the validity claim is not regarded as problematic from the start; the patient does not take up a hypothetical attitude toward what is said; on his side, it is by no means the case that all motives except that of cooperatively seeking the truth are put out of play; the relations between the partners in dialogue are not symmetrical, and so on."[292] In light of the above, a skeptic should say that this is characteristic of everyday relations, that their participants do not presuppose and do not respect the conditions that are necessary for free and undistorted communication. Accordingly, they do not assume a hypothetical attitude toward, for example, what is being said. Habermas has argued that such a situation can be changed by means of the healing power of conversation and the persuasive power of arguments used in its course. He wrote that he would like "to take account of these special circumstances by always speaking of 'critique' instead of 'discourse' when arguments are employed in situations in which participants need not presuppose that the conditions for speech free of external and internal constraints are fulfilled."[293]

Linguistic communication free from external and internal coercion shall not occur unless agreement—or rejection—of the content of an articulated statement is related to assuming an attitude toward the validity claim in question. If the claim is an arbitrary request—an "imperative"—and is not normatively rooted, agreement or its lack, acceptance or disapproval, shall result in following or opposing the will of the other. Then we will be faced with a power claim instead of a validity claim. The difference between them rests on the fact that "yes/no positions on validity claims mean that the healer agrees or does not agree with a criticizable expression and does so *in light of reasons or grounds*; such positions are the expression of *insight or understanding*."[294] Power claims, however, have to be based on "supplementary sanctions" in order to be successful.[295]

A skeptic, taking into account the presence of power claims, should ask once again: is it actually possible to provide conditions for undistorted communication so that no elements of coercion or repression—that we can talk of in a situation when one of the parties is more privileged than the other—appear within it? Undoubtedly, it is difficult to satisfy the condition of equality of parties participating in dialogue. As Rorty said, "[T]he principal source of conflict between human communities is the belief that I have no reason to justify my beliefs to you, and none in finding out what alternative beliefs you may have, because you are, for example, an infidel, a foreigner, a woman, a child, a slave."[296] For even if the participants recognize themselves as its equal parties and if they believe that they can agree on certain issues by presenting their points of view, they may not be aware, for example, of how deeply certain convictions and beliefs are planted in them; so deeply that they will not be able to revise them, to be critical toward them. If a consensus is reached in such conditions, it is undoubtedly to be a "false consensus"—a "pseudoconsensus" based upon mistake and illusion. It will consist in the participants of the interaction being mistaken about their own strategic attitude. And all this will take place due to "violations of necessary conditions for processes of consensus formation."[297] The situation is much more evident, of course, when none of the parties of the dialogue is able to support their claim, or when only one party is able to do that, and the other one is but willing to conform. Certainly, in all these cases, it is not possible to talk of undistorted communication.

In accordance with what Habermas himself has been well aware of, that is, that "pure modes of using language are the exception," that "negotiated descriptions of situations, and agreements based on the intersubjective recognition of criticisable validity-claims, are diffuse, fleeting, occasional and fragile," that "communicative acts take on explicitly linguistic forms only in exceptional cases,"[298] a skeptic would say that in most situations—if not in each of them—we are faced with "critique" and not "discourse." That is why Rorty said, "I have no use for the claim that any communicative action contains a claim to universal validity, because this so-called 'presupposition' seems to us to have no role to play in the explanation of linguistic behaviour."[299] He also said, "I think that the *only* ideal presupposed by discourse is that of being able to justify your beliefs to a *competent* audience."[300] Habermas would undoubtedly respond that even if it is so in most cases, it does not need to be so, and he would point to the "healing power of conversation" and the "persuasive power of arguments used in its course" that contribute to the emergence of undistorted communication. And he would add, with all certainty, that we should not lose hope. But is this enough?

On Role of Philosophy and Philosophers, and on Responsibility

Due to the fact that there is no "natural" order for justifying one's beliefs and desires, and that "there is no center to the self, then there are only different ways of weaving new candidates for belief and desire into antecedently existing webs of belief and desire."[301] Thus, if a liberal utopia is to ever come into being, it is necessary, in Rorty's opinion, to introduce egalitarian politics into the language of multiple cultural traditions with due calm and patience. It shall be necessary to persuade us to change "our habit of basing political decisions on the difference between people like us, the paradigmatic human beings, and such dubious cases of humanity as foreigners, infidels, untouchables, women."[302] Rorty thought that the role of introducing these new habits of engaging with others should be taken up by philosophers whose "moral concern should be with continuing the conversation of the West, rather than with insisting upon a place for the traditional problems of modern philosophy within that conversation."[303] In its course, they would illuminate the human suffering and oppression that have become ostensibly visible since the French Revolution, and the numerous attempts at implementing its ideals.[304] In Rorty's opinion, they would also be politically useful: just like poets, playwrights, economists, and engineers they would warn against particular projects in particular times, they would persuade people to be free. These philosophers would refer to themselves as "servants of [...] freedom, servants of democracy."[305]

This might seem like a striking claim, after having read Rorty's criticism of the role of philosophy, "that no philosophical thesis, either about contingency or about truth, does anything *decisive* for democratic politics."[306] He did not think that philosophy could do much for democratic politics. Philosophical reflections "can do little more than rearrange previously existent intuitions, rather than creating new ones or erasing old ones."[307] But one has to understand that he criticized a particular kind of philosophy—the one that is looking for truth—and that is why he said that "philosophy should not be the basis for creating political visions—only bad things happen like with Nietzsche and Hitler."[308]

In accordance with the above stated view, Rorty claimed that for both himself and for other pragmatists, "the best hope for philosophy is not to practice Philosophy."[309] When trying to sketch his vision of a liberal utopia, he did not seek its justification outside our context. But Habermas has not sought such justification either, for he has defended the view that modern culture does not need philosophical justification.[310] Therefore, he has written about his utopian project of an ideal communicative community and undistorted intersubjectivity that would involve free and reciprocal recognition of the parties of dialogue and would rest on common and supportive actions, just like Rorty, who described his project as historically rooted in the communicative reason that incited it.[311] Here, philosophy may only highlight the situation in which we "can contribute to our learning to understand the ambivalences that we come up against as just so many appeals to increasing responsibilities within a diminishing range of options."[312] This ever more common attitude of responsibility is to be present in actions consisting in considering the multiplicity of our approaches and interests. As Habermas has observed, this is what the modern sense of humanism is related to, the humanism that has already been expressed in the ideas of self-conscious life, authentic self-realization, and autonomy:

> Given the postmetaphysical thinking characterizing the modern condition, where ontological and theological background assumptions became more and more controversial, practical philosophy has gone on to sacrifice even its substantive content. For, in view of what is now considered as a legitimate pluralism of worldviews, modern philosophical ethics is no longer able to commend particular models for how to lead a good life [...] [and] ethics [...] must confine itself to the more formal aspects of the basic question of who I am and would like to be, and of what is good for me in the long run.[313]

V

POSTSCRIPT

From Dewey to Rorty and Habermas

The Main Themes

This work has focused on the texts of Dewey, Rorty, and Habermas. In order to not take a single step toward either critique or approval that could not be justified by their careful analyses, and to not fall under the sway of other interpretations, this work has presented some of the central threads of the sociopolitical thought of these three philosophers. The aim of this work has not been to deliberate on who is mistaken and to what extent people misinterpret these thinkers, but to present certain issues and problems, reflecting on them and pointing to the potential pragmatist consequences for sociopolitical thought. The aim has been, then, inter alia, to point to what such a perspective can give us today, what possibilities it opens for us. The writing of this work was accompanied by the idea of taking a step forward as far as formulating a clear articulation of present pragmatist thought. For, despite critique, such a message does exist, and we can consider it when proceeding forward in taking certain kinds of action.[1]

In order to recapitulate the contents of this volume, we shall now present the main themes of the sociopolitical thought of Rorty and of Habermas, which shall be juxtaposed with the categories crucial for Dewey's philosophy, so that one can find out that it is indeed possible to talk of a common pragmatist voice.[2] By doing so, we will make good on the promises made in the introduction of this work. Once again, it is a direct reference to the texts that will serve as a basis for further reflection. At the same time, it shall allow us to point to some of the ideas that prove the main intuitions accompanying the process of writing this book; that is, mostly, the intuition that the sociopolitical thought of Rorty and of

Habermas converges to a large extent when we speak about foundations. They both recognize the value of democracy and share an understanding of the category of freedom. Based on their thoughts, it is also possible to present in the future an attempt to work out new understanding of freedom: freedom as responsibility. The main themes that shall be pointed to include the issue of the tasks that philosophy is faced with, the proper attitude toward the categories of truth and freedom, and the nature of democracy, the nature of communication, the possibility of progress, the role of pragmatism, and the importance of utopias.

Philosophy

As has already been said, Rorty and Habermas have hoped that their similar sociopolitical projects will perhaps spread broadly throughout our society and motivate communicative action. As has been demonstrated, these projects, as well as the categories on which they are based, are to a great extent convergent with the central themes of Dewey's sociopolitical thought (discussed in the introduction). They do not rest on any stable and unchanging "philosophical foundations." Rorty and Habermas have treated philosophy the same way Dewey did; Dewey wrote that it can offer us hypotheses that prove valuable only when they make our minds more sensitive to the present.[3] Philosophy thus understood should be, accordingly, more of a method than a theoretical system that takes on different shapes.[4] It should not search for ultimate descriptions of the world or its stable and unchanging elements. As Habermas put it, "Philosophy can no longer refer to the whole of the world, of nature, of history, of society, in the sense of a totalizing knowledge. Theoretical surrogates for worldviews have been devalued, not only by the factual advance of empirical science but even more by the reflective consciousness accompanying it."[5] In consequence, the task of philosophy no longer consists in discovering ultimate knowledge but in criticism toward our values and beliefs.[6] It should investigate whether beliefs and institutions correspond to the existing circumstances and goals that society has created. In *The Need for a Recovery of Philosophy*, Dewey wrote that philosophy "recovers itself when it ceases to be a device for dealing with the problems of philosophers and becomes a method, cultivated by philosophers, for dealing with the problems of men."[7]

This is also what Rorty and Habermas have thought; they have seen philosophy as a tool for facilitating human freedom, equality, and responsibility. As Rorty wrote, the philosophical tradition should be "utilized, as one utilizes a bag of tools."[8] In a situation when its "conceptual instruments" are no longer useful, it is necessary to develop a new one.

It is important for such a tradition to be vital, to be efficacious for our circumstances and to allow for coping with them effectively. As Habermas wrote, "The traditions that survive are only those which change in order to fit new situations."[9] Philosophical traditions that can address normative issues of the just or well-ordered society, as Habermas argued, would not, however, exist without freedom. Philosophy and democracy are both dependent on freedom, apart from the fact that they emerge from the same historical context.[10]

From Truth to Freedom

Rorty and Habermas—just like Dewey—opposed the doctrines of representationalism and the concept of truth as correspondence. They have bade farewell to the hope for acquiring the truth and the philosophy that—as Dewey wrote in *Reconstruction in Philosophy*—"under the cover of communing with an ultimate reality, coped with the values rooted in social traditions."[11] What they have deemed most important is to attempt to reach for the common welfare and happiness of as many people as possible, by presenting the possibility of changing the language, the customs, and the institutions that impede it.[12] They give up creating a metaphysical background and exercise the independence that individuals thus obtain. By doing that, they follow the steps of Dewey, who, as Rorty wrote, "assumed that no good achieved by earlier societies would be worth recapturing if the price were a diminution in our ability to leave people alone, to let them try out their private visions of perfection in peace. He admired the American habit of giving democracy priority over philosophy by asking, about any visions of the meaning of life, 'Would not acting out this vision interfere with the ability of others to work out their own salvation?'"[13] Asking such a question is synonymous with taking into consideration the fact that our actions affect others and that we need to be careful not to limit their freedom and opportunities for self-realization. This is the behavior that Rorty and Habermas have expected of the members of liberal societies. Accordingly, the freedom that they wish for all individuals becomes more specific, inter alia, through the awareness that we are not alone, that we live and act within minorities and within greater communities in which we affect them and they affect us. In other words, individuals need to conceive of this freedom in the context of the community in which it exists, and the community needs to be able to exercise freedom, bearing in mind how important it is for proper individual growth. Without basic freedoms, as Dewey remarked, individuals cannot grow, and society is deprived of what they could contribute.[14] Freedom allows for unconstrained scientific research and for the unconstrained discussion necessary for the proper development and welfare of societies.[15]

The category of growth is of great import to pragmatist thought, for it points to the necessity of creating conditions for individuals to fully realize themselves.[16] These conditions are also crucial for the emergence of understanding in the course of undistorted communication.[17] As far as the aforementioned is concerned, Habermas said, "In contemporary philosophy, wherever coherent argumentation has developed around constant thematic cores—in logic and the theory of science, in the theory of language and meaning, in ethics and action theory, even in aesthetics—interest is directed to the formal conditions of rationality in knowing, in reaching understanding through language, and in acting."[18] These formal conditions, to which our attention is being drawn, include, inter alia, the equality of the parties in dialogue and the freedom of speech. These need to be constantly taken care of, and therefore what Dewey saw as the basis of individual human greatness is—as Rorty rightly observed—our contribution to building social freedom, which is understood in accordance with the tradition of the French Revolution.[19] It is simply "sociopolitical freedom, the sort of freedom found in bourgeois democracies."[20] In order not to negate it, we need to get rid of all the doctrines that prevent us from exercising it. In other words, freedom is much more important than any truth. This thought is present in the philosophies of Rorty and of Habermas, but it has also been articulated by Dewey.[21] As Rorty said, "Dewey put a new twist on the idea that if you take care of freedom, truth will take care of itself [...]. He taught us to call 'true' whatever belief results from a free and open encounter of opinions, without asking whether this result agrees with something beyond that encounter."[22] Rorty shared this stance and repeatedly emphasized that we should take care of freedom and then the truth shall take care of itself. It is not important whether we tell the truth, it is important to be free and to speak of what we think is true. As Rorty himself admitted, for him, Dewey remained the original author of the view that it is possible to do without "views about truth save that it is more likely to be obtained in [...] 'free and open encounter' of opinions."[23] Thus, both he and Habermas have conceived of truth in the way Dewey did, that is, as "warranted assertability"[24]: as "a social phenomenon rather than a transaction between 'the knowing subject' and 'reality.'"[25] According to such a perspective, we can call true any stance that has been commonly created and accepted, and the search for objectivity is nothing but pursuing an intersubjective understanding.[26] And as Rorty claimed, such a belief "goes hand in hand with the thesis that no language is more adequate to reality than any other language."[27]

Democracy—One of the Ways

Just like Dewey, Rorty and Habermas have also advocated for liberal democracy, democracy that Dewey and Habermas called a radical one.[28] They have not tried to justify it by referring to something fundamental in the world, so as to show that it is the only right political form. As Habermas wrote, "All attempts at discovering ultimate foundations, in which the intentions of First Philosophy live on, have broken down."[29] In light of that, Rorty pointed out that the difference between him and Habermas has been no difference in practice: "[W]e both have the same utopias in mind, and we both engage in the same sort of democratic politics. So why quibble about whether to call utopian communication practices 'oriented to truth' or not?"[30] In another place he said that "we should be retrospective rather than prospective: inquiry should be driven by concrete fears of regression rather than by abstract hopes of universality."[31] He did not agree with Habermas that "as soon as the concept of truth is eliminated in favour of a context-dependent, epistemic validity-for-us, the normative reference-point [...] that would explain why a proponent should struggle to secure acceptance for '*p*' *beyond the bounds of his own group* is missing."[32] Rorty did not think that there is some higher obligation to go beyond the bounds of our own group, and that is why he said, "I regard it as a fortunate historical accident that we find ourselves in a culture—the high culture of the West in the twentieth century—which is highly sensitized to the need to go beyond such borders. This sensitization is a result of our awareness of the blind cruelty which has resulted from not doing so in the past, and our fear of falling back into barbarism."[33]

What we can, however, talk about when choosing between democracy and totalitarianism is a "moral obligation" and to giving such a notion "a respectable, secular, non-transcendental sense by relativizing it to a historically contingent sense of moral identity."[34] The followers of Dewey, such as Rorty, would like "to praise parliamentary democracy and the welfare state as very good things, but only on the basis of invidious comparisons with suggested concrete alternatives, not on the basis of claims that these institutions are truer to human nature, or more rational, or in better accord with the universal moral law, than feudalism or totalitarianism."[35] However, such an approach faces much criticism. Dewey himself was criticized that his radical democracy is depriving us of the weapons against the enemies of liberalism, not offering us in return anything with which we could reply to the Nazis.[36] In response, Rorty wrote that "it is not clear how to argue for the claim that human beings ought to be liberals rather than fanatics without being driven back on a theory of human nature, on philosophy."[37] Accordingly, we need to presume that liberalism is, alongside fanaticism or totalitarianism, nothing but one of many ways that humans can follow, that it is one of many vocabularies which are there to be used. In the opinion of the pragmatists, it does not make any sense to claim "the *real* vocabulary for describing what's *really* going on."[38] Thus, Rorty believed that no attitude can be privileged, unless we deem "privileged" the attitude that has been shared by a given community in some sort of a special way. Therefore, our attitude, which has been to some extent disseminated, is but one of many ways to conceive of and approach certain issues. In consequence, "the utopian world community envisaged by the Charter of the United Nations and the Helsinki Declaration of Human Rights is no more the destiny of humanity than is an atomic holocaust or the replacement of democratic governments by feuding warlords."[39] And there is also no reason to believe that "the promise of American democracy will find its final fulfillment in America, any more than Roman law reached its fulfillment in the Roman Empire or literary culture its fulfillment in Alexandria."[40]

A lot depends on the circumstances. Things can turn out not the way we wanted them to when another attitude wins more appreciation. As Jean-Paul Sartre noted, some may decide on establishing fascism, while others, cowardly or slack, may allow it.[41] What can we do in such a situation? As Rorty remarked, it is impossible to convince the adherents of totalitarian regimes by means of argumentation, referring to universally accepted premises. It is also pointless to pretend "that a common human nature makes the totalitarians unconsciously hold such premises."[42] What we can do in such a situation is speak out about the advantages of our community and of our way of perceiving the world. All we can do "is to show how the other side looks from our point of view."[43] And this is also the point of view held by Dewey, who would certainly agree with the stance that the value of his philosophy comes down to the value of the life that it advocates. Philosophy should not justify the affiliation to a given community by referring to some ahistorical construct called "reason" or "transcultural rules," but simply present the advantages of this community over others in as much detail as possible. This can be pursued due to discussion: for instance, between those who deem contemporary democratic societies as "hopeless" and those who see them as our only hope with reference to the real problems that we encounter.[44]

Talking about the advantages that our community has over others is important not only during dialogue with other communities but also for our own community and society. For talking about equality, tolerance, or freedom, we arrive at an ever more widespread dissemination of these values. As Rorty noted, society will eventually get used to the fact that "social policy needs no more authority than successful accommodation among individuals, individuals who find themselves heir to the same historical traditions and faced with the same problems. It will be a society that encourages the 'end of ideology', that takes reflexive equilibrium as the only method needed in discussing social policy."[45] It shall be a society that appreciates the wisdom of novels much more than the wisdom of philosophy. The former manifests itself, as Milan Kundera wrote, in the fact that it "does not by nature serve ideological certitudes, it contradicts them."[46] In Rorty's as well as in Habermas's opinion (having in mind his defense of validity claims), the ideological certitudes and the threat of ideologization shall cease to exist once we abandon the idea of universal and absolute foundations, on which our lives supposedly rest. Challenging the idea of a transhistorical, important set of concepts results in a—both in Rorty's and Habermas's, as well as in Dewey's opinion—strengthening, and not weakening, of liberal institutions.[47] Still, this is not all that we need in order to strengthen our values and democratic institutions.

Progress and Free Communication

Pragmatists such as Dewey, Habermas, and Rorty believe that the world in which we live is capable of self-repair and that it allows for progress. And this is what we need. Progress is not understood here as "a matter of a self gradually gaining a more clear and objective perspective on the intrinsic nature of its surroundings, but as a series of experiments, an adventure, in the course of which we are constantly creating new self-descriptions: descriptions which cannot be verified by anything but our descendants' belief in their utility, arrived at in retrospection."[48] Writing in a similar manner, Dewey pointed to the relation between the growth of rationality, which emerges alongside modern science and technology, and the rationality that is synonymous with tolerance. He believed that with time, it will be ever easier to acquire this type of rationality.[49]

This has also been pointed out by Habermas; he believed that rationality becomes pronounced when decentration occurs. As a consequence of this decentration, there emerges a growing need for understanding, which we are no longer granted a priori, but which is created in the course of domination-free communication.[50] Writing in a manner similar to Dewey and Rorty, in *The Theory of Communicative Action*, Habermas reconstructed the conditions necessary for communication, assuming that in everyday communicative practices, socialized individuals cannot avoid using speech in a way that would not be oriented to reaching understanding. Further, he has tried to prove his intuition that they need to be pursued in accordance with a concrete, practical presupposition. According to it, wherever we think what we say, our expressions are accompanied with claims for validity, rightness, and honesty.[51] By pointing, inter alia, to the importance of communicative rationality, Habermas, however, has aimed not at presenting the basic norms of a well-organized society but the formal conditions necessary for creating different visions of what the society could be like. In doing that he followed Dewey, whom he cited in *Between Facts and Norms*: "Majority rule, just as majority rule, is as foolish as its critics charge it with being. But it never is *merely* majority rule. . . . 'The means by which a majority comes to be a majority is the more important thing': antecedent debates, modification of views to meet the opinions of minorities. . . . The essential need, in other words, is the improvement of the methods and conditions of debate, discussion and persuasion."[52] It is thanks to them, the conditions of debate, the formal conditions of communication, important for appearance of Habermas's radical democracy of Dewey's radical democracy, and complying with them, that undistorted communication shall occur, and that it will be possible to cope with the complex situations that make us reach for understanding anew. Alongside widening the space that it encompasses, we will come closer to democracy through freedom of speech, equality, and tolerance for difference, about which Rorty has written.[53] In such a democracy, according to Dewey, free social action is to be inextricably linked with vivid communication.[54]

It needs to be remarked, though, that not everyone would agree with the above. There are also those, like Michel Foucault, who see the contemporary West as a panoptic society, in which rationality, meant as a greater dose of tolerance, is less and less likely to occur.[55] Is it possible to state who is right? Rorty answered that perhaps the forces of Western culture support a panoptic society "in which individuality—and thus rationality—is becoming increasingly impossible."[56] He stressed, however, that he was not convinced that it is the philosophers who are able to decide whether this is what will actually happen. Thus, he wished "to replace the search for universal validity with utopian social hope."[57] This has already been pursued by Dewey. He wanted to replace the knowledge of "the will of God," "the moral law," "the laws of history," or "scientific facts" with a utopian dream of an ideal, decent, and civilized society.[58] In spite of a certain rhetoric of hope, Dewey's philosophy, as Rorty noted, did not teach "that the combination of American institutions and the scientific method would produce the Good Life for Man. Its attitude was best expressed by Sidney Hook in an essay called *Pragmatism and the Tragic Sense of Life*, which closes by saying, 'Pragmatism [. . .] is the theory and practice of enlarging human freedom in a precarious and tragic world by the arts of intelligent social control. It may be a lost cause. I do not know of a better one.'"[59] The project of facilitating this human freedom is undertaken not only by Dewey, whose works are filled with the nineteenth-century faith in human history as a story of the growth of human freedom, but also by Rorty and Habermas, whose philosophies, like Dewey's, are dominated by the question, what sort of philosophical vocabulary and approach would serve human-freedom best?[60] As Rorty wrote, Habermas is here "the contemporary philosopher who most resembles Dewey—not only in doctrine but in his attitude toward his society, and in the role which he has played in the day-to-day, nitty-gritty political debates of his time. Like Dewey, Habermas's thought is dominated by [...] the conviction that the modern industrialized technological world is not hopeless, but, on the contrary, capable of continual self-improvement."[61] This improvement can happen thanks to the growth of solidarity based on freedom, pluralism, and diversity, and thanks to overcoming the sharp dichotomy between individual and community.[62]

Pragmatism and Utopias

In light of the above, we may ask how to briefly define pragmatism and its role. An answer can be found in Rorty's words: "In the form John Dewey gave it, pragmatism is a philosophy tailored to the needs of political liberalism, a way of making political liberalism look good to persons with philosophical tastes. It provides a rationale for nonideological, compromising, reformist muddling-through."[63] According to Rorty, then, pragmatism can be conceived of as "clearing the ground for democratic politics," and not a justification for it.[64] It needs to be treated as drawing attention to certain possibilities that are in front of us, and not as something that is ultimate enough to be a solid argument.[65] Of course, the pragmatists believe that their words are true, but that does not mean that anyone is obliged to think alike. All they do is present their point of view, from which they preach, among other things, that philosophy can be revived by giving up the dualisms that modern science, as well as the more flexible and open kinds of sociopolitical institutions, have worked to make obsolete.[66] Also, they have presented the view that the obligation of being rational is nothing but an obligation of being willing to converse and of being tolerant, of also taking into consideration the point of view of others.[67]

This type of pragmatism is a core interest for both Rorty and Habermas. Habermas has argued that only pragmatism builds upon the spirit of radical democracy in a convincing way. Habermas has written that pragmatism comes up "as the only approach that embraces modernity in its most radical forms, and acknowledges its contingencies, without sacrificing the very purpose of Western philosophy—namely to try out explanations of who we are and who we would like to be, as individuals, as members of our communities."[68] Habermas has undertaken this radical project, and while he acknowledges all different kinds of contingencies, he has presented a utopian vision of who we—as individuals, as members of communities, and as human beings—could be. He has continued to believe that what we need are precisely such utopian images, for without them nothing will change. It is they that facilitate the innovativeness of social activism and allow us to effectively release the energy hidden in social movements.[69]

Rorty also believed that these utopian visions and redescriptions are what we actually need. What we dispose of are metaphors and imaginings. The conviction that these cannot be ignored is, in his opinion, in accordance with "Habermas's and Dewey's claim that rationality is a matter of finding agreement among human beings, rather than of finding ideas which are adequate to reality."[70] The answer to the question of what to do in order to make humans live in harmony not with nature but with other humans who have different visions of who they are and who they should be, to make them tolerate the different visions of their own selves, remains problematic. Rorty claimed that society should be glued together by the conviction that tolerance toward those who disagree with the presently shared opinions of a culture is the best way to ensure that our descendants know more truths than we do.[71]

Tolerating the aforementioned metaphors and utopias is crucial, according to Rorty, for "redescribing ourselves is the most important thing we can do."[72] Creating them is accompanied with the hope that perhaps one day they shall come true.[73] Of course, the utopias and hopes about which Dewey, Habermas, and Rorty—or anyone else—write will always seem controversial in the eyes of some.[74] But when advocating something questionable, we can still say "[A]t present there is too little justification for believing this, but a world may arise in which it seems just common sense."[75] And even though these redescriptions or, as Habermas has seen them, social theories, are quite abstract, both are convinced that they can make us *more sensitive* to the emerging ambiguities of life. They can open our eyes to the dilemmas that we cannot avoid and for which we need to be prepared.[76] They can also help us to develop an attitude of greater responsibility in an ever more demanding reality. Such great responsibility is required by democracy, and thanks to it, as Dewey argued, we can see a fuller sense of democracy.[77]

CONCLUSION

Aims

The writing of this work was guided by the question, to what extent are the philosophical standpoints of Richard Rorty and Jürgen Habermas—leading modern philosophers—convergent, and to what extent are they divergent? They themselves have often pointed out the general convergence of their work. My aim was to show that the supposed differences between these two philosophers do not appear to be as big as many believe them to be. Such an impression is of course justifiable, for—as it has already been said above—both Rorty and Habermas misinterpret, or even overinterpret, each other's arguments, and then come to the wrong conclusions. They do so, however, only to a certain extent, and only to a certain point. For, as was discussed in chapter3, due to their ongoing dialogue, the gap between them grew ever smaller. The analysis in this chapter was possible after the selected threads, important for demonstration of the basis on which their sociopolitical thought rests, were presented. What was important in the preceding chapters was not only presenting their stances but also preparing the grounds for illuminating how convergent they are in their thought, for further reflection on the consequences of their sociopolitical thought, and especially for answering the question about what kind of politics we need. Those chapters also pointed to the possibility of recognizing in their thought the foundations for developing a new understanding of the category of freedom as responsibility.

In order to present the possible practical meaning for sociopolitical thought of Rorty's and Habermas's thinking, this book has offered a reconstruction of the visions of coexistence that they developed; these are visions that will allow us, as Habermas argued, to upkeep dignity in community. Their proposals are certain projects presenting what would happen if these visions were popularized. They are suggestions of a new vocabulary that would allow us to describe reality via categories that are much more appropriate in light of the aims we designate and the problems we encounter.

At this point, using such expressions as "new vocabulary" or "popularizing" should no longer be surprising, even though they may have seemed so when they first appeared. Just in case, in this conclusion, which covers all of the most important issues touched upon in this text, I will stress once again the sense in which they have been used. At the very end, I shall articulate the answer to Rorty's question quoted in the introduction.

Validity Claims

Another dimension to the aforementioned question that guides this work is whether, in light of Habermas's thought being rooted in pragmatism, we can say that his perspective is convergent with Rorty's. Is Habermas willing to ascribe to his vision of a community the same status Rorty ascribes to his community of solidarity, that is, the status of a specific project that is to come true once it is disseminated? Recapitulating the considerations included in the above chapters, it is worth saying once again, at the very end, that Habermas's ideal communicative community is to come true due to the effective dissemination of the idea of undistorted communication and respect for the formal conditions on which it is to rest, as well as by ongoing historical processes, in the course of which communicative rationality, residing in communicative action, is "revealed." In other words, the process of its realization is influenced not only by our engagement and actions but also by something quite commonplace: that is, validity claims, strictly connected with communicative rationality and constituting Habermas's project. This conviction about the common character of validity claims is what distinguishes him from Rorty.

Therefore, there is a difference between Rorty and Habermas: it concerns universal validity claims. Habermas has continued to affirm that his thought reconciles the fact that validity claims are a characteristic element of our culture and language, and the fact that they have a universal character, that they are something universal as a basic element of formal and procedural properties of justification that—though they are not always institutionalized—are present in all cultures.[1] Rorty could not accept the universality of validity claims, to their transcending the borderlines of the contexts in which they appear and to their universally serving as a formal condition for communication and consensus. He believed that it is possible to do without universal validity claims, and he thought even the idea of them causes more trouble than it is worth.[2] And it is plausible to agree with Rorty in this respect. Habermas's attempts to convince us seem to be insufficient.

It looks like, however, that Habermas has also been aware of this fact. At the end of *Theory of Communicative Action*, he states that it would be necessary to come up with "the test case" advocating the theory of rationality, thanks to which "the modern understanding of the world is to ascertain its own universality."[3] Unfortunately, Habermas, as noted in chapter 2, does not offer us such a "test case." What he does is refer to the works of Ernest Gellner and Robin Horton, and present us with a specific perspective, within which communicative rationality emerges in the course of Occidental rationalization and becomes the key to understanding other forms of rationality. It is not enough, though, and therefore Habermas's arguments are not convincing.[4] It was not convincing for Rorty either, even after the exchange of arguments being published in the volume *Rorty and His Critics*. Still, as far as the conspicuous difference between himself and Habermas was concerned, Rorty stated (as mentioned in chapter 3) that it is not that significant. In other words, the issue of universal validity claims divided Rorty and Habermas, but not to a considerable extent, especially in light of the convergence of the elements of their sociopolitical perspectives analyzed in this book.[5]

Formal Conditions

Despite the aforesaid difference, all the succeeding issues discussed here have affirmed the main intuition that was present during the process of writing this book. Accordingly, in seeking validation for the thesis that it is plausible to talk of a convergence of philosophical perspectives in Rorty and Habermas, it was also important to answer the question whether we can assume that Habermas and Rorty propose a new vocabulary, new rhetoric, and new idea of education aimed at constituting a society in which its members, bound by solidarity, do not long for acontextual and ahistorical truth. Such an intuition has been proven in the course of the analysis of the texts in chapters 1 and 2. For Habermas, there is no substantial, acontextual, and ahistorical truth that we ought to yearn for. He has accepted Rorty's critique of the realistic conceptions of truth as correspondence, and he has adopted, after John Dewey, the idea of truth as "warranted assertability." Habermas, like Rorty, has tried to erase the category of truth from its central place in our culture, and—as he himself has written—has bidden farewell to philosophers' hopes for reaching such a truth. He has not wanted to present any single truth, or any single worldview. He has wished to create a number of minor truths, borrowing from other theories, and he has also tried to present a perspective of his own.

Of course, we should also bear in mind what has been said above: that is, that in Habermas's theory, what is crucial is referring to the common elements inherent in any linguistic communication. However, these idealizing tenets of communicative action, in Habermas's opinion, cannot be considered ideal conditions by which ultimate understanding shall be achieved. Therefore, Habermas has not presented us with any concrete model of the life-form. He has concluded that we do not have any prospects for such forms, and even if they could be realized, it would happen only in the course of cooperative effort, marked by conflict.[6] In other words, he has not proposed any particular form of coexistence; he has claimed, however, that it is possible to point to a different approach in which autonomy and dependence can be in concordance, without renouncing differences as such. He has presented a formal and procedural vision that, once accepted, will enable the particular forms of coexistence to be formulated and discussed. Undoubtedly, he has prioritized certain values, such as the idea of appropriate formal conditions, and in this very respect his proposition is not neutral, but it is a minimum to which we need to agree if we want to create space for any perspective to be presented.

However, as was argued in chapter 3, such a formal and procedural vision is present also in Rorty's perspective. Thus, it is hardly difficult to answer the question whether it is the vision presented by Habermas or the vision presented by Rorty that comprises the form of coexistence for which we strive, consisting in, inter alia, not causing others to suffer. It is to be the vision that emerges while analyzing both Rorty's and Habermas's thought. That said, it is important to remember here that this form of coexistence, if we can use such an expression in light of the above conclusions, is not connected with any ultimate solutions as to how we should live but with acknowledging certain formal and procedural conditions allowing us to arrive at how we should live in given circumstances. Of course, the choice of such a formal and procedural form is rooted in certain values, but, as it has already been said, even our procedures are not free from such roots. In other words, in the course of considerations included in the sections "What Kind of Politics?" and "Toward Freedom as Responsibility" in chapter 4, it has become apparent that we do not need to choose between Rorty's and Habermas's visions, trying to decide which of them would better contribute to the project of realizing liberal ideas and of not causing others to suffer to a fuller extent. The perspectives of the tow are in this respect convergent, and it seems that they can further form the basis for developing the understanding of freedom as responsibility.

Accordingly, it is impossible to actually agree with the stance that Rorty advocated: that there is an inevitable existence of different axiological and ideological systems, hoping to create a fragile agreement between them as to the necessary foundations for the emergence of democratic debate, and that Habermas's approach can be characterized by certainty that it is possible to work out such a common consensus as to the aims chosen if certain conditions, the significance of which he stressed, are satisfied. This is a quite inaccurate account in light of the analysis presented in chapters 1 and 2, as Habermas can be said to be not certain but hopeful; he has acknowledged, just as Rorty did, the differences between axiological and ideological systems. Despite them, though, he has hoped to accomplish a fragile agreement as to the principles of democratic debate, though he has also hoped, just as Rorty did, that the agreement will actually grow less and less fragile. What is more, it is not only the pursuit of common consensus concerning our aims that is important—an issue to which Rorty also pointed—but also the procedures in which both philosophers see a hope for agreement. They offer to us procedures that could aid us in solving ethical, social, and political problems, and that could support our actions aimed at forming the common will. This common will is likely to be formed if we turn toward the concept of communicative rationality that is strictly connected with the necessity for certain formal conditions for undistorted communication.

Arriving at a Consensus

On the basis of the above, we can say then that Rorty's and Habermas's perspectives do not seem as different as some critics claim, and that their utopian projects are, to a great extent, convergent. When characterizing the social projects of both Rorty and Habermas in such a way it is important to bear in mind that they are not based upon any absolute truths. The perspective present in communicative rationality is restricted to presenting formal conditions for communication.[7] These conditions are necessary for undistorted communication, based on free and unconstrained exchange of arguments, to occur. A similar stance was shared by Rorty, who also cared about the free exchange of arguments, and who also pointed to the necessity of meeting certain conditions in order for it to occur. This communication will be possible due to the emergence of appropriate formal conditions, such as freedom of speech and equality of parties, and it shall lead, in his opinion, to understanding, or—in other words—arriving at a consensus, as Habermas would put it.

Rorty, however, also referred to a consensus. We can thus say that arriving at a "consensus" in the course of dialogue is important not only for Habermas but also for Rorty. For example, it is clear that Rorty valued such consensus building when he opposed those who treated certain events as signs of the "bankruptcy" of any long-term efforts to reform society. As presented in chapter 3, he claimed that in order to talk of such efforts, we need to follow Dewey and Habermas and use such phrases as "persuasion" or "consensus" so as to express our political aims. In Rorty's case, this aim is "global democracy" or a moment in politics when there will be only one tradition, consisting in respecting equality, freedom, and difference. In short, both of them care about the emergence of undistorted communication and the space to challenge different views as free and open encounters, for arriving at a consensus of a certain kind, though each of them has given a slightly different framing. For Habermas the ideal consists in common, argument-based agreement, while for Rorty common acceptance would be more than enough, even though it would have to be, in his opinion, rational, that is, a result of rational dialogue.[8]

However, at this point it is important to remember what has been said in chapter 3, that is, that Habermas—unlike Rorty—has continued to believe that in the course of the process of communication, accompanied by us assuming a given attitude, a historical process of a particular kind occurs: it consists in communicative action causing a release of rationality inherent in it and, consequently, putting an end to the archaic core of rationality. In other words, "the release of a potential for reason embedded in communicative action" takes place.[9] It is in this reason that Habermas has desired to discern the common conditions for communication; he has offered a vision of communication based on formal conditions of unconstrained intersubjectivity. He has continued to believe that these structures of unconstrained intersubjectivity contain the conditions necessary for our coercion-free understanding of each other. He has stressed, however, that the theory that wishes to affirm universality, the common character of these structures cannot originate from a transcendental position, cannot transcend the reality of its own reasoning. Its status is purely hypothetical: it has the status of a certain kind of practical hypothesis even though it contains claims to universal validity.[10]

Answering the Main Question

After extensive consideration, we shall now proceed to the very heart of this book. Rorty and Habermas, when they presented their projects, attempted at the same time to approach the problems of the past and the present. Thus, they sought the answer to the question that is of critical importance to us, the significance of which both of them acknowledged.

It is the question that appeared at the very beginning of this volume, voiced through Rorty's words. What can we draw on "at times like that of Auschwitz, when history is in upheaval and traditional institutions and patterns of behaviour are collapsing"?[11] What is the answer? Many wish to draw on something that is beyond history and institutions, something like the humanity we share, like solidarity. But are there any grounds for drawing on these supposedly external sources?

According to Rorty, as presented in chapter 1, when models collapse, there is nothing beyond culture that we can draw on for support. What may serve us as a point of reference are our values and beliefs, and not some one and only truth about the world or humanity. In light of the above, Rorty advocated solidarity with the members of our community as well as all those outside of it. He opposed causing others to suffer and using violence. He preached tolerance for difference and respect for equality for all. However, he became an advocate of all those values not because they are right or true but because he was raised in a liberal society, and because peace and respect for other human beings brings more advantages to individuals and to the society within which they live. Only then are individuals able to grow to a full extent, and the society to utilize what the individuals contribute. And undoubtedly Habermas would also agree to that view, as we can assume on the basis of chapter 2. He also advocated the values of equality, freedom, and difference. Just like Rorty, Habermas latter on has opposed the totalitarian visions of order and the hopes for reaching the truth that would determine our actions forever.

In short, there is no single truth that should accompany us and that could become our sole point of reference. What we may refer to, and what we rely on, are the values of our culture.[12] Is there, however, anything that could aid us in developing our social and political space so that the events that happened in the past do not happen again? Both Habermas and Rorty have answered in the affirmative. Still, Habermas has continued to believe that, as discussed in chapter 2, it is possible to point to the forms of coexistence in which autonomy and dependence can be compatible; it is possible to preserve ones dignity in a community, and without renouncing difference; and it is possible to reach some unity in diversity. The form to which he and Rorty point is a society based upon coercion-free communication.

One of the main intuitions that initiated this work is that Habermas has sought for the possibilities of unity in cultural life. Living in a time of the fear of regression, after the tragic experiences of the war, he tried to find here and there the traces of reason "that binds without unnaming difference, that points out the common and the shared among strangers, without depriving the other of otherness."[13] However, here, the possible unity is not connected with any substantial unity of reason. It is unity not in the theoretical dimension but in the practical one. It is accomplished in the course of communication—acknowledging this communication as a means of solving problematic situations. It is accomplished each time anew, alongside the changing circumstances and the advocating of formal conditions such as freedom of speech and equality of the parties in a dialogue, which are crucial for arriving at a consensus.[14]

Rorty also saw an opportunity for developing such a unity, as we saw in chapters 1 and 3. He claimed that perhaps the time will come when only one tradition will exist in politics and it will consist in respect for equality, difference, and freedom. He believed that returning to such a "Deweyan outlook might leave us in a better position to carry on whatever conversation between nations," and, articulating his thought in more general terms, it would enable us to take a better position in dialogue with other citizens.[15] For that to occur, however, certain additional institutional solutions need to be implemented. Thus, we need an appropriate kind of politics. Habermas and Rorty agreed that it should consist in a proceduralist policy of negotiation, based upon the institutionalization of particular procedures and creating conditions for free communication. Acting on the basis of these procedures may allow for successful coercion-free agreement.[16]

What to Do in Order for It Not to Happen Again?

In order to answer the question of what to do in order for what happened in the past not to happen again, grasping at the same time what has been discussed in this book, we can say—in accordance with Dewey's, Rorty's, and Habermas's thought—that concrete absolute truths should be dethroned from their central place in our culture, and so should the interests accompanying them. This step can be made in the name of the value of freedom. Justification of such a step is purely practical. When a certain truth becomes common, it can so happen that we will disagree with it. When the secret service knocks at our door one night, perhaps it will be that we are innocent. In both cases, our only rescue will consist in the right to speak that it is this way, and not the other, that we have been unjustly accused. Freedom of speech and the right of defense should be at least as important as truth. This freedom and this right should be praised and popularized, for we do not know when they will become our only means of rescue, our only chance for communication or for survival.

Once we recognize the value of freedom of speech, we encounter new possibilities of redescribing the world and creating new metaphors. While using them, we ought to remember, however, that we will always rely on our vocabularies, though sometimes transformed by the "experiences" we gather, by certain "knowledge" we gain about "others." Therefore, it is important to add that we should be cautious, and when using our language to describe the world surrounding us we should not become deaf to the voices of others, not describe them in such a way that would part us from understanding their point of view, which would make it impossible for us to hear their call for help. We need to make sure that our nets made of categories, notions, and values have loose enough meshes for those trapped in them to be able to free themselves as soon as they begin to be tethered or strangled. Only then will it be possible, in the case of an encounter, to arrive at a consensus via linguistic communication, acknowledging the equality of parties and respecting each other's otherness.

It Will Be the Way We Decide

Given what we have written, we may ask, is it only a utopia? Is it likely to ever cease being one? Today, the fear of utopia and utopian change is common. Characterizing a thought as "utopian" is most often used to depreciate its adherents. Moreover, many claim that utopias are of little advantage. That common view, however, according to Judith Shklar, is not a reason for abusing utopias. At the very end of her essay "What Is the Use of Utopia?," Shklar voiced her hope that perhaps they will once again enlighten us.[17] Hopefully, this is to be the result of studying the thought of Dewey, Rorty, and Habermas, even though they do not create utopias that would rest upon any absolute truths but rather point to the necessity of certain formal and institutional conditions, giving each and every individual a chance for growth while being part of a community.[18] What the existence of certain formal and institutional conditions depends on to a great extent is accurately expressed in Jean-Paul Sartre's words quoted by Rorty in *Consequences of Pragmatism*: "In reality, things will be as man has decided they are."[19]

It is to a great extent up to us whether the sociopolitical perspectives of Rorty and Habermas can come true. It depends on the conditions for undistorted communication and on our treating our partners in dialogue as equals, and allowing them to exercise their freedom of speech. For, regardless of whether each instance of linguistic communication contains universal validity claims (as Habermas has continued to believe) or does not (as Rorty believed), undistorted communication shall not occur if "discussion" begins with depreciating one of the parties, if the partners in dialogue are considered as persons of a worse category. In other words, it is the popularization of Dewey's, Habermas', and Rorty's perspectives that determines the emergence of a world in which the Orwellian boot shall not stomp on a human face forever. And when I speak of popularization, I mean the dissemination of those elements of their philosophies that are connected with pointing to the need of existence of conditions for undistorted communication based upon such values as equality of parties in dialogue and based on freedom. This freedom is an element crucial for constituting a liberal society. It is, according to the philosopher's perspective, "specified." It is linked with the necessity of following formal rules.[20] It is respecting rules responsibly that supports individual growth and social progress. Respecting this rules and acting in a responsible way in accordance with this rules will lead to individual growth and social progress. In other words, individual growth and social progress depend on responsibility for our actions and the consequences that they lead to, on whether they will not restrict the freedom of others.[21] In this perspective, freedom is perceived as a category referring to the individual and to the community, both of which should be supported and respected in the name of common and individual good. Such a perspective opens up the possibility of developing a new understanding of freedom: "freedom as responsibility."[22]

It is up to each member of our society to decide whether it is language, and not violence, that is to become our means of communication, whether in a discussion we will treat our partners as our equals and whether we will give them a chance to speak, freely and without constraint.[23] This is why at the very beginning of this work I wrote that the philosophers in question create visions of a better future, hoping that these visions will be disseminated.[24] Perhaps one day the idea of the "Great Community" of the "ideal liberal society" or of the "ideal communicative community" will become ever more common.[25] It could help us in dealing with many of the concrete problems of today. Undoubtedly, this will not happen without our help.[26]

NOTES

Notes to From the Author

1. R. Rorty, "There Is a Crisis Coming," interview by Z. Stanczyk, in *Take Care for Freedom and Truth Will Take Care of Itself: Interviews with Richard Rorty*, ed. E. Mendieta (Stanford University Press, Stanford 2006), 57.

2. The record of this debate is J. Niżnik and T. Sanders, *Debating the State of Philosophy: Habermas, Rorty, and Kolakowski* (Westport, CT: Praeger Publishers, 1996), one of the key materials analyzed when writing this volume.

Notes to the Acknowledgments

1. Many countries are turning toward authoritarian rule today. For an account, see, for example, T. Snyder, *The Road to Unfreedom, Russia, Europe, America* (New York: Tim Duggan Books, 2018) or M. Albright, *Fascism: A Warning* (New York: Harper Collins, 2018).

2. See, for example, J. Gerhards, H. Lengfeld, Z. Ignácz, F. K. Kley, and M. Priem, *European Solidarity in Times of Crisis: Insights from a Thirteen-Country Survey* (New York: Routledge, 2019).

3. See, for example, Y. Mounk, *The People vs. Democracy: Why Our Freedom Is in Danger and How to Save It* (Cambridge, MA: Harvard University Press, 2018); S. Levitsky and D. Ziblatt, *How Democracies Die* (New York: Crown, 2018); T. Piketty, *Capital and Ideology* (Cambridge, MA: Harvard University Press, 2020; H. Landemore, *Open Democracy: Reinventing Popular Rule for the Twenty-First Century* (Princeton, NJ: Princeton University Press, 2020); A. Applebaum, *Twilight of Democracy: The Seductive Lure of Authoritarianism* (New York: Doubleday, 2020).

Introduction

1. Z. Brzeziński, *The Grand Failure: The Birth and Death of Communism in the Twentieth Century* (London: MacDonald, 1989), 7.

2. R. Rorty, *Contingency, Irony, and Solidarity* (Cambridge: Cambridge University Press, 1989), 189.

3. J. Habermas, "The Dialectics of Rationalization," in *Autonomy and Solidarity: Interviews with Jürgen Habermas*, ed. P. Dews (London: Verso, 1992), 125.

4. On the meaning of Auschwitz for Habermas, see J. Habermas, *Between Naturalism and Religion: Philosophical Essays* (Cambridge: Polity Press, 2008), 20. On Habermas being deeply disturbed by Nazism, see also M. G. Specter, *Habermas: An Intellectual Bibliography* (Cambridge: Cambridge University Press, 2010), 148.

5. To clarify, I shall add that I call these projects "utopian" since not only does Rorty call them so in his works, but so does Habermas, for instance, in *Theory of Communicative Action*. In "A Reply to My Critics," he wrote again about communicative rationality, which is crucial for the theory of action: "To be sure, the concept of communicative rationality does contain a utopian perspective"; J. Habermas, "A Reply to My Critics," in *Habermas: Critical Debates*, ed. J. B. Thompson and D. Held, (London: MIT Press, 1982), 227–228. This issue will be touched upon again further on in this work.

6. Some of the problems mentioned are well described by Thomas Piketty, Branco Milanovic, Leif Wenar, Peter Termin, and David Hoffman. See T. Piketty, *The Economics of Inequality* (Cambridge, MA: Belknap Press, 2015); I. Golding, *Divided Nations, Why Global Governance Is Failing and What We Can Do about It* (Oxford: Oxford University Press, 2013); Leif Wenar, *Blood Oil: Tyrants, Violence, and the Rules that Run the World* (Oxford: Oxford University Press, 2017); B. Milanović, *Global Inequality: A New Approach for the Age of Globalization* (Cambridge: Belknap Press, 2018); Peter Termin, *The Vanishing Middle Class: Prejudice and Power in a Dual Economy* (Cambridge, MA: MIT Press, 2018); D. Hoffman, *The Dead Hand: The Untold Story of the Cold War Arms Race and Its Dangerous Legacy* (New York: Doubleday, 2009).

7. On that issue, see, for example, J. Klein, *Politics Lost: How American Democracy Was Trivialized by People Who Think You're Stupid* (New York: Doubleday, 2007).

8. J. Habermas, "Die Krise des Wehlwahrfstaates und die Erschörfung utopischer Energie," in *Die neue Unübersichtlichkeit: Suhrkamp* (Frankfurt: Suhrkamp, 1985), 143.

9. R. Rorty, "Emancipating Our Culture," in Niżnik and Sanders, *Debating the State of Philosophy*, 26.

10. See appendix 3 in Niżnik and Sanders, *Debating the State of Philosophy*, 121.

11. R. Rorty, *Objectivity, Relativism, and Truth: Philosophical Papers I* (Cambridge: Cambridge University Press, 1991), 23.

12. When we read pragmatic philosophy, we can be regularly surprised because, as Susan Haack wrote, "the history of pragmatism is both confusing and disturbing." See S. Haack ed., *Pragmatism Old and New* (Amherst, NY: Prometheus Books, 2006), 18.

13. Some interpreters of Habermas's work are conscious of that. As Richard Posner pointed out, pragmatism in Europe begun to attract Habermas, "who has acknowledged an affinity with the American pragmatists." See R. Posner, "Legal Pragmatism," in *The Range of Pragmatism and the Limits of Philosophy*, ed.

R. Shusterman (Oxford: Blackwell Publishing, 2004), 146. On Habermas being put into the pragmatist camp, see also J. Appleby, L. Hunt, M. Jacob, *Telling the Truth about History* (New York: W. W. Norton, 1994), 284.

14. For more on some of these categories, see M. Aboulafia, M. Orbach Bookman, and C. Kemp, eds., *Habermas and Pragmatism* (London: Routledge, 2002).

15. It is important though to point out that such a distinction is a bit too radical, for American pragmatism has appeared in many variants. For example, the pragmatist philosophy of Charles S. Peirce had a Kantian character.

16. J. Habermas, "A Philosophico-Political Profile," in *Autonomy and Solidarity: Interviews with Jürgen Habermas*, ed. P. Dews (London: Verso, 1992), 148–149. Bracketed ellipses have been used to indicate omissions in quoted text.

17. See "A Philosophico-Political Profile," 148–149.

18. J. Habermas, *Truth and Justification*, ed. Barbara Fultner (Cambridge, MA: The MIT Press, 2003), 1.

19. On Rorty as a postmodernist, see S. Seidman, ed., *The Postmodern Turn: New Perspectives on Social Theory* (Cambridge: Cambridge University Press, 1994). See also S. Sim, *Irony and Crisis: A Critical History of Postmodern Culture* (Cambridge: Icon Books, 2002), 69–72.

20. On Rorty being "still too universalist," see, for example, Terry Eagleton, *The Illusions of Postmodernism* (Oxford: Blackwell Publishing, 1996), 114. On Habermas's departure from universalism, see A. G. Scherer and M. Patzer, "Beyond Universalism and Relativism: Habermas's Contribution to Discourse Ethics and Its Implications for Intercultural Ethics and Organization Theory," in *Philosophy and Organization Theory*, Research in the Sociology of Organizations, vol. 32, ed. H. Tsoukas and R. Chia (Bingley, UK: Emerald Group Publishing Limited, 2011).

21. Habermas held a series of debates with leading philosophers such as Gadamer, Foucault, and Derrida. For more on the arguments exchanged during these debates, see J. Mendelson, "The Habermas-Gadamer Debate," *New German Critique*, no. 18 (Autumn 1979), 44–73; R. Coles, "Communicative Action & Dialogical Ethics: Habermas & Foucault," *Polity* 25, no. 1 (Autumn 1992): 71–94; D. Ingram, "Foucault and Habermas on the Subject of Reason," in *The Cambridge Companion to Foucault*, ed. Gary Gutting (Cambridge: Cambridge University Press, 1994), 215–261; M. Kelly, ed., *Critique and Power: Recasting the Foucault/Habermas Debate* (Cambridge, MA: MIT Press, 1994).

22. Habermas, "Philosophico-Political Profile," 150.

23. J. Habermas, "Modernity: An Unfinished Project," in *Habermas and the Unfinished Project of Modernity*, ed. M. P. d'Entrèves and S. Benhabib (Cambridge, MA: The MIT Press, 1997), 44.

24. See Habermas, "Modernity," 52–53.

25. Rorty, *Contingency, Irony, and Solidarity*, xvi.

26. Rorty wrote, "My position differs from Dewey's mainly in offering a somewhat different account of the relation of natural science to the rest of culture, and in stating the problematic of representationalism vs. antirepresentationalism in terms of words and sentences rather than in terms of ideas and experiences. But I do not see these differences as very great"; Rorty, *Objectivity, Relativism, and Truth*, 16–17.

27. Rorty, *Objectivity, Relativism, and Truth*, 17.

28. For an interesting account of differences between Dewey and Rorty in their understanding of the notion of freedom, see R. Shusterman, "Pragmatism and Liberalism between Dewey and Rorty," in *Political Theory* 22, no. 3 (August 1994): 391–413.

29. Habermas, "Dialectics of Rationalization," 96.

30. John McCumber said that Habermas and Rorty "are not necessarily so very different from one another." See J. McCumber, *Philosophy as Freedom: Derrida, Rorty, Habermas, Foucault* (Bloomington: Indiana University Press, 2000). On that point, see also M. Festenstein, *Pragmatism and the Political Theory from Dewey to Rorty* (Chicago: University of Chicago Press, 1997); R. Bernstein's *Philosophical Profiles: Essays in a Pragmatic Mode* (Philadelphia: University of Pennsylvania Press, 1986); R. Bernstein, *The New Constellation: The Ethical-Political Horizons of Modernity/Postmodernity* (Cambridge, MA: MIT Press, 1991); The work of George Trey on Habermas and Derrida was also very inspirational for me. See G. Trey, *Solidarity and Difference: The Politics of Enlightenment in the Aftermath of Modernity* (New York: SUNY Press, 1998).

31. It is worth noting other attempts to see Rorty and Habermas in dialogue, which are, however, narrower in scope, as in the case of the book by Pierre-Luc Proulx, who focuses on the notion of truth understood by both philosophers or equally engaged in analyzing philosophical positions of both philosophers, as in the case of the book by Barbara Weber, who wants to answer the question of which better serves the goal of building solidarity and protecting human rights: reason or compassion. See P.-L. Proulx, *Réalisme et vérité: Le Débat entre Habermas et Rorty* (Paris: L'Harmattan, 2012); Barbara Weber, *Zwischen Vernunft und Mitgefühl, Jürgen Habermas und Richard Rorty im Dialog über Wahrheit, politische Kultur, und Menschenrechte* (Freiburg: Alber Publisher, 2013).

32. For other introductions to philosophy of Rorty or Habermas, see A. Malachowski, *Richard Rorty* (Princeton, NJ: Princeton University Press, 2002); J. Finlayson, *Habermas: A Very Short Introduction* (Oxford: Oxford University Press, 2005); D. Ingram, *Habermas: Introduction and Analysis* (Ithaca, NY: Cornell University Press, 2010); A. Edgar, *The Philosophy of Habermas* (New York: Routledge, 2014); K. Baynes, *Habermas* (New York: Routledge, 2016).

33. See, for example, Joshua Cohen, who wrote in his "Reflection on Habermas on Democracy," "I will put to the side claims about the bases of democracy in a theory about the nature and competence of reason, and come back to the substance of Habermas's radical account of democracy." See J. Cohen, "Reflection on Habermas on Democracy," *Ratio Juris* 12, no. 4 (December 1999): 387.

34. That is what Joshua Cohen is interested in when he said, "I steer clear of the wider philosophical framework—Habermas's post-metaphysical theory of human reason, communicative action, and argumentation—because I think that political argument should not be made to depend, or presented as dependent on, a philosophical theory about the nature of reason. Philosophical theories about the nature and competence of reason do not provide the common ground for equal citizens that is desirable in public argument in a democracy. An appeal to reason cannot

help us 'get behind' the plurality of competing moral, political, religious, metaphysical outlooks, because the nature and competence of reason is one matter on which such outlooks disagree." Cohen, "Reflection," 386.

35. J. Habermas, *Between Facts and Norms* (Cambridge: Polity Press, 2004), 373.

36. See R. Rorty, "Emancipating Our Culture," in Niżnik and Sanders, *Debating the State of Philosophy*, 28.

37. Rorty, "Emancipating Our Culture," 26.

38. For a preliminary account of such an approach, see, for example, J. T. Kloppenberg, "Democracy and Disenchantment: From Weber and Dewey to Habermas and Rorty," in *The Virtues of Liberalism*, ed. J. T. Kloppenberg (Oxford: Oxford University Press, 1998).

Notes to Chapter I

1. These works were very influential from the very beginning; see C. D. Morris, "Pragmatism and the Crisis of Democracy," in *Public Policy Pamphlets: No. 12*, ed. H. D. Gideonse (Chicago: University of Chicago Press, 1934). For more on that and on Dewey's thought in the wider context of pragmatic philosophy, see I. Sheffler, *Four Pragmatists: A Critical Introduction to Peirce, James, Mead, and Dewey* (London: Routledge & Kegan Paul, 1986).

2. *The Public and Its Problems*; *Individualism, Old and New*; and *Liberalism and Social Action* were published alongside the rest of Dewey's works in *Collected Works of John Dewey, 1882–1953* (Carbondale: Southern Illinois Press, 1991). The collected works are divided into three sections: *The Early Works: 1882–1898* [EW], *The Middle Works: 1899–1924* [MW], and *The Later Works: 1925–1953* [LW].

3. Dewey, *Liberalism and Social Action*, LW 11:27.

4. Dewey, *Individualism*, LW 5:84–85.

5. For more, see J. Campbell, *The Community Reconstructs: The Meaning of Pragmatic Social Thought* (Champaign: University of Illinois Press, 1992).

6. For more on liberal principles, the individual, and enterprise, see C. Anderson, *Pragmatic Liberalism* (Chicago: University of Chicago Press, 1990), 17–45.

7. J. Dewey, *Democracy and Education*, MW 9:105.

8. Dewey, *Individualism*, LW 5:121.

9. Dewey, *Individualism*, LW 5:74.

10. J. Dewey, *Critique of American Civilization*, LW 3:144.

11. J. Dewey, *Philosophy*, LW 5:164.

12. Dewey, *Public and Its Problems*, LW 2:332. Individuals' activities are manifested with their reason and intelligence, which is not their private property but a social creation. See Dewey, *Liberalism*, LW 11:52.

13. Dewey, *Public*, LW 2:328.

14. Robert Westbrook calls Dewey's approach a "hybrid form of liberal-communitarianism"; see R. B. Westbrook, *John Dewey and American Democracy* (Ithaca, NY: Cornell University Press, 1991), 550. Among the followers of Dewey's approach, Westbrook mentions Benjamin Barber, William M. Sullivan, Robert Dahl, Amy Gutmann, and David Held, among others. See, for example, B. Barber, *Strong*

Democracy: Participatory Politics for a New Age (Berkeley: University of California Press, 1984); W. M. Sullivan, *Reconstructing Public Philosophy* (Berkeley: University of California Press, 1982); R. Dahl, *Dilemmas of Pluralist Democracy* (New Haven, CT: Yale University Press, 1982); A. Gutmann, *Democratic Education* (Princeton, NJ: Princeton University Press, 1987); D. Held, *Models of Democracy* (Stanford, CA: Stanford University Press, 1985).

15. Dewey, *Individualism*, LW 5:75. It is important to add that while Dewey was concerned with the value of community, he was not a communitarian. As we saw, he was equally concerned with the value of individual liberty. On that subject, see W. Kymlicka, *Liberalism, Community, and Culture* (Oxford: Clarendon Press, 1989), 209.

16. On how that approach affects the idea of self-realization, see R. J. Roth, *John Dewey and Self-Realization* (Englewood Cliffs, NJ: Prentice-Hall, 1982).

17. J. Dewey, *Quest for Certainty*, LW 4:20. Dewey argued that people have created for themselves a strange dreamworld in which once they do not have a ready-made ideal of good, they do not recognize the need for freeing themselves of present problems; seeDewey, *Human Nature and Conduct*, MW 14:195.

18. J. Dewey, *Experience and Nature*, LW 1:325.

19. Dewey, *Individualism*, LW 5:121.

20. J. Dewey, *Ethics*, LW 7:298–302.

21. J. Dewey, *Creative Democracy—The Task before Us*, LW 14:226–228. For more on individual and cooperation with others, see A. Damico, *Individual and Community: The Social and Political Theory of John Dewey* (Gainesville: University of Florida Press, 1978). For more on democracy as a "culture" of cooperation and communication, see T. M. Alexander, *John Dewey and the Roots of Democratic Imagination*, in *Recovering Pragmatism's Voice: The Classical Tradition, Rorty, and the Philosophy of Communication*, ed. L. Langsdorf and A. R. Smith (New York: SUNY Press, 1995), 152.

22. Dewey, *Democracy Is Radical*, LW 11:299.

23. Michael Sandel nicely considers Dewey's democracy "the political expression of an experimental, pragmatic attitude to the world." See M. J. Sandel, *Public Philosophy: Essays on Morality in Politics* (Cambridge, MA: Harvard University Press, 2005), 188.

24. Dewey, *Liberalism*, LW 11:46.

25. Dewey, *Liberalism*, LW 11:59.

26. Dewey, *Liberalism*, LW 11:298.

27. J. Dewey, *Democracy Is Radical*, LW 11:287.

28. Dewey, *Ethics*, LW 7:227.

29. J. Dewey, *Outlines of Critical Theory of Ethics*, EW 3:322. In Dewey's text, this reflection is written in capital letters.

30. Dewey, *Public*, LW 2:275, 282; Dewey, *Ethics*, LW 7:350.

31. Dewey, *Outlines*, EW 3:320. On that subject, see also J. Campbell, "Dewey's Conception of Community," in *Reading Dewey: Interpretations for a Postmodern Generation*, ed. L. A. Hickman (Bloomington: Indiana University Press, 1998).

32. Dewey, *Public*, LW 2:350.

33. J. Dewey, *Reconstruction in Philosophy and Essays*, MW 12:198.
34. Dewey, *Creative Democracy*, LW 14:227.
35. Dewey, *Ethics*, LW 7:329.
36. Dewey, *Individualism*, LW 5:115.
37. J. Dewey, *Challenge to Liberal Thought*, LW 15:273. Dewey understood science in quite a specific way. Its task is not to uncover the everlasting and absolute truths about reality. For Dewey, science is connected with experimental problem solving, forming hypotheses and verifying them not against some externally existing world but against what we deem right or true at a particular moment.
38. Dewey, *Public*, LW 2:344.
39. Dewey, *Democracy Is Radical*, LW 11:219.
40. Dewey, *Liberalism*, LW 11:40.
41. Dewey, *Democracy and Education*, MW 9:105.
42. Dewey, *Liberalism*, LW 11:44.
43. For more on Dewey and his theory of education, see M. Jay, *The Education of John Dewey: A Biography* (New York: Columbia University Press, 2002); and M. Gordon, "John Dewey's 'Democracy and Education' in an Era of Globalization," *Educational Philosophy and Theory* 48, no. 10 (2016): 977–980. For more on social reform according to Dewey, see T. Hoy, *The Political Philosophy of John Dewey: Towards a Constructive Renewal* (Westport, CT: Praeger, 1998).
44. Dewey, *Democracy and Education*, MW 9:54.
45. Dewey, *Public*, LW 2:365.
46. J. Dewey, *Freedom and Culture*, LW 13:177.
47. Dewey, *Public*, LW 2:329; Dewey, *Individualism*, LW 5:57.
48. J. Dewey, *A Common Faith*, LW 9:57–58. The one that agrees with Dewey is J. J. Stuhr. See J. J. Stuhr, "Dewey's Social and Political Philosophy," in *Reading Dewey*, ed. L. A. Hickman (Bloomington: Indiana University Press, 1998).
49. For such criticism, see, for example, R. Niebuhr, *Moral Man and Immoral Society: A Study in Ethics and Politics* (Louisville, KY: Westminster John Knox Press, 2013); R. Niebuhr, *The Children of Light and the Children of Darkness* (Chicago: University of Chicago Press, Chicago 2011); Charles Dunn Hardie, *Truth and Fallacy in Educational Theory* (Chicago: University Press, 1942). See also Sidney Morgenbesser, *Dewey and His Critics: Essays from the Journal of Philosophy* (New York: The Journal of Philosophy, 1977).
50. Dewey, *Creative Democracy*, LW 14:225.
51. J. Dewey, *The Need for a Recovery of Philosophy*, MW 10:48. The traditional values of liberalism—equity, freedom, and fraternity—are, according to Dewey, but aspects of freedom; they do have a moral dimension. Equality is a basis for self-realization; it means unrestrained participation in the life of a community. Freedom is an element crucial for the growth of individual abilities. Fraternity consists in deliberate participation in the community's relations, defining the direction of social activity that is connected with dialogue and communication; see Dewey, *Public*, LW 2:330.
52. This is the way to overcome alienation or cultural deterioration. On that subject, see F. F. Cruz, *John Dewey's Theory of Community* (New York: Peter Lang, 1987).

53. For other accounts of the return to the thought of Dewey, see *Classical American Pragmatism and Its Contemporary Vitality*, ed., S. B. Rosenthal, C. R. Hausman, and D. R. Anderson (Urbana–Champaign: University of Illinois Press, 1999; J. J. Stuhr, ed., *Classical American Philosophy* (New York: Oxford University Press, 1987). See also J. Margolis, "Dewey in Dialogue with Continental Philosophy," in *Reading Dewey*, ed. L. A. Hickman (Bloomington: Indiana University Press, 1998).

54. In doing such important work, Rorty was sometimes accused of misrepresenting Dewey's thought. See M. Elderidge, *Transforming Experience: John Dewey's Cultural Instrumentalism* (Nashville, TN: Vanderbilt University Press, 1998), 16; H. Joas, *Pragmatism and Social Theory* (Chicago: Chicago University Press, 1993), 258–259; Westbrook, *John Dewey*, 537–552. Rorty was, however, aware of that claim and, as Westbrook pointed out, "Rorty himself sometimes openly admits that his use of 'Deweyan' [Dewey's position] for purposes of self-identification is distorting if taken too literally." Westbrook, *John Dewey*, 539.

55. R. Rorty, *Objectivity, Relativism, and Truth*, 211.

56. Rorty, *Objectivity*, 17.

57. This thought is also "preserved" in the twenty-first century thanks to the scholars that see a great potential in it; see M. K. Williams, "John Dewey in the 21st Century," *Journal of Inquiry & Action in Education* 9, no. 1 (2017): 91–102; R. Bruno-Jofré and J. Schriewer, *The Global Reception of John Dewey's Thought* (London: Routledge International Studies in the Philosophy of Education, 2013).

58. Z. Brzeziński, *The Grand Failure: The Birth and Death of Communism in the Twentieth Century* (London: MacDonald, 1989), 8.

Notes to Chapter II

1. Despite the deep interest in Dewey's philosophy by even such notable philosophers as Alfred North Whitehead, Bertrand Russell, and Hans Reichenbach, Dewey was forgotten about until Rorty renewed interest in his philosophy. For more on Whitehead's, Russell's, and Reichenbach's accounts of Dewey, see P. A. Schilpp, ed., *The Philosophy of John Dewey*, vol. 1. of *The Library of Living Philosophers* (Evanston: Northwestern University, 1939).

2. R. Rorty, "Relativism—Finding and Making," in *Debating the State of Philosophy: Habermas, Rorty, and Kolakowski*, ed. J. Niżnik and T. Sanders (Westport, CT: Praeger, 1996), 32.

3. R. Rorty, *Philosophy and the Mirror of Nature* (Princeton, NJ: Princeton University Press, 1979), 13.

4. For example, R. B. Talisse, "A Pragmatist Critique of Richard Rorty's Hopeless Politics," *Southern Journal of Philosophy* 39 (2001): 611–626; Paul Giladi, "A Critique of Rorty's Conception of Pragmatism," *European Journal of Pragmatism and American Philosophy* 7, no. 2 (2015): 1–16.

5. As an example, see N. Geras, *Solidarity in the Conversation of Humankind: The Ungroundable Liberalism of Richard Rorty* (London: Verso, 1995); R. Bernstein, "One Step Forward, Two Steps Backward: Richard Rorty on Liberal Democracy and Philosophy," *Political Theory* 15, no. 4 (1987): 538–563.

6. Rorty, *Philosophy and the Mirror of Nature*, 12.

7. R. Rorty, "Edukacja i wyzwanie postnowoczesności" [Education and the challenge of postmodernity], trans. L. Witkowski, in *Spory o edukację: Dylematy i kontrowersje we współczesnych pedagogikach* [Debates on education: Dilemmas and controversies in contemporary pedagogy], ed. Z. Kwieciński and L. Witkowski (Warsaw: Instytut Badań Edukacyjnych, 1993), 99–100. The text was originally delivered by Rorty during a seminar conducted by Professor Zbigniew Kwieciński and coorganized by Professor Lech Witkowski on June 6, 1992, at Nicolaus Copernicus University. Further on in the text, he wrote that what is deemed a vivid intellectual option is to differ across communities, depending on their traditions. And these traditions are what they are because of past conflicts over power.

8. For more on the rejection of "Truth" in the wider context of postmodern philosophy, see M. A. Diaconu, "Truth and Knowledge in Postmodernism," *Social and Behavioral Sciences* 137 (July 2014): 165–169.

9. R. Rorty, *Objectivity, Relativism, and Truth: Philosophical Papers I* (Cambridge: Cambridge University Press, 1991), 193.

10. R. Rorty, *Truth and Progress: Philosophical Papers III* (Cambridge: Cambridge University Press, 1998), 45.

11. See R. Rorty, *Contingency, Irony, and Solidarity* (Cambridge: Cambridge University Press, 1989), 8.

12. See Rorty, *Objectivity*, 110.

13. R. Rorty, "Wstęp do polskiego wydania esejów Stanleya Fisha" [Introduction to the Polish edition of Stanley Fish's essays], in *Stanley Fish: Interpretacja, retoryka, polityka: Eseje wybrane* [Stanley Fish: Interpretation, rhetoric, politics: Selected essays], trans. and ed. A. Szahaj (Kraków, Poland: Universitas, 2002), 8.

14. Rorty, *Contingency*, 86.

15. Rorty, *Edukacja i wyzwanie*, 102.

16. Rorty, *Philosophy and the Mirror of Nature*, 9–10.

17. Rorty, *Contingency*, 40.

18. Rorty, *Objectivity*, 212.

19. R. Rorty, *Consequences of Pragmatism: Essays, 1972–1980* (Minneapolis: University of Minnesota Press, 1982), 167.

20. Rorty, *Objectivity*, 15.

21. Rorty, *Objectivity*, 16.

22. Rorty, *Objectivity*, 218.

23. See Rorty, *Edukacja i wyzwanie*, 101.

24. R. Rorty, "Foucault, Dewey, Nietzsche," *Raritan* 9, no. 4 (Spring 1990): 5.

25. The problem has also been recognized by Matthew T. Jones. See M. T. Jones , "Rorty's Post-Foundational Liberalism: Progress or the Status Quo?" August 11, 2013, https://ssrn.com/abstract=2308651.

26. J. Habermas, "Coping with Contingencies," in Niżnik and Sanders, *Debating the State of Philosophy*, 4–5.

27. Habermas, "Coping with Contingencies," 5.

28. Habermas, "Coping with Contingencies," 5. There are others who ask a similar question. See A. Nehamas, "Can We Ever Quite Change the Subject? Richard

Rorty on Science, Literature, Culture, and the Future of Philosophy," *boundary 2* 10, no. 3 (Spring 1982): 395–413.

29. Rorty, *Edukacja i wyzwanie*, 98.

30. See R. Rorty, *Philosophy and Social Hope* (London: Penguin Books, 1999).

31. In reference to Rorty's humanistic project and style, Randall Auxier wrote, "Rorty is a humanist in the sense that one might apply the term to Cicero, Seneca, and Epictetus, the *eloquent* humanist; or to Pico della Mirandola and Montaigne, the *wise* humanist; or to Emerson and Dewey, the *prudent* humanist." See R. E. Auxier, preface to *The Philosophy of Richard Rorty*, ed. R. E. Auxier and L. E. Hahn, Library of Living Philosophers (LaSalle, IL: Open Court, 2010), xix.

32. Rorty, *Consequences of Pragmatism*, 92.

33. Rorty, *Contingency*, 5.

34. Rorty, *Consequences of Pragmatism*, xiii.

35. Rorty, *Objectivity*, 24.

36. F. Nietzsche, "On Truth and Lie in Extra-Moral Sense," in *The Viking Portable Nietzsche*, trans. W. Kaufmann (London: Penguin Books, 1977), 46–47. For more on Rorty and Nietzsche, see P. Sedgwick, "The Future of Philosophy: Nietzsche, Rorty, and Post-Nietzscheanism," *Nietzsche Studien* 29, no. 1 (2000): 234–251; J. M. Boffetti, "Rorty's Nietzschean Pragmatism: A Jamesian Response," *Review of Politics* 66, no. 4 (Autumn 2004): 605–631.

37. Rorty, *Contingency*, 5.

38. Rorty, *Contingency*, 6.

39. Rorty, *Contingency*, 11.

40. Rorty, *Contingency*, 10.

41. For more on Rorty and Davidson, see J. Malpas, "Mapping the Structure of Truth: Davidson Contra Rorty," in *Truth and Its Nature (if Any)*, ed. J. Peregrin, Synthese Library (Studies in Epistemology, Logic, Methodology, and Philosophy of Science), vol. 284 (Dordrecht: Springer, 1999); T. W. Schick Jr., "Rorty and Davidson on Alternate Conceptual Schemes," *Journal of Speculative Philosophy* 1, no. 4 (1987): 291–303; A. Bilgrami, "Is Truth a Goal of Inquiry? Rorty and Davidson on Truth," in *Rorty and His Critics*, ed. Robert B. Brandon (Cambridge, MA: Blackwell, 2000), 242–262.

42. As Rorty noted, Donald H. Davidson discussed the phenomenon in a similar fashion in his philosophy of language, where he perceived language "as new forms of life constantly killing off old forms—not to accomplish a higher purpose, but blindly"; see Rorty, *Contingency*, 19.

43. Rorty, *Contingency*, 18.

44. Rorty, *Contingency*, 16.

45. For more on that subject, see T. Edwards, "Rorty on the Literalization of Metaphor," *Method & Theory in the Study of Religion* 9, no. 2 (1997): 127–138.

46. Rorty argued further on that the only way of justifying this stance is to follow philosophers such as Davidson and Hilary Putnam, and "exhibit the sterility of attempts to give a sense to phrases like 'the way the world is' or 'fitting the facts'"; Rorty, *Contingency*, 20.

47. Rorty, *Contingency*, 9. For a complex study of the role of metaphors, see G. Lakoff and M. Johnson, *Metaphors We Live By*, University of Chicago Press, Chicago 1980.

48. Rorty, *Contingency*, 30.

49. For a broadened account on Freud and Rorty, see, for example, see M. Casey, *Meaninglessness: The Solutions of Nietzsche, Freud, and Rorty*, Religion, Politics, and Society in the New Millennium (Lanham, MD: Lexington Books, 2002).

50. Rorty, *Contingency*, 39.

51. Rorty, *Contingency*, 48.

52. For Rosa Cacaterra it is a feature of what she calls "linguistic pragmatism." See R. M. Cacaterra, *Contingency and Normativity: The Challenges of Richard Rorty* (Leiden: Brill /Rodopi, 2019), 23.

53. Rorty, *Contingency*, 75.

54. R. Rorty, "A Pragmatist View of Rationality and Cultural Difference," *Philosophy East and West* 42, no. 4 (1992): 581.

55. Rorty, *Objectivity*, 37.

56. Rorty, *Objectivity*, 220.

57. R. Rorty, "Emancipating Our Culture," in Niżnik and Sanders, *Debating the State of Philosophy*, 28.

58. For example, see H. Putnam, *Realism with a Human Face* (Cambridge, MA: Harvard University Press, Cambridge 1990); H. Putnam, *Ethics without Ontology* (Cambridge, MA: Harvard University Press, 2004).

59. See Rorty, *Contingency*, 48–49.

60. On that subject, see A. C. Hutchinson, "The Three 'Rs': Reading/Rorty/Radically," *Harvard Law Review* 103, no. 2 (December 1989): 555–585.

61. See M. Dell'utri, "The Threat of Cultural Relativism: Hilary Putnam and the Antidote of Fallinilism," *European Journal of Analitic Philosophy* 4. no. 2 (2008): 75–86.

62. Rorty, *Objectivity*, 30.

63. Rorty, *Consequences of Pragmatism*, 166.

64. Rorty, "Relativism—Finding and Making," 33.

65. Rorty, "Relativism—Finding and Making," 33.

66. Rorty, *Contingency*, 8.

67. Rorty, *Consequences of Pragmatism*, xiv.

68. Rorty, *Objectivity*, 23–24.

69. Rorty, *Objectivity*, 24.

70. Rorty, "Relativism—Finding and Making," 47.

71. Rorty, *Objectivity*, 30.

72. Rorty, "Relativism—Finding and Making," 34.

73. For example, see Susan Hack's allegations in S. Haack, *Evidence and Enquiry: Towards Reconstruction in Epistemology* (Oxford: Blackwell, 1993); S. Haack, *Manifesto of a Passionate Moderate* (Chicago: The University of Chicago Press, 1998).

74. Rorty, *Contingency*, 44. Rorty's suggestion is, then, to simply "change the subject"; Rorty, *Consequences of Pragmatism*, xxxi.

75. Rorty, *Objectivity*, 33.

76. Rorty, *Objectivity*, 22–23.
77. Rorty, *Consequences of Pragmatism*, xiii.
78. Rorty, *Contingency*, 83.
79. Rorty, *Objectivity*, 29.
80. Rorty, "Relativism—Finding and Making," 37.
81. Thus Rorty wrote that pragmatists "start with a Darwinian account of human beings as animals doing their best to cope with the environment—doing their best to develop tools which will enable them to enjoy more pleasure and less pain"; Rorty, "Relativism—Finding and Making," 38.
82. Rorty, *Consequences of Pragmatism*, 203.
83. Rorty, *Consequences of Pragmatism*, 32–33.
84. Rorty, "Relativism—Finding and Making," 39.
85. Rorty, "Relativism—Finding and Making," 40.
86. Rorty, *Contingency*, 4.
87. Rorty, *Contingency*, 183.
88. Rorty, "Relativism—Finding and Making," 41–42.
89. Rorty, *Contingency*, 182.
90. Rorty, *Contingency*, 188.
91. Rorty, *Contingency*, 185.
92. Rorty, *Contingency*, 183.
93. Rorty, *Contingency*, 175–176.
94. For more on Rorty and Orwell, see J. Conant, "Freedom, Cruelty, and Truth: Rorty versus Orwell," in *Rorty and His Critics*, ed. R. B. Brandom (Oxford: Blackwell, 2002), 199–202.
95. We may ask, who is the ironist? The one who hides behind the figure of the ironist is no one else but Rorty himself. This was manifested in the way in which the author of *Contingency, Irony, and Solidarity* opened particular sentences, writing, "We ironists . . ." or "For us ironists . . ."; Rorty, *Contingency*, 79, 80.
96. Rorty, *Contingency* 76.
97. See Rorty, *Contingency* 74.
98. Rorty, *Contingency* 73. Further, Rorty argued, "Those words are as far as he [its user] can go with language; beyond them there is only helpless passivity or a resort to force."
99. Rorty, *Contingency* 74.
100. Rorty, *Contingency* 80.
101. Rorty, *Contingency* 78. On the following page, Rorty wrote, "A more up-to-date word for what I have been calling 'dialectic' would be 'literary criticism.'" He understood this criticism as a constant comparison of descriptions, one of them overcoming the other.
102. Rorty, *Contingency* 73.
103. Rorty, *Contingency*.
104. Rorty, *Contingency* 102.
105. More on irony further within the chapter.
106. Rorty, *Contingency* 87.

107. For example, see M. L. Rogers, "Rorty's Straussianism; Or, Irony against Democracy," *Contemporary Pragmatism* 1, no. 2 (2004): 95–121.

108. Rorty, *Contingency*, xv.

109. M. Kundera, *The Art of the Novel*, 7, in R. Rorty, "Heidegger, Kundera, Dickens," in *Essays on Heidegger and Others: Philosophical Papers II* (Cambridge: Cambridge University Press, 1991), 75.

110. Kundera, *Art of the Novel*, 159, in Rorty, "Heidegger," 75.

111. Rorty, *Contingency*, 46. See also J. Schumpeter, *Capitalism, Socialism, and Democracy* (London: George, Allen & Unwin, 1943), 243.

112. Rorty, *Objectivity*, 6.

113. Rorty, *Objectivity*, 30.

114. Rorty, *Objectivity*, 177.

115. Of course, the tradition or the consensus should be understood as something more than the tradition of the whole of our community, for it would be difficult to talk of a community, or a culture, within which there would be only one commonly shared tradition, or a specific consensus. What is common within them are rather several beliefs that we respect and a number of those that do not deserve our respect. The likelihood of one, common voice does not seem plausible in light of the increasing diversification of our communities.

116. Rorty, *Objectivity*, 29.

117. Rorty, *Objectivity*, 30.

118. Rorty, *Consequences of Pragmatism*, xliv.

119. Rorty, *Contingency*, 198.

120. Rorty, *Objectivity*, 2.

121. Rorty, *Contingency*, 61.

122. Rorty, *Contingency*, 174.

123. Rorty, *Objectivity*, 16.

124. Rorty, *Objectivity*, 213.

125. Rorty's democratic utopia is sometimes perceived in positive terms, and sometimes criticized. For a sympathetic account of Rorty's utopia, see R. J. Bernstein, "Rorty's Liberal Utopia," *Social Research* 57, no. 1 (Spring 1990): 31–72. For a critical account, see K. Wain, "Strong Poets and Utopia: Rorty's Liberalism, Dewey and Democracy," *Political Studies* 41, no. 3 (1993): 394–407.

126. Rorty, "Heidegger," 75.

127. Rorty is not alone in opposing the use of violence. For an interesting account of Rorty's approach to suffering in a larger context of Buddhist thought, see S. Harris, "Antifoundationalism and the Commitment to Reducing Suffering in Rorty and Madhyamaka Buddhism," *Contemporary Pragmatism* 7, no. 2 (2010): 71–89.

128. Rorty, *Objectivity*, 33.

129. Rorty, *Objectivity*, 14.

130. Rorty, *Objectivity*, 213.

131. Rorty, *Objectivity*, 207.

132. Rorty, *Objectivity*, 207.

133. For more on Rorty and tolerance, see C. B. Miller, "Rorty and Tolerance," *Theoria: A Journal of Social and Political Theory*, no. 101 (June 2003): 94–108.

134. Rorty, "Pragmatist View," 587.

135. On difficulties of such an approach in practice, see J. C. Isaac, "Is the Revival of Pragmatism Practical, or What Are the Consequences of Pragmatism?," in *A Pragmatist's Progress? Richard Rorty and American Intellectual History*, ed. J. Petegrew (Lanham. MD: Rowman & Littlefield, 2000).

136. Rorty, *Objectivity*, 218.

137. Rorty, *Essays on Heidegger and Others*, 15.

138. Rorty, *Objectivity*, 214.

139. Rorty, *Objectivity*, 212. Rorty's belief in progress was so strong that he was even willing to write that we are a part of the historical procession of progress that is gradually embracing all humankind.

140. Deliberating on such a possibility, Rorty tried to respond to the critique of Jean-François Lyotard included in *Histoire universelle*.

141. Rorty, *Objectivity*, 214.

142. Rorty, *Contingency*, 61.

143. Rorty, *Contingency*, 189.

144. Rorty, *Objectivity*, 21.

145. Rorty, *Objectivity*, 22.

146. Rorty, *Objectivity*, 28.

147. Rorty, *Objectivity*, 27–28.

148. See Rorty, *Objectivity*, 16.

149. On the probability of achieving Rorty's claims, see F. Selim, "Postmodern Liberalims and Solidarity: Richard Rorty," *International Journal of Social Sciences* 3 no. 2 (2017): 654–671.

150. Rorty, *Objectivity*, 95.

151. R. Rorty, *Truth and Progress: Philosophical Papers III* (Cambridge: Cambridge University Press, 1998), 181.

152. For a critical examination of Rorty's proposal, see P. Hayden, "Sentimentality and Human Rights: Critical Remarks on Rorty," *Philosophy in the Contemporary World* 6, no. 3/4 (1999): 59–66.

153. Rorty, *Contingency*, 40.

154. Rorty, *Contingency*, 177.

155. R. Rorty, *Consequences of Pragmatism*, xlii.

156. Rorty, *Contingency*, 31–32.

157. Rorty, *Essays on Heidegger and Others*, 198.

158. Rorty, *Consequences of Pragmatism*, xlii.

159. See Rorty, *Contingency*, 197.

160. Rorty, *Contingency*, 189.

161. Rorty, *Contingency*, 189.

162. Rorty, *Contingency*, xiii.

163. Rorty, *Contingency*, xiii.

164. Rorty, *Contingency*, 191.

165. Rorty, *Contingency*, 195.

166. Rorty wrote pretty much in the same way about such abstract categories as "humanity" and "human nature." These concepts have opened the door for political

and cultural transformations, but, as Rorty wrote, they were nothing but a "handy bit of rhetoric"; Rorty, *Contingency*, 195.

167. Rorty distinguished between human solidarity as identifying oneself with "humanity as such" and human solidarity in the form of uncertainty: the uncertainty of one's own sensitivity to others' suffering and humiliation. The uncertainty of whether the existing institutional solutions are ample to manage this suffering and humiliation.

168. R. Rorty, "On Moral Obligation, Truth, and Common Sense," in Niżnik and Sanders, *Debating the State of Philosophy*, 48.

169. Rorty, *Contingency*, 60.

170. Rorty, *Contingency*, 52.

171. Rorty, *Objectivity*, 41.

172. Rorty, *Objectivity*, 39.

173. Rorty, *Objectivity*, 218.

174. Rorty, "Relativism—Finding and Making," 44. Accomplishing common goals should be perceived in the context of the increasing sense of radical diversity of private goals and the definitely poetic character of individual biographies; Rorty, *Contingency*, 67.

175. Rorty, *Contingency*, 84.

176. Rorty, *Contingency*, 84–85.

177. Rorty, *Contingency*, 84.

178. Rorty, *Contingency*, 84.

179. It is worth adding that Rorty wrote a great deal about the history of accruing human freedom, but still he did not think that there is a force supporting such a freedom, that there is any rationality, being an additional ingredient, that human beings dispose of. He wrote about the accrual of human freedom as about a narrative that usefully connects the contingent historical point of view of a culture with the events of the past and the possibilities of the future; Rorty, "Pragmatist View," 585.

180. Rorty, *Contingency*, 85.

181. Regarding the objections to and the inconsistencies in Rorty's philosophy, see D. Rothlede, *The Work of Friendship: Rorty, His Critics, and the Project of Solidarity* (Albany: State University of New York Press, 1999), 75–76.

182. Rorty, *Contingency*, 85.

183. About such doubts, see Sami Pihlström, *Pragmatist Metaphysics: An Essay on the Ethical Grounds of Ontology* (London: Bloomsbury, 2009), 112–115.

184. Rorty, *Contingency*, 85.

185. Rorty, *Contingency*, 86.

186. What Rorty would write later on in his career was also controversial. He believed that religious faith, faith in the immortal soul, has been weakened by scientific discoveries and philosophers' attempts at keeping up with the natural sciences. It is worth noticing that Rorty dismissed religious faith quite easily, assuming that "scientific discoveries" have weakened it. Further, it is surprising that, all of a sudden, "scientific discoveries" have become for Rorty something more than one of the paradigms, one of the narratives, with the help of which we describe the world. Were things the way Rorty said they were (there is nothing apart from our vocabularies),

it should be said that religious faith is one thing, and science and its discoveries are another. These are two different, disproportionate vocabularies. It would be more just if Rorty wrote that the vocabulary of scientific discoveries supplanted or began to replace the vocabulary of religious faith. His thought would then retain some of its coherence. This is, however, not what he has written.

187. Rorty, *Contingency*, 86.

188. It is striking that for Rorty the hope for heaven is something different from social hope. The former has been, in his opinion, weakened by "scientific discoveries and philosophers' attempts at keeping up with natural sciences," while the latter is not susceptible to changes in philosophical convictions.

189. Rorty, *Contingency*, 86. Further on, he wrote, "The vocabularies are, typically, parasitic on the hopes—in the sense that the principal function of the vocabularies is to tell stories about future outcomes which compensate for present sacrifices." Best and Kellner added that "social glue" consists also in "conversation." See S. Best and D. Kellner, "Richard Rorty and Postmodern Theory," in *Richard Rorty: Education, Philosophy, and Politics*, ed. M. A. Peters and Paulo Ghiraldelli, Jr. (Lanham, MD: Rowman & Littlefield, 2001), 103.

190. Rorty, *Contingency*, 190–200.

191. Rorty, *Contingency*, 52.

192. Rorty did not write about philosophical foundations per se but about a set of rules held by a liberal society that we should search for within literature and politics; Rorty, *Contingency*, 53.

193. Rorty, *Contingency*, 87.

194. Rorty, *Contingency*, 87.

195. Rorty, *Contingency*, 88.

196. Rorty, *Contingency*, 86.

197. Rorty, *Contingency*, 88.

198. Rorty, *Contingency*, 83.

199. Rorty, *Contingency*, 100.

200. Rorty, *Contingency*, 92.

201. The phrase used here was coined by Judith Shklar, and Rorty himself often used it in *Contingency, Irony, and Solidarity*. See J. Shklar, *Ordinary Vices* (Cambridge, MA: Harvard University Press, 1984), 44. For more on Rorty and Shklar, see J. Keks, "Cruelty and Liberalism," *Ethics* 106, no. 4 (July 1996): 162–166.

202. Rorty, *Contingency*, 93. What Rorty meant here are transcultural reasons.

203. In the context of the significance that Rorty ascribed to suffering, we can ask, does he not uncover a common denominator for us all—a thing characteristic of a liberal metaphysician—when he pointed to the susceptibility to experience humiliation and pain that we all share? Such a common denominator is to serve the metaphysician to describe his own self and to describe his relations with others, for both private and public purposes. Answering this question, one could come up with an interpretation according to which Rorty did indeed introduce a certain common denominator. This, however, shall not be elaborated on here.

204. Or thus said Rorty. But can things be different? See the footnote above.

205. R. Rorty, "Reply to J. B. Schneewind," in Auxier and Hahn, *Philosophy of Richard Rorty*, 509.

206. Rorty, *Objectivity*, 43.
207. Rorty, *Objectivity*, 43.
208. Rorty, "Foucault, Dewey, Nietzsche," 5.
209. Rorty, *Contingency*, 197. He did state, however, that it is impossible to justify such a request, for "there is no *neutral*, noncircular way to defend the liberal's claim that cruelty is the worst thing we do . . ."; Rorty, *Contingency*, 197.
210. For more on Rorty and Foucault, see H. F. Haber, *Beyond Postmodern Politics: Lyotard, Rorty, Foucault* (New York: Routledge, 1994).
211. Rorty, *Contingency*, 57.
212. Rorty, *Contingency*, 41.
213. Rorty, "Putnam and the Relativist Menace," 445.
214. See Rorty, *Contingency*, 85–86.
215. For more on self-enlarging as encompassing the private and public, see Tracy Llanera, "Redeeming Rorty's Private–Public Distinction," *Contemporary Pragmatism* 13, no. 3 (2016): 316–340.
216. Rorty himself observed that making ourselves sensitive to suffering is greatly facilitated by novels, such as *Uncle Tom's Cabin*, whose language and metaphors have permeated our consciousness, and have shaped the vocabulary we use in the public sphere. Thus, regardless of whether it is possible to point to those "responsible," whether it is possible to determine the roots of our beliefs or positions, the vocabulary that we use in the public sphere is shaped by private vocabularies.
217. Rorty, *Contingency*, 41.
218. Rorty, *Contingency*, 41.
219. R. Rorty, "Toward a Post-Metaphysical Culture," interview with Michael O'Shea, *Harvard Review of Philosophy* 5 (Spring 1995): 58–66.
220. Rorty, "Toward a Post-Metaphysical Culture," 62.
221. Rorty, "Relativism—Finding and Making," 40. Any new vocabulary is a new belief, a new way of acting.
222. Rorty, "Pragmatist View," 593. Rorty opposed theory as connected with the simplicity, structure, and abstraction, characteristic of an ascetic monk. Instead, he favored theory that is a narrative, which is inclined toward detail and diversity, and manifests itself in the figure of a novelist.
223. Rorty, *Heidegger*, 80.
224. Rorty, "Toward a Post-Metaphysical Culture," 62.
225. Rorty, "Toward a Post-Metaphysical Culture," 62.
226. Rorty, *Contingency*, 96.
227. It can be said that by suggesting that others' private idiosyncrasies are just elements of their private spheres, he cast doubt over his own position, for, in consequence, everything he said should be considered as his own construct, an effect of his attempt at self-creation.
228. Rorty, *Contingency*, xv.
229. Rorty, *Contingency*, 62.
230. It can be exemplified with the "private" conviction that the Holocaust did not happen. In Germany, for instance, disseminating such a conviction is punishable, as it is believed that, once it is uttered out loud, it becomes a part of the public sphere.

231. Rorty, *Contingency*, 62. This is why Michael Dellwing argues that for Rorty private sphere is not a fixed realm but a moving army of stop signs the setting of which is always in social dispute, see M. Dellwing, "Fences: Rorty's Private-Public-Dichotomy as a Situational Game," *Minerva: An Internet Journal of Philosophy* 16 (2012): 62–82.

232. Rorty, "Reply to J. B. Schneewind," 509.

233. Rorty, *Contingency*, 175.

234. Rorty, *Contingency*, 175–176.

235. Subjective convictions usually exhibit a tendency to become objective once they are considered such by the vast majority of people. Accordingly, there is not much difference between an objective reality and a widespread belief, which is not a belief anymore, but our "objective reality." Only a few will be willing to remember that some of our convictions were only assumptions at first. The more comfortable we begin to feel within a set of certain beliefs, the faster we tend to forget about their origins.

236. Even Rorty pointed to the role of interests when he claimed that we ought to give up the idea of research as discovering what the world is like in itself, as detached from human interests and desires. Rorty, *Edukacja i wyzwanie*, 99.

237. For more on that line of argumentation, see M. Kilanowski, "Abandoning Truth Is Not a Solution: A Discussion with Richard Rorty," *Diametros* 61 (2019): 34–50.

238. Rorty, *Objectivity*, 13.

239. Rorty, *Contingency*, 87.

240. Habermas would agree as well. He said, "[T]he functional fit of Platonism with present circumstances provides sufficient legitimation for continuing that language game"; Habermas, "Coping with Contingencies," 20.

241. Rorty, *Edukacja i wyzwanie*, 100.

242. Rorty, *Objectivity*, 192.

243. Moreover, we would not have to fear a less liberal and tolerant truth if we ranked equality, freedom, and tolerance for difference a common truth as well. The objective truth, meaning preaching the superiority of freedom, would not result in tyranny and violence.

244. Rorty, "Is It Desirable to Love Truth?," in *Truth, Politics, and "Post-Modernism"* (Assen, Netherlands: Van Gorcum, 1997), 9.

245. Rorty, *Contingency*, 84.

246. Rorty, *Contingency*, xiii.

247. Rorty, *Contingency*, 176. It should be added that Rorty meant political freedom, for elsewhere he wrote, "[I]f we take care of political freedom, truth and goodness will take care of themselves"; Rorty, *Contingency*, 84.

248. G. Orwell, *1984*, in Rorty, *Contingency*, 172.

249. Rorty, *Contingency*, 173.

250. Rorty, *Contingency*, 176.

251. R. Rorty, "Philosophy and the Future," in *Rorty and Pragmatism: The Philosopher Responds to His Critics*, ed. H. J. Saatkamp (Nashville, TN: Vanderbilt University Press, 1995), 205.

252. Rorty, *Contingency*, 68.

Notes to Chapter III

1. R. Rorty, *Essays on Heidegger and Others: Philosophical Papers II* (Cambridge: Cambridge University Press, 1991), 24.

2. J. Habermas, *The Theory of Communicative Action*, Vol. 2, *Lifeworld and System: A Critique of Functionalist Reason*, trans. T. McCarthy (Boston: Beacon Press, 1987), 382. Further on, he wrote, "In the totally administered society only instrumental reason, expanded into a totality, found embodiment; everything that existed was transformed into a real abstraction. In that case, however, what was taken hold of and deformed by these abstractions escaped the grasp of empirical inquiry."

3. For more on that subject, see S. Benhabib, *Critique, Norm, and Utopia: A Study of the Foundations of Critical Theory* (New York: Columbia University Press, 1986).

4. J. Habermas, "The Dialectics of Rationalization," in *Autonomy and Solidarity: Interviews with Jürgen Habermas*, ed. P. Dews (London: Verso, 1992), 102.

5. For more on Habermas's thought in the context of critical theory, see J. Always, *Critical Theory and Political Possibilities: Conceptions of Emancipatory Politics in the Works of Horkheimer, Adorno, Marcuse, and Habermas* (London: Greenwood Press, 1995); T. McCarthy, *Critical Theory* (Boston: Beacon Press, 1978).

6. Habermas, "Dialectics of Rationalization," 100.

7. Habermas, *Theory of Communicative Action*, 2:397.

8. The path that Habermas followed is one of the three he himself listed. The other paths include: (a) formal-pragmatist analysis of a propaedeutically set forth concept of communicative rationality—such a project heads toward hypothetical reconstructions of pretheoretical knowledge, which the competent users of language employ in the course of reaching an agreement; and (b) estimating the empirical usefulness of formal-pragmatist findings.

9. J. Habermas, *The Theory of Communicative Action*, Vol. 1, *Reason and the Rationalization of Society*, trans. T. McCarthy (Boston: Beacon Press, 1984), 139–140.

10. Habermas, "Dialectics of Rationalization," 112.

11. Habermas, *Theory of Communicative Action*, 1:xl.

12. Habermas, *Theory of Communicative Action*, 2:2.

13. Habermas, *Theory of Communicative Action*, 1:9.

14. Habermas, *Theory of Communicative Action*, 1:9.

15. Habermas, *Theory of Communicative Action*, 1:9.

16. Habermas, *Theory of Communicative Action*, 1:10.

17. Habermas, *Theory of Communicative Action*, 1:10.

18. Habermas, *Theory of Communicative Action*, 1:15.

19. Habermas, *Theory of Communicative Action*, 1:15. It needs to be added that as far as other types of expression are concerned, Habermas listed the expressions that articulate judgments that are not accompanied with a clearly profiled validity claim.

20. Habermas, *Theory of Communicative Action*, 1:16.

21. Habermas, *Theory of Communicative Action*, 1:17–18.

22. Habermas, *Theory of Communicative Action*, 1:25.

23. Habermas, *Theory of Communicative Action*, 1:25.

24. Habermas, *Theory of Communicative Action*, 1:26.

25. Habermas, *Theory of Communicative Action*, 1:22.

26. On the "force" of a batter argument in Habermas's thought, see A. Allen, "The Unforced Force of the Better Argument: Reason and Power in Habermas's Political Theory," *Constellations* 19, no. 3 (September 2012): 353–368.

27. Habermas, *Theory of Communicative Action*, 1:22.

28. For a further comprehensive account of the intersubjectivity of validity claims, see H. H. Grady and S. Wells, "Toward a Rhetoric of Intersubjectivity: Introducing Jürgen Habermas," *Journal of Advanced Composition* 6 (1985/1986): 33–47.

29. J. Habermas, "A Philosophico-Political Profile," in *Autonomy and Solidarity: Interviews with Jürgen Habermas*, ed. P. Dews (London: Verso, 1992), 159.

30. Habermas, "Philosophico-Political Profile," 159–160.

31. Habermas, *Theory of Communicative Action*, 1:38.

32. Habermas, *Theory of Communicative Action*, 1:39.

33. Habermas, *Theory of Communicative Action*, 1:39.

34. Habermas, *Theory of Communicative Action*, 1:42.

35. See Habermas, *Theory of Communicative Action*, 1:18.

36. As far as this impartiality is concerned, he said that it is "to be found not in the construction of the arguments employed; it can be explained only in connection with the conditions for discursively redeeming validity claims"; Habermas, *Theory of Communicative Action*, 1:35.

37. Habermas, *Theory of Communicative Action*, 2:399.

38. Habermas, "The Unity of Reason in the Diversity of Its Voices," in *Postmetaphysical Thinking*, trans. W. M. Hohengarten (Cambridge, MA: The MIT Press, 1992), 144.

39. See Habermas, "A Reply to My Critics," in *Habermas: Critical Debates*, ed. J. B. Thompson and D. Held (London: MIT Press, 1982), 236.

40. Habermas, *Theory of Communicative Action*, 1:285.

41. Habermas, "Reply to My Critics," 234. Further, Habermas wrote that communication "viewed from the perspective of the participants, it then serves to establish interpersonal relations; from the perspective of social science, it is the medium through which the life-world shared by the participants in communication is reproduced"; Habermas, "Reply to My Critics," 234.

42. Habermas, *Theory of Communicative Action*, 1:286.

43. For more on this distinction, see T. Cohen, "Illocutions and Perlocutions," *Foundations of Language* 9, no. 4 (March 1973): 492–503.

44. Habermas, *Theory of Communicative Action*, 1:289.

45. Habermas, *Theory of Communicative Action*, 1:289.

46. Habermas, *Theory of Communicative Action*, 1:289. This overview of the distinction introduced by John Austin has been included here, for Habermas used the terms introduced by him while presenting his own position.

47. Habermas, *Theory of Communicative Action*, 1:287.

48. As far as speech acts are concerned, Habermas said, "As the medium for achieving understanding, speech acts serve: (1) to establish and renew interpersonal relations, whereby the speaker takes up a relation to something in the world of legitimate (social) orders; (b) to represent (or presuppose) states and events, whereby the speaker takes up a relation to something in the world of existing states

of affairs; (c) to manifest experiences—that is, to represent oneself—whereby the speaker takes up a relation to something in the subjective world to which he has privileged access"; Habermas, *Theory of Communicative Action*, 1:308.

49. Habermas, *Theory of Communicative Action*, 1:305. Thus, the force to coordinate action by means of linguistic acts results not from authoritative power or from social norms, as it is the case with linguistic acts bound institutionally; neither does it result from the potential of accidentally available sanctions, as it is the case with imperative expressions of will; see Habermas, *Theory of Communicative Action*, 1:296–297.

50. Habermas, "Dialectics of Rationalization," 109.

51. Habermas, *Theory of Communicative Action*, 1:335.

52. Habermas, *Theory of Communicative Action*, 1:335–336.

53. Habermas, *Theory of Communicative Action*, 1:336.

54. Habermas referred also to the work of Ludwig Wittgenstein, for whom implicit knowledge is manifested through commonsensical certitudes, ingredients of our world-image, which are perceived as unquestionable and indubitable. It is this nonproblematic knowledge that determines literal meanings, which, by that process, are relative.

55. Habermas, *Theory of Communicative Action*, 1:336.

56. Habermas, *Theory of Communicative Action*, 2:125. Habermas also argued that culture and language do not count as situation constituents—they are not restricted to the sphere of free action and they do not fall under any of the formal world-concepts. It is only when culture and language fail as resources, when we are faced with nontransparent traditions or incomprehensible utterances, that they need to be interpreted as cultural facts that limit the scope of freedom in acting. Institutional order and identity structures are quite different in this respect; they can limit the freedom of actors' initiatives and exist alongside as the situational constituents. They do fall under one of the formal world-concepts. However, they can also have a double status: on the one hand, they appear as the elements of a certain social or subjective world, and on the other, they appear as the structural components of the lifeworld.

57. Habermas, *Theory of Communicative Action*, 1:69.

58. Habermas, *Theory of Communicative Action*, 1:69.

59. Habermas, *Theory of Communicative Action*, 1:70. It needs to be added that, according to Habermas, "the concept of a subjective world permits us to contrast not only our own internal world, but also the subjective worlds of others, with the external world"; Habermas, *Theory of Communicative Action*, 1:69.

60. Habermas, *Theory of Communicative Action*, 2:125.

61. Habermas, *Theory of Communicative Action*, 2:126.

62. Habermas, *Theory of Communicative Action*, 2:126.

63. Habermas, *Theory of Communicative Action*, 2:135.

64. Habermas, *Theory of Communicative Action*, 2:139.

65. Habermas, *Theory of Communicative Action*, 2:139.

66. Habermas, *Theory of Communicative Action*, 2:148.

67. Habermas, *Theory of Communicative Action*, 2:150.

68. Habermas, *Theory of Communicative Action*, 2:118.
69. Habermas, *Theory of Communicative Action*, 1:70.
70. See Habermas, *Theory of Communicative Action*, 1:340.
71. Habermas, *Theory of Communicative Action*, 2:145.
72. Habermas, *Theory of Communicative Action*, 2:145–146.
73. Habermas, *Theory of Communicative Action*, 2:146.
74. Habermas, *Theory of Communicative Action*, 2:146.
75. Habermas, *Theory of Communicative Action*, 2:146.
76. Habermas, *Theory of Communicative Action*, 2:147.
77. See Habermas, *The Theory of Communicative Action*, 1:341.
78. Habermas referenced the three levels of moral consciousness developed by Lawrence Kohlberg, that is, preconventional, conventional, and postconventional. Then he used this distinction to present the levels of the development of law.
79. Habermas, *Theory of Communicative Action*, 2:174.
80. Habermas, *Theory of Communicative Action*, 2:174. Law as authorized by the state becomes an institution detached from the ethical motivations of legal entities.
81. For more on that subject, see J. Habermas, "The Internal Relation between Law and Politics," in *Between Facts and Norms* (Cambridge, MA: The MIT Press, 1998), 133–150.
82. See Habermas, *Theory of Communicative Action*, 2:179.
83. Habermas, *Theory of Communicative Action*, 2:180.
84. Habermas, *Theory of Communicative Action*, 2:180.
85. It is worth mentioning that Habermas's concept of reaching a consensus is questioned by some as limiting the possibility for deliberation. See K. Jezierska, "With Habermas against Habermas, Deliberation without Consensus," *Journal of Public Deliberation* 15, no. 1 (2019): 4–23.
86. Habermas, *Theory of Communicative Action*, 2:352–353.
87. Habermas, *Theory of Communicative Action*, 2:403.
88. Habermas, *Theory of Communicative Action*, 2:354.
89. Habermas, *Theory of Communicative Action*, 2:355.
90. Habermas, *Theory of Communicative Action*, 2:355.
91. Habermas, *Theory of Communicative Action*, 2:180.
92. Habermas, *Theory of Communicative Action*, 2:181.
93. Habermas, *Theory of Communicative Action*, 2:185.
94. Habermas, *Theory of Communicative Action*, 2:183.
95. Habermas, *Theory of Communicative Action*, 2:327.
96. Habermas, *Theory of Communicative Action*, 1:341.
97. Habermas, *Theory of Communicative Action*, 1:342.
98. Habermas, *Theory of Communicative Action*, 1:342–343.
99. Habermas, *Theory of Communicative Action*, 1:342.
100. For clarification, it needs to be added that the colonization of the lifeworld can occur only after the deconstructing of traditional life-forms and the development of the structural components of the lifeworld, i.e., culture, society, and personality.
101. Habermas, *Theory of Communicative Action*, 2:323.

102. Habermas used the example of capitalist growth, which "triggers conflicts within the lifeworld chiefly as a consequence of the expansion and the increasing density of the monetary-bureaucratic complex; this happens, first of all, where socially integrated contexts of life are redefined around the roles of consumer and client and assimilated to systematically integrated domains of action"; Habermas, *Theory of Communicative Action*, 2:351.

103. A disharmony of material reproduction can be avoided at the cost of disturbances in the symbolic reproduction of the lifeworld. Habermas said on this point, "In the advanced industrial societies of the West, containment of class conflict by the welfare state sets in motion the dynamics of a reification of communicatively structures areas of action"; Habermas, *Theory of Communicative Action*, 2:302.

104. Habermas, *Theory of Communicative Action*, 2:392.

105. Habermas, *Theory of Communicative Action*, 2:303.

106. Habermas, *Theory of Communicative Action*, 2:330.

107. Habermas is not alone in presenting a critical analysis of the role experts play today. For more on that subject, see S. Turner, "What Is the Problem with Experts?," *Social Studies of Science* 31, no. 1 (February 2001): 123–149.

108. For a detailed analysis of this process, see M. Hertogh and S. Halliday, eds., *Judicial Review and Bureaucratic Impact, International, and Interdisciplinary Perspectives*, (Cambridge: Cambridge University Press, 2009).

109. Habermas, *Theory of Communicative Action*, 2:365.

110. For more on law as a steering medium in Habermas's thought, see M. Deflem, "The Legal Theory of Jürgen Habermas," in *Law and Social Theory*, ed. R. Banakar and M. Travers (Oxford: Hart, 2013), 70–95.

111. Habermas, *Theory of Communicative Action*, 2:365.

112. For more on this subject, see J. Habermas, "Crisis Theories and the Proceduralist Understanding of Law," in *Between Facts and Norms* (Cambridge: MIT Press, 1998), 427–446.

113. Habermas, *Theory of Communicative Action*, 2:365.

114. Habermas, *Theory of Communicative Action*, 2:365.

115. Habermas, *Theory of Communicative Action*, 2:372–373.

116. It is worth noting that such an approach is debatable according to Frank Michelman. See F. Michelman, "How Can the People Ever Make the Laws? A Critique of Deliberative Democracy," in *Pluralism and Pragmatic Turn: The Transformation of Critical Theory*, ed. W. Rehg and J. Bohman (Cambridge, MA: The MIT Press, 2001)..

117. Habermas, *Theory of Communicative Action*, 2:330.

118. Habermas, *Theory of Communicative Action*, 2:356.

119. Habermas, *Theory of Communicative Action*, 2:327.

120. For arguments supporting Habermas's perspective on the role of feeling in shaping distinctively human cultures, see A. Damasio, *The Strange Order of Things: Life, Feeling, and the Making of Cultures* (New York: Vintage, 2018).

121. For more on this problem, see R. Grundmann, "The Problem of Expertise in Knowledge Societies," *Minerva* 55, no. 1 (2017): 25–48.

122. See J. Habermas, "Modernity: An Unfinished Project," in *Habermas and the Unfinished Project of Modernity*, ed. M. P. d'Entrèves and S. Benhabib (Cambridge, MA: The MIT Press, 1997), 46.

123. Habermas, "Modernity," 45.

124. For arguments in support of such solution, see D. Kennedy, *A World of Struggle: How Power, Law, and Expertise Shape Global Political Economy* (Princeton, NJ: Princeton University Press, 2016).

125. Kennedy, *World of Struggle*, 397.

126. Habermas follows Kant on this particular matter. For more, see F. Rush, "Dialectic, Objectivity, and the Unity of Reason," in *The Oxford Handbook of Continental Philosophy*, ed. B. Leiter and M. Rosen. (Oxford: Oxford University Press, 2007).

127. Habermas, *Theory of Communicative Action*, 1:137.

128. The internal rational structure of the processes of reaching understanding includes: "(a) the three world-relations of actors and the corresponding concepts of the objective, social, and subjective worlds; (b) the validity claims of propositional truth, normative rightness, and sincerity or authenticity; (c) the concept of a rationally motivated agreement, that is, one based on the intersubjective recognition of criticizable validity claims; and (d) the concept of reaching understanding as the cooperative negotiation of common definitions of the situation"; Habermas, *Theory of Communicative Action*, 1:137.

129. Habermas, *Theory of Communicative Action*, 1:137.

130. See Habermas, *Theory of Communicative Action*, 2:143.

131. Habermas, *Theory of Communicative Action*, 2:144.

132. Habermas, *Theory of Communicative Action*, 2:400.

133. Habermas, *Theory of Communicative Action*, 2:400.

134. The original quotation comes from a preface to the third edition of the first volume of *The Theory of Communicative Action* in Polish; see J. Habermas, *Teoria działania komunikacyjnego: Racjonalność działania a racjonalność społeczna*, vol. 1, trans. A. M. Kaniowski (Warsaw: Wydawnictwo Naukowe PWN, 2002), 4.

135. Habermas, *Theory of Communicative Action*, 2:398–399.

136. Habermas, *Theory of Communicative Action*, 2:397.

137. Habermas, "Reply to My Critics," 227.

138. Habermas, *Theory of Communicative Action*, 1:50–51.

139. Habermas, *Theory of Communicative Action*, 2:50.

140. Habermas, *Theory of Communicative Action*, 2:50–51. Habermas said all of this in order to present the differences between the mythical and the modern understanding of the world. In the mythical world, worldviews do not allow us to get rid of the categorical conjugation of nature and culture, for it includes a categorical intertwining of the objective and the subjective world as well as reification of the linguistic worldview, which results in dogmatic inclusion of certain contents in the conceptions of the world: contents with respect to which it is impossible to assume a rational attitude and to be able to criticize them.

141. Whether the dialogue he entered into with those of opposing views is conducted as it should be and whether he did refute the objections of the universalistic

position is one issue; the other is what point of view he tried to present in his answers.

142. Habermas, *Theory of Communicative Action*, 2:58.
143. Habermas, *Theory of Communicative Action*, 2:55.
144. Habermas, *Theory of Communicative Action*, 2:58.
145. We can of course assume that other worldviews or other cultures can be based on the same validity claims; this does not, however, need to be the case. The fact that in our "modern attitude" what counts are the claims for truth, honesty, or rightness does not change the "fact" that other attitudes may favor sophisticated speech, humor, and the rhythm of the contents to be presented. Habermas acknowledges only one option. This is expressed, for instance, in the following passage: "When the interpreter takes up the reasons that an actor gives—or would under suitable circumstances give—for his expression, he is moving to a level where he has to take a positive or negative position on criticizable validity claims"; Habermas, *Theory of Communicative Action*, 2:55.
146. Habermas, *Theory of Communicative Action*, 2:62.
147. Habermas, *Theory of Communicative Action*, 2:63–64.
148. Habermas, *Theory of Communicative Action*, 2:64.
149. Habermas, *Theory of Communicative Action*, 2:63.
150. Habermas, *Theory of Communicative Action*, 2:64.
151. Habermas, *Theory of Communicative Action*, 2:65.
152. This is Peter G. Winch's thesis from his book *The Idea of a Social Science and Its Relation to Philosophy*, with which Habermas struggles. See P. Winch, *The Idea of a Social Science and Its Relation to Philosophy* (London: Routledge, 1990).
153. This means that even if we assume that truth is a universal validity claim and that, taking such an assumption as a basis, we can compare other worldviews from the perspective of cognitive adequacy, it does not change the fact that this comparison is to be made within our language, and adequacy is to be understood according to our standards. We will be faced with such a situation also in the case of observing the contradictions in the reasoning or actions of other cultures, which will depend on our own ways of recognizing such contradictions. This is what Winch has claimed and what Habermas—as it has been mentioned—has tried to polemicize.
154. Habermas, *Theory of Communicative Action*, 2: 140.
155. Habermas, *Theory of Communicative Action*, 2: 140.
156. Habermas, *Theory of Communicative Action*, 2: 66.
157. Habermas, *Theory of Communicative Action*, 2: 44.
158. Habermas, *Theory of Communicative Action*, 2: 400
159. For other critical approaches to *Theory of Communicative Action*, see, for example, J. C. Alexander, "Habermas's New Critical Theory: Its Promise and Problems," *American Journal of Sociology* 91, no. 2 (September 1985): 400–424; H. Haferkamp, "Critique of Habermas's Theory of Communicative Action," in *Social Action*, ed. G. Seebass and R. Tuomela (Dordrecht: D. Reidel, 1985), 197–205; M. Plot, "Communicative Action's Democratic Deficit: A Critique of Habermas's

Contribution to Democratic Theory," *International Journal of Communication* 3 (2009): 825–852.

160. Habermas, *Theory of Communicative Action*, Habermas, *Theory of Communicative Action*, 1:xxxix.

161. Habermas, *Theory of Communicative Action*, 2:187.

162. See Habermas, *Theory of Communicative Action*, 2:187.

163. Habermas, *Theory of Communicative Action*, 1:337.

164. Habermas, *Theory of Communicative Action*, 1:339.

165. See Habermas, *Theory of Communicative Action*, 1:339.

166. See Habermas, *Theory of Communicative Action*, 1:286.

167. Habermas, *Theory of Communicative Action*, 1:59.

168. Habermas, "Reply to My Critics," 228.

169. Habermas, *Theory of Communicative Action*, 1:73.

170. Habermas, *Theory of Communicative Action*, 1:73.

171. Habermas took a different approach here than in his previous attempts to present such an idea. For more on the attempts to see Habermas's project in a wider context, see Ryan K. Balot, "Utopian and Post-Utopian Paradigms in Classical Political Thought," *Arion: A Journal of Humanities and the Classics* 3rd series, 16, no. 2 (Fall 2008): 75–90.

172. Habermas, "Unity of Reason," 144.

173. Habermas, "Reply to My Critics," 235.

174. In light of this clarification, Habermas would not agree that his philosophy expresses ambivalence between the tolerance for diversity and commitment to unity that may deny that diversity. For an opposing view, see Axel Van den Berg, "Habermas and Modernity: A Critique of the Theory of Communicative Action," *Current Perspectives in Social Theory* 10 (January 1990): 161–193.

175. Habermas, "Reply to My Critics," 262. In the above quote, Habermas has used the fragment of A. Wellmer's text "Thesen über Vernunft, Emanzipation und Utopie," in *Ethik und Dialog*, ed. A. Wellmer (Frankfurt am Main: Suhrkamp, 1986), 203.

176. Habermas, "Philosophico-Political Profile," 166.

177. A. Wellmer, "Thesen über Vernunft," in Habermas, *Theory of Communicative Action*, 1:74. See also Habermas, "Reply to My Critics," 262–263.

178. Habermas, "Unity of Reason," 146.

179. Habermas, "Die Krise des Wehlwahrfstaates und die Erschörfung utopischer Energie," in *Die neue Unübersichtlichkeit* (Frankfurt: Suhrkamp, 1985), 161.

180. For more on the utopian dimension of Habermas's theory, see S. Benhabib, "The Utopian Dimension in Communicative Ethics," special issue on Jürgen Habermas, *New German Critique*, no. 35 (Spring–Summer 1985): 83–96.

181. Habermas, "Reply to My Critics," 228.

182. See P. Johnson, "Are Our Utopian Energies Exhausted?," *European Journal of Political Theory* 3, no. 3 (2004): 267–291.

183. Habermas, *Theory of Communicative Action*, 2:401.

184. McCarthy, *Critical Theory*, 255–256.

185. McCarthy, *Critical Theory*, 254–255.

186. Habermas, "Reply to My Critics," 252–253. It is worth adding that Habermas is just one of many philosophers that argue in favor of the ethics of discourse. For a fuller account, see W. Rehg, "Discourse Ethics," in *The Ethical*, ed. E. Wyschogrod and G. P. McKenny (Oxford: Blackwell, 2003), 5–83.
187. Habermas, *Theory of Communicative Action*, 1:43.
188. Habermas, *Theory of Communicative Action*, 1:43.
189. Habermas, *Theory of Communicative Action*, 1:43.
190. See Habermas, "Philosophico-Political Profile," 180.
191. Habermas, "Philosophico-Political Profile," 180.
192. Habermas, "Philosophico-Political Profile," 180–181.
193. Habermas, "Reply to My Critics," 245.
194. Habermas, "Reply to My Critics," 235.
195. Habermas, "Reply to My Critics," 250.
196. In *Between Facts and Norms* Habermas has added that it is crucial how since French Revolution, "one can reconcile equality with liberty, unity with variety, or the rights of the majority with the rights of the minority." J. Habermas, *Between Facts and Norms* (Cambridge: Polity Press, 2004), 472. Habermas's answer is that it can be possible to reconcile them in the course of communication.
197. For a reflection on to what extent such a view affected thinking about shaping the public sphere anew, see, for example, R. Benson, "Shaping the Public Sphere: Habermas and Beyond," *American Sociologist* 40, no. 3 (February 2014): 175–197.
198. For more on how such a view is supportive and enhances the principles and requirements of the public sphere, at both the national and global level in a period of significant global change, see M. Z. Khan, I. S. Gilani, and A. Nawaz, "From Habermas Model to New Public Sphere: A Paradigm Shift," *Global Journal of Human Social Science* 12, no. 5 (March 2012): 43–51. Also, for how such a view, as well as the political and legal philosophy based on Habermas's pluralist vision, is best suited to confront the problems of the twenty-first century, see M. Rosenfeld, *Law, Justice, Democracy, and the Clash of Cultures: A Pluralist Account* (Cambridge: Cambridge University Press, 2011).
199. For an account how important is such an approach for public deliberation, see T. Christiano, "The Significance of Public Deliberation," in *Deliberative Democracy: Essays on Reason and Politics*, ed. W. Rehg and J. Bohman (Cambridge, MA: The MIT Press, 1997).
200. R. Rorty, *Contingency, Irony, and Solidarity* (Cambridge: Cambridge University Press, 1989), 68.
201. Rorty, *Contingency*, 68.

Notes to Chapter IV

1. R. Rorty, *Contingency, Irony, and Solidarity* (Cambridge: Cambridge University Press, 1989), 67.
2. J. Habermas, *Truth and Justification*, ed. Barbara Fultner (Cambridge, MA: The MIT Press, 2003), 9.

3. See, for example, E. J. Grippe, *Richard Rorty's New Pragmatism: Neither Liberal nor Free* (New York: Continuum, 2007).

4. Rorty, *Contingency*, 82.

5. Among others it is worthwhile to mention Richard J. Bernstein, Hilary Putnam, Daniel C. Dennett, Robert B. Brandom, and James Conant. For detailed argumentation of the critics of Rorty's philosophy, see H. J. Saatkamp Jr., ed., *Rorty and Pragmatism: The Philosopher Responds to His Critics* (Nashville, TN: Vanderbilt University Press, 1995); R. B. Brandom, *Rorty and His Critics* (Oxford: Blackwell, 2000).

6. Rorty, *Contingency*, 62.

7. Rorty, *Contingency*, 62.

8. Rorty, *Contingency*, 62.

9. Rorty, *Contingency*, 83.

10. R. Rorty, "On Moral Obligation, Truth, and Common Sense," in *Debating the State of Philosophy: Habermas, Rorty, and Kolakowski*, ed. J. Niżnik and T. Sanders (Westport, CT: Praeger, 1996), 51.

11. J. Habermas, "An Alternative Way Out of the Philosophy of the Subject: Communicative versus Subject-Centered Reason," in *The Philosophical Discourse of Modernity* (Cambridge, MA: The MIT Press, 1987), 321.

12. Habermas, "Alternative Way Out," 322.

13. Rorty is not the only one who was critical of Habermas's perspective. For other critical approaches on *The Philosophical Discourse of Modernity*, see M. P. d'Entrèves and S. Benhabib, eds., *Habermas and the Unfinished Project of Modernity: Critical Essays on the Philosophical Discourse of Modernity* (London: Polity Press, 1996).

14. J. Habermas, "The Unity of Reason in the Diversity of Its Voices," in *Postmetaphysical Thinking*, trans. W. M. Hohengarten (Cambridge, MA: The MIT Press, 1992), 136.

15. Rorty, "On Moral Obligation," 50–51.

16. R. Rorty, "Universality and Truth," in Brandom, *Rorty and His Critics*, 18.

17. R. Rorty, *Philosophy and Social Hope* (London: Penguin Books, 1999), 36.

18. For more on the way Putnam understood the notion of truth, see H. Putnam, *Ethics without Ontology* (Cambridge, MA: Harvard University Press, 2004), 21–26; H. Putnam, *Realism with a Human Face* (Cambridge, MA: Harvard University Press, Cambridge 1990), 111–121.

19. Habermas, *Truth and Justification*, 38.

20. Habermas, *Truth and Justification*, 36.

21. Habermas, "Unity of Reason," 136.

22. Habermas, "Unity of Reason," 137. See also Rorty, "Universality and Truth," 20.

23. J. Habermas, *Past as Future* (Lincoln: University of Nebraska Press, 1994), 102.

24. J. Habermas, "What Theories Can Accomplish—and What They Can't," in *The Past as Future*, 102. In *Rorty and His Critics* Habermas added, "What is at stake is not the correct representation of reality but everyday practices that must not fall apart [. . .]. Reaching understanding cannot function unless the participants refer to a single objective world, thereby stabilizing the intersubjectively shared public space with which everything that is merely subjective can be contrasted. This

supposition of an objective world that is independent of our descriptions fulfills a functional requirement of our processes of cooperation and communication." See J. Habermas, "Richard Rorty's Pragmatic Turn," Brandom, *Rorty and His Critics*, 41.

25. For more on this subject, see Habermas, *Truth and Justification*, 36–42.

26. Habermas, "Unity of Reason," 136. This ethnocentric point of view means that all alien utterances must be tested by us against our own standards.

27. J. Habermas, "Coping with Contingencies," in *Debating the State of Philosophy: Habermas, Rorty, and Kolakowski*, ed. J. Niżnik and T. Sanders (Westport, CT: Praeger, 1996), 23.

28. In consequence, as Yao Dazhi and Xiang Yunhua have pointed out, Rorty on the one hand criticized the Enlightenment but on the other forcefully defended it. See Y. Dazhi and X. Yunhua, "Postmodernist Liberalism: A Critique of Richard Rorty's Political Philosophy," *Frontiers of Philosophy in China* 3, no. 3 (September 2008): 455–463.

29. See R. Rorty, "The Notion of Rationality," in Niżnik and Sanders, *Debating the State of Philosophy*, 85.

30. A sympathetic account of such perspective can be found in M. Asghari, "Has Richard Rorty a Moral Philosophy?," *Philosophical Investigations* 9, no. 17 (Fall–Winter 2015): 55–74. Asghari pointed out that the central aim of Rorty's moral philosophy was experiencing solidarity with others, which is "the basis of a democratic society and should be strengthened so that moral life could improve, namely, the reduction of all forms of cruelty and suffering through strengthening our moral solidarity with others." Asghari, "Richard Rorty," 72.

31. R. Rorty, *Philosophy as Cultural Politics* (Cambridge: Cambridge University Press, 2007), 53.

32. Rorty, *Philosophy as Cultural Politics*, 53.

33. Rorty, "On Moral Obligation," 49–50.

34. Habermas, "Unity of Reason," 135–136.

35. See R. Rorty, "Response to Habermas," in Brandom, *Rorty and His Critics*, 56.

36. Habermas, "Coping with Contingencies," 18.

37. He also wrote, "It is not that there is anything wrong with reason, truth, and knowledge. All that is wrong is the Platonic attempt to put them in the center of culture, in the center of our sense of what is to be a human being"; R. Rorty, "Emancipating Our Culture," in Niżnik and T. Sanders, *Debating the State of Philosophy*, 27–28.

38. Habermas, "Coping with Contingencies," 20.

39. J. Habermas, "The Dialectics of Rationalization," in *Autonomy and Solidarity: Interviews with Jürgen Habermas*, ed. P. Dews (London: Verso, 1992), 129.

40. Habermas, "Dialectics of Rationalization," 128.

41. On such new theories and their role in shaping reality, see R. Blaug, *Democracy, Real and Ideal: Discourse Ethics and Radical Politics* (New York: SUNY Press, 1999).

42. Habermas, "Coping with Contingencies," 19.

43. Habermas, "Coping with Contingencies," 23.

44. Rorty, "On Moral Obligation," 52.

45. J. Habermas, *The Philosophical Discourse of Modernity* (Cambridge, MA: The MIT Press, 1987), 206.
46. Rorty, *Contingency*, 66.
47. Habermas, "Coping with Contingencies," 24.
48. Habermas, "Coping with Contingencies," 24.
49. See Rorty, "Notion of Rationality," 87.
50. Rorty, "Notion of Rationality," 88.
51. Rorty "would agree" if he would accept that the redescriptions that he wanted to propose are not that radical. For more on this subject, see K. Topper, "Richard Rorty, Liberalism and the Politics of Redescription," *American Political Science Review* 89 (1995): 954–965.
52. Habermas, "Coping with Contingencies," 24.
53. Habermas, "Unity of Reason," 145.
54. Habermas, "Unity of Reason," 138.
55. Habermas, "Unity of Reason," 139.
56. Habermas, "Unity of Reason," 139.
57. Habermas, "Unity of Reason," 139.
58. Habermas, *Philosophical Discourse*, 206.
59. Rorty, *Contingency*, 68.
60. J. Habermas, "Modernity: An Unfinished Project," in *Habermas and the Unfinished Project of Modernity*, ed. M. P. d'Entrèves and S. Benhabib (Cambridge, MA: The MIT Press, 1997), 50.
61. Habermas, "Unity of Reason," 140.
62. Rorty, "Universality and Truth," 18.
63. Rorty, *Contingency*, 67.
64. Rorty, "Universality and Truth," 18.
65. Rorty, *Contingency*, 67–68.
66. Habermas, "Richard Rorty's Pragmatic Turn," 41.
67. Rorty, "Emancipating Our Culture," 28.
68. After Rorty admitted that *The Philosophical Discourse of Modernity* made an enormous impression on him, he added, "Ever since I read it I have thought of the 'linguistic turn' as subsumable within the larger movement from subject-centered rationality to communicative rationality." See Rorty, "Response to Habermas," 56.
69. Such a view is also shared by Robert B. Westbrook when he said, "Sometimes Rorty suggests that his pragmatism does include a modest, context-independent notion of rationality as 'reasonable.'" See R. B. Westbrook, *Democratic Hope, Pragmatism, and the Politics of Truth* (Ithaca, NY: Cornell University Press, 2005), 163.
70. In light of that he said, "Communicative reason is not a source of anything, but simply the activity of justifying claims by offering arguments rather than threats." See Rorty, *Philosophy as Cultural Politics*, 51.
71. Habermas, "Coping with Contingencies," 21–22.
72. These formal rules are important for Rorty's philosophy, which Miklos Nyiro calls a "practice in cultural politics." See M. Nyiro, "Rorty on Politics, Culture, and Philosophy: A Defence of His Romanticism," *Human Affairs* 19 (2009): 60–67.
73. Habermas, *Truth and Justification*, 1.

74. Rorty, "Emancipating Our Culture," 28.

75. See Rorty, "Response to Habermas," 56. Rorty added in a different place that the insistence of Habermas that the "regulative ideal of universal validity can save us from relativism" seemed to him inconsistent with his own account of reason as communicative rather than subject centered. See R. Rorty, *Philosophy as Poetry* (Charlottesville: University of Virginia Press, 2008), 55.

76. Habermas, *Truth and Justification*, 40.

77. Habermas, *Truth and Justification*, 40.

78. Habermas, "Unity of Reason," 145.

79. Habermas's awareness has, however, been limited, as Piet Strydom has argued, because he overlooked the problem of "triple contingency," which is the contingency that the public brings into the social process. For more on this subject, see P. Strydom, "The Problem of Triple Contingency in Habermas," *Sociological Theory* 19, no. 2 (July 2001): 165–186.

80. Strydom, "Problem of Triple Contingency," 140. Habermas added in *Truth and Justification*, "The reality facing our propositions is not 'naked', but is itself already permeated by language. The experience against which we check our assumptions is linguistically structured and embedded in contexts of action." Habermas, *Truth and Justification*, 36.

81. Habermas, *Truth and Justification*, 36.

82. For Rorty this was also a concession to Platonism. He said, "But I regard Habermas's insistence that we retain the ideal of universal validity as an unfortunate concession to Platonism." Rorty, *Philosophy as Cultural Politics*, 78.

83. Rorty, *Philosophy as Cultural Politics*, 138.

84. For Rorty, the "claim is disputable" in light of "poeticized culture of a liberal utopia" as being too theoretical and detached from the contingencies of a daily life. It is worth noting that his "poeticized culture" is, however, also described by Christopher M. Duncan as failing to accept its burdens and possibilities and as being too theoretical. See C. M. Duncan, "A Question for Richard Rorty," *Review of Politics* 66, no. 3 (2004): 385–414.

85. Rorty, "Notion of Rationality," 85.

86. Rorty, *Contingency*, 68.

87. Rorty, *Contingency*, 67.

88. Rorty also said, "As I see it, the notion of a 'universal validity claim', as used by Habermas and Apel, is just the claim to such a medal, and is thus dispensable. Although I entirely agree with Habermas about the desirability of substituting what he calls 'communicative reason' for 'subject-centred reason', I think of his insistence on universality, and his dislike for what he calls 'contextualism' and 'relativism', as leftovers from a period of philosophical thought in which it seemed that an appeal to the universal was the only alternative to immersion in the contingent status quo." See Rorty, *Philosophy and Social Hope*, 89n16.

89. Rorty, "Emancipating Our Culture," 28. Rorty referred to Ralph W. Emerson, for he "restated the Protagorean thesis that human beings are on their own—that their own imagination will have to do what they had hoped the gods, or a scientific

knowledge of the intrinsic nature of reality, might do"; Rorty, "Emancipating Our Culture," 26.

90. See R. Roderick, *Habermas and the Foundations of Critical Theory* (London: Pelgrave Macmillan, 1986), 84.

91. Rorty, *Contingency*, 84.

92. R. Rorty, *Essays on Heidegger and Others* (Cambridge, MA: Cambridge University Press, 1991), 197.

93. Rorty, *Contingency*, 64.

94. See J. Habermas, *The Future of Human Nature* (Cambridge: Polity, 2003). See also D. C. Henrich, "Human Nature and Autonomy: Jürgen Habermas' Critique of Liberal Eugenic," *Ethical Perspectives* 18, no. 2 (June 2011): 249–268.

95. R. Rorty, "Relativism—Finding and Making," in Niżnik and Sanders, *Debating the State of Philosophy*, 31.

96. This is why Critchley has pointed out that Rorty's pragmatic liberalism cannot be pragmatic all the way down. See S. Critchley, "Metaphysics in the Dark: A Response to Richard Rorty and Ernesto Laclau," *Political Theory* 26, no. 6 (December 1998): 812.

97. Habermas, "Coping with Contingencies," 23–24. Anton van Niekerk, who agreed with Habermas on the need of idealizations, pointed out that Rorty's position problematizes the possibility of international moral consensus that could make "more difficult for despots like Milosevich and Saddam Hussein to persist in their atrocities." For van Niekerk, Rorty's argumentation shows on the point idealizations both intellectual and moral poverty. See A. van Niekerk, "Contingency and Universality in the Habermas-Rorty Debate," *Acta Academica Suplementum* 2 (2005): 38.

98. Rorty, *Contingency*, 67.

99. Some of their critics also arrive at this conclusion. For more on Rorty's perspective, see J. B. Elshtain, "Don't Be Cruel: Reflections on Rortyan Liberalism," in *Richard Rorty*, ed. C. Guignon and D. R. Hiley (Cambridge: Cambridge University Press, 2003), 139–157. For more on Habermas's perspective, see H. Joas, *Pragmatism and Social Theory* (Chicago: Chicago University Press, 1993), 126–153.

100. For more on this subject, see Blaug, *Democracy*, 141–157.

101. It is worth mentioning that when Simon Critchley said that "possibly Habermas and Derrida share more with each other than they both share with Rorty [. . .] especially when it comes to political matters" he used the word "possibly." Besides, his belief is not contradicting the claim that what Habermas and Rorty share, "especially when it comes to political matters," is significant or very significant. See Critchley, *Metaphysics in the Dark*, 804.

102. Critchley, *Metaphysics in the Dark*, 66–67.

103. See J. Habermas, "A Philosophico-Political Profile," in *Autonomy and Solidarity: Interviews with Jürgen Habermas*, ed. P. Dews (London: Verso, 1992), 180.

104. J. Habermas, *The Theory of Communicative Action*, vol. 2, *Lifeworld and System: A Critique of Functionalist Reason*, trans. T. McCarthy (Boston: Beacon Press, 1987), 395.

105. R. Rorty, *Objectivity, Relativism, and Truth* (Cambridge: Cambridge University Press, 1991), 211.

106. J. Habermas, "Three Normative Models of Democracy," in *Constellations* 1, no. 1, (1994): 1.
107. Habermas, "Three Normative Models," 1.
108. Habermas, "Three Normative Models," 4.
109. M. Sandel, *Liberalism and the Limits of Justice* (Cambridge: Cambridge University Press, 1982), 49, in Rorty, *Objectivity*, 182.
110. Rorty, *Objectivity*, 188.
111. Rorty, *Objectivity*, 192.
112. For more on Rorty and communitarianism, see, for example, W. Kymlicka, *Liberalims, Community, and Culture* (Oxford: Clarendon Press, 1991), 64–70.
113. J. Rawls, "Justice as Fairness: Political not Metaphysical," *Philosophy and Public Affairs* 14, no. 3. (Summer 1985): 230; Rorty, *Objectivity*, 182.
114. Rorty, *Objectivity*, 191.
115. It is worth noticing, however, that Habermas disagreed with Rorty as far as his interpretation of John Rawls is concerned; see J. Habermas, *Between Facts and Norms* (Cambridge: Polity Press, 2004), 62. For more on Habermas and Rawls, see K. Baynes, *The Normative Grounds of Social Criticism: Kant, Rawls, Habermas* (New York: SUNY Press, 1992).
116. Rorty, *Objectivity*, 196.
117. Habermas, "Richard Rorty's Pragmatic Turn," 51.
118. Rorty, "Universality and Truth," 8.
119. Rorty, "Universality and Truth," 9.
120. Rorty, "Universality and Truth," 23.
121. Rorty, "Universality and Truth," 25.
122. Rorty, "Response to Habermas," 62.
123. Habermas, Habermas, "Three Normative Models," 6. In *Between Facts and Norms* Habermas also said, "According to this view, practical reason no longer resides in universal human rights, or in the ethical substance of a specific community, but in the rules of discourse and forms of argumentation that borrow their normative content from the validity basis of action oriented to reaching understanding. In the final analysis, this normative content arises from the structure of linguistic communication and the communicative mode of sociation." Habermas, *Between Facts and Norms*, 297.
124. In light of what Habermas said, Dryzek argued that "Habermas's democratic theory differs from republican theories, from communitarian theories and liberal theories." See J. S. Dryzek, *Deliberative Democracy and Beyond, Liberals, Critics, Contestation*, Oxford University Press, Oxford 1998, 26.
125. Habermas, *Between Facts and Norms*, 297.
126. Habermas, *Between Facts and Norms*, 298.
127. Habermas, Habermas, "Three Normative Models," 7–8. Habermas also repeated that point in *Between Facts and Norms*, see; Habermas, *Between Facts and Norms*, 298.
128. Habermas, Habermas, "Three Normative Models," 8. In *Between Facts and Norms* Habermas also referred to that issue by saying, "Discourse theory drops al those motifs employed by the *philosophy of consciousness* that lead one either

to ascribe the citizens' practice of self-determination to a macrosocial subject or to refer the anonymous rule of law to competing individual subjects." Habermas, *Between Facts and Norms*, 299.

129. See J. Habermas, *Theory and Practice*, Beacon Press, Boston 1973.

130. J. Habermas, "A Reply to My Critics," in *Habermas: Critical Debates*, ed. J. B. Thompson and D. Held (London: MIT Press, 1982), 262.

131. See Habermas, Habermas, "Three Normative Models," 10.

132. To properly place Habermas's arguments here in the historical context see J. S. Fishkin, *Deliberative Democracy*, in *The Blackwell Guide to Social and Political Philosophy*, ed. R. L. Simon, Blackwell Publishers Ltd, Oxford 2002, 221–238. On deliberative politics, see also J. Cohen, *Deliberation and Democratic Legitimacy*, in *Democracy*, ed. D. Estlund, Blackwell Publishers, Oxford 2002, 85–106.

133. Rorty, *Essays on Heidegger and Others*, 193. It is worth adding that Rorty perceived Habermas as a philosopher also concerned, just as he was, with questions such as "how we might change our social and political institutions so as better to combine freedom with order and justice." See Rorty, *Philosophy as Poetry*, 26.

134. Rorty, *Objectivity*, 209.

135. Rorty, *Objectivity*, 43.

136. Rorty, *Objectivity*, 45.

137. Rorty, "Heidegger, Kundera, and Dickens," 78.

138. Rorty, *Contingency*, 85.

139. Rorty, *Contingency*, 84.

140. Rorty, "Appendix 3," in Niżnik and Sanders, *Debating the State of Philosophy*, 124. As Richard Bernstein noted, Rorty sometimes also mentions a commitment to social justice, but "he rarely spells out what precisely he means—except for few general catchy phrases." R. J. Bernstein, "Rorty's Inspirational Liberalism," in *Richard Rorty*, ed. Charles B. Guignon and David R. Hiley (Cambridge: Cambridge University Press, 2003), 130.

141. Habermas, *Between Facts and Norms*, 398.

142. Habermas, *Between Facts and Norms*, 304.

143. Habermas, *Between Facts and Norms*, 299.

144. As announced, these threads will not be developed here because they were not the subject of the Rorty-Habermas debate.

145. Habermas, *Between Facts and Norms*, 310.

146. Habermas, *Between Facts and Norms*, 311.

147. I. Berlin, "Two Concepts of Liberty," in *Four Essays on Liberty* (Oxford: Oxford University Press, 1958), 2.

148. Berlin, "Two Concepts of Liberty," 6.

149. Berlin, "Two Concepts of Liberty," 4.

150. See Berlin, "Two Concepts of Liberty," 11.

151. Berlin, "Two Concepts of Liberty," 8.

152. Unfortunately, Berlin did not point out when precisely that happened.

153. Berlin, "Two Concepts of Liberty," 9.

154. For an example, inter alia, pointing to the same problems, see H. Arendt, *Essays in Understanding, 1930–1954: Formation, Exile, and Totalitarianism* (New

York: Schocken, 2005). See also F. A. Hayek, *The Constitution of Liberty* (Chicago: University of Chicago Press, 1978).

155. Hayek, *Constitution of Liberty*, 8.

156. For more on Berlin and Rorty, see E. Myers, "From Pluralism to Liberalism: Rereading Isaiah Berlin," *Review of Politics* 72, no. 4 (Fall 2010): 599–625; Jonny Steinberg, "Post-enlightenment Philosophy and Liberal Universalism," in *The Political Thought of Isaiah Berlin and Richard Rorty* (Oxford: University of Oxford, 1998). For more on Habermas and Berlin, see B. Walker, "Habermas and Pluralist Political Theory," *Philosophy and Social Criticism* 18, no. 1 (1992): 81–102.

157. Berlin, "Two Concepts of Liberty," 29.

158. Rorty, *Essays on Heidegger and Others*, 197.

159. Rorty, 195.

160. Rorty, 194.

161. Rorty, *Contingency*, 65.

162. Rorty, *Contingency*, 65.

163. On the present day difficulties with such approach, see J. F. Mowbray, "Autonomy, Identity and Self-knowledge: A New 'Solution' to the Liberal-Communitarian 'Problem'?," in *Human Rights: Old Problems, New Possibilities*, ed. D. Kinley, W. Sadurski, and K. Walton (Cheltenha, UK: Edward Elgar), .212–214.

164. Rorty, *Objectivity*, 14.

165. Rorty, "Relativism—Finding and Making," 31.

166. Rorty, "Relativism—Finding and Making," 43, 44.

167. Rorty, "Relativism—Finding and Making," 44.

168. For more on the role of emotions in Rorty's thought, see J.-M. Barreto, "Rorty and Human Rights: Contingency, Emotions and How to Defend Human Rights Telling Stories," *Utrecht Law Review* 7, no. 2 (April 2011): 93–112; R. Lamb, "Pragmatism, Practices, and Human Rights," *Review of International Studies* 45, no. 4 (October 2019): 550–568.

169. For a defense of human nature, see, for example, also I. Hacking, *The Social Construction of What?* (Cambridge, MA: Harvard University Press, 1999). It is worth noting that some critics, even though they recognize that some categories are indeed social constructions, at the same time provide arguments to defend the category of human nature and back up their argumentation by referring to psychology or cognitive science. See, for example, S. Pinker, *The Blank Slate: The Modern Denial of Human Nature* (New York: Penguin Books, 2003), 202.

170. Berlin, "Two Concepts of Liberty," 32.

171. Berlin, "Two Concepts of Liberty," 32.

172. Berlin, "Two Concepts of Liberty," 32.

173. While Berlin was well aware of the relativity of principles, he was not a relativist but a pluralist. For more on this subject, see I. Berlin and B. Polanowska-Sygulska, *Unfinished Dialogue* (Amherst, NY: Prometheus Books, 2006); J. Gray, *Isaiah Berlin: An Interpretation of His Thought* (Princeton, NJ: Princeton University Press, 2013).

174. Gray, *Isaiah Berlin*, 31.

175. For more on pluralism as a feature of Rorty's philosophy and of his pragmatism, see J. R. Shook, "Pragmatism, Pluralism, and Public Democracy," *Revue française d'études américaines* 2, no. 124 (2010): 11–28. For more on Habermas and pluralism, see Walker, "Habermas and Pluralist Political Theory," 81–102.

176. Habermas, *The Theory of Communicative Action*, vol. 1, *Reason and the Rationalization of Society*, trans. T. McCarthy (Boston: Beacon Press, 1984), 70.

177. Habermas, "Philosophico-Political Profile," 171.

178. J. Habermas, "Reply to My Critics," 238. As he put it, "Post-empiricist philosophy of science has provided good reasons for holding that the unsettled ground of rationally motivated agreement among participants in argumentation is our only foundation—in questions of physics no less than in those of morality." Habermas, "Reply to My Critics," 238.

179. Habermas, "Dialectics of Rationalization," 129.

180. Habermas, "Dialectics of Rationalization," 125.

181. Habermas, *Theory of Communicative Action*, 1:140.

182. Habermas, *Theory of Communicative Action*, 1:140.

183. By means of the theory of communication, as Habermas noted, it is possible to "explain the symbolic reproduction of the lifeworld of a social group [. . .] if we approach the matter from an internal perspective"; Habermas, *Theory of Communicative Action*, 1:2. He highlighted, however, that it is impossible to explain to a satisfactory extent the reproduction of a society by referring to the conditions of communicative rationality. For apart from symbolic reproduction, there is also material reproduction that is realized through the medium of purposive activity. By its means individuals influence the world in order to realize their objectives.

184. Habermas, *Theory of Communicative Action*, 1:137.

185. Habermas, "Reply to My Critics," 227.

186. Rorty, *Contingency*, 67–68.

187. Rorty, *Objectivity*, 42.

188. Rorty, *Objectivity*, 199.

189. Rorty, *Contingency*, 195.

190. For more on Sellars's arguments, see J. O'Shea, *Wilfrid Sellars: Naturalism with a Normative Turn* (London: Polity Press, 2007).

191. Rorty, *Contingency*, 59.

192. Rorty, *Contingency*, 59.

193. Rorty, *Contingency*, 59.

194. M. Oakeshott, *On Human Conduct* (Oxford: Oxford University Press, 1975), 78–79.

195. Rorty, *Contingency*, 58.

196. For more on Oakeshott and his understanding of contingency, see D. R. Mapel, "Civil Association and the Idea of Contingency," *Political Theory* 18, no. 3 (August 1990): 392–410.

197. Rorty, "Relativism—Finding and Making," 43.

198. Rorty, *Essays on Heidegger and Others*, 196. The moral identity that is supposed to be characteristic of the public sphere is, for Rorty, the opposite to the private identity characteristic of the private sphere. Thus, it is important to bear

in mind that moral identity does not exhaust the self-description of a "Romantic intellectual" who does not think that the relation to other human beings should be of the utmost significance for oneself. What is more important for a "Romantic intellectual," as Rorty noted, is looking for their own private autonomy.

199. Rorty, *Essays on Heidegger and Others*, 196.

200. R. Rorty, *Consequences of Pragmatism: Essays, 1972–1980* (Minneapolis: University of Minnesota Press, 1994), xv.

201. Rorty, *Contingency*, 84.

202. See Habermas, "Reply to My Critics," 248.

203. Rorty, Rorty, "Universality and Truth," 17. Rorty also said that the "distinction between social practice and what transcends such practice is an undesirable remnant of logocentrism." Rorty, "Universality and Truth," 7.

204. Habermas, *Theory of Communicative Action*, 1:20.

205. Habermas, *Theory of Communicative Action*, 1:42.

206. See Rorty, *Objectivity*, 198. Rorty refers to the adherents of such a perspective as "Hegelians."

207. Rorty, *Objectivity*, 197.

208. Rorty, *Objectivity*, 199.

209. Rorty, *Objectivity*, 198. This is an opinion held by Hegelians, and by Rorty as well.

210. Rorty, "Universality and Truth," 19–20.

211. Rorty, *Essays on Heidegger and Others*, 198.

212. Here, Rorty's thought is quite unlike the position of Michel Foucault, who perceived our involvements in the "networks of power" as negative.

213. Habermas has labeled this process socialization; however, he does not understand it in a negative way, as an imposition of a given perspective. It is related not to subjugation but to teaching, so that individuals can pursue to their full extent responsible self-realization.

214. Habermas, *Theory of Communicative Action*, 2:141.

215. Habermas, "Unity of Reason," 146.

216. Habermas, *Truth and Justification*, 34.

217. Rorty, *Objectivity*, 41.

218. Rorty, *Philosophy as Cultural Politics*, 54.

219. Rorty, *Philosophy as Cultural Politics*, 31–32.

220. R. Rorty, "Edukacja i wyzwanie postnowoczesności" [Education and the challenge of postmodernity], trans. L. Witkowski, in *Spory o edukację: Dylematy i kontrowersje we współczesnych pedagogikach* [Debates on education: Dilemmas and controversies in contemporary pedagogy], ed. Z. Kwieciński and L. Witkowski (Warsaw: Instytut Badań Edukacyjnych, 1993), 100. What we teach is tolerance, equality, and liberty, and the better objective we aim at is agreement arrived at via communication.

221. R. Rorty, "Amerykanizm i pragmatyzm" [Americanism and pragmatism], trans. A. Grzeliński, in *Filozofia amerykańska dziś* [American philosophy today], ed. T. Komendziński and A. Szahaj (Toruń, Poland: Wydawnictwo Naukowe UMK, 1999), 122.

222. Habermas, *Theory of Communicative Action*, 1:36.
223. Habermas, *Theory of Communicative Action*, 2:145.
224. Habermas, *Theory of Communicative Action*, 1:19.
225. Rorty, *Objectivity*, 212–213.
226. J. Habermas, "Die Krise des Wehlwahrfstaates und die Erschörfung utopischer Energie," in *Die neue Unübersichtlichkeit* (Frankfurt: Suhrkamp, 1985), 161.
227. Answering such a question is especially important in light of Rorty's claim that his "basic disagreement with Habermas concerns his attempt to retain the notion of the intrinsically better argument while adopting a theory of the sociality of reason." See Rorty, *Philosophy as Cultural Politics*, 83.
228. Rorty, "On Moral Obligation," 48. Rorty wrote about moral progress, though at another point, he also observed that making people more sensitive would lead to a progress in sentiment. The intuition that underlies those seemingly different kinds of progress is the same: we should search for similarities and not for differences between us, and we should not be motivated only by the ability to acquire knowledge but also by the ability to develop friendships. It is not morality based upon rationality that should form the foundations of our actions but morality based upon sentimentality, on empathy with the pain and the suffering of "others"; see R. Rorty, *Truth and Progress: Philosophical Papers III* (Cambridge: Cambridge University Press, 1998), 184–185.
229. See Habermas, "Dialectics of Rationalization," 125.
230. See Habermas, *Theory of Communicative Action*, 1:341; Habermas, "Unity of Reason," 146.
231. For more on the importance of compassion for Habermas, see Habermas, "Reply to My Critics," 245–247.
232. Rorty, "On Moral Obligation," 48.
233. Rorty, *Contingency*, 59.
234. Apart from books that help us to become less cruel, Rorty also mentioned books that help us achieve autonomy. The former concern our relations with others. The latter are connected with idiosyncratic contingencies. We may mention here the works of Vladimir Nabokov, who described cruelty from the inside, helping us see how the private pursuit of aesthetic pleasure gives rise to cruelty.
235. Rorty, *Contingency*, 141. Books of the former kind may be exemplified by *Uncle Tom's Cabin*; books of the latter kind, with the aforesaid works by Nabokov. We may also say that, on the one hand, there is George Orwell, and on the other, Nabokov. Both, as Rorty claimed, warn the ironist liberal intellectual against the tendency to be cruel, and both highlight the tension between private irony and liberal hope; Rorty, *Contingency*, 144. For more on the role of literature in Rorty's philosophy, see M. Fisher, "Refefining Philosophy as Literature: Richard Rorty's 'Defense' of Literary Culture," *Interdisciplinary Journal* 67, no. 3 (Fall 1984): 312–324. See also L. Bredella, "Richard Rorty on Philosophy, Literature and Hermeneutics," in *Literature and Philosophy*, ed. Herbert Grabes (Tübingen: Narr Francke Attempto Verlag, 1997), 103–124.
236. Rorty, *Essays on Heidegger and Others*, 196.
237. Habermas, "Unity of Reason," 146.

238. J. Dewey, *Individualism, Old and New*, LW 5:75.
239. Habermas, *Between Facts and Norms*, 314.
240. See Berlin, "Two Concepts of Liberty," 30.
241. Berlin, "Two Concepts of Liberty," 32.
242. Rorty, *Contingency*, 46.
243. Rorty, *Contingency*, 46.
244. For an interesting account of application of such an approach, see, for example, E. Brigham, *Sustaining the Hope for Unity: Ecumenical Dialogue in a Postmodern World* (Wilmington, NC: Michel Glazier, 2012).
245. Rorty, *Objectivity*, 193.
246. As far as rationality is concerned, the approaches of Habermas and Rorty, as it has already been said, are convergent. This approach refers to undistorted communication and tolerance.
247. Berlin, "Two Concepts of Liberty," 30.
248. Rorty, *Objectivity*, 194.
249. Rorty, *Essays on Heidegger and Others*, 196.
250. In such a way we can establish conditions for moral progress. For more on this subject, see M. Nussbaum, "On Moral Progress: A Response to Richard Rorty," *University of Chicago Law Review* 74, no. 3 (Summer 2007): 939–960.
251. R. Rorty, *An Ethics for Today: Finding Common Ground Between Philosophy and Religion* (New York: Columbia University Press, 2008), 22.
252. Rorty, *Contingency*, 86.
253. Rorty, *Contingency*, 86.
254. R. Rorty, *Essays on Heidegger and Others* (Cambridge: Cambridge University Press, 1991), 26. Rorty believed that so far no one has offered a proposal of how to put an end to the at the close of the twentieth century, a proposal that would use new conceptual resources, new vocabularies and metaphors. He wrote, "Our political imagination has not been enlarged by the philosophy of our century. This is not because of the irrelevance or cowardice or irresponsibility of philosophy professors, but because of the sheer recalcitrance of situation into which the human race has stumbled." However, these words had been put down, as Rorty himself noted, before the appearance of Mikhail Gorbachev. He would never have thought that this protégé of Yuri Andropov would become the Abraham Lincoln of Central and Eastern Europe; see Rorty, *Essays on Heidegger and Others*, 26.
255. R. Rorty, *Essays on Heidegger and Others* (Cambridge: Cambridge University Press, 1991), 81.
256. Rorty, *Contingency*, 63.
257. For an approach outlining how that new vocabulary can help with transition toward "antiauthoritarian" society and what role the intellectual might play in contemporary life, see M. Bacon, *Richard Rorty: Pragmatism and Political Liberalism* (Lanham, MD: Lexington Books, 2007); C. Voparil, *Richard Rorty: Politics and Vision* (Lanham, MD: Rowman & Littlefield, 2006); W. Curtis, *Defending Rorty: Pragmatism and Liberal Virtue* (Cambridge: Cambridge University Press, 2015); N. Gascoigne, *Richard Rorty: Liberalism, Irony, and the Ends of Philosophy*

(Cambridge: Polity Press, 2008); J. Tomborino, "Philosophy as the Mirror of Liberalism: The Politics of Richard Rorty," *Polity* 30 (1997): 57–78.

258. R. Rorty, "A Pragmatist View of Rationality and Cultural Difference," *Philosophy East and West* 42, no. 4 (1992): 587–588.

259. Rorty, "Heidegger, Kundera, and Dickens," 75.

260. Rorty, "Edukacja," 101. Interestingly Westbrook noted, "[W]hat most distinguishes the American hope of the pragmatists from that of others—and makes it so intriguing—is that it is hope without transcendental foundations." See Westbrook, *Democratic Hope*, 141.

261. For more on this subject, see D. S. Owen, *Between Reason and History: Habermas and the Idea of Progress* (Albany: State University of New York Press, 2002).

262. Habermas, "Die Krise des Wehlwahrfstaates," 143.

263. For more on the complex role science and technology played in development of the twentieth century, see J. Lukács, *A Short History of the Twentieth Century* (Cambridge, MA: Belknap Press, 2013; T. Judt, *Postwar: A History of Europe since 1945* (London: Vintage Books, 2010).

264. Habermas, *Theory of Communicative Action*, 2:326.

265. Habermas, *Theory of Communicative Action*, 2:326–327.

266. Habermas, "Modernity: An Unfinished Project," in *Habermas and the Unfinished Project of Modernity*, ed. M. P. d'Entrèves and S. Benhabib (Cambridge, MA: The MIT Press, 1997), 51.

267. Rorty, "Notion of Rationality," 85.

268. Rorty, *Objectivity*, 220.

269. He is supported by those that, despite the challenges brought by the twentieth century, critically examine the views of many contemporary skeptics and consider the potential for progressive social change. See, for example, G. Teeple, *Globalization and the Decline of Social Reform: Into the Twenty-First Century* (Toronto: University of Toronto Press, 2000).

270. Rorty, *Objectivity*, 220. Such citations prove that claims that Rorty and Habermas represent "totally different conceptions" on the role and function of language, and on truth and rationality in dialogue, are incorrect. See K. Kyung-Man, "Beyond Justification: Habermas, Rorty and the Politics of Cultural Change," *Theory, Culture and Society* 31, no. 6 (2014): 103–123.

271. R. Rorty, "Philosophy and the Future," in *Rorty and Pragmatism: The Philosopher Responds to His Critics*, ed. H. J. Saatkamp (Nashville, TN: Vanderbilt University Press, 1995), 203.

272. Rorty, "Philosophy and the Future," 204.

273. See Rorty, "Notion of Rationality," 85.

274. Habermas, "Dialectics of Rationalization," 125.

275. Rorty, *Objectivity*, 218.

276. Habermas, when writing about the rational structures of arriving at an agreement, hoped that they would be recognized as universal; still, sometimes, as it has already been said, he has tried to justify their universality.

277. Rorty, *Objectivity*, 190.

278. Rorty, *Objectivity*, 191.
279. Rorty, *Objectivity*, 191.
280. Rorty, "Universality and Truth," 22.
281. Rorty, "Universality and Truth," 17.
282. Rorty, "Appendix 3," 125.
283. Rorty, "Universality and Truth," 22.
284. Rorty, *Philosophy as Cultural Politics*, 54. Rorty also backed up his argument by referring to Isaiah Berlin, who argued in his "Two Concepts of Liberty" that some goods are incompatible with one another, "no matter what sociopolitical setup we come to agree on, some-thing will be lost. Somebody will get hurt." Berlin, "Two Concepts of Liberty," 81.
285. Habermas, *Theory of Communicative*, 1:42. Validity claims include the truthfulness of statements, rightfulness of norms regulating moral actions, and comprehensiveness or correctness of formulated symbolic expressions. In order to affirm these validity claims it is not necessary to "introduce" them by means of transcendental deduction; it is enough to follow a reliable procedure based upon testing of reconstructional hypotheses. The validity of each of the claims can be intersubjectively tested by referring to one's "reasons."
286. What is more, forms of argumentation also differentiate according to these universal validity claims. These forms often become recognizable only in relation to certain contexts of expression; however, as Habermas has pointed out, they are not constituted by them.
287. Habermas, *Theory of Communicative Action*, 2:383. In order to do that, he analyzed the theory of speech acts so as to point out that the primary aim of using language is to reach understanding.
288. See Habermas, "Reply to My Critics," 233–234.
289. Habermas, "Philosophico-Political Profile," 165.
290. J. Habermas, *Theory of Communicative Action*, 2:174–175. We owe new forms of social integration to the utilization and institutionalization of knowledge forms acquired individually, and then transmitted and collectively made accessible. The process of their implementation in the social sphere is pursued alongside political struggles and social movements, with the involvement of marginal and innovative groups.
291. Habermas, *Theory of Communicative Action*, 2:183.
292. Habermas, *Theory of Communicative Action*, 1:41.
293. Habermas, *Theory of Communicative Action*, 1:42.
294. Habermas, *Theory of Communicative Action*, 1:38.
295. Habermas, *Theory of Communicative Action*, 1:305.
296. Rorty, "Universality and Truth," 15.
297. Habermas, "Reply to My Critics," 236.
298. See Habermas, "Reply to My Critics," 235.
299. Rorty, "Universality and Truth," 16–17.
300. Rorty, "Universality and Truth," 9.
301. Rorty, *Contingency*, 83–84.
302. Rorty, "Philosophy and the Future," 204.

303. Rorty, *Philosophy and the Mirror of Nature* (Princeton, NJ: Princeton University Press, 1979), 394.

304. Rorty, *Essays on Heidegger and Others*, 25.

305. Rorty, "Philosophy and the Future," 205.

306. Rorty, "Universality and Truth," 14.

307. Rorty, "Response to Habermas," 63.

308. E. Mendieta, ed., *Take Care of Freedom and Truth Will Take Care of Itself: Interviews with Richard Rorty*, (Stanford, CA: Stanford University Press, 2005), 51.

309. Rorty, *Consequences of Pragmatism*, xv.

310. Proceeding with this thought, he wrote, "With modern science, with positive law and principled secular ethics, with autonomous art and institutionalized art criticism, three moments of reason crystallized without help from philosophy. Even without the guidance of the critiques of pure and practical reason, the sons and daughters of modernity learned how to divide up and develop further the cultural tradition under these different aspects of rationality—as questions of truth, justice, or taste"; Habermas, *Theory of Communicative Action*, 2:397.

311. Habermas, "Unity of Reason," 146. It is worth remembering that achieving this undistorted intersubjectivity cannot be regarded as achieving an ideal life-form.

312. Habermas, *Theory of Communicative Action*, 2:423.

313. Habermas, *Truth and Justification*, 279.

Notes to Chapter V

1. Pragmatism, in other words, does more than just "signal ... an attitude, an orientation"; it "clears the underbrush without planting a forest," as Richard Posner claimed. See R. A. Posner, "What Has Pragmatism to Offer Law?," *Southern California Law Review* 63 (1990): 1670.

2. For other attempts to position Dewey in relation to Habermas's philosophy, see J. Gouinlock, "Dewey and Contemporary Moral Philosophy," in *Philosophy and the Reconstruction of Culture: Pragmatic Essays after Dewey*, ed. J. J. Stuhr (State University of New York Press, 1993), 79–96; P. Deen, "Dewey, Habermas, and the Unfinished Project of Modernity in Unmodern Philosophy and Modern Philosophy," in *The Oxford Handbook of Dewey*, ed. Steven Fesmire (Oxford: Oxford University Press, 2019); R. Antonio and D. Kellner, "Communication, Modernity and Democracy in Habermas and Dewey," *Symbolic Interaction* 15, no. 3 (Fall 1992): 77–298; S. B. Rosenthal, "Habermas, Dewey, and Democratic Self," in *Habermas and Pragmatism*, ed. A. Michell, M. Orbach Bookman, and C. Kemp (London: Routledge, 2002)210–222. On Dewey in reference to Rorty's philosophy, see R. W. Sleeper, "The Pragmatics of Deconstruction and the End of Metaphysics," in *Philosophy and the Reconstruction of Culture: Pragmatic Essays after Dewey*, ed. J. J. Stuhr (Albany: State University of New York Press, 1993), 241–256; C. Voparil, "Rorty and Dewey Revisited: Toward a Fruitful Conversation," *Transactions of the Charles S. Peirce Society* 50, no. 3 (Summer 2014): 373–404.

3. J. Dewey, *Reconstruction in Philosophy and Essays*, MW 12:91–91.

317. Philosophy is understood here as social criticism. It is worth adding that such an understanding of philosophy can be seen in Dewey as well as in Habermas, and it affects the way both have thought about democracy. Alan Rayan said, "[T]here are many connections between Habermas's ideas about emancipatory forms of social theory and Dewey's conception of philosophy as social criticism; there is a clear affinity between the way Dewey's *Democracy and Education* links human communication and democracy and the way Habermas develops an account of democracy in communicative terms." See A. Rayan, *John Dewey and the High Tide of American Liberalism* (New York: W. W. Norton & Company, 1997), 357.

5. Habermas, *Theory of Communicative Action*, 1:1.
6. J. Dewey, *Quest for Certainty*, LW 4:226.
7. J. Dewey, *Essays in Experimental Logic*, MW 10:46.
8. Rorty, *Essays on Heidegger and Others*, 9.
9. Habermas, Habermas, "Dialectics of Rationalization," 96.
10. Habermas, *Truth and Justification*, 290.
11. J. Dewey, "Reconstruction in Philosophy," in Rorty, "Pragmatyzm," 112.
12. See Rorty, *Essays on Heidegger and Others*, 20.
13. Rorty, *Objectivity*, 194.
14. J. Dewey, *Democracy Is Radical*, LW 11:220. As James Campbell said, "Dewey's conception of our goal is thus not *freedom from involvement* but rather *free and full participation*." See J. Campbell, *Understanding John Dewey: Nature and Cooperative Intelligence* (Chicago: Open Court, 1995), 169.
15. J. Dewey, *Liberalism and Civil Liberties*, LW 11:374.
16. For more on this subject, see P. Kitcher, "Pragmatism and Progress," *Transactions of the Charles S. Peirce Society* 51, no. 4 (Winter 2015): 475–494. See also, R. J. Bernstein, "American Pragmatism: The Conflict of Narratives," in *Rorty and Pragmatism: The Philosopher Responds to His Critics*, ed. H. J. Saatkamp (Nashville, TN: Vanderbilt University Press, 1995), 54–67.
17. Rorty rightly pointed out that "for Dewey, as for Habermas, what takes the place of the urge to represent reality accurately is the urge to come to free agreement with our fellow human beings—to be full participating members of a free community of inquiry." See Rorty, *Philosophy and Social Hope*, 119.
18. Habermas, *Theory of Communicative Action*, 1:2.
19. See Rorty, *Essays on Heidegger and Others*, 18.
20. Rorty, *Philosophy and Social Hope*, 119.
21. For more on this subject, see Campbell, *Understanding John Dewey*, 166–177.
22. Rorty, *Philosophy and Social Hope*, 118.
23. Rorty, *Objectivity*, 1.
24. Habermas, "Coping with Contingencies," 20.
25. Rorty, *Philosophy and the Mirror of Nature*, 9.
26. For more on this subject, see J. Cohen, "Discourse Ethics and Civil Society," in Saatkamp, *Rorty and Pragmatism*, 83–101.
27. R. Rorty, "Is It Desirable to Love Truth?," in *Truth, Politics, and "Post-Modernism"* (Assen, Netherlands: Van Gorcum, 1997), 22.

28. Their vision of liberal democracy reaches outside of liberal tradition. It might be said that it reconciles liberalism and communitarianism. See B. Singer, "Reconciling Liberalism and Communitarianism," in *Pragmatism, Rights, and Democracy* (New York: Fordham University Press, 1999).

29. Habermas, *The Theory of Communicative Action*, 1:2.

30. Rorty, "Universality and Truth," 7–8.

31. R. Rorty, "Response to Jürgen Habermas," in Brandom, *Rorty and His Critics*, 61.

32. Habermas, "Richard Rorty's Pragmatic Turn," 51.

33. R. Rorty, "Response to Jürgen Habermas," in R. Brandom, *Rorty and His Critics*, 61.

34. Rorty, "Response to Jürgen Habermas," 61.

35. Rorty, *Objectivity*, 211.

36. Robert Westbrook has found such accusations inappropriate, however, he saw such a danger when analyzing Rorty's philosophy. He said that "Rortyan pragmatism, unlike Deweyan pragmatism, must entertain the possibility of a fascist brother and of a pragmatized culture that would be a very nasty and illiberal affair." Westbrook, *Democratic Hope*, 163.

37. Rorty, *Objectivity*, 190.

38. Rorty, "Appendix 3," 123.

39. Rorty, "Relativism—Finding and Making," 47.

40. Rorty, *Consequences of Pragmatism*, 70.

41. See J. P. Sartre, *Existentialism Is a Humanism* (New Haven, CT: Yale University Press, 2007), 36.

42. Rorty, *Objectivity*, 42. However, Rorty did not state that it is impossible to justify in a rational way the superiority of liberal societies over totalitarian ones on the basis of the fact that it is impossible to step out of the community onto neutral grounds of some sort. Such a conclusion would require the concept of "rationality" understood as a set of ahistorical rules, an idea that the pragmatists reject; see Rorty, *Objectivity*, 42.

43. Rorty, *Philosophy and the Mirror of Nature*, 364–365.

44. Rorty, *Essays on Heidegger and Others*, 25. He argued that theoretical reflection can be of little help with respect to solving our current problems, for "once we have criticized all the self-descriptive sophistry, and exposed all the 'false consciousness', the result of our efforts is to find ourselves just where our grandfathers suspected we were: in the midst of a struggle for power between those who currently possess it [. . .] and those who are starving or terrorized because they lack it"; Rorty, *Essays on Heidegger and Others*, 25–26.

45. Rorty, *Objectivity*, 184. It is worth adding that he saw the criticism of ideology as based on the distinction between what is ideological and what is not. As he noted, it is "an occasionally useful tactical weapon in social struggles," but only one of many; see Rorty, *Essays on Heidegger and Others*, 135.

46. M. Kundera, *The Art of Novel*, 160, in Rorty, "Heidegger, Kundera, and Dickens," 73. For more on Kundera and Rorty, see E. Gander, *The Last Conceptual Revolution: A Critique of Richard Rorty's Political Philosophy* (Albany: State University of New York, 1998), 170–174.

47. Rorty, *Contingency*, 57.

48. Rorty, "Wstęp do polskiego wydania esejów Stanleya Fisha" [Introduction to the Polish edition of Stanley Fish's essays], in *Stanley Fish: Interpretacja, retoryka, polityka: Eseje wybrane* [Stanley Fish: Interpretation, rhetoric, politics: Selected essays], trans. and ed. A. Szahaj (Kraków, Poland: Universitas, 2002), 12.

49. Rorty, "Pragmatist View," 581.

50. Habermas, *Theory of Communicative Action*, 1:70.

51. Habermas, "What Theories Can Accomplish," 101–102.

52. Habermas, *Between Facts and Norms*, 304. Habermas has quoted Dewey's *The Public and Its Problems* (Chicago, 1954). In this citation Dewey quoted Samuel J. Tilden.

53. R. Rorty, *Filozofia i przyszłość*, s. 93.

54. J. Dewey, *The Public and Its Problems*, LW 2:350. In *Ideologies and Political Theory: A Conceptual Approach*, Michael Freeden, following that line of argument, has pointed out that there are no absolute standards independent of the vocabularies we employ, but he also said that we need enlightened deliberation and factual knowledge (that torture brings suffering) about what may lead to human flourishing without universal validity. M. Freeden, *Ideologies and Political Theory: A Conceptual Approach* (Oxford: Clarendon Press, 1996), 91–92.

55. For more on this subject, see W. Brown, *Regulating Aversion: Tolerance in the Age of Identity and Empire* (Princeton, NJ: Princeton University Press, 2006).

56. Rorty, "Pragmatist View," 591.

57. Rorty, "Emancipating Our Culture," 26.

58. Rorty, *Achieving Our Country* (Cambridge, MA: Harvard University Press, 1998), 106–107.

59. S. Hook, *Pragmatism and the Tragic Sense of Life*, in Rorty, *Consequences of Pragmatism*, 69–70.

60. Rorty, "Pragmatyzm," 112; Rorty, *Essays on Heidegger and Others*, 24.

61. Rorty, *Essays on Heidegger and Others*, 24.

62. As Rosenthal said, "Both Habermas and Dewey are concerned with community solidarity within the context of pluralism and diversity, avoiding the extremes of the homogeneity of the communitarian vision and the fragmented, heterogeneous pluralism of the libertarian vision." See Rosenthal, "Habermas, Dewey, and Democratic Self," 210. On that issue, see also K. Baynes, "The Liberal/Communitarian Controversy and Communicative Ethics," in *Universalism vs. Communitarianism: Contemporary Debates in Ethics*, ed. D. Rasmussen (Cambridge, MA: The MIT Press, 1995).

63. Rorty, *Objectivity*, 211.

64. Rorty, *Objectivity*, 13.

65. R. Rorty, "Appendix 2," in Niżnik and Sanders, *Debating the State of Philosophy*, 114–115.

66. Rorty, "Pragmatyzm," 117–118.

67. Rorty, "Is It Desirable?," 30.

68. J. Habermas, "Postscript—Reflections on Pragmatism," in *Habermas and Pragmatism*, ed. M. Aboulafia, M. Orbach Bookman, and C. Kemp (London: Routledge, 2002), 229.

69. J. Habermas, "A Conversation about Questions of Political Theory," in *A Berlin Republic: Writings on Germany*, trans. S. Rendall (Cambridge: Polity Press, 1997), 133–134.

70. R. Rorty, "Is It Desirable?," 21.

71. Rorty, "Edukacja," 102.

72. Rorty, *Philosophy and the Mirror of Nature*, 358–359.

73. That hope was already present in the works of Whitman and Dewey. As Rorty wrote, "Whitman and Dewey tried to substitute hope for knowledge. They wanted to put shared utopian dreams—dreams of an ideally decent and civilized society—in the place of knowledge of God's Will, Moral Law, the Laws of History, or the Facts of Science." See Rorty, *Achieving Our Country*, 106–107.

74. Dewey's and Rorty's philosophies can be even called "philosophies of hope." See C. Koopman, "Pragmatism as a Philosophy of Hope: Emerson, James, Dewey, Rorty," *Journal of Speculative Philosophy—New Series* 20, no. 2 (2006): 106–116.

75. See Rorty, "On Moral Obligation," 50.

76. J. Habermas, "What Theories Can Accomplish," 116–117. Habermas has written on some of these dilemmas in J. Habermas, "The Tendency toward a Mutual Infiltration of Public and Private Spheres," in *The Structural Transformation of The Public Sphere* (Cambridge, MA: MIT Press, Cambridge 1991), 141–151.

77. James Campbell has also added that "the level of work necessary to fulfill the responsibilities of democracy makes Dewey's democrats active participants in communal life." See Campbell, *Understanding John Dewey*, 180.

Notes to the Conclusion

1. J. Habermas, "Rorty's pragmatische Wende," in J. Habermas, *Warheit und Rechtferigung* (Frankfurt am Main: Suhrkamp, 1999), 258.

2. Rorty said, "We can work toward intersubjective agreement without being lured by the promise of universal validity." See R. Rorty, *Philosophy as Cultural Politics*, vol. 4, *Philosophy as Cultural Politics: Philosophical Papers IV* (Cambridge: Cambridge University Press, 2007), 85.

3. J. Habermas, *The Theory of Communicative Action*, vol. 2, *Lifeworld and System: A Critique of Functionalist Reason*, transl. T. McCarthy (Boston: Beacon Press, 1987), 400.

4. For a critique of universality in the theory of communicative action, see also J. McCumber, *Philosophy as Freedom: Derrida, Rorty, Habermas, Foucault* (Bloomington: Indiana University Press, 2000), 91–96. On what to do with these troubling claims about universality, see McCumber, *Philosophy as Freedom*, 105–108. For more on communicative ethics and the controversies surrounding it, see also S. Benhabib and F. Dallmayr, eds., *Communicative Ethics Controversy* (Cambridge, MA: MIT Press, 1990).

5. To sum up in Rorty's own words, "As I see it, the only serious or interesting disagreement between Habermas and myself is about whether you need notions like 'unconditionality' and 'universal validity' in order to justify social democratic institutions." R. Rorty, "Response to Richard Shusterman," in *Richard Rorty: Critical Dialogues*, ed. M. Festenstein and S. Thompson (Cambridge: Polity Press, 2001), 153.

6. See J. Habermas, "The Unity of Reason in the Diversity of Its Voices," in *Postmetaphysical Thinking*, trans. W. M. Hohengarten (Cambridge, MA: The MIT Press, 1992), 146.

7. Habermas wrote, "[T]his perspective comprises *only* formal determinations of the communicative infrastructure of *possible* forms of life and life-histories"; see J. Habermas, "A Reply to My Critics," in *Habermas: Critical Debates*, ed. J. B. Thompson and D. Held (London: The MIT Press), 228.

8. This view is supported by Jari I. Niemi, who argues that Habermas's understanding of speech acts as oriented toward understanding, and which raise three different kinds of validity claims simultaneously (claims to truth, truthfulness, and normative rightness), receives cogent support only from the argument from understanding and reaching understanding, and only if the notion of 'understanding' is expanded to that of 'agreement.'" See Jari I. Niemi, "Habermas and Validity Claims," *International Journal of Philosophical Studies* 13, no. 2 (2005): 227–244.

9. J. Habermas, "A Philosophico-Political Profile," in *Autonomy and Solidarity: Interviews with Jürgen Habermas*, ed. P. Dews (London: Verso, 1992), 180.

10. Such a perspective is also presented by Peter Dews. He added that "the assumptions and values which structure the lifeworld are not projections on to the blank screen of a value-neutral reality, but rather perspectival ways of experiencing the world as such." See P. Dews, *Habermas: A Critical Reader* (Oxford: Blackwell Publishers, 1999), 21.

11. R. Rorty, *Contingency, Irony, and Solidarity* (Cambridge: Cambridge University Press, 198), 189.

12. This is the difficulty, this is the "tragedy," as Bert van den Brink would say, which liberalism must face. See Bert van den Brink, *The Tragedy of Liberalism, An Alternative Defense of a Political Tradition* (Albany: State University of New York Press, 2000).

13. J. Habermas, "What Theories Can Accomplish—and What They Can't," in *The Past as Future* (Lincoln: University of Nebraska Press, 1994), 120.

14. It is also important to mention one more time that Habermas would like to find certain common elements in the process of arriving at a consensus. He has tried to point to the validity claims accompanying our expressions in communicative action as having universal character. However, as has been said in chapter 2, the arguments he has given us are not convincing.

15. R. Rorty, *Objectivity, Relativism, and Truth: Philosophical Papers I* (Cambridge: Cambridge University Press, 1991), 201.

16. In light of those procedures, Habermas has mentioned Rorty's convergence with his own thought. On the discursively structured public sphere as a requirement for democracy, see J. Habermas, "Postscript—Reflections on Pragmatism," in *Habermas and Pragmatism*, ed. M. Aboulafia, M. Orbach Bookman, and C. Kemp (London: Routledge, 2002), 228.

17. J. Shklar, "What Is the Use of Utopia?," in *Political Theory and Political Thinkers*, ed. S. Hoffmann (Chicago: University of Chicago Press, 1998), 190.

18. In "Postscript—Reflections on Pragmatism," Habermas has additionally explained, "Pragmatism emerges as the only approach that embraces modernity in its most radical forms, and acknowledges its contingencies, without sacrificing

the very purpose of Western philosophy—namely to try out explanations of who we are and who we would like to be, as individuals, as members of our communities." See Habermas, "Postscript—Reflections on Pragmatism," 229. On that issue, see also W. Rehg, *Insight and Solidarity: The Discourse Ethics of Jürgen Habermas* (Berkeley: University of California Press, 1994).

19. J. P. Sartre, *L'Existentialisme est un humanisme* (Paris Nagel, 1946), 53–54.

20. It is worth adding that Habermas has said that "moral rules are fragile constructions [. . .]. The individual self will only emerge through the course of social externalization, and can only by stabilized within the network of undamaged relations of mutual recognition." J. Habermas, *The Future of Human Nature* (Cambridge: Polity Press, 2003), 33–34.

21. In *The Future of Human Nature*, Habermas has recognized that this is a very difficult task. He said, "The programmed person, being no longer certain about the contingency of the natural roots of her life, may feel the lack of mental precondition for coping with the moral expectation to take, even if only in retrospect, the *sole* responsibility for her own life." See Habermas, *Future of Human Nature*, 81.

22. For examples of the work that is facing that direction where Rorty's philosophy is concerned, see C. J. Voparil, "Taking Other Human Beings Seriously: Rorty's Ethics of Choice and Responsibility," *Contemporary Pragmatism* 11 (2014): 83–102; C. Voparil, "Contingency and Responsibility in Rorty's Ethics," *Iride: Filosofia e discussione pubblica* 3 (2019): 585–600; C. J. Voparil, "Rorty's Ethics of Responsibility," in *A Companion to Rorty*, ed. A. Malachowski (Hoboken, NJ: Wiley-Blackwell, 2020), 490–504.

23. The value of this approach can be seen in its fruitful application to the modern problems of corporate management; see W. R. Caspary, *Dewey on Democracy* (Ithaca, NY: Cornell University Press, 2000); M. Kilanowski, "Deep Capture: The Hidden Role of Rationalizations, Psychology and Corporate Law, and What Philosophy Can Do about It," in *Philosophy in the Time of Economic Crisis, Pragmatism, and Economy*, ed. K. W. Stikker and K. P. Skowroński (New York: Routledge, 2018), 108–125. It is also fruitful when applied to problems of language rights or role of mass media in the United States; see S. Chambers, *Reasonable Democracy: Jürgen Habermas and the Politics of Discourse* (Ithaca, NY: Cornell University Press, 1996); J. Braaten, *Habermas's Critical Theory of Society* (Albany: State University of New York Press, 1991). See also other examples in W. Rehg and J. Bohman, eds., *Deliberative Democracy: Essays on Reason and Politics* (Cambridge, MA: The MIT Press, 1997).

24. In Rorty's view, people need alternatives, and they have no interest in getting rid of the present view until they are offered details about the new alternative. See R. Rorty, *Achieving Our Country* (Cambridge, MA: Harvard University Press, 1998), 104.

25. On how this idea influenced the narrative about the responsible society during the Clinton presidency, see A. Rayan, *John Dewey and the High Tide of American Liberalism* (New York: W. W. Norton, 1997), 358. On the influence of pragmatic ideas on the politics of hope of President Obama, see J. T. Kloppenberg, *Reading Obama: Dreams, Hope and the American Political Tradition* (Princeton, NJ:

Princeton University Press, 2011). For more on the ideas of the Great Society and Great Community and possibilities to achieve them today, see also M. J. Sandel, *Public Philosophy: Essays on Morality in Politics* (Cambridge, MA: Harvard University Press, 2005), 194.

26. Habermas and Rorty also tried to help by dealing with concrete issues themselves. See Rorty, *Achieving Our Country*; J. Habermas, *The Crisis of the European Union: A Response*, trans. Ciaran Cronin (Cambridge: Polity Press, 2012); Habermas, *Future of Human Nature*; J. Habermas, *The Inclusion of the Other: Studies in Political Theory*, ed. Ciaran Cronin and Pablo de Greiff (Cambridge, MA: The MIT Press, 1996); J. Habermas et al., *An Awareness of What Is Missing: Faith and Reason in a Post-Secular Age* (Cambridge: Polity Press, 2011); G. Borradori, *Philosophy in the Times of Terror: Dialogues with Jürgen Habermas and Jacques Derrida* (Chicago: University of Chicago Press, 2003).

BIBLIOGRAPHY

I. Works by Dewey, Habermas, and Rorty

Dewey, J. *Challenge to Liberal Thought*, LW 15.*
Dewey, J. *A Common Faith*, LW 9.
Dewey, J. *Creative Democracy—The Task before Us*, LW 14.
Dewey, J. *A Critique of American Civilization*, LW 3.
Dewey, J. *Democracy and Education*, MW 9.
Dewey, J. *Democracy Is Radical*, LW 11.
Dewey, J. *Essays in Experimental Logic*, MW 10.
Dewey, J. *Ethics*, LW 7.
Dewey, J. *Experience and Nature*, LW 1.
Dewey, J. *Freedom and Culture*, LW 13.
Dewey, J. *Human Nature and Conduct*, MW 14.
Dewey, J. *Individualism, Old and New*, LW 5.
Dewey, J. *Liberalism and Civil Liberties*, LW 11.
Dewey, J. *Liberalism and Social Action*, LW 11.
Dewey, J. *The Need for a Recovery of Philosophy*, MW 10.
Dewey, J. *Outlines of Critical Theory of Ethics*, EW 3.
Dewey, J. *Philosophy*, LW 5.
Dewey, J. *The Public and Its Problems*, LW 2.
Dewey, J. *Quest for Certainty*, LW 4.
Dewey, J. *Reconstruction in Philosophy and Essays*, MW 12.
Habermas, J. "An Alternative Way Out of the Philosophy of the Subject: Communicative versus Subject-Centered Reason." In *The Philosophical Discourse of Modernity*, 294–326. Cambridge, MA: The MIT Press, 1987.
Habermas, J. *Between Facts and Norms*. Cambridge: Polity Press, 2004.
Habermas, J. *Between Naturalism and Religion: Philosophical Essays*. Cambridge: Polity Press, 2008.

Habermas, J. "A Conversation about Questions of Political Theory." In *A Berlin Republic: Writings on Germany*, 131–158. Translated by S. Rendall. Cambridge: Polity Press, 1997.

Habermas, J. "Coping with Contingencies: : The Return of Historicism." In *Debating the State of Philosophy: Habermas, Rorty, and Kolakowski*, edited by J. Niżnik and T. Sanders, 1–23. Westport, CT: Praeger, 1996.

Habermas, J. *The Crisis of the European Union: A Response*. Translated by Ciaran Cronin. Cambridge: Polity Press, 2012.

Habermas, J. "Crisis Theories and the Proceduralist Understanding of Law." In *Between Facts and Norms*, 427–446. Cambridge: MIT Press, 1998.

Habermas, J. "The Dialectics of Rationalization." In *Autonomy and Solidarity: Interviews with Jürgen Habermas*, edited by P. Dews, 63–76. London: Verso, 1992.

Habermas, J. "Die Krise des Wehlwahrfstaates und die Erschörfung utopischer Energie." In *Die neue Unübersichtlichkeit*, 141–163. Frankfurt: Suhrkamp, 1985.

Habermas J. *The Future of Human Nature*. Cambridge: Polity Press, 2003.

Habermas, J. *The Inclusion of the Other: Studies in Political Theory*. Edited by Ciaran Cronin and Pablo de Greiff. Cambridge, MA: The MIT Press, 1998.

Habermas, J. "The Internal Relation between Law and Politics." In *Between Facts and Norms*, 133–150. Cambridge, MA: The MIT Press, 1998.

Habermas, J. "Modernity: An Unfinished Project." In *Habermas and the Unfinished Project of Modernity*, edited by M. P. d'Entrèves and S. Benhabib, 38–55. Cambridge, MA: The MIT Press, 1997.

Habermas, J. *Past as Future*. Lincoln: University of Nebraska Press, 1994.

Habermas, J. *The Philosophical Discourse of Modernity*. Cambridge, MA: MIT Press, 1987.

Habermas, J. "A Philosophico-Political Profile." In *Autonomy and Solidarity: Interviews with Jürgen Habermas*, edited by P. Dews, 147–186. London: Verso, 1992.

Habermas, J. "Postscript—Reflections on Pragmatism." In *Habermas and Pragmatism*, edited by M. Aboulafia, M. Orbach Bookman, and C. Kemp, 223–233. London: Routledge, 2002.

Habermas, J. "A Reply to My Critics." In *Habermas: Critical Debates*, edited by J. B. Thompson and D. Held, 219–282. London: The MIT Press, 1982.

Habermas, J. "Richard Rorty's Pragmatic Turn." In *Rorty and His Critics*, edited by R. B. Brandon, 31–55. Oxford: Blackwell, 2002.

Habermas, J. *The Structural Transformation of the Public Sphere*. Cambridge, MA: MIT Press, 1991.

Habermas, J. *Theory and Practice*. Translated by J. Viertel. Boston: Beacon Press, 1973.

Habermas, J. *The Theory of Communicative Action*. Vol. 1, *Reason and the Rationalization of Society*. Translated by T. McCarthy. Boston: Beacon Press, 1984.

Habermas, J. *The Theory of Communicative Action*. Vol. 2, *Lifeworld and System: A Critique of Functionalist Reason*. Translated by T. McCarthy. Boston: Beacon Press, 1987.

Habermas, J. "Three Normative Models of Democracy." In *Constellations* 1, no. 1 (1994): 1–10.

Hambermas, J. *Truth and Justification*. Edited by Barbara Fultner. Cambridge, MA: The MIT Press, 2003.

Habermas, J. "The Unity of Reason in the Diversity of Its Voices." In *Postmetaphysical Thinking*, 115–148. Translated by W. M. Hohengarten. Cambridge, MA: The MIT Press, 1992.

Habermas, J. *Warheit und Rechtfertigung*. Frankfurt am Main: Suhrkamp, 1999.

Habermas, J. "What Theories Can Accomplish—and What They Can't." In *The Past as Future*, 99–120. Lincoln: University of Nebraska Press, 1994.

Habermas, J., et al. *An Awareness of What Is Missing: Faith and Reason in a Post-Secular Age*. Translated by Ciaran Cronin. Cambridge: Polity Press, 2011.

Rorty, R. *Achieving Our Country*. Cambridge, MA: Harvard University Press, 1998.

Rorty, R. "Amerykanizm i pragmatyzm" [Americanism and pragmatism]. Translated by A. Grzeliński. In *Filozofia amerykańska dziś* [American philosophy today], edited by T. Komendziński and A. Szahaj, 119–144. Toruń, Poland: Wydawnictwo Naukowe UMK, 1999.

Rorty, R. "Appendix II." In *Debating the State of Philosophy: Habermas, Rorty, and Kolakowski*, edited by J. Niżnik and T. Sanders, 113–115. Westport, CT: Praeger, 1996.

Rorty, R. "Appendix III." In *Debating the State of Philosophy: Habermas, Rorty, and Kolakowski*, edited by J. Niżnik and T. Sanders, 121–125. Westport, CT: Praeger, 1996.

Rorty, R. *Consequences of Pragmatism: Essays, 1972–1980*. Minneapolis: University of Minnesota Press, 1994.

Rorty, R. *Contingency, Irony, and Solidarity*. Cambridge: Cambridge University Press, 1989.

Rorty, R. "Deconstruction and Circumvention." *Critical Inquiry* 11, no. 1 (September 1984): 1–23.

Rorty, R. Rorty, *Philosophy and Social Hope*. London: Penguin Books, 1999.

Rorty, R. "Edukacja i wyzwanie postnowoczesności" [Education and the challenge of postmodernity]. Translated by L. Witkowski. In *Spory o edukację: Dylematy i kontrowersje we współczesnych pedagogikach* [Debates on education: Dilemmas and controversies in contemporary pedagogy], edited by Z. Kwieciński and L. Witkowski, 96–102. Warsaw: Instytut Badań Edukacyjnych, 1993.

Rorty, R. "Emancipating Our Culture." In *Debating the State of Philosophy: Habermas, Rorty, and Kolakowski*, edited by J. Niżnik and T. Sanders, 24–29. Westport, CT: Praeger, 1996.

Rorty, R. *Essays on Heidegger and Others: Philosophical Papers II*. Cambridge: Cambridge University Press, 1991.

Rorty, R. *An Ethics for Today: Finding Common Ground between Philosophy and Religion*. New York: Columbia University Press, 2008.

Rorty, R. "Foucault, Dewey, Nietzsche." *Raritan* 9, no. 4 (Spring 1990): 1–8.

Rorty, R. "Is It Desirable to Love Truth?" In *Truth, Politics, and "Post-Modernism,"* 11–32. Assen, Netherlands: Van Gorcum, 1997.

Rorty, R. "The Notion of Rationality." In *Debating the State of Philosophy: Habermas, Rorty, and Kolakowski*, edited by J. Niżnik and T. Sanders, 84. Westport, CT: Praeger, 1996.

Rorty, R. *Objectivity, Relativism, and Truth*. Cambridge: Cambridge University Press, 1991.
Rorty, R. "On Moral Obligation, Truth, and Common Sense." In *Debating the State of Philosophy: Habermas, Rorty, and Kolakowski*, edited by J. Niżnik and T. Sanders, 48–51. Westport, CT: Praeger, 1996.
Rorty, R. *Philosophy and Social Hope*. London: Penguin Books, 1999.
Rorty, R. "Philosophy and the Future." In *Rorty and Pragmatism: The Philosopher Responds to His Critics*, edited by H. J. Saatkamp, 197–205. Nashville, TN: Vanderbilt University Press, 1995.
Rorty, R. *Philosophy and the Mirror of Nature*. Princeton, NJ: Princeton University Press, 1979.
Rorty, R. *Philosophy as Cultural Politics: Philosophical Papers IV*. Cambridge: Cambridge University Press, 2007.
Rorty, R. *Philosophy as Poetry*. Charlottesville: University of Virginia Press, 2016.
Rorty, R. "A Pragmatist View of Rationality and Cultural Difference." *Philosophy East and West* 42, no. 4 (1992): 581–596.
Rorty, R. "Pragmatyzm" [Pragmatism]. In *Filozofia amerykańska dziś* [American Philosophy Today], edited by T. Komendziński and A. Szahaj, n.p. Toruń, Poland: Wydawnictwo Naukowe UMK, 1999.
Rorty, R. "Relativism—Finding and Making." In *Debating the State of Philosophy: Habermas, Rorty, and Kolakowski*, edited by J. Niżnik and T. Sanders, 31–47. Westport, CT: Praeger, 1996.
Rorty, R. "Response to Habermas." In *Rorty and His Critics*, edited by R. B. Brandon, 56–64. Oxford: Blackwell, 2002.
Rorty, R. "There Is a Crisis Coming." Interview by Z. Stanczyk. In *Take Care for Freedom and Truth Will Take Care of Itself: Interviews with Richard Rorty*, edited by E. Mendieta, 56–65. Stanford, CA: Stanford University Press, 2006.
Rorty, R. "Toward a Post-Metaphysical Culture." Interview with Michael O'Shea. *Harvard Review of Philosophy* 5 (Spring 1995): 58–66.
Rorty, R. *Truth and Progress: Philosophical Papers III*. Cambridge: Cambridge University Press, 1998.
Rorty, R. "Universality and Truth." In *Rorty and His Critics*, edited by R. B. Brandon, 1–30. Oxford: Blackwell, 2002.
Rorty, R. "Wstęp do polskiego wydania esejów Stanleya Fisha" [Introduction to the Polish edition of Stanley Fish's essays]. In *Stanley Fish: Interpretacja, retoryka, polityka: Eseje wybrane* [Stanley Fish: Interpretation, rhetoric, politics: Selected essays], 5–12. Translated and edited by A. Szahaj. Kraków, Poland: Universitas, 2002.

II. Other Works

Aboulafia, M., M. Orbach Bookman, and C. Kemp, eds. *Habermas and Pragmatism*. London: Routledge, 2002.
Albright, M. *Fascism: A Warning*. New York: Harper Collins, 2018.
Alexander, J. C. "Habermas's New Critical Theory: Its Promise and Problems." *American Journal of Sociology* 91, no. 2 (September 1985): 400–424.

Alexander, T. M. "John Dewey and the Roots of Democratic Imagination." In *Recovering Pragmatism's Voice: The Classical Tradition, Rorty, and the Philosophy of Communication*, edited by L. Langsdorf and A. R. Smith, 131–154. Albany: State University of New York Press, 1995.

Allen, A. "The Unforced Force of the Better Argument: Reason and Power in Habermas's Political Theory." *Constellations* 19, no. 3 (September 2012): 353–368.

Always, J. *Critical Theory and Political Possibilities: Conceptions of Emancipatory Politics in the Works of Horkheimer, Adorno, Marcuse, and Habermas*. London: Greenwood Press, 1995.

Anderson, C. *Pragmatic Liberalism*. Chicago: University of Chicago Press, 1990.

Antonio, R. J., and D. Kellner. "Communication, Modernity and Democracy in Habermas and Dewey." *Symbolic Interaction* 15, no. 3 (Fall 1992): 277–298.

Applebaum, A. *Twilight of Democracy: The Seductive Lure of Authoritarianism*. New York: Doubleday, 2020.

Appleby, J., L. Hunt, and M. Jacob. *Telling the Truth about History*. New York: W. W. Norton, 1994.

Arendt, H. *Essays in Understanding, 1930–1954: Formation, Exile, and Totalitarianism*. New York: Schocken, 2005.

Asghari, M. "Has Richard Rorty a Moral Philosophy?" *Philosophical Investigations* 9, no. 17 (Fall–Winter 2015): n.p.

Auxier, R. E. Preface to *The Philosophy of Richard Rorty*, edited by R. E. Auxier and L. E. Hahn, Library of Living Philosophers, xvii–xxxi. LaSalle, IL: Open Court, 2010.

Bacon, M. *Richard Rorty: Pragmatism and Political Liberalism*. Lanham, MD: Lexington Books, 2007.

Balot, R. K. "Utopian and Post-Utopian Paradigms in Classical Political Thought." *Arion: A Journal of Humanities and the Classics* 3rd series, 16, no. 2 (Fall 2008): 75–90.

Barber, B. *Strong Democracy: Participatory Politics for a New Age*. Berkeley: University of California Press, 1984.

Barreto, J.-M. "Rorty and Human Rights: Contingency, Emotions and How to Defend Human Rights Telling Stories." *Utrecht Law Review* 7, no. 2 (April 2011): 93–112.

Bauman, Z. *Does Ethics Have a Chance in a World of Consumers?* Cambridge, MA: Harvard University Press, 2008.

Baynes, K. *Habermas*. New York: Routledge, 2016.

Baynes, K. "The Liberal/Communitarian Controversy and Communicative Ethics." In *Universalism vs. Communitarianism: Contemporary Debates in Ethics*, edited by D. Rasmussen, 61–81. Cambridge, MA: The MIT Press, 1995.

Baynes, K. *The Normative Grounds of Social Criticism: Kant, Rawles, Habermas*. Albany: State University of New York Press, 1992.

Benhabib, S. *Critique, Norm, and Utopia: A Study of the Foundations of Critical Theory*. New York: Columbia University Press, 1986.

Benhabib, S. "The Utopian Dimension in Communicative Ethics." Special issue on Jurgen Habermas, *New German Critique*, no. 35 (Spring–Summer 1985): 83–96.

Benhabib, S., and F. Dallmayr, eds. *Communicative Ethics Controversy*. Cambridge, MA: MIT Press, 1990.

Benson, R. "Shaping the Public Sphere: Habermas and Beyond." *American Sociologist* 40, no. 3 (February 2014): 175–197.

Berlin, I. *Four Essays on Liberty*. Oxford: Oxford University Press, 1958.

I. Berlin. "Two Concepts of Liberty." In *Four Essays on Liberty*. Oxford: Oxford University Press, 1958.

Berlin, I., and B. Polanowska-Sygulska. *Unfinished Dialogue*. Amherst, NY: Prometheus Books, 2006.

Bernstein, R. J. "American Pragmatism: The Conflict of Narratives." In *Rorty and Pragmatism: The Philosopher Responds to His Critics*, edited by H. J. Saatkamp, 54–67. Nashville, TN: Vanderbilt University Press, 1995.

Bernstein, R. *The New Constellation: The Ethical-Political Horizons of Modernity/Postmodernity*. Cambridge, MA: MIT Press, 1991.

Bernstein, R. "One Step Forward, Two Steps Backward: Richard Rorty on Liberal Democracy and Philosophy." *Political Theory* 15, no. 4 (1987): 538–563.

Bernstein, R. J. *Philosophical Profiles: Essays in a Pragmatic Mode*. Philadelphia: University of Pennsylvania Press, 1986.

Bernstein, R. "Rorty's Inspirational Liberalism." In *Richard Rorty*, edited by Charles B. Guignon and David R. Hiley, 124–138. Cambridge: Cambridge University Press, 2003.

Bernstein, R. "Rorty's Liberal Utopia." *Social Research* 57, no. 1 (Spring 1990): 31–72.

Best, S., and D. Kellner. "Richard Rorty and Postmodern Theory." In *Richard Rorty: Education, Philosophy, and Politics*, edited by M. A. Peters and Paulo Ghiraldelli, Jr., 101–110. Lanham, MD: Rowman & Littlefield, 2001.

Bilgrami, A. "Is Truth a Goal of Inquiry? Rorty and Davidson on Truth." In *Rorty and His Critics*, edited by Robert B. Brandon, 242–262. Cambridge, MA: Blackwell, 2000.

Blaug, R. *Democracy, Real and Ideal: Discourse Ethics and Radical Politics*. Albany: State University of New York Press, 1999.

Blewett, J., ed. *Dewey John: His Thought and Influence*. New York: Fordham University Press, 1960.

Boffetti, J. M. "Rorty's Nietzschean Pragmatism: A Jamesian Response." *Review of Politics* 66, no. 4 (Autumn 2004): 605–631.

Bohman, J. "Habermas, Marxism and Social Theory." In *Habermas: A Critical Reader*, edited by Peter Dews, 53–86. Oxford: Blackwell, 1999.

Borradori, G. *Philosophy in the Times of Terror: Dialogues with Jürgen Habermas and Jacques Derrida*. Chicago: University of Chicago Press, 2003.

Braaten, J. *Habermas's Critical Theory of Society*. Albany: State University of New York Press, 1991.

Bran, R. *Rorty and His Critics*. Oxford: Blackwell, 2000.

Bredella, L. "Richard Rorty on Philosophy, Literature and Hermeneutics." In *Literature and Philosophy*, edited by Herbert Grabes, 103–124. Tübingen: Narr Francke Attempto Verlag, 1997.

Brigham, E. *Sustaining the Hope for Unity: Ecumenical Dialogue in a Postmodern World*. Wilmington, NC: Michel Glazier, 2012.

Brown, W. *Regulating Aversion: Tolerance in the Age of Identity and Empire*. Princeton, NJ: Princeton University Press, 2006.

Bruno-Jofré, R., and J. Schriewer, eds. *The Global Reception of John Dewey's Thought*. Routledge International Studies in the Philosophy of Education. London: Routledge, 2012.

Brzeziński, Z. *The Grand Failure: The Birth and Death of Communism in the Twentieth Century*. London: MacDonald, 1989.

Cacaterra, R. M. *Contingency and Normativity: The Challenges of Richard Rorty*. Leiden: Brill/Rodopi, 2019.

Campbell, J. *The Community Reconstructs: The Meaning of Pragmatic Social Thought*. Champaign: University of Illinois Press, 1992.

Campbell, J. "Dewey's Conception of Community." In *Reading Dewey*, edited by L. A. Hickman, 23–42. Bloomington: Indiana University Press, 1998.

Campbell, J. *Understanding John Dewey: Nature and Cooperative Intelligence*. Chicago: Open Court, 1995.

Casey, M. *Meaninglessness: The Solutions of Nietzsche, Freud, and Rorty*. Religion, Politics, and Society in the New Millennium. Lanham, MD: Lexington Books, 2002.

Caspary, W. R. *Dewey on Democracy*. Ithaca, NY: Cornell University Press, 2000.

Chambers, S. *Reasonable Democracy: Jürgen Habermas and the Politics of Discourse*. Ithaca, NY: Cornell University Press, 1996.

Christiano, T. "The Significance of Public Deliberation." In *Deliberative Democracy. Essays on Reason and Politics*, edited by W. Rehg and J. Bohman, 243–278. Cambridge, MA: The MIT Press, 1997.

Cohen, J. "Deliberation and Democratic Legitimacy." In *Democracy*, edited by David Estlund, 87–106. Oxford: Blackwell, 2002.

Cohen, J. "Discourse Ethics and Civil Society." In *Universalism vs. Communitarianism: Contemporary Debates in Ethics*, edited by David Rasmussen, 83–105. Cambridge, MA: The MIT Press, 1995.

Cohen, J. "Reflection on Habermas on Democracy." *Ratio Juris* 12 no. 4 (December 1999): 385–416.

Cohen, T. "Illocutions and Perlocutions." *Foundations of Language* 9, no. 4 (March 1973): 492–503.

Coles, R. "Communicative Action & Dialogical Ethics: Habermas & Foucault." *Polity* 25, no. 1 (Autumn 1992): 71–94.

Conant, J. "Freedom, Cruelty, and Truth: Rorty versus Orwell." In *Rorty and His Critics*, edited by R. B. Brandon, 268–324. Oxford: Blackwell, 2002.

Critchley, S. "Metaphysics in the Dark: A Response to Richard Rorty and Ernesto Laclau." *Political Theory* 26, no. 6 (December 1998): 803–817.

Cruz, F. F. *John Dewey's Theory of Community*. New York: Peter Lang, 1987.

Curtis, W. *Defending Rorty: Pragmatism and Liberal Virtue*. Cambridge: Cambridge University Press, 2015.

d'Entrèves, M. P., and S. Benhabib, eds. *Habermas and the Unfinished Project of Modernity: Critical Essays on the Philosophical Discourse of Modernity*. London: Polity Press, 1996.

Dahl, R. *Dilemmas of Pluralist Democracy*. New Haven, CT: Yale University Press, 1982.

Damasio, A. *The Strange Order of Things: Life, Feeling, and the Making of Cultures*. New York: Vintage, 2018.

Damico, A. *Individual and Community: The Social and Political Theory of John Dewey*. Gainesville: University of Florida Press, 1978.

Dazhi, Y., and X. Yunhua. "Postmodernist Liberalism: A Critique of Richard Rorty's Political Philosophy." *Frontiers of Philosophy in China* 3, no. 3 (September 2008): 455–463.

Deen, P. "Dewey, Habermas, and the Unfinished Project of Modernity in Unmodern Philosophy and Modern Philosophy." In *The Oxford Handbook of Dewey*, edited by Steven Fesmire, 537–550. Oxford: Oxford University Press, 2019.

Deflem, M. "The Legal Theory of Jürgen Habermas." In *Law and Social Theory*, edited by R. Banakar and M. Travers, 70–95. Oxford: Hart, 2013.

Dell'utri, M. "The Threat of Cultural Relativism: Hilary Putnam and the Antidote of Fallinilism." *European Journal of Analitic Philosophy* 4. no. 2 (2008): 75–86.

Dellwing, M. "Fences: Rorty's Private-Public-Dichotomy as a Situational Game." *Minerva: An Internet Journal of Philosophy* 16 (2012): 62–82.

Dews, P., ed. *Habermas: A Critical Reader*. Oxford: Blackwell, 1999.

Diaconu, M. A. "Truth and Knowledge in Postmodernism." *Social and Behavioral Sciences* 137 (July 2014): 165–169.

Duncan, C. M. "A Question for Richard Rorty." *Review of Politics* 66, no. 3 (2004): 385–414.

Dryzek, J. S. *Deliberative Democracy and Beyond: Liberals, Critics, Contestations*. Oxford: Oxford University, 1998.

Eagleton, T. *The Illusions of Postmodernism*. Oxford: Blackwell, 1996.

Edgar, A. *The Philosophy of Habermas*. New York: Routledge, 2014.

Edwards, T. "Rorty on the Literalization of Metaphor." *Method & Theory in the Study of Religion* 9, no. 2 (1997): 127–138.

Elderidge, M. *Transforming Experience: John Dewey's Cultural Instrumentalism*. Nashville, TN: Vanderbilt University Press, 1998.

Elshtain, J. B. "Don't Be Cruel: Reflections on Rortyan Liberalism." In *Richard Rorty*, edited by C. Guignon and D. R. Hiley, 139–157. Cambridge: Cambridge University Press, 2003.

Estlund, D., ed. *Democracy*. Oxford: Blackwell, 2002.

Festenstein, M. *Pragmatism and the Political Theory from Dewey to Rorty*. Chicago: University of Chicago Press, 1997.

Festenstein, M., and S. Thompson, eds. *Richard Rorty: Critical Dialogues*. Cambridge: Polity Press, 2001.

Finlayson, J. *Habermas: A Very Short Introduction*. Oxford: Oxford University Press, 2005.

Fisher, M. "Refefining Philosophy as Literature: Richard Rorty's 'Defense' of Literary Culture." *Interdisciplinary Journal* 67, no. 3 (Fall 1984): 312–324.

Fishkin, J. S. "Deliberative Democracy." In *The Blackwell Guide to Social and Political Philosophy*, edited by Robert L. Simon, 221–238. Oxford: Blackwell, 2002.

Flower, E., and M. G. Murphy. *A History of Philosophy in America*. Vol. 2. New York: Capricorn Books, 1977.
Freeden, M. *Ideologies and Political Theory: A Conceptual Approach*. Oxford: Clarendon Press, 1996.
Gander, E. *The Last Conceptual Revolution: A Critique of Richard Rorty's Political Philosophy*. Albany: State University of New York Press, 1998.
Gascoigne, N. *Richard Rorty: Liberalism, Irony, and the Ends of Philosophy*. Cambridge: Polity Press, 2008.
Geras, N. *Solidarity in the Conversation of Humankind: The Ungroundable Liberalism of Richard Rorty*. London: Verso, 1995.
Gerhards, J., H. Lengfeld, Z. Ignácz, F. K. Kley, and M. Priem. *European Solidarity in Times of Crisis: Insights from a Thirteen-Country Survey*. New York: Routledge, 2019.
Giladi, P. "A Critique of Rorty's Conception of Pragmatism." *European Journal of Pragmatism and American Philosophy* 7, no. 2 (2015): 1–16.
Golding, I. *Divided Nations: Why Global Governance Is Failing and What We Can Do about It*. Oxford: Oxford University Press, 2013.
Gordon, M. "John Dewey's 'Democracy and Education' in an Era of Globalization." *Educational Philosophy and Theory* 48, no. 10 (2016): 977–980.
Gouinlock, J. "Dewey and Contemporary Moral Philosophy." In *Philosophy and the Reconstruction of Culture: Pragmatic Essays after Dewey*, edited by J. J. Stuhr, 79–96. Albany: State University of New York Press, 1993.
Grady, H. H., and S. Wells. "Toward a Rhetoric of Intersubjectivity: Introducing Jürgen Habermas." *Journal of Advanced Composition* 6 (1985/1986): 33–47.
Gray, J. *Isaiah Berlin: An Interpretation of His Thought*. Princeton, NJ: Princeton University Press, 2013.
Greenwood, J. "Organized Civil Society and Democratic Legitimacy in the European Union." *British Journal of Political Science* 37, no. 2 (2007): 333–357.
Grippe, E. J. *Richard Rorty's New Pragmatism: Neither Liberal nor Free*. New York: Continuum, 2007.
Grundmann, R. "The Problem of Expertise in Knowledge Societies." *Minerva* 55, no. 1 (2017): 25–48.
Guignon, C., and D. E. Hiley, eds. *Richard Rorty*. Cambridge: Cambridge University Press, 2003.
Gutmann, A. *Democratic Education*. Princeton, NJ: Princeton University Press, 1987.
Haack, S. *Evidence and Enquiry: Towards Reconstruction in Epistemology*. Oxford: Blackwell, 1993.
Haack, S. *Manifesto of a Passionate Moderate*. Chicago: University of Chicago Press, 1998.
Haack, S., ed. *Pragmatism Old and New*. Amherst, NY: Prometheus Books, 2006.
Haber, H. F. *Beyond Postmodern Politics: Lyotard, Rorty, Foucault*. New York: Routledge, 1994.
Hacking, I. *The Social Construction of What?* Cambridge, MA: Harvard University Press, 1999.

Haferkamp, H. "Critique of Habermas's Theory of Communicative Action." In *Social Action*, edited by G. Seebass and R. Tuomela, 197–205. Dordrecht: D. Reidel, 1985.

Hardie, C. D. *Truth and Fallacy in Educational Theory*. Chicago: University Press, 1942.

Harris, S. "Antifoundationalism and the Commitment to Reducing Suffering in Rorty and Madhyamaka Buddhism." *Contemporary Pragmatism* 7, no. 2 (2010): 71–89.

Hayden, P. "Sentimentality and Human Rights: Critical Remarks on Rorty." *Philosophy in the Contemporary World* 6, no. 3/4 (1999): 59–66.

Hayek, F. A. *The Constitution of Liberty*. Chicago: University of Chicago Press, 1978.

Held, D. *Models of Democracy*. Stanford, CA: Stanford University Press, 1985.

Henrich, D. C. "Human Nature and Autonomy: Jürgen Habermas' Critique of Liberal Eugenic." *Ethical Perspectives* 18, no. 2 (June 2011): 249–268.

Hertogh, M., and S. Halliday, eds. *Judicial Review and Bureaucratic Impact, International, and Interdisciplinary Perspectives*. Cambridge: Cambridge University Press, 2009.

Hickman, L. A. "Liberal Irony and Social Reform." In *Philosophy and the Reconstruction of Culture: Pragmatic Essays After Dewey*, edited by J. J. Stuhr, 223–239. Albany: State University of New York Press, 1993.

Hickman, L. A. *Reading Dewey: Interpretations for a Postmodern Generation*. Bloomington: Indiana University Press, 1998.

Hoffman, D. *The Dead Hand: The Untold Story of the Cold War Arms Race and Its Dangerous Legacy*. New York: Doubleday, 2009.

Hook, S. *Pragmatism and the Tragic Sense of Life*. New York: Basic Books, 1974.

Hoy, T. *The Political Philosophy of John Dewey: Towards a Constructive Renewal*. Westport, CT: Praeger, 1998.

Hutchinson, A. C. "The Three 'Rs': Reading/Rorty/Radically." *Harvard Law Review* 103, no. 2 (December 1989): 555–585.

Ingram, D. "Foucault and Habermas on the Subject of Reason." In *The Cambridge Companion to Foucault*, edited by Gary Gutting, 215–261. Cambridge: Cambridge University Press, 1994.

Ingram, D. *Habermas: Introduction and Analysis*. Ithaca, NY: Cornell University Press, 2010.

Isaac, J. C. "Is the Revival of Pragmatism Practical, or What Are the Consequences of Pragmatism?" *Constellation* 6, no. 4 (December 1999): 561–887.

Jay, M. *The Education of John Dewey: A Biography*. New York: Columbia University Press, 2002.

Jezierska, K. "With Habermas against Habermas, Deliberation without Consensus." *Journal of Public Deliberation* 15, no. 1 (2019): 4–23.

Joas, H. *Pragmatism and Social Theory*. Chicago: Chicago University Press, 1993.

Johnson, P. "Are Our Utopian Energies Exhausted?" *European Journal of Political Theory* 3, no. 3 (2004): 267–291.

Jones, T. M. "Rorty's Post-Foundational Liberalism: Progress or the Status Quo?" August 11, 2013. SSRN. https://ssrn.com/abstract=2308651.

Judt, T. *Postwar: A History of Europe Since 1945*. London: Vintage Books, 2010.

Kaniowski, A. M. *Filozofia społeczna Jürgena Habermasa: W poszukiwaniu jedności teorii i praktyki.* Warsaw: Kolegium Ottyckie, 1990.
Kaniowski, A. M. *Jürgen Habermas wobec sporów filozoficznych wokół epoki nowoczesności. Colloquia Communia*, no. 4–5 (1986): n.p.
Kekes, J. "Cruelty and Liberalism." *Ethics* 106, no. 4 (July 1996): 834–844.
Kelly, M., ed. *Critique and Power: Recasting the Foucault/Habermas Debate.* Cambridge, MA: MIT Press, 1994.
Kennedy, D. *A World of Struggle: How Power, Law, and Expertise Shape Global Political Economy.* Princeton, NJ: Princeton University Press, 2016.
Khan, M. Z., I. S. Gilani, and A. Nawaz. "From Habermas Model to New Public Sphere: A Paradigm Shift." *Global Journal of Human Social Science* 12, no. 5 (March 2012): 43–51.
Kilanowski, M. "Abandoning Truth Is Not a Solution: A Discussion with Richard Rorty." *Diametros* 61 (2019): 34–50.
Kilanowski, M. "Deep Capture: The Hidden Role of Rationalizations, Psychology and Corporate Law, and What Philosophy Can Do about It." In *Philosophy in the Time of Economic Crisis, Pragmatism, and Economy*, edited by K. W. Stikker and K. P. Skowroński, 108–125. New York: Routledge, 2018.
Kilanowski, M. "Towards a Responsible and Rational Ethical Discussion: A Critique of Putnam's Pragmatic Approach." In *Philosophy of Hilary Putnam*, Library of Living Philosophers, edited by R. E. D. R. Auxier and L. E. Hahn, 827–862. Chicago: Open Court, 2015.
Kitcher, P. "Pragmatism and Progress." *Transactions of the Charles S. Peirce Society* 51, no. 4 (Winter 2015): 475–494.
Klein, J. *Politics Lost: How American Democracy Was Trivialized by People Who Think You're Stupid.* New York: Doubleday, 2007.
Kloppenberg, J. T. "Democracy and Disenchantment: From Weber and Dewey to Habermas and Rorty." In *The Virtues of Liberalism*, edited by J. T. Kloppenberg, 81–99. Oxford: Oxford University Press, 1998.
Kloppenberg, J. T. *Reading Obama: Dreams, Hope, and the American Political Tradition.* Princeton, NJ: Princeton University Press, 2011.
Koczanowicz, L. *Politics of Dialogue: Non-consensual Democracy and Critical Community.* Edinburgh: Edinburgh University Press, 2015.
Kolenda, K. *Rorty's Humanistic Pragmatism: Philosophy Democratized.* Tampa: University of South Florida Press, 1990.
Koopman, C. "Pragmatism as a Philosophy of Hope: Emerson, James, Dewey, Rorty." *Journal of Speculative Philosophy—New Series* 20, no. 2 (2006): 106–116.
Kundera, M. *The Art of the Novel.* New York: HarperCollins, 2003.
Kwiek, M. *Rorty's Elective Affinities: The New Pragmatism and Postmodern Thought.* Poznań, Poland: Wydawnictwo Naukowe IF UAM, 1996.
Kymlicka, W. *Liberalism, Community, and Culture.* Oxford: Clarendon Press, 1991.
Kyung-Man, K. "Beyond Justification: Habermas, Rorty and the Politics of Cultural Change." *Theory, Culture and Society* 31, no. 6 (2014): 103–123.
Lakoff, G., and M. Johnson. *Metaphors We Live By.* Chicago: University of Chicago Press, 1980.

Lamb, R. "Pragmatism, Practices, and Human Rights." *Review of International Studies* 45, no. 4 (October 2019): 550–568.
Landemore, H. *Open Democracy: Reinventing Popular Rule for the Twenty-First Century*. Princeton, NJ: Princeton University Press, 2020.
Langsdorf, L., ed. *Reinterpreting the Political: Continental Philosophy and Political Theory*. Albany: State University of New York Press, 1998.
Langsdorf, L., and A. R. Smith, eds. *Recovering Pragmatism's Voice: The Classical Tradition, Rorty, and the Philosophy of Communication*. Albany: State University of New York Press, 1995.
Levitsky, S., and D. Ziblatt. *How Democracies Die*. New York: Crown, 2018.
Llanera, T. "Redeeming Rorty's Private–Public Distinction." *Contemporary Pragmatism* 13, no. 3 (2016): 316–340.
Lukács, J. *A Short History of the Twentieth Century*. Cambridge, MA: Belknap Press, 2013.
Malachowski, A. *Richard Rorty*. Philosophy Now. Princeton, NJ: Princeton University Press, 2002.
Malpas, J. "Mapping the Structure of Truth: Davidson Contra Rorty." In *Truth and Its Nature (if Any)*, edited by J. Peregrin, 117–127. Synthese Library (Studies in Epistemology, Logic, Methodology, and Philosophy of Science). Vol. 284. Dordrecht: Springer, 1999.
Mapel, D. R. "Civil Association and the Idea of Contingency." *Political Theory* 18, no. 3 (August 1990): 392–410.
Margolis, J. "The Benign Antimony of a Constructive Realism." In *Pragmatic Naturalism and Realism*, edited by John R. Shook, 29–42. Amherst, NY: Prometheus Books, 2003.
Margolis, J. "Dewey in Dialogue with Continental Philosophy." In *Reading Dewey*, edited by L. A. Hickman, 231–256. Bloomington: Indiana University Press, 1998.
Marsoobian, A. T., and J. Ryder, eds. *The Blackwell Guide to American Philosophy*. Oxford: Blackwell, 2004.
McCarthy, T. *Critical Theory*. Boston: Beacon Press, 1978.
McCumber, J. *Philosophy as Freedom: Derrida, Rorty, Habermas, Foucault*. Bloomington: Indiana University Press, 2000.
Mendelson, J. "The Habermas-Gadamer Debate." *New German Critique*, no. 18 (Autumn 1979): 44–73.
Mendieta, E., ed. *Take Care of Freedom and Truth Will Take Care of Itself: Interviews with Richard Rorty*. Stanford, CA: Stanford University Press, 2005.
Michelman, F. "How Can the People Ever Make the Laws? A Critique of Deliberative Democracy." In *Deliberative Democracy*, edited by W. Rehg and J. Bohman, 145–171. Cambridge, MA: The MIT Press, 1997.
Milanović, B. *Global Inequality: A New Approach for the Age of Globalization*. Cambridge, MA: Belknap Press, 2018.
Miller, C. B. "Rorty and Tolerance." *Theoria: A Journal of Social and Political Theory*, no. 101 (June 2003): 94–108.
Morgenbesser, S. *Dewey and His Critics: Essays from the Journal of Philosophy*. New York: The Journal of Philosophy, 1977.

Morris, C. D. "Pragmatism and the Crisis of Democracy." In *Public Policy Pamphlets: No. 12*, edited by H. D. Gideonse, 1–25. Chicago: University of Chicago Press, 1934.
Mouffe, C., ed. *Deconstruction and Pragmatism*. London: Routledge, 1996.
Mounce, H. O. *The Two Pragmatisms*. London: Routledge, 1997.
Mounk, Y. *The People vs. Democracy: Why Our Freedom Is in Danger and How to Save It*. Cambridge, MA: Harvard University Press, 2018.
Mowbray, J. F. "Autonomy, Identity and Self-knowledge: A New 'Solution' to the Liberal-Communitarian 'Problem'?" In *Human Rights: Old Problems, New Possibilities*, edited by D. Kinley, W. Sadurski, and K. Walton, 212–214. Cheltenha, UK: Edward Elgar, .
Myers, E. "From Pluralism to Liberalism: Rereading Isaiah Berlin." *Review of Politics* 72, no. 4 (Fall 2010): 599–625.
Nehamas, A. "Can We Ever Quite Change the Subject? Richard Rorty on Science, Literature, Culture, and the Future of Philosophy." *boundary 2* 10, no. 3 (Spring 1982): 395–413.
Niebuhr, R. *The Children of Light and the Children of Darkness*. Chicago: University of Chicago Press, 2011.
Niebuhr, R. *Moral Man and Immoral Society: A Study in Ethics and Politics*. Louisville, KY: Westminster John Knox Press, 2013.
Nielsen, K. *After the Demise of the Tradition: Rorty, Critical Theory, and the Fate of Philosophy*. Boulder, CO: Westview Press, 1991.
Niemi, J. I. "Habermas and Validity Claims." *International Journal of Philosophical Studies* 13, no. 2 (2005): 227–244.
Nietzsche, F. "On Truth and Lie in Extra-Moral Sense." In *The Viking Portable Nietzsche*, translated by W. Kaufmann. London: Penguin Books, 1977.
Niżnik, J., and T. Sanders. *Debating the State of Philosophy: Habermas, Rorty, and Kolakowski*. Westport, CT: Praeger Publishers, 1996.
Nussbaum, M. "On Moral Progress: A Response to Richard Rorty." *University of Chicago Law Review* 74, no. 3 (Summer 2007): 939–960.
Nyiro, M. "Rorty on Politics, Culture, and Philosophy: A Defence of His Romanticism." *Human Affairs* 19 (2009): 60–67.
Oakeshott, M. *On Human Conduct*. Oxford: Oxford University Press, 1975.
Orwell, G. *1984*. New York: Signet Classic, 1977.
O'Shea, J. *Wilfrid Sellars: Naturalism with a Normative Turn*. London: Polity Press, 2007.
Outhwait, W. *Habermas: A Critical Introduction*. Cambridge, MA: Polity Press, 1994.
Owen, D. S. *Between Reason and History: Habermas and the Idea of Progress*. Albany: State University of New York Press, 2002.
Peterson, R. T. *Democratic Philosophy and the Politics of Knowledge*. University Park: The Pennsylvania State University Press, 1996.
Pihlström, S. *Pragmatist Metaphysics: An Essay on the Ethical Grounds of Ontology*. London: Bloomsbury, 2009.
Piketty, T. *Capital and Ideology*. Cambridge, MA: Harvard University Press, 2020.

Piketty, T. *The Economics of Inequality*. Cambridge, MA: Belknap Press, 2015.
Pinker, S. *The Blank Slate: The Modern Denial of Human Nature*. New York: Penguin Books, 2003.
Plot, M. "Communicative Action's Democratic Deficit: A Critique of Habermas's Contribution to Democratic Theory." *International Journal of Communication* 3 (2009): 825–852.
Posner, R. "Legal Pragmatism." In *The Range of Pragmatism and the Limits of Philosophy*. edited by Richard Shusterman, 144–156. Oxford: Blackwell, 2004.
Posner, R. "What Has Pragmatism to Offer Law?" *Southern California Law Review* 63 (Summer 1990): 1653–1670.
Proulx, P.-L. *Réalisme et vérité: Le Débat entre Habermas et Rorty*. Paris: L'Harmattan, 2012.
Putnam, H. *The Collapse of the Fact/Value Dichotomy*. Cambridge, MA: Harvard University Press, 2002.
Putnam, H. *Ethics without Ontology*. Cambridge, MA: Harvard University Press, 2004.
Putnam, H. *Realism with a Human Face*. Cambridge, MA: Harvard University Press, MA 1990.
Rasmussen, D., ed. *Universalism vs. Communitarianism: Contemporary Debates in Ethics*. Cambridge, MA: The MIT Press, 1995.
Rayan, A. *John Dewey and the High Tide of American Liberalism*. New York: W. W. Norton, 1997.
Rehg, W. "Discourse Ethics." In *The Ethical*, edited by E. Wyschogrod and G. P. McKenny, 5–83. Oxford: Blackwell, 2003.
Rehg, W. *Insight and Solidarity: The Discourse Ethics of Jürgen Habermas*. Berkeley: University of California Press, 1994.
Rehg, W., and J. Bohman. *Deliberative Democracy: Essays on Reason and Politics*. Cambridge, MA: The MIT Press, 1997.
Rehg, W., and J. Bohman, eds. *Pluralism and Pragmatic Turn: The Transformation of Critical Theory*. Cambridge, MA: The MIT Press, 2001.
Roderick, R. *Habermas and the Foundations of Critical Theory*. London: Pelgrave Macmillan, 1986.
Rogers, M. L. "Rorty's Straussianism; Or, Irony against Democracy." *Contemporary Pragmatism* 1, no. 2 (2004): 95–121.
Rosenfeld, M. *Law, Justice, Democracy, and the Clash of Cultures: A Pluralist Account*. Cambridge: Cambridge University Press, 2011.
Rosenthal, S. B. "Habermas, Dewey, and Democratic Self." In *Habermas and Pragmatism*, edited by A. Michell, M. Orbach Bookman, and C. Kemp, 210–222. London: Routledge, 2002.
Rosenthal, S. B., C. R. Hausman, and D. R. Anderson, eds. *Classical American Pragmatism and Its Contemporary Vitality*. Urbana–Champaign: University of Illinois Press, 1999.
Roth, R. J. *John Dewey and Self-Realization*. Englewood Cliffs, NJ, Prentice-Hall, 1982.
Rothlede, D. *The Work of Friendship: Rorty, His Critics, and the Project of Solidarity*. Albany: State University of New York Press, 1999.

Rush, F. "Dialectic, Value Objectivity, and the Unity of Reason." In *The Oxford Handbook of Continental Philosophy*, edited by B. Leiter and M. Rosen, 287–333. Oxford: Oxford University Press, 2007.

Saatkamp, H. J., Jr., ed., *Rorty and Pragmatism: The Philosopher Responds to His Critics*. Nashville, TN: Vanderbilt University Press, 1995.

Sandel, M. *Liberalism and the Limits of Justice*. Cambridge: Cambridge University Press, 1982.

Sandel, M. *Public Philosophy: Essays on Morality in Politics*. Cambridge, MA: Harvard University Press, 2005.

Sartre, J. P. *Existentialism Is a Humanism*. New Haven, CT: Yale University Press, 2007.

Scheffler, S. *Bouddaries and Allegiances: Problems of Justice and Responsibility in Liberal Thought*. Oxford: Oxford University Press, 2001.

Scherer, A. G., and M. Patzer. "Beyond Universalism and Relativism: Habermas's Contribution to Discourse Ethics and Its Implications for Intercultural Ethics and Organization Theory." In *Philosophy and Organization Theory*, Research in the Sociology of Organizations, vol. 32, edited by H. Tsoukas and R. Chia, 155–180. Bingley, UK: Emerald Group, 2011.

Schick Jr., T. W. "Rorty and Davidson on Alternate Conceptual Schemes." *Journal of Speculative Philosophy* 1, no. 4 (1987): 291–303.

Schilpp, P. A., ed. *The Philosophy of John Dewey*. Vol. 1 of *The Library of Living Philosophers*, Evanston, WY: Northwestern University, 1939.

Schumpeter, J. *Capitalism, Socialism, and Democracy*. London: George, Allen & Unwin, 1943.

Sedgwick, P. "The Future of Philosophy: Nietzsche, Rorty, and Post-Nietzscheanism." *Nietzsche Studien* 29 (2000): 234–251.

Seidman, S., ed. *The Postmodern Turn: New Perspectives on Social Theory*. Cambridge: Cambridge University Press, 1994.

Selim, F. "Postmodern Liberalims and Solidarity: Richard Rorty." *International Journal of Social Sciences* 3 no. 2 (2017): 654–671.

Sheffler, I. *Four Pragmatists: A Critical Introduction to Peirce, James, Mead, and Dewey*. London: Routledge & Kegan Paul, 1986.

Shklar, J. *Ordinary Vices*. Cambridge, MA: Harvard University Press, 1984.

Shklar, J. "What Is the Use of Utopia?" In *Political Theory and Political Thinkers*, edited by S. Hoffmann, 175–190. Chicago: University of Chicago Press, 1998.

Shook, J. R., ed. *Pragmatic Naturalism and Realism*. Amherst, NY: Prometheus Books, 2003.

Shook, J. R. "Pragmatism, Pluralism, and Public Democracy." *Revue française d'études américaines* 2, no. 124 (2010): 11–28.

Shusterman, R. "Pragmatism and Liberalism between Dewey and Rorty." *Political Theory* 22, no. 3 (August 1994): 391–413.

Shusterman, R. "Reason and Aesthetics between Modernity and Postmodernity Habermas and Rorty." In *Richard Rorty: Critical Dialogues*, edited by M. Festenstein and S. Thompson, 134–152. Cambridge: Polity Press, 2001.

Sim, S. *Irony and Crisis: A Critical History of Postmodern Culture*. Cambridge: Icon Books, 2002.

Simon, R. L., ed. *The Blackwell Guide to Social and Political Philosophy*. Oxford: Blackwell, 2002.

Singer, B. J. *Pragmatism, Rights, and Democracy*. New York: New York University Press, 1999.

Sleeper, R. W. "The Pragmatics of Deconstruction and the End of Metaphysics." In *Philosophy and the Reconstruction of Culture: Pragmatic Essays after Dewey*, edited by J. J. Stuhr, n.p. Albany: State University of New York Press, 1993.

Snyder, T. *The Road to Unfreedom: Russia, Europe, America*. New York: Tim Duggan Books, 2018.

Specter, M. G. *Habermas and Intellectual Bibliography*. Cambridge: Cambridge University Press, 2010.

Stanley, R. *Habermas, Lyotard, and the Concept of Justice*. London: Macmilian, 1992.

Steinberg, J. *Post-enlightenment Philosophy and Liberal Universalism in the Political Thought of Isaiah Berlin and Richard Rorty*. Oxford: University of Oxford, 1998.

Strydom, P. "The Problem of Triple Contingency in Habermas." *Sociological Theory* 19, no. 2 (July 2001): 165–186.

Stuhr, J. J., ed. *Classical American Philosophy*. New York: Oxford University Press, 1987.

Stuhr, J. J. "Dewey's Social and Political Philosophy." In *Reading Dewey*, edited by L. A. Hickman, 82–99. Bloomington: Indiana University Press, 1998.

Stuhr, J. J., ed. *Philosophy and the Reconstruction of Culture: Pragmatic Essays after Dewey*. Albany: State University of New York Press, 1993.

Sullivan, W. M. *Reconstructing Public Philosophy*. Berkeley: University of California Press, 1982.

Szahaj, A. *Ironia i miłość: Neopragmatyzm Richarda Rorty'ego w kontekście sporu o postmodernizm*. Wrocław, Poland: Wydawnictwo Leopoldinum, 1996.

Talisse, R. B. "A Pragmatist Critique of Richard Rorty's Hopeless Politics." *Southern Journal of Philosophy* 39 (2001): 611–626.

Teeple, G. *Globalization and the Decline of Social Reform: Into the Twenty-First Century*. Toronto: University of Toronto Press, 2000.

Termin, P. *The Vanishing Middle Class: Prejudice and Power in a Dual Economy*. Cambridge, MA: MIT Press, 2018.

Tomborino, J. "Philosophy as the Mirror of Liberalism: The Politics of Richard Rorty." *Polity* 30 (1997): 57–78.

Topper, K. "Richard Rorty, Liberalism and the Politics of Redescription." *American Political Science Review* 89 (1995): 954–965.

Trey, G. *Solidarity and Difference: The Politics of Enlightenment in the Aftermath of Modernity*. Albany: State University of New York Press, 1998.

Turner, S. "What Is the Problem with Experts?" *Social Studies of Science* 31, no. 1 (February 2001): 123–149.

van den Berg, A. "Habermas and Modernity: A Critique of the Theory of Communicative Action." *Current Perspectives in Social Theory* 10 (January 1990): 161–193.

van den Brink, B. *The Tragedy of Liberalism: An Alternative Defense of a Political Tradition*. Albany: State University of New York Press, 2000.

van Niekerk, A. "Contingency and Universality in the Habermas-Rorty Debate." *Acta Academica Suplementum* 2 (2005): 21–41.

Voparil, C. "Contingency and Responsibility in Rorty's Ethics." *Iride: Filosofia e discussione pubblica* 3 (2019): 585–600.
Voparil, C. *Richard Rorty: Politics and Vision*. Lanham, MD: Rowman & Littlefield, 2006.
Voparil, C. "Rorty and Dewey Revisited: Toward a Fruitful Conversation." *Transactions of the Charles S. Peirce Society* 50, no. 3 (Summer 2014): 373–404.
Voparil, C. J. "Rorty's Ethics of Responsibility." In *A Companion to Rorty*, edited by A. Malachowski, 490–504. Hoboken, NJ: Wiley-Blackwell, 2020.
Voparil, C. J. "Taking Other Human Beings Seriously: Rorty's Ethics of Choice and Responsibility." *Contemporary Pragmatism* 11 (2014): 83–102.
Wain, K. "Strong Poets and Utopia: Rorty's Liberalism, Dewey and Democracy." *Political Studies* 41, no. 3 (1993): 394–407.
Walker, B. "Habermas and Pluralist Political Theory." *Philosophy and Social Criticism* 18, no. 1 (1992): 81–102.
Weber, B. *Zwischen Vernunft und Mitgefühl: Jürgen Habermas und Richard Rorty im Dialog über Wahrheit, politische Kultur, und Menschenrechte*. Freiburg: Alber, 2013.
Welchman, J. *Dewey's Ethical Thought*. Ithaca, NY: Cornell University Press, 1995.
Wellmer, A. "Thesen über Vernunft, Emanzipation und Utopie." In *Ethik und Dialog*, edited by A. Wellmer, n.p. Frankfurt am Main: Suhrkamp, 1986.
Wenar, L. *Blood Oil: Tyrants, Violence, and the Rules that Run the World*. Oxford: Oxford University Press, 2017.
Westbrook, R. B. *Democratic Hope, Pragmatism, and the Politics of Truth*. Ithaca, NY: Cornell University Press, 2005.
Westbrook, R. B. *John Dewey and American Democracy*. Ithaca, NY: Cornell University Press, 1991.
White, M. *The Origins of Dewey's Instrumentalism*. New York: Columbia University Press, 1943.
White, M. *Pragmatism and the American Mind: Essays and Reviews in Philosophy and Intellectual History*. New York: Oxford University Press, 1973.
White, S. K. *Political Theory and Postmodernism*. Cambridge: Cambridge University Press, 1991.
Williams, M. K. "John Dewey in the 21st Century." *Journal of Inquiry & Action in Education* 9, no. 1 (2017): 91–102.
Winch, P. *The Idea of a Social Science and Its Relation to Philosophy*. London: Routledge, 1990.

INDEX

Aboulafia, Mitchell, 213, 255, 257, 262, 264
Adorno Theodor, 7, 75, 229, 265
Albright, Madeleine, 211, 264
Alexander, Jeffrey C., 235, 264
Alexander, Thomas M., 216, 265
Allen, Amy, 230
Anderson, Charles, 215, 265
Anderson, Douglas R., 218, 274
Andropow, Jurij, 249
Applebaum, Anne, 211, 265
Appleby, Joyce, 213
Arendt, Hannah, 244, 265
Asghari, Mohammad, 239, 265
Austin, John, 89, 230
Auxier, Randall E., xvi, 220, 226, 265, 271

Bacon, Michael, 249, 265
Balot, Ryan, 236, 265
Banakar, Reza, 233, 268
Barber, Benjamin, 215, 265
Barreto, José-Manuel, 245, 265
Bauman, Zygmunt, 265
Baynes, Kenneth, 214, 243, 255, 265
Benhabib, Seyla, 213, 229, 234, 238, 240, 250, 256, 262, 265, 266, 267
Benson, Rodney, 237, 266
Berlin, Isaiah, 160–62, 164–65, 168, 177–78, 244–45, 249–51, 256, 262, 266, 269, 273, 276

Bernstein, Richard J., 7, 214, 218, 238, 244, 253, 266
Best, Steven, 226, 266
Bilgrami, Akeel, 220, 266
Bohman, James, 233, 237, 258, 266-267, 272, 274
den Brink, Bert, xvi, 257
Blaug, Ricardo, 239, 242, 246
Blewett, John, 266
Boffetti, Jason M., 220, 266
Bohman, James, 233, 237, 258, 266, 267, 272, 274
Borradori, Giovanna, 259, 266
Braaten, Jane, 258, 266
Brandon, Robert, 262, 264, 266–67
Bredella, Lothar, 248, 266
Brigham, Erin, 249, 266
Brown, Wendy, 255, 267
Bruno-Jofré, Rosa, 267
Brzeziński, Zbigniew, 211, 218, 267

Cacaterra, Rosa M., 221, 267
Campbell, James, 215, 216, 253, 256, 267
Casey, Michael, 221, 267
Caspary, William R., 258, 267
Chambers, Simone, 258, 267
Chia, Robert, 213, 275
Christiano, Thomas, 237, 267
Cicero, 220
Cohen, Joshua, 214, 215, 244, 253, 267

Cohen, Ted, 230
Coles, Romand, 213, 267
Conant, James, 222, 238, 267
Condorcet, Nicolas de, 181
Copernicus, 137
Critchley, Simon, 242, 267
Cruz, Feodor F., 217 267
Curtis, William, 249, 267

Dahl, Robert, 215, 216, 268
Damasio, Antonio, 233, 268
Damico, Alfonso, 216, 268
Darwin, Charles, 137
Davidson, Donald H., 32, 220, 266, 272, 275
Dazhi, Yao 239, 268
Deen, Phillip, 252, 268
Deflem, Mathieu, 233, 268
Dell'utri, Massimo, 221, 268
Dellwing, Michael, 228, 268
Dennett, Daniel C., 238
Derrida, Jacques, 61, 213, 214, 242, 256, 259, 266, 272
Dewey John, vii, x, xi, xv, 7, 9, 12, 13, 15–23, 25, 49, 55, 62, 63, 66, 70, 73, 125, 128, 136, 139, 154, 173, 177, 178, 180, 182, 191–200, 203, 206, 208–10, 213–20, 223, 227, 249, 252–56, 258, 261, 263, 265–77
Dews, Peter, 212, 213, 229, 230, 239, 242, 257, 262, 266, 268
Diaconu, Mircea A., 219, 268
Duncan, Christopher M., 241, 266
Durkheim, Émile, 77, 78,
Dryzek, John S., 243, 268

Eagleton, Terry, 213, 268
Edgar, Andrew, 214, 268
Edwards, Tony, 220, 268
Elderidge, Michael, 218, 268
Elshtain, Jean B., 242, 268
Emerson, Ralph W., 220, 241, 256, 271
d'Entrèves, Maurizio Passerin, 213, 234, 238, 240, 250, 262, 267
Epictetus, 220
Estlund, David, 244, 267, 268

Festenstein, Matthew, 7, 214, 256, 268, 27
Fesmire, Steven, 252, 268

Finlayson, James, 214, 268
Fisher, Michael, 248, 268,
Fishkin, James S., 244, 268
Flower, Elizabeth 269
Foucault, Michel, 61, 64, 163 198, 213, 214, 219, 227, 247, 256, 263, 267, 269, 270, 271, 272
Freeden, Michael, 255, 269
Freud, Zygmunt, 32, 52, 137, 168, 221, 267

Galileo, 137
Gander, Eric, 154, 169
Gascoigne, Neil, 249, 269
Gellner, Ernest, 113, 114, 203
Geras, Norman, 218, 269
Gerhards, Jürgen, 213, 269
Ghiraldelli, Paulo, 226, 266
Gideonse, Harry D., 215 273
Giladi, Paul, 218, 269
Gilani, Ijaz, S 237, 271
Golding, Ian, 212, 269
Gorbachev, Mikhail, 249
Gordon, Mordechai, 217, 269
Gouinlock, James, 252, 265
Grady, Hugh H., 230, 269
Gray, John, 245, 269
Greenwood, Justin, 269
Grippe, Edward J., 238, 264
Grundmann, Reiner, 233, 269
Grzeliński, Adam, 247, 263
Guignon, Charles, 242, 244, 266, 268, 269
Gutmann, Amy, 215, 216, 269
Gutting, Gary, 213, 270

Haack, Susan, 212, 221, 269
Haber, Honi F., 227, 269
Habermas, Jürgen, ix–xvi, 1-13, 15, 22, 29, 75–75, 177–83, 185–95, 197–277
Hacking, Ian, 245, 269
Haferkamp, Hans, 235, 270
Hahn, Lewis E., 220, 226, 265, 271
Hardie, Charles D., 217, 270
Harris, Stephen, 233, 270
Hausman, Carel R., 218, 274
Hayden, Patrick, 224, 270
Hayek, Friedrich A., 245, 270
Hegel, Georg Wilhelm Friedrich, 3, 61, 122, 247

Held, David, 12, 215, 216, 220, 244, 257, 262, 270
Henrich, Daniel C., 242, 270
Hertogh, Marc, 233, 270
Halliday, Simon, 233, 270
Heidegger, Martin, 25, 28, 64, 223, 224, 227, 229, 242, 244, 245, 246, 247, 248, 249, 250, 252, 253, 254, 255, 263
Hitler, Adolf, 22, 64, 67, 139, 162, 178
Hoffmann, Stanley, 257, 275
Hook, Sidney, 198, 255, 270
Horkheimer, Max, 75, 229, 265
Horton, Robin, 113, 114, 203
Hoy, Terry, 217, 270
Hickman, Larry A., 216, 217, 218, 267, 270, 272, 276
Hiley, David R., 242, 244, 266, 268, 269
Hunt, Lynn, 213, 265
Hutchinson, Allan C., 221, 270

Ignácz, Zsófia S., 211, 269
Ingram, David, 213, 214, 270
Isaac, Jeffrey C., 224, 270

Jacob, Margaret, 213, 265
Jay, Martin, 217, 270
Jezierska, Katarzyna, 232, 270
Joas, Hans, 218, 242, 270
Johnson, Mark, 221, 271
Johnson, Pauline, 236, 270
Jones, Matthew, 219, 270
Judt, Tony, 250, 271

Kaniowski, Andrzej M., xvi, 234, 271
Kant, Immanuel, 24, 129, 234, 243, 265
Kekes, John, 226
Kelly, Michael, 213, 271
Kemp, Cathy (Catherine), 213, 252, 255, 257, 262, 264, 274
Kennedy, David, 234, 271
Kennedy, Duncan, xiv
Khan, Zubair M., 237 271
Kilanowski, Marcin, 228, 258, 271
Kellner, Douglas, 226, 252, 265, 266
Kinley, David, 245, 273
Kitcher, Philip, 253, 271
Klein, Joe, 212, 271
Kley, Florian K., 211, 269

Kloppenberg, James T., 215, 258, 271
Koczanowicz, Leszek, 271
Kohlberg, Lawrence, 232
Kolenda, Konstanti, 271
Kołakowski, Leszek, 211, 218, 238, 239, 262, 263, 264, 273
Komendziński, Tomasz, 247, 263, 264
Koopman, Colin, 256, 271
Kundera, Milan, 43, 197, 223, 244, 250, 254, 271
Kwiek, Marek, 271,
Kwieciński, Zbigniew, 219, 247, 263
Kymlicka, Will, 216, 243, 271
Kyung-Man, Kim, 250, 271

Laclau, Ernesto, 242, 267
Lakoff, George, 221, 271
Lamb, Robert, 245, 272
Landemore, Hélène, 211, 272
Lengfeld, Holger 211, 269
Langsdorf, Lenor, 216, 265, 272
Leiter, Brian, 234, 275
Levitsky, Steven, 211, 272
Llanera, Tracy, 227, 272
Lukács, John, 250, 272
Luther, 137
Lyotard, Jean-François, 244, 227, 269, 276

Malachowski, Alan, 258, 272, 277
Malpas, Jeff, 220, 272
Mao, Zedong, 64, 67, 139, 162
Mapel, David R., 246, 272
Marcuse Herbert, 75, 229, 265
Margolis, Joseph, 218, 272
Marx, Karl, 63
Marsoobian, Armen T., 272
McCarthy, Thomas, 120, 129, 236, 242, 246, 256, 262, 272
McCumber, John, 7, 214, 256, 272
McKenny, Gerald P., 237, 274
Mead, George H., 77, 78, 108, 215, 275
Mendelson, Jack, 213, 272
Mendieta, Eduardo, 211, 252, 264, 272
Michelman, Frank, 233, 272,
Milanović, Branko, 212, 272
Mill, John Stuart, 160, 180
Miller, Chris B., 223, 272
Mirandola, Giovanni Pico della, 220

Montaigne, Michel de, 220
Morgenbesser, Sidney 217, 272
Morris, Charles D., 215, 272
Mouffe, Chantal, 273
Mounce, Howard O., 273
Mounk, Yascha, 211, 273
Mowbray, Jacqueline F., 245, 273
Murphy, Murray G., 269
Myers, Ella, 245, 273

Nabokov, Vladimir, 248,
Nawaz, Allah, 237, 271
Nehamas, Alexander, 219, 273
Niebuhr, Reinhold, 217, 273
Nielsen, Kai, 273
Niemi, Jari I., 273
Nietzsche, Friedrich Wilhelm, 31, 61, 64, 129, 163, 188, 219, 220, 221, 227, 263, 266 267, 273, 275
Niżnik, Jozef, 211, 212, 215, 218, 219, 221, 225, 238, 239, 242, 244, 255, 262
Nussbaum, Martha, 249, 273
Nyiro, Miklos, 240, 273

Oakeshott, Michael, 168, 169, 246, 273
Orbach Bookman, Mary, 213, 252, 255, 257, 262, 264, 274
Orwell, George, 39, 69, 73, 210, 222, 228, 248, 267, 273
O'Shea, James, 227, 246, 264, 273
Outhwait, William, 273
Owen, David S., 250, 273

Parsons, Talcott, 77, 98
Patzer, Moritz, 213, 275
Peirce, Charles S., 130, 134, 172, 213, 215, 252, 253, 271, 275, 277
Peters, Michael A., 226, 266, 273
Peterson, Richard T., 273
Piaget, Jean, 92, 96
Pihlström, Sami, 225, 273
Piketty, Thomas, 211, 212, 273, 274
Pinker, Steven, 245, 274
Plato, 63, 64, 136
Plot, Martin, 235, 274
Polanowska-Sygulska, Beata, 245, 266
Posner, Richard, 212, 252, 274
Priem, Maximilian, 211, 269
Proulx, Pierre-Luc, 214, 274

Putnam, Hilary, xvi, 130, 131, 134, 139, 145, 220, 221, 227, 238, 268, 271, 274

Rasmussen, David, 255, 265, 267, 274
Rawls, John, 154, 243
Rayan, Allan, 253, 258, 274
Rehg, Willima, 233, 237, 258, 267, 272, 274
Reichenbach Hans, 218
Rendall, Steven, 256, 262,
Roderick, Rick, 242, 274
Rogers, Melvin L., 223, 274
Rosenfeld, Michel, 237, 274
Rosenthal, Sandra B., 218, 252, 255, 274
Roth, Robert J., 216, 274
Rorty, Richard, ix–xiii, 1–75, 125–59, 261–77
Rothlede, Dianne, 225, 274
Rush, Fred, 234, 252, 275
Russell, Bertrand, 218
Rosen, Michael, 234, 275
Ryder, John, 272

Saatkamp, Herman J., Jr., 228, 238, 250, 253, 264, 266, 275
Sadurski, Wojciech, xvi, 245, 273
Sandel, Michael, 153, 154, 216, 243, 259, 275
Sanders, John T., 211, 212, 215, 218, 219, 221, 225, 238, 239, 242, 244, 255, 262, 263, 264, 273
Sartre, Jean-Paul, 196, 209, 254, 258, 275
Scheffler, Samuel, 275
Scherer, Andreas G., 213, 275
Schick, Theodore W., Jr., 220, 275
Schilpp, Paul Arthur, 218, 275
Schriewer, Jürgen, 218, 267
Schumpeter, Joseph A., 43, 44, 177, 233, 275
Searle, John R., 91
Sedgwick, Peter, 220, 275
Seebass, Gottfried, 235, 270,
Seidman, Steven, 213, 275
Selim, Ferdi, 224, 275
Seneca, Lucius Annaeus, 220
Sheffler, Israel, 275
Shklar, Judith, 209, 226, 257, 275
Shook, John R., 246, 272, 275
Shusterman, Richard, 213, 214, 256, 274, 275
Sim, Stuart, 275
Simon, Robert L., 244, 268, 276

Singer, Beth J., 254, 276
Skowroński, Krzysztof P., 258, 271
Sleeper, R. W., 252, 276
Smith, Andrew R., 216, 265, 272
Snyder, Tymothy, 211, 276
Specter, Matthew G., 212, 276
Spencer, Herbert, 136
Stanley, Raffel, 276
Stalin, Joseph, 22
Steinberg, Jonny, 245
Stikker, Kenneth W., 258. 271
Strydom, Piet, 241, 276
Stuhr, John J., 217, 218, 252, 269, 270, 276
Sullivan, William M., 215, 216, 276

Talisse, Robert B., 218, 276
Teeple, Gary, 250, 276
Termin, Peter, 212, 276
Thompson, John B., 212, 230, 244, 257, 262
Thompson, Simon, 256, 268, 275
Tomborino, John, 250, 276
Topper, Keith, 240, 276
Travers, Max, 233, 268
Trey, George, 214, 276
Tsoukas, Haridimos, 213, 275
Tuomela, Raimo, 235, 270
Turner, Stephen, 233, 276

Unger, Roberto Mangabeira, xvi, 27, 163
van Niekerk, Anton, 242, 276

Wain, Kenneth, 223, 277
Walker, Brian, 245, 246, 277
Walton, Kevin, 245, 273
Weber, Barbara, 214, 277
Weber, Max, 77, 215, 271
Welchman, Jennnifer, 277
Wellmer, Albrecht, 119, 236, 277
Wells, Susan, 230, 269
Wenar, Leif, 212, 277
Westbrook, Robert B., 215, 218, 240, 250, 254, 277
White, Morton, 277
Whitehead Alfred North, 218
Whiteman, Walt, 173
Williams, Morgan K., 218, 277
Winch, Peter G., 235, 277
Witkowski, Lech, xiv, 219, 247, 263
Wittgenstein, Ludwig, 25, 66, 231
Winch, Peter, 235, 277
Wyschogrod, Edith, 237, 274

Voparil, Christopher, 249, 252, 258, 277

Yunhua, Xiang, 239, 268

Ziblatt, Daniel, 211, 272

www.ingramcontent.com/pod-product-compliance
Lightning Source LLC
Chambersburg PA
CBHW020640230426
43665CB00008B/246